SEXUALITY IN ADOLESCENCE

Sexuality in Adolescence: The digital generation provides a comprehensive and up-to-date overview of research and theory about adolescent sexuality in today's world. The book examines biological, social and health-related approaches and reviews qualitative and quantitative research from psychology, sociology, epidemiology and medicine, emphasizing the interplay between perspectives and privileging the voices of young people as they discuss the joys and pains of sexual awakening. The focus is on understanding healthy sexual development and its many variations, but problems and issues arising as young people make their journey to adult sexuality are also considered.

The book presents global research on many key issues of our time, including the impact of media and technology on adolescent sexuality, changes in adolescent sexual behaviours and beliefs, sexual risk-taking, sex education, and teen pregnancy and abortion. *Sexuality in Adolescence* also addresses the crucial issues of sexual diversity, sexual safety and sexual communication, including coercion, peer pressure and double standards.

In *Sexuality in Adolescence* the authors aim to promote sexual wellbeing, and argue for the importance of the adolescent period as a time for engendering healthy sexual attitudes and practices. This book will be valuable reading for students in the social, behavioural and health sciences who are interested in adolescent development and the topic of sexuality, as well as for professionals working with young people and families.

Meredith Temple-Smith is an Associate Professor and a Director of Research Training in the Melbourne Medical School at The University of Melbourne, Australia.

Susan Moore is Emeritus Professor of Psychology at Swinburne University, Melbourne, Australia, and Fellow of the Australian Psychological Society.

Doreen Rosenthal was Founding Director of the Australian Research Centre in Sex, Health and Society and is Emeritus Professor in the Melbourne School of Population Health at The University of Melbourne, Australia.

Adolescence and Society
Series Editor: John C. Coleman
Department of Education, University of Oxford

In the 20 years since it began, this series has published some of the key texts in the field of adolescent studies. The series has covered a very wide range of subjects, almost all of them being of central concern to students, researchers and practitioners. A mark of its success is that a number of books have gone to second and third editions, illustrating its popularity and reputation.

The primary aim of the series is to make accessible to the widest possible readership important and topical evidence relating to adolescent development. Much of this material is published in relatively inaccessible professional journals, and the objective of the books has been to summarise, review and place in context current work in the field, so as to interest and engage both an undergraduate and a professional audience.

The intention of the authors is to raise the profile of adolescent studies among professionals and in institutions of higher education. By publishing relatively short, readable books on topics of current interest to do with youth and society, the series makes people more aware of the relevance of the subject of adolescence to a wide range of social concerns.

The books do not put forward any one theoretical viewpoint. The authors outline the most prominent theories in the field and include a balanced and critical assessment of each of these. Whilst some of the books may have a clinical or applied slant, the majority concentrate on normal development.

The readership rests primarily in two major areas: the undergraduate market, particularly in the fields of psychology, sociology and education; and the professional training market, with particular emphasis on social work, clinical and educational psychology, counselling, youth work, nursing and teacher training.

SEXUALITY IN ADOLESCENCE

The digital generation

Meredith Temple-Smith, Susan Moore and Doreen Rosenthal

Routledge
Taylor & Francis Group

LONDON AND NEW YORK

First published 2016
by Routledge
27 Church Road, Hove, East Sussex BN3 2FA

and by Routledge
711 Third Avenue, New York, NY 10017

Routledge is an imprint of the Taylor & Francis Group, an informa business

British Library Cataloguing in Publication Data
A catalogue record for this book is available from the British Library

Library of Congress Cataloging in Publication Data
Moore, Susan, 1945-
Sexuality in adolescence : the digital generation / Meredith
Temple-Smith, Susan Moore, Doreen Rosenthal.—[Third edition].
pages cm. — (Adolescence and society)
Includes bibliographical references and index.
1. Youth—Sexual behavior. 2. Teenagers—Sexual behavior.
3. Risk-taking (Psychology) in adolescence. 4. Youth—Sexual
behavior—Australia. 5. Youth—Australia—Attitudes. 6. Risk-taking
(Psychology) in adolescence—Australia. I. Temple-Smith, M. J.
(Meredith J.) II. Rosenthal, Doreen, 1938- III. Title.
HQ27.M635 2015
306.70835—dc23
2015006898

ISBN: 978-1-84872-301-6 (hbk)
ISBN: 978-1-84872-302-3 (pbk)
ISBN: 978-1-315-84934-8 (ebk)

Typeset in Bembo
by Swales & Willis Ltd, Exeter, Devon, UK

Printed and bound in the United States of America by
Edwards Brothers Malloy on sustainably sourced paper

CONTENTS

ACKNOWLEDGEMENTS

We would like to thank our colleagues and institutions (the Department of General Practice, Melbourne Medical School at The University of Melbourne; the Centre for Women's Health, Gender and Society, Melbourne School of Population Health at The University of Melbourne and the Department of Psychological Sciences, Faculty of Health, Arts and Design at Swinburne University of Technology) for providing the resources that enabled us to complete this book. We are particularly grateful to the research assistants and students who helped us gather information about adolescent sexuality over many years of research. Special thanks are due to Belinda Garth and Lucian Chaffey for their recent contributions.

Our picture of what it is like to be an adolescent and a sexual being in today's world would not have been possible without the involvement of many young people who contributed to our research and trusted us with such sensitive information. Interactions with our own offspring and their peers also contributed to our understanding of adolescent sexuality; Jasmine, Tobyn and Cassia Temple-Smith are the most recent addition to this group. Special thanks go to all the adolescents who have talked to us, whose experiences enrich the text and have provided a framework for this book.

We thank our publisher for encouraging us to continue to update our understanding of adolescent sexuality in the twenty-first century.

Finally our thanks to Mark, Ian and David who have supported and tolerated us while we wrote this book.

1

INTRODUCING ADOLESCENT SEXUALITY

> I want my first time to actually be something I remember in a good way,
> not in a bad way.
>
> *(Carmody, 2009:30)*

Two decades ago, when we first started on the journey of describing research on adolescent sexuality, there was little to document. Certainly, textbooks on adolescence addressed this topic but they covered mostly issues such as biological changes, teen pregnancy and the negative correlates of adolescent sexual expression. It was difficult to undertake research on adolescent sexuality; there was little funding available and either the subject was considered off limits, or there was not a great deal of interest in adolescents' sex lives. How things have changed! In preparing for this book we searched two key data bases for scholarly papers using the terms 'adolescent' and 'sexual', and found, by using these terms, that 50 years ago there were zero and four citations respectively. By 1993, the publication year of our first book, citations had increased to 1065 in one data base and 1325 in the other. Two decades later, in 2013, there was an even greater increase to 2456 and 8460 citations. Why the upsurge in focus on adolescents and their sexual lives? In the late 1980s and 1990s, increases in liberal attitudes to sexual and the spectre of HIV/AIDS raised issues of sexual safety and homosexuality, among others. It also made clear the need to know more about the context of adolescent sexual expression in order to develop programmes that would help adolescents to ensure that their sexual lives could unfold in ways that were safe, physically and psychologically.

A decade or more after publication of our first book, our second involved a major rewrite. In Australia alone, there were considerable concerns about adolescent sexual wellbeing, with the federal government providing substantial funds for a Centre for HIV Social Research, one of whose directors was Doreen Rosenthal. This intensified focus on research was accompanied by a considerable attitudinal shift in most western countries towards greater acceptance and understanding of adolescent sexuality and sexual diversity. By the time our second book was published, medical research had brought new forms of contraception, the morning-after pill, greater concern about sexually transmitted infections other than HIV, and there were more enlightened sex education programmes in schools. At this time, we began to recognize the potential for good or harm provided by the internet and we touched on this as an influencing factor. We also discussed one of the key issues in sex education, especially in the United States – whether teens should be taught about abstinence only or armed with knowledge based on the reality of their sexual practices.

Why a third book?

In part, some of the issues that were key in 2006 remain so and needed to be revisited. There are timeless questions such as how parents talk to their adolescents about sex, how young people cope with the changes of puberty, how the sexual lives of young men and women are shaped by biology and nurture, and how social institutions influence young people's sexuality. In addition, the heavy emphasis on deviance, risk-taking, disease and unwanted pregnancy remains in today's research and discourse about adolescent sexuality, often overshadowing a positive focus on health, growth and pleasure. Finally, young people across the globe live in different social, cultural and economic circumstances, yet their sexual worlds reveal commonalities as well as differences. Most of the research we review is from western countries, but in the present volume we have tried to present studies from developing countries wherever possible to provide a sense of the wider global context.

New issues and new areas of research have emerged that are central to young people's sexual health and wellbeing. Perhaps one of the most significant growth areas in adolescent research is the greater understanding of brain plasticity and the nature of the adolescent brain. How this affects decision-making, especially in the highly charged arena of sexual behaviour, is an important feature of adolescent development. Another emerging issue relates to online technologies. In the past decade, an absolute tidal wave of social media has markedly changed youth culture. Although this has a bearing on their relationships in general, social media now is a major means of communication in developing sexual relationships. It has had an impact on dating and courtship rituals; it provides opportunities for lonely and isolated young people to engage with others, but also has potential for dangerous outcomes. Knowing how social media functions in this regard is essential for understanding at least some of adolescents' current sexual practices.

Two important and related areas in which social attitudes have changed over the past decade are, first, a greater understanding of what constitutes unacceptable sexual behaviour (and a lower tolerance towards it) and second, that such behaviours and their consequences should be exposed rather than shamefully hidden. Given a culture in which young women's desires have long been subordinate to men's passions and sexual urges, it is pleasing to see a greater research interest in and acceptance of young girls' sexual desire (Tolman, 2012).

We should add that attitudinal change has accelerated, particularly in relation to sexual diversity; although coming out as gay, lesbian or bisexual can still be a risky exercise, it is much less so than previously.

Sexuality: a defining feature of adolescent development

Sexual questions, conflicts and crises may begin prior to adolescence and may certainly continue after this phase of life, but there is no doubt that, for most people, adolescence is a 'critical period' in the upsurge of sexual drives, the development of sexual values and the initiation of sexual behaviours. The advent of puberty, the power of peer group expectations, and the communication of mixed messages about sex from the adult generation make dealing with sexuality a difficult but exciting challenge for adolescents.

For healthy outcomes, adolescents need the information, skills, commitment to the future and, sometimes, protection that will enable them to avoid risky sex, unplanned or unwanted pregnancies, sexually transmissible infections and threats to their fertility. They need the skills to establish healthy and adaptive, non-exploitative sexual relationships. Adolescent sexuality need not be defined as problem behaviour. Sexual activity that is non-exploitative and safe, from the point of view of mental and physical health, can make a positive contribution to young people's development through increased independence, social competence and self-esteem. This is not to say that all adolescent sexual behaviour is adaptive, healthy and moral. Clearly sexual activity can occur too early and in contexts that are inappropriate. The view taken in this book is that sexuality is a normative event in adolescent development, with the potential for both positive and negative consequences.

All theories of adolescent development give sexuality a central place in negotiating the transition from child to adult. The sexual urges that emerge at puberty must be blended with other aspects of adolescents' lives and channelled adaptively. It is especially important that the adolescent is able to integrate his or her sexual feelings, needs and desires into a coherent and positive self-identity that contains, as one aspect, a sexual self. Unlike many of the activities we engage in, expression of our sexuality (for the most part) involves a relationship, no matter how limited or fleeting, with another individual. Sexual expression allows, indeed requires, a unique exposure of the self to another. On the one hand there is the possibility of validating one's sense of self-worth and achieving a deeply satisfying intimate relationship. On the other hand, wrong choices can lead to destructive outcomes, to feelings of anxiety and guilt, and to a sense of unworthiness. For adolescents who are in the process of forging a satisfying and satisfactory sense of their own identity and their place in the world, dealing with these issues is a crucial part of their development.

The task is a complex one. If we are to understand the significance of sexuality during adolescence, we need to consider how it fits into the biological, psychological and social aspects of adolescent development. At the biological level, sexuality is a central feature, marked by the onset of puberty which signals maturation of the reproductive organs, the possibility of becoming a parent and an increasing sex drive. Changes at the psychological level have to do with readiness for taking on adult roles, including sex and procreation. There is a shift from a primary orientation to one's family to a reliance on peers for providing guidelines for attitudes and behaviour, as well as a clarification of goals and the development of interpersonal skills. This occurs within a context of expanded cognitive skills that allow the adolescent to evaluate alternative points of view. At a broader level, social forces shape adolescents' sexuality by establishing and re-establishing values and norms relating to sexuality and expectations tied to gender.

Education enabling young people to develop sexual and relationship knowledge and skills is likely to be most effective if educators take into account the current beliefs and practices of their target audience. Sex education that stresses fear-arousing messages, punitive outcomes of experimentation or value stances considered 'out-of-date' will fail to reach those most needing intervention. Educators need to know about the different sexual subcultures of youth if their programmes are to be effective. But education about sexuality does not just occur in schools. It is pervasive in our culture through modelling adult behaviour, through the media, through talking with each other and family, and through our laws as well as religious and other values.

Focus of this book

One major focus for research on adolescent sexuality is documenting sexual behaviours, usually within a biological framework. How many adolescents are sexually active? What are they doing? Are they using contraception? What is the incidence of adolescent pregnancy? These are still important questions and current practices (and changes in these) are addressed in this book. Other research examines the sociocultural underpinnings of sexuality since biological approaches have limited explanatory power. They do not fit with observed gender, ethnic and class differences in behaviours and beliefs. Recognizing those aspects of sexuality that are socially constructed enables us to raise questions about the social context and how this channels adolescents' sexual experiences.

In line with this focus, there have been changes in the methods used to explore aspects of young people's sexuality. Although there is still an emphasis on large-scale quantitative surveys, increasingly qualitative techniques are being used. These enable us to understand better the meanings and motives underlying behaviours and to generate richer explanations. Together these methods allow for educational programmes that are more effectively targeted and take account of young people's own reality.

We have two starting points for this book. The first is our definition of adolescence. Historically, adolescence was defined by the World Health Organization (WHO) as encompassing the stage from 10 to 19 years (WHO, 2001). However, the lengthening of the period between childhood and adulthood, created by the decreasing age of puberty coupled with an older age at which adulthood is achieved, has resulted in the use of the term adolescence to refer to those aged between 10 and 24 years (Sawyer et al., 2012). Our other starting point for this book is the concept of sexual health. Recognizing that sexual health is more than the absence of disease, WHO provides a working description that takes into account the qualities of healthy sexual relationships and access to pleasure, as well as absence of discomfort.

> Sexual health is a state of physical, emotional, mental and social wellbeing related to sexuality; it is not merely the absence of disease, dysfunction or infirmity. Sexual health requires a positive and respectful approach to sexuality and sexual relationships, as well as the possibility of having pleasurable and safe sexual experiences, free of coercion, discrimination and violence. For sexual health to be attained and maintained, the sexual rights of all persons must be respected, protected and fulfilled.
>
> *(WHO, 2014a)*

We take up the challenge of this holistic view of sexual health, covering topics such as normative biological changes, romantic and sexual relationships, adolescent pregnancy, unwanted, forced or manipulative sex and healthy and unhealthy attitudes towards gender differences and sexual diversity. Where possible, we include research from non-western countries to provide a view of adolescent sexuality in an ever-increasingly globalized world.

2

SEXUAL BEHAVIOURS AND ATTITUDES

What is happening now?

[Premarital sex is] totally natural and practically a rite of passage, teenagers are meant to drink and get high and have sex . . . why go against your natural urges and 'self control' for no reason. Sex is fun. It feels good. It makes people happy and closer. Why not do it as much as possible! (American female, 16 years)

(Yahoo Answers, 2010)

[H]ow should we control our sexual desires? When we don't know how we should behave in our first sexual relationship and how we should show our feelings? (Iranian female, 18 years)

(Javadnoori, Roudsari, Hasanpour, Hazavehei &
Taghipour, 2012:542)

These quotes come from young women living in very different worlds, with correspondingly different attitudes to premarital sex. In the past two or three decades there have been remarkable changes in social norms around the expression of adolescent sexuality, particularly in the west. In relation to sex, the past was a simpler place than now in western societies, mirroring to some extent the current situation for young people in more conservative developing nations. Girls protected their virginity in order to attract a suitable husband and then became wives and mothers. Boys' lives were career-oriented and it was expected they would sow their sexual wild oats prior to taking on their family role of provider. Today, with changing social expectations, these goals are not so clearly defined, and ideas about 'right' and 'wrong' sexual behaviour are less rigid. Young people are delaying or dispensing with marriage, and at the same time, the age at which puberty begins is decreasing. This extension of the period between physical maturation and the taking up of traditional roles, together with the fact that contraception (together with the 'morning-after' pill and abortion) is often available, has led to the uncoupling of sexuality, marriage and child-bearing in the last few decades of the twentieth century. Prohibitions about premarital adolescent sex are difficult to enforce and far less prevalent, but there is also a huge diversity of views within the subgroups that make up society. There are many more possible pathways for healthy sexual development for adolescents in the twenty-first century than there were in the 1950s or even the 1990s – more possibilities, but also more pitfalls.

In this chapter, we examine contemporary sexual attitudes and practices, and provide an overview of what young people are doing sexually, some influences on their sexual practices and the context in which their sexuality is developing. In particular, we note changes that have occurred in the past decade.

Patterns of sexual behaviour

Generalizing about the sexual practices of adolescents is a dangerous procedure, given the wide range of behaviours included under this rubric, the individual differences that distinguish adolescents from each other and the diversity of societal influences experienced by adolescents in different subgroups. No less important are the differences one might expect in comparing the behaviour of 13-year-olds with that of older adolescents. With this caveat in mind, we turn to what adolescents do sexually, with whom and when.

What do young people do and with whom do they do it?

There have been significant changes in the patterning of young people's relationships with each other. 'Falling in love', developing crushes and forming romantic relationships may or may not precede sexual intercourse. These aspects of young people's sexual development are dealt with in a later chapter. Here we focus on specific sexual acts. Several studies have shown the robustness of a sequence of adolescent sexual behaviour which starts at around the age of 13 with embracing and kissing, moving through petting or fondling of breasts and external genitalia, and ending, sooner or later, with oral, vaginal or anal intercourse (e.g. Shtarkshall, Carmel, Jaffe-Hirschfield & Woloski-Wruble, 2009; Smith, Rissel, Richters, Grulich & de Visser, 2003). In the past, many adolescents, especially young women, moved gradually towards more intimate sexual behaviour – 'heavy' petting and intercourse – through the experience of 'dating' or 'going steady' and perhaps on to co-habitation or marriage. This may still happen today, but it is certainly not the only, or even most common, pathway to first intercourse.

There is greater diversity in the nature of relationships than previously. Casual encounters, often facilitated by social media, define the sex lives of many western youth. Young people text message, or 'talk' and they may or may not 'hook up'. Hooking up is generally defined as a casual sexual encounter that may or may not include intercourse and typically occurs during a singular occasion between strangers or recently met acquaintances. Unlike dating, a unique feature of hooking up is that there is little or no expectation of future romantic commitment.

Both casual and more continuing relationships provide young people with the opportunities for sexual exploration and discovery. For example, it has often been suggested that non-vaginal premarital petting, especially to orgasm, has been practised to protect girls' virginity – an important com-modity in many cultures even today. In this way girls can remain technically virgins while experiencing sexual intimacy. At an interpersonal level, the successes and failures, pleasures and disappointments of these relationships help young people to acquire the skills in intimacy that are necessary to establish adaptive long-term partnerships.

Are young people more likely to have premarital sex as a casual event or as part of a regular relationship? It depends on culture, gender and attitudes, among other factors. Among sexually active American adolescents in a study reported by the Guttmacher Institute (2014), three-quarters of females and more than half of the males reported that their first sex was with a steady partner and 16 per cent of females and 28 per cent of males first had sex with someone they had just met or a friend.

Sexual initiation

> I think that girls should start having sex when they feel like they found the right one, or like if they feel like they've been talking to that person for a long amount of time, and if they know them for a long amount of time. (African-American female, 15 years)
>
> *(Timmons, 2014:61)*

How many young people are virgins and how many are sexually experi-enced? We have seen that there was a substantial increase in adolescents' sexual activity in the last decades of the twentieth century. In a British study of boys and girls aged 15–19 years interviewed in the early 1960s, Schofield

(1968) found that only 20 per cent of boys and 12 per cent of girls had had sexual intercourse. Most studies in the late 1980s and 1990s, across a number of western countries, suggested that by the end of high school about 35–40 per cent of teenagers were non-virgins. Australian studies monitoring high school students' sexual practices showed a continuing increase from 1992 to 2002 in the numbers who had ever had sex (Lindsay, Smith & Rosenthal, 1997; Smith et al., 2003). The most recent survey, conducted in 2013, found a further increase in the numbers of sexually active high schoolers (Mitchell, Patrick, Heywood, Blackman & Pitts, 2014) although Lim, Bowring, Gold, Aitken and Hellard (2012) found no increase in those reported ever having had sex across the time period of 2006–2011. The discrepancy between these Australian studies is partly explained by sampling differences – high school students in the former, music festival attendees in the latter – as well as data collection methods. It is possible, of course, that music festival attendees started from a higher level of sexual activity in 2006 than Mitchell et al.'s high school students.

How many young people are sexually active?

Although there have always been adolescents who have engaged in sexual activity, what is new is the increasing numbers of young people engaging in this behaviour in the past 50 years. In particular, there has been a dramatic rise over this period in the numbers of teenage girls who are sexually active outside marriage. Although historically young boys were more sexually active than young girls, the gap between the sexes began to narrow in the 1980s. One early US study showed an increase in the number of White American 16-year-old girls having intercourse from 7 per cent in 1950 to 44 per cent in 1982 (Brooks-Gunn & Furstenberg, 1989). More recent studies confirm a continuing increase in recent years. For example, an analysis of data from national health surveys in four Central American countries – El Salvador, Guatemala, Honduras and Nicaragua – showed that the number of adolescent females aged 15 to 19 years who had experienced sexual intercourse has increased over time in El Salvador, Honduras and Nicaragua, but has remained stable in Guatemala (Samandari & Speizer, 2010).

Some studies now reveal that, in addition to higher levels of sexual activity, young women are as sexually active as their male peers, for example among Swedish (Häggström-Nordin, Borneskog, Eriksson & Tyden, 2011), Australian (Mitchell et al., 2014), Israeli (Shtarkshall et al., 2008) and French adolescents (Bajos et al., 2010). Nevertheless, the gender gap remains in some populations, for example among the US-based urban minority youth studied by O'Donnell, Myint-U, O'Donnell and Stueve (2003) and in some countries such as China where girls' sexual experience is especially frowned upon (Yu, 2012; Yu, Guo & Sun, 2013; see also Godeau *et al.*, 2008).

Undoubtedly the increase in the 1980s was due, at least partially, to the contraceptive pill and to the influence of the women's movement of the 1960s and 1970s, with its demands for equality of sexual expression and sexual fulfilment. More recently, too, there appear to be more opportunities for women to be sexually active. In a review of studies of late adolescents' sexual behaviour from 1900 to 1980, Darling, Kallen and VanDusen (1984) identified three historical periods, each characterized by different sexual standards. The earliest, which lasted until the 1940s or early 1950s, was the period of the 'double standard', with sexual activity accepted for boys but prohibited for girls, although in Chapter 7 we present evidence that this attitude still exists albeit in different forms. During the next 20 or so years, it seemed that premarital sex was allowed for young people provided that it occurred in a love relationship that was a prelude to marriage. The 'sexual revolution' of the 1960s and 1970s, which was characterized by more permissive attitudes towards sexuality and greater concern for personal fulfilment, brought with it a lessening of the prohibition on premarital sex. The trend towards later marriage may well have contributed to this shift in attitude, since many believe it to be unrealistic to expect young people to abstain from sexual activity until their late twenties or longer. Since then we have seen a greater tolerance for sex outside of a romantic relationship.

In an analysis of sexual behaviour data available from 59 countries, Wellings and her colleagues found considerable diversity by region and sex but, in general, an increase in premarital sex, with higher prevalence in developed than developing countries and in men compared with women (Wellings *et al.*, 2006). Several recent US surveys place the prevalence of sexual intercourse higher than in previous decades, at around two-thirds of high school seniors and of 18- to 19-year-olds (e.g. Chandra, Mosher, Copen & Sionean, 2011).

Nevertheless, the rapid increase in rates of sexual activity among young people that characterized the latter part of the twentieth century has plateaued in some western countries and many teenagers do not engage in premarital sex. A significant proportion of young people advocate no sex before marriage, although it is difficult to assess whether this attitude is always consistent with behaviour. Some young people prefer to wait until they find the 'right' person; others do not experience opportunities for sexual engagement because of their family, community or personal characteristics. In a recent Australian study (Mitchell *et al.*, 2014), 50 per cent of Year 12 students had not yet experienced intercourse.

Even in countries where premarital sex has long been proscribed there is increasing evidence that young people are sexually active. A review of research in China (Yu, 2012) and a survey of adolescents in 24 countries (Godeau *et al.*, 2008) confirm this. While adolescents in non-western countries may not be as sexually active as their western counterparts, substantial numbers report engaging in sex. These include young people in Africa (Gupta & Mahy, 2003; Hoque, 2011) and Eastern Europe (Gyarmathy *et al.*, 2002). Even in Asian and Middle Eastern countries, where discussion of sex is often taboo and strict traditional prohibitions on premarital sex are still in place, the numbers who have experienced sex is surprisingly high, and it is likely that these numbers are an underestimate given that some young people may be unwilling to disclose sexual activity (e.g. Farahani, Cleland & Mehryar, 2011; Mohammadi *et al.*, 2006; Wu, 2003).

Age of sexual initiation

There is conflicting evidence as to whether the age of sexual initiation is decreasing (Bajos *et al.*, 2010; Mercer *et al.*, 2013; Shtarkshall *et al.*, 2008) or is delayed compared to earlier cohorts. Häggström-Nordin *et al.* (2011) report a decline across a number of countries including Nordic countries in the average age at which young people have intercourse for the first time. In Sweden, the age of initiation into sex has dropped from an average of 19 years to 16 years in the past four decades. In contrast, among unmarried young American women and men aged 15–19 years in 2013, 11 per cent and 14 per cent respectively had had sex before age 15 compared with 19 per cent and 21 per cent respectively in 1995 (Finer & Philbin, 2013). In the UK, Wellings *et al.* (2006) found no universal trend towards earlier sexual intercourse in their review.

It is misleading to talk of an average age for loss of virginity because there are so many individual, gender, cultural group and even neighbourhood group differences. Studies from a range of countries indicate different levels of sexual experience for similarly aged young people from different social, religious, ethnic and racial groups. For example, African-American and Hispanic adolescents become sexually active at a younger age than White American adolescents (Halpern & Haydon, 2012; O'Donnell *et al.*, 2003).

Our interviews with young people suggest that the majority of adolescents themselves believe that 15 is too young an age to begin intercourse, and that although the ideal age for loss of virginity 'depends on the person' (their level of maturity), sexual initiation too early can have a damaging psychological effect. Some express considerable ambivalence in their decisions about having their first sexual intercourse (Pinquart, 2010) and some regret that decision. For example, Osorio *et al.* (2012) found that many high schoolers aged 14–18 years (and more girls than boys) living in the Philippines, El Salvador and Peru regretted having already had sexual relationships which were often the result of pressure from their partner or from a belief that their friends had already engaged in sex. We take up these issues in other chapters but note here that loss of control of sexual decision-making can lead to negative outcomes for teens.

Variety of practices

Just as the numbers of adolescents engaging in sex have increased, so too they are becoming more sexually adventurous. Young people are engaging in a wider variety of sexual behaviours than before and with more partners. The practice of oral sex is now widespread among adolescents, with one US study reporting that three-quarters of males and half the females had had oral sex by age 18 years (Halpern & Haydon, 2012). In the UK, 70 per cent of 16- to 24-year-olds had given or received oral sex with opposite sex partners in the previous 12 months (Mercer *et al.*, 2013). In Sweden, 37 per cent of high school boys had given and 37 per cent had received oral sex. Somewhat more girls had engaged in oral sex – nearly half in the former and half in the latter case (Häggström-Nordin *et al.*, 2011). In a recent study, substantial numbers of Australian high school students reported giving or receiving oral sex (39 per cent in each case), with somewhat fewer girls than boys receiving oral sex (Mitchell *et al.*, 2014).

There is a significant proportion of young people now for whom the practice of oral sex precedes coitus. Smith *et al.* (2003) found that about half (55 per cent) of their high school students had experienced oral sex but not vaginal intercourse with one partner, a finding consistent with US data (Chandra *et al.*, 2011). In a rare study examining the sexual timetables for oral, vaginal and anal sex, Halpern and Haydon (2012) found that, overall, about two-thirds of adolescents had had oral intercourse by age 18, although this varied by race, with non-Hispanic Black and Hispanic adolescents having lower rates than non-Hispanic White adolescents. They found no evidence for one consistent pattern. Similar percentages (33 per cent) of their partici-pants either had vaginal intercourse first or initiated two sexual behaviours (usually oral–genital and vaginal sex) and only 15 per cent reported initiating oral sex first. Halpern and Haydon concluded that there were multiple types of first experience, with overlap between oral and vaginal intercourse being most common.

The emergence of oral sex as a common practice needs to be recog-nized, particularly as there is evidence that young people may not equate oral sex with vaginal sex (Rissel, Richters, Grulich, deVisser & Smith, 2003; Sanders *et al.*, 2010) or that they may deem it significantly less risky and more acceptable than vaginal sex (Halpern-Felsher, Cornell, Kropp & Tschann, 2005). This separation of oral sex and vaginal sex suggests that if young people engage in oral sex without intercourse, they may not recognize the risk of disease transmission. Although oral sex is potentially less risky than vaginal intercourse with respect to HIV transmission, it is not entirely safe and a range of sexually transmitted infections (STIs) can be spread by these practices, particularly if semen, blood or vaginal fluids enter the mouth.

The incidence of anal sex, although relatively low, occurs with more frequency among some groups and more often with regular than with casual partners. The recent survey of Australian high schoolers (Mitchell *et al.*, 2014) found that 11 per cent of boys and 7 per cent of girls had experienced anal sex, while the UK study reported by Mercer *et al.* (2013) found that nearly one-fifth of 16- to 24-year-olds had experienced anal sex with an opposite sex partner in the preceding 12 months. Eleven per cent of UK participants in Halpern and Haydon's study reported having experienced anal sex by age 18 years, although again there were gender and race differences. Less than 1 per cent of respondents reported anal sex as their first sexual experience.

In a review of research on heterosexual anal sex, mostly among adults, McBride and Fortenberry (2010) noted one study of adolescents aged 12–18 years that showed similar and moderately high prevalence rates of anal intercourse among individuals with a main partner and those with casual partners (16 per cent vs. 12 per cent, respectively). However they question, as do others, the extent to which underreporting has influenced the accuracy of estimations of incidence and prevalence of anal sex, given the taboo nature of this practice in most cultures.

In one recent interview study of young African-American women (Timmons, 2014), oral and anal sex were the only sexual acts that were regarded by participants as being inappropriate for adolescents and as likely to be unsafe. The reasons given for this did not appear to reflect gender, culture or religion. As one young woman put it:

> I think – okay – like not the anal and oral sex, because that's just too much. That's when you're supposed to wait 'til you married for real because you don't know if he with somebody else. He could bring something back, and it be in your mouth. I think just regular vaginal sex is okay. (Female, 16 years)
>
> *(Timmons, 2014:65)*

There are many anecdotal reports from adolescents, as well as in the study by Houston and colleagues (2007), that anal intercourse is not defined as sex. Thus a young woman who engages in anal intercourse but abstains from vaginal sex may still label herself a 'virgin'. It seems that there are at least two reasons, seemingly related to sexual 'safety', why young people engage in anal sex: as a means of remaining a 'virgin' and as a contraceptive (Houston, Fang, Husman & Peralta, 2007). There is also a documented influence of pornography, as we describe in Chapter 6, where anal sex is commonly performed. Easy online access to pornography may have led to it being perceived as a 'model' for sexual practice by some young people.

The practice of withdrawal of the penis before ejaculation during vaginal intercourse (known as withdrawal) is often not included as a category separate from vaginal intercourse in adolescent sexuality research. Nevertheless it is an important practice to note from the point of view of both pregnancy protection and transmission of STIs. The belief that withdrawal eliminates risk is mistaken. Even withdrawal that successfully averts conception – less likely among those sexually inexperienced – still carries risk through possible infection carried in the pre-ejaculate or vaginal fluids. In the most recent study of Australian secondary students (Mitchell *et al.*, 2014), 15 per cent engaged in withdrawal at their last sexual encounter in spite of education messages about the risks to sexual health associated with this practice.

We do need to be cautious in accepting too readily the evidence for an increase in the frequency and variety of sexual activity. Attitudes to sexuality are more liberal than in previous decades so that the adolescents of today may be more willing to admit to these behaviours than their predecessors. Nevertheless, the generality of these findings across studies in different countries, using different samples and different information-gathering strategies, suggests that real changes have occurred.

Solo sex

It should not be forgotten that sexual behaviours can occur without a partner and that these practices can be intensely gratifying. They can be involuntary, like nocturnal emissions, or behaviours that are deliberate, like erotic fantasy and masturbation. In 2006 we noted that there was very little research published on any of these sexual behaviours, no doubt in part because they were, and still are, regarded as intensely private and somewhat shameful activities. Today there is more to report.

More than two decades ago Katchadourian (1990) wrote that erotic fantasy is the most common sexual activity of all, either on its own or as part of other sexual behaviours, suggesting that these fantasies fulfil a number of functions in the adolescent's erotic life. They are a source of pleasurable sexual arousal. They act as a substitute for the satisfaction of unattainable or inappropriate sexual needs or goals, performing a 'compensatory, wish-fulfilment function'. Finally, they provide an opportunity for adolescents to recognize their sexual needs and preferences, and to rehearse these in a way that is non-threatening for most teenagers (Pilon, 2011). However, for some, erotic fantasies provoke anxieties and guilt about sexual feelings that may be perceived as perverted or forbidden.

Contemporary writers have focused on the positive aspects of sexual fantasies. Despite popular belief, sexual fantasizing is not the sole province of those who lack sexual opportunity or who do not engage in sex. There is evidence that sexual fantasy and actual sex can and do go hand in hand (Boubli & Elbez, 2010; Doskoch, 2014). Gender differences are as might be predicted: boys often start having sexual fantasies earlier than girls, fantasize more and indulge in a greater variety of fantasies (Leitenberg & Henning, 1995). It is also true that fantasizing about someone of the same sex does not necessarily mean one is homosexual. Heterosexuals can have fantasies about same-sex peers without having to question their sexual orientation, as this 13-year-old young girl worries:

> I'm a girl and I like boys. But I've been feeling anxious for months now because sometimes I have thoughts about girls that excite me. I've always been straight so I'd really like to stop feeling anxious. (Female, 13 years)
>
> *(Pilon, 2011:6)*

Homosexuals sometimes have fantasies about people of the opposite sex (Kahr, 2008, cited in *The Sex Educator*, 2011). Although creating sexual fantasies may be intensely pleasurable, and revealing one's fantasies may have the effect of increasing intimacy between young people, there is a potential downside to disclosure of this very intimate aspect of oneself, leaving one vulnerable to criticism and gossip (Kahr, 2008, cited in *The Sex Educator*, 2011). As the research reveals, there is no doubt that the common act of engaging in sexual fantasies is one shared by many adolescents and, on balance, its benefits may well outweigh negative aspects of this activity.

Unlike menarche, which signals girls' entry into sexual maturity, little is known about the incidence of boys' wet dreams; those disconcerting, involuntary nocturnal emissions which cause so many young boys embarrassment and, possibly, guilt in the morning. We know a little more about masturbation – but it is surprising how little research has been conducted on this activity. Although in some cultures masturbation is accepted as a normal part of human sexuality, there are many cultures in which this behaviour is regarded as unacceptable. Certainly among the great religions of the world there are prohibitions against this practice. Western society, in the past, maintained a strong injunction against this behaviour. At the beginning of this century, physicians, including the US surgeon general, warned that masturbation was a cause of cancer, heart disease, hysteria, impotence and insanity.

On the other side of the Pacific Ocean, in 1906, one eminent medical authority of the day, Dr William Henry Symes, claimed that masturbation led to imbecility and epilepsy, that 75 per cent of those addicted to this filthy habit could be 'rescued from insanity and probably death' by forcible vasectomies, and that the 'moral defectives' who remained uncured should be put on an island and flogged with the cat-o'-nine-tails. Even as late as the 1980s, a textbook on adolescent development placed the topic of masturbation in a section entitled 'Special problems of psychosexual development' (Rogers, 1981). In spite of these awful dangers, many young people continued to engage, albeit surreptitiously, in this behaviour. It is not difficult to imagine the guilt, conflict and depression caused by a seeming addiction to such a taboo and dangerous practice. More recently, there has been a shift towards greater openness and acceptance, perhaps reflecting a more general move from a focus on sex for reproduction to sex for pleasure. It is perhaps telling, however, that in popular culture in those few occasions where masturbation is the topic, it is treated as comedy rather than as a pleasurable sexual experience.

Masturbation

Masturbation is the most common source of orgasm in young people of both sexes and the source of a boy's first ejaculation. There is evidence of a sex difference in masturbatory practices. Fewer girls than boys admit to this practice but whether girls' lower rates of reporting masturbatory behaviour reflect a real difference or simply a difference in willingness to admit to a 'stigmatized' behaviour is not known. Certainly it seems that acceptance of masturbation among boys is greater than for girls. As early as the late 1940s Kinsey and his colleagues reported that observation of peers masturbating was common for boys, prior to their own masturbatory experience (Kinsey, Martin, Pomeroy & Gregg, 1948). Most knowledge about masturbation among boys comes from their peer group. For girls, masturbation is a more closeted experience. Girls are more likely than boys to report learning about masturbation from books and magazines, or sex education in schools, and less likely to learn from peers.

It is difficult to get accurate figures on masturbatory practices but several studies suggest that most boys and many girls engage in this behaviour. In a recent Swedish study, 94 per cent of male and 70 per cent of female high school students reported ever having masturbated (Häggström-Nordin *et al.*, 2011). Analysis by Mercer *et al.* (2013) of a national UK study found that 83 per cent of adolescent males but only 37 per cent of females reported having masturbated in the preceding four weeks. A report of findings from the US National Survey of Sexual Health and Behavior revealed that teenage boys masturbated more frequently than girls and started earlier. At age 14 years, 43 per cent of boys said they had masturbated 'recently' while 68 per cent of those aged 17 did so, a figure that was considerably lower for girls (Mozes, 2011).

Clearly cultural attitudes affect both young people's preparedness to masturbate and their willingness to report that they do so and their feelings associated with this practice. In her comparison of Dutch and American teenagers, Schalet (2010) reported that Dutch girls were more likely to describe feeling sexual pleasure and exercising sexual agency than their American counterparts. Although masturbation remains shrouded in taboo for many American girls, two-thirds of Dutch 17-year-old girls report having masturbated. Only 13 per cent of Dutch girls agreed that 'after masturbating I often feel guilty'. But for some young girls, masturbating is an activity that they could not contemplate. In an interview study of 16- to 18-year-olds, Hogarth and Ingham (2009) reported immense diversity of views.

> I would never touch myself . . . I think that's really disgusting . . . it's just not right 'cos only a boy suppose to touch you there and even then it's not that great. (Female, 17 years)
>
> *(Hogarth & Ingham, 2009:561)*

> It felt really good. . . . I felt a million dollars and then so calm and feeling so good inside myself . . . it was as if I had at last done something just for me. . . . It was just this incredible release and I knew that if I ever felt . . . really uptight I could do this again and I could feel good again. (Female, 18 years)
>
> *(Hogarth & Ingham, 2009:563)*

In the developing world, especially, masturbation is accompanied by many myths. As Shelton (2010) notes, one common myth is that losing semen saps men of energy and vital fluids. There is also a pervasive taboo against even talking about masturbation that reinforces the idea that there is something wrong with it. However Shelton reports studies that show that masturbation was common in an urban Chinese sample and unmarried adolescents in Tanzania, albeit at lower levels than in western countries.

Although self-stimulation may still cause some anxiety for adolescents, the reality is that masturbation may be both enjoyable and tension reducing, as the comment above demonstrates, and that it does not cause physical harm. What is particularly injurious is the attitude taken towards this practice. The severe condemnation expressed by many parents when they discover that their teenager (or small infant or toddler) is masturbating can be a disturbing drawback to the young person's psychosexual development. There is no indication that masturbation causes later sexual maladjustment. It may lessen parents' anxiety to know that most researchers have failed to find a relationship between ever having masturbated and engaging in sexual intercourse. Indeed masturbation may have benefits. Masturbation can help inexperienced youngsters learn how to give and receive sexual pleasure, and allow for the expression of sexual feelings without entering into a relationship for which the teenager is not emotionally ready. The fantasies associated with masturbation can help the adolescent develop a sexual identity and establish sexual preferences. As with many behaviours, however, excess is potentially problematic. In some cases, masturbation may reflect adjustment problems, especially when used not just as a substitute for 'real' sex when this is unavailable, but as a refuge from or replacement for satisfactory sexual relationships with peers. It may also be a problem if masturbation develops an obsessional quality, and this may be associated with disturbances of attachment that carry through to adult relationships.

The sexual context

Studies that investigate the age of sexual initiation rarely tell us much about the context in which this significant event occurs. Is early initiation related to regular and frequent subsequent sexual activity? Who are the partners of these young people? How often is initiation of sexual activity not voluntary (a topic we take up in Chapter 11)? Is it a pleasurable experience or one fraught with negative emotions? It seems that having had intercourse once (and at an early age) does not necessarily mean that the young person maintains a high level of sexual activity. For some young adolescents, sexual intercourse is sporadic and rare, often a one-off experience. However, once the transition to non-virgin is made, subsequent acts of intercourse are likely to follow quite quickly.

Partners

To what extent is partner changing a feature of adolescent and young adult sexual practice? Several recent studies suggest that the stereotype of high activity among this age group is not borne out by the data. In the most recent national study of Australian high school students, half of the young men who had experienced sexual intercourse in the preceding 12 months reported having only one partner, as did nearly two-thirds of the young women. It was more common for young men (28 per cent) than young women (20 per cent) to report having three or more partners (Mitchell *et al.*, 2014). In a review of South African studies of young people's sexual behaviour, Eaton, Flisher and Aaro (2003) found that the majority reported ever having only one partner, although a small proportion of females (1–5 per cent) and about one-quarter of males had had more than four partners in the previous year. In the UK study reported by Mercer *et al.* (2013), half of the 16- to 24-year-old young women and 40 per cent of the boys had only had one partner in the previous year while one-third of the males and one-quarter of the females had had two or more partners.

As might be expected, frequency of intercourse is still related to the nature of the relationship with one's partner – the more committed the relationship, the more frequent the sexual activity. In US and Australian studies, young girls tend to engage in fewer acts of intercourse with 'casual' partners or someone they had met for the first time than do boys, and are more likely to report that sexual activity occurs with regular or steady partners (Martinez, Copen & Abma, 2011; Mitchell *et al.*, 2014). Of course, it is possible that these young girls are avoiding the socially unacceptable role – at least for women – of taking part in a casual one-off sexual encounter by deluding themselves that the relationship with a new partner will last. Certainly, boys seem to be more willing than girls to engage in uncommitted sex. Mitchell *et al.* found that four times as many male than female high school students reported their most recent sexual partner was someone they had met for the first time.

It is not surprising that young women whose sexual experiences begin early report that their partners are older than themselves – on average about three years – whereas teenage boys report their partners to be the same age as themselves or slightly younger (Mitchell *et al.*, 2014). But in some cultures it is not uncommon for the age gap between young girls and their partners to be much greater. There is evidence from African research that some young women are engaging in sex with partners who are significantly older than they are (Jewkes, Levin & Penn-Kekana, 2003; Pettifor *et al.*, 2005). As Nkosana and Rosenthal (2007a, 2007b) noted in studies of intergenerational sex, there are multiple reasons why teenage girls have sex with older men. These include financial benefits:

> These men have supernatural buying power. They have money. They give us whatever we want. They buy us special watches, necklaces, earrings, cell-phones and clothes. (Adolescent female)
> *(Nkosana & Rosenthal, 2007a:183)*

Material gain was sometimes associated with envy and peer pressure. Some girls expressed a desire to have the things that their peers have and to enjoy the services enjoyed by their peers.

> The other motivating factor is envy; we are envious if we see one of the girls living a luxurious life, so we end up also joining the game of dating older people. (Adolescent female)
>
> *(Nkosana & Rosenthal, 2007a:183)*

The findings revealed that not all girls were passive and controlled by their older sexual partners. Some derived pleasure, enjoyment, love and equal partnership in these sexual relationships. They displayed a capacity to take charge of their own sexual lives by insisting on and engaging in safe sex behaviours. It is interesting that nearly one-third of these young women, when approached for sex by an older man, refused. Most cited personal factors, such as wanting to retain their decision-making power without being intimidated by someone who is older. Others had a strong sense of their own self-worth.

> I am not a commodity that can be purchased. I value myself so much and I believe there is no one who can attach any price to me. I don't look down upon myself, I believe I am special and that's what I am. Even though I don't have what my peers have materially, at least I have my freedom and peace of mind and I am happy with that. (Adolescent female)
>
> *(Nkosana & Rosenthal, 2007b:5)*

Regretting sex

This quote from an adolescent boy expresses a tone of regret that is not uncommon among young people.

> If I could change it I probably would . . . to keep it [my virginity] a bit longer and find someone more to connect with. I was pretty pissed so I don't even remember most of it. So yeah something I regret, being drunk for the first time. (Male, 14 years)
>
> *(Carmody, 2009:31)*

If we turn to the quality of adolescents' earliest experience of sexual intercourse, for many young people, their first act of coitus is not a pleasurable or satisfying one. Bettelheim captures something of the flavour of the experience for an earlier generation of adolescents.

American middle-class youth learns about sex in the back seat of a car, or during a slightly drunken party, or because there was nothing better to do to kill boredom. . . . The first sexual experience often leaves ineffaceable impressions, marred by a total lack of experience on either side. Both partners feeling anxious and insecure, neither one can offer encouragement to the other, nor can they take comfort from the accomplished sex act, since they cannot be sure they did it well.

(Bettelheim, 1962:68)

From virgin to non-virgin

We know from past research that even when sex is wanted, some young women find the transition from 'virgin' to 'non-virgin' is accompanied by feelings of ambivalence and/or distress (Pinquart, 2010). Even for those young people who are prepared for their first sexual experience, often through childhood sexual experimentation, masturbation or other explorations of their body, or through discussions with parents (usually their mother), first coitus can fail to live up to expectations. First sex is rarely the stuff of movies and magazine stories, romantic and wonderful. The reality can be painful and uninspiring.

Once again, even in western societies, there are differences in young people's responses to first intercourse. Albert (2007) reports a majority of American teenagers who say they wish they had waited longer to have sex, while in a national study of Dutch adolescents aged 12–24, the vast majority say their first sexual experiences – broadly defined – were wanted, well timed and fun (de Graaf, Meijer, Poelman & Vanwesenbeeck, 2005, cited in Schalet, 2010). Nevertheless, the same study found that 27 per cent of female respondents regularly or always have trouble reaching orgasm – and a majority felt pain at least sometimes during sex. Still, more than four out of five Dutch girls and young women said that they were (very) satisfied with the physical pleasure as well as the contact with their partner they experienced during sex (de Graaf *et al.*, 2005).

Recent evidence (Mitchell *et al.*, 2014) suggests that attitudes among Australian students are similar to those of their Dutch counterparts. In general, high school students reported feeling positive after their last sexual encounter. Almost all reported that they had wanted to have sex and about half the students reported feeling extremely happy, good or loved and less commonly reported negative feelings. The majority felt not at all upset (79 per cent), used (73 per cent) or guilty (69 per cent). It is true, however, that young women were less likely than their male counterparts to endorse the 'extreme' positive response. But although most students felt good about their last sexual experience, there was a substantial minority (20–30 per cent) who did not. A qualitative study of girls aged 14–19 years (Skinner, Smith, Fenwick, Fyfe & Hendriks, 2008) suggested some reasons for these feelings. Skinner *et al.* found that teenage girls who lose their virginity when they are not ready, often at an early age, are more likely to feel disappointed and regret the experience. She concluded that the degree of personal control over the situation that led to intercourse determined how these young women felt. Idealistic perceptions about sex and relationships, peer pressure, coercion from sexual partners and being drunk were common reasons for premature first experience of sexual intercourse.

A study of over 8000 young people in the Philippines, El Salvador and Peru (Osorio *et al.*, 2012) confirmed that first sex in these cultures was often the result of pressure or being 'carried away' by desire and was regretted even when love was associated with this sexual encounter, with young women more likely than young men to regret having already had sex. But in talking about pressure as a reason for unwanted sex, we need to ask which of the partners is using pressure. Stephanie and John had their first sexual intercourse unprotected, but Stephanie talks about self-pressure that resulted in this risky sex: 'My boyfriend never pressured me ever to do any of that.' Still she felt pressure, 'like I was obligated to because we were going out for so long' (Schalet, 2010:319).

Finally, we know that for a substantial minority of young people, the initiation of sex is not voluntary. Sufficient to say here that in the recent study by Mitchell and her colleagues cited above, over one-quarter of young women and one-fifth of young men had experienced an unwanted sexual encounter. The most common reasons for this were that they were too drunk, too high or their partner wanted them to. Interestingly, many more females than males had been pressured to have sex. One-third of females reported having sex because they were 'frightened', compared with 14 per cent of young men. Although it may be thought that unwanted sex provides an excellent example of the gendered power dynamics operating in the sexual world of young people, this study and an earlier one by Arbes-Dupuy (2000) hint at a more complex story showing that young men can be the recipients of unwanted sex, just as young women can be the perpetrators.

We should not leave this issue without reporting briefly some of the reasons Australian high school students gave for not having sexual intercourse (that is, remaining virgins). The most important of these were not feeling ready, being proud to be able to say no and mean it, with girls reporting these reasons as 'extremely important' more than boys (64 vs. 32 per cent and 62 vs. 37 per cent, respectively). Religious and cultural beliefs and parental disapproval were less important in the decision not to have sex (Mitchell *et al.*, 2014).

Sex and gender

The complex interaction of sex and gender is discussed later as another critical influence on the sexual context in which young people enact their sexuality. Here we touch on only a small aspect of the contribution of gender to sexual behaviours. Prior to the 'sexual revolution' of the 1960s, there were strong gender differences in attitudes to premarital sex. For young girls sex was equated with love and was only acceptable in a love relationship. Adolescent boys, on the other hand, were more likely to hold permissive attitudes and be favourably disposed to casual sexual adventures. This double standard extended to virginal status at marriage and is still held today by some, as this quote from one of our adolescent girls indicates.

> [Virginity] is something you should take care of, something special. I think it symbolises that you are clean and that there is nothing dirty about you. . . . You should keep it for your future husband even though he may have slept around. (Female, 16 years)
>
> *(Moore & Rosenthal, 2006:27)*

Most young boys, although wanting to be sexually experienced, required their wives to be virgins at marriage. There was considerable social support for this double standard, the most prevalent view being that girls 'set the standard' for sexual behaviour and that boys have the right to 'get what they can'.

These issues are taken up in Chapter 7; the point here is that although there has been a considerable increase in the extent of adolescent sexual activity, the changes in attitudes are neither as substantial nor as clear-cut as might be expected if behaviour is used as an indicator of attitudes. If sexual attitudes are imperfect predictors of adolescent sexual activity (and vice versa), what other factors help us understand young people's sexuality? This question provides a major focus for the remainder of this book.

The most important biological, psychological and sociological influences on sexual behaviour are dealt with in later chapters. These include the impact of puberty as well as factors such as family and peer influences, and the role of social and cultural norms that pervade the adolescent's daily life. Social institutions such as the family and religion exert their influence in three ways: they provide the norms for acceptable sexual behaviour; individuals in powerful roles in these institutions use norms as the basis for informal controls; and, finally, there are often formal rules that constrain sexual behaviour through fear of institutional sanctions.

The influence of sociocultural factors

One of the most powerful influences on adolescents' sexual experience is cultural background, irrespective of whether one talks about countries with a single national culture or about multicultural societies such as Australia, Britain and the US. Earlier in this chapter variations between countries in young people's sexual behaviours were noted. So, too, are there differences in societies where a mix of racial or ethnic groups live together. For example, differences are regularly reported in the US between African-American young people and their White and Latino peers, with the former sexually active earlier (Belgrave, 2009; Boyar, Levine & Zensius, 2011; Halpern & Haydon, 2012). The reasons for this difference are complex. Some writers believe that the socioeconomic differences between Black and White populations account for the disparity in sexual behaviour; others take a cultural norms approach, arguing that there are significant differences in the acceptability of early sexual experience. These two explanations may not be mutually exclusive. Long-term poverty may lead to different outlooks on marriage and child-bearing that affect attitudes to early sexual activity.

In one of our early studies in multicultural Australia, we found a relatively high level of sexual activity among older boys of Greek descent, and extremely low rates of premarital sex reported by Greek girls. Both the high rate for boys and the disparity between the sexes can be explained by the greater sexual freedom given to boys in the Greek culture and the strong emphasis on chastity for girls, at least at that time. We found similar attitudes among younger Greek-Australian adolescents, especially in matters of chastity and fidelity, particularly among girls (Moore & Rosenthal, 2006). As one girl told us:

> It is important for a girl to be a virgin on her wedding day. Because [if you were not a virgin] when you did get married and you tried to walk down the aisle wearing white, God would strike you down. In front of everyone! (Female, 16 years)
>
> (Moore & Rosenthal, 2006:26)

Social class has been frequently implicated as a key factor in studies of adolescent sexual behaviour. Living in poverty is associated with early sexual activity, possibly through the impact of poor life satisfaction and even poorer prospects. Although many adolescents aspire to good jobs and adequate incomes, with all the security that these imply, the reality is that many are trapped in a cycle of poverty. Small wonder that the perceived lack of options and desirable alternatives for the future lead some young people to increased sexual activity as a way of achieving immediate, if short-lived, pleasure. The nature of the inner-city environment may be another reason for the association between poverty and early sexual activity. Living in an environment characterized by poor and crowded housing and serious social disorganization, young people are often exposed to a street culture that valorizes male virility, as expressed in a variety of sexual exploits. Certainly the finding that rural youth, usually part of a close-knit homogenous culture, are less sexually experienced than their urban peers (Lammers, Ireland, Resnick & Blum, 2000) may be interpreted as resulting, at least in part, from the diffusion of a sense of community among urban young people as well as the increased opportunities for sexual activity.

A final influence is that of education. It seems that higher levels of educational achievement and clear educational goals are related to delayed premarital sex for both boys and girls, as is positive adjustment (Lammers *et al.*, 2000; Wheeler, 2010). The association between educational outcomes and sexual behaviour is mediated by a number of factors, including those discussed above. The achieving student is likely to come from a relatively well-to-do family, to place a high value on achievement, to be more goal-oriented and to be able to plan for the future. All these characteristics may lead to a low likelihood of sexual involvement at an early age.

We have by no means exhausted the sociocultural factors associated with early sexual adolescent activity, nor have we attempted here anything more than a brief description and a limited explanation of the effects of these factors. Later chapters will place these and other influences in the context of the adolescent's struggle to develop a sense of his or her sexual identity. For now we turn to one other aspect of sexual behaviour that is a source of particular concern, in the light of the reported increases in sexual activity.

Responsible sex? Contraception and STI prevention

The increased sexual activity among adolescents has led to concerns about young women's heightened risk of unplanned and/or unwanted pregnancies and, more recently, the dangers for both sexes of STIs. We might expect, in the light of these threats to adolescents' wellbeing and sexual health, that young people would have adopted contraceptive methods – and particularly condoms – with great alacrity. What do the figures on contraceptive use show? Alarmingly, whether we take as a measure contraceptive use at first intercourse, or the extent to which contraceptives are ever used, there is evidence that many adolescents are still ignoring (or not receiving) sexual health messages. This is especially so in developing countries or countries where there is a pervasive impact of poverty and lack of knowledge (Eaton *et al.*, 2003; Harris *et al.*, 2014).

Using condoms

We do not deal here with the wide range of contraceptive techniques available today, although the rates of unwanted pregnancies among young women indicate that their contraceptive practices leave them vulnerable; we take up this issue in Chapter 10. Here we focus on young people's use of condoms in the context of increasing rates of STIs, and the continuing threat of HIV/AIDS, especially in developing countries. Although there has been considerable increase in young people's acceptance of condoms during the past few decades, recent studies of condom use across many countries show that many young people use them inconsistently or not at all (Godeau *et al.*, 2008; Harris *et al.*, 2014; Martinez *et al.*, 2011; Mitchell *et al.*, 2014; Yu *et al.*, 2013). Most studies show greater use of condoms with casual than regular partners (Hock-Long *et al.*, 2013; Lim *et al.*, 2012).

The increase in prevalence of condom use appears to have occurred largely because many young people now use condoms 'sometimes'. The meaning of this is complex from the point of view of adolescent sexual health. On the positive side it indicates increased exposure to condoms and the potential for improved skill in negotiating their use. But protection is not consistent. Young people are being influenced by situational factors that occur in sexual encounters, such as high arousal, alcohol and drug use, or partner reluctance, or making judgements about particular partners ('this partner looks too good to be diseased', 'this partner is someone I love therefore must be safe') and/or sexual situations ('bodily fluids are not going to be exchanged in this sexual situation', i.e. withdrawal is practised) which lead them to reject the need to use condoms. A nonchalant attitude to condoms was expressed by this young man in a qualitative study of males aged 15–25 years by J.L. Smith *et al.* (2012).

> There can be all the adverts in the world out there but if you don't have a condom then you're still going to have unsafe sex in my experience. It doesn't tend to stop me. (Male, 22 years)
>
> *(J.L. Smith* et al.*, 2012:491)*

The young man quoted above was categorized by the authors as 'lacking consequential thought' (J.L. Smith *et al.*, 2012:490). On a positive note, they also identified a group of young men who were clear in their intentions to stay safe, especially with casual partners.

> I've had times when I've met girls who don't want to use them. I say, hey, that's how it is. I'm not going to take a chance for one night of lust for the rest of my life in pain, no way. (Male, 24 years)
>
> (J.L. Smith et al., 2012:490)

In a 'companion' study of young women, J.L. Smith, Skinner and Fenwick (2011) provide fascinating insights into why they fail to use contraception, including condoms. They identify three categories of approaches to contraception among these young women. 'Holding the reins' represents authority and control on the part of these girls, exemplified by their assertive and uncompromising approach to condom use, among other forms of contraception.

> I'm pretty like headstrong, like I wouldn't really falter. Like if a guy was saying, oh come on you know let's do it without protection, I am just like, no you're an idiot. It's my way or the highway. (Female, 18 years)
>
> (J.L. Smith et al., 2011:630)

A second class of response, 'Letting nature take its course', was related to a lowered concern about becoming pregnant:

> At first we were using condoms and stuff but then after we were like properly seeing each other he didn't cause we were in love then, so there was no need. (Female, 18 years)
>
> (J.L. Smith et al., 2011:631)

The final category, 'Lowering the guard', was particularly relevant for young women who had low perceptions of pregnancy risk and were shocked when this occurred.

> We used condoms for a couple of months and then I don't know what happened, we just fell in love with each other too soon. (Female, 15 years)
>
> (J.L. Smith et al., 2011:631)

As the authors note, the narrative of 'being in love' is one driver of the experience of condom non-use. They comment '[T]hemes of procrastination, reluctance, forgetting, and lost inhibitions emerged as the main reasons for not using contraception and accounted for their greater willingness to have unprotected sex' (J.L. Smith *et al.*, 2011:631).

With greater sexual experience the responsibility for contraception often falls on the young woman. There is evidence that many young people stop using condoms when the female partner is using an oral contraceptive or other long-acting reversible contraception (Mitchell *et al.*, 2014), rationalizing this through assuming safety as J.L. Smith *et al.* (2012) found.

> If you know that someone's on the Pill then there's not that same incentive to use a condom. (Male, 18 years)
>
> *(J.L. Smith et al., 2012:491)*

Unfortunately the disease prevention role of condoms is either not recognized or is forgotten in favour of protection from pregnancy. It is interesting to speculate about the reason(s) for discarding condoms when the pill is used. Young people appear to be subject to two potentially conflicting discourses around sexual health that are related to condom use. The 'safe sex' discourse is a more recent phenomenon, arising out of the HIV/AIDS pandemic. This discourse emphasizes the use of condoms for protection against STIs and HIV. The other discourse ('pregnancy prevention') has been around a lot longer – the emphasis here is on effective contraception rather than disease prevention and the best way to ensure this is by using a contraceptive pill. The problem for many young people is that these two become conflated. Safe sex (no exchange of bodily fluids) equals contraception, but the converse does not hold.

It seems that the term 'safe sex' has been hijacked to mean contraception. Although the condom has long been used for contraception, it was only at the start of the HIV/AIDS epidemic that the condom was grafted on to the notion of disease prevention, and the term 'safe sex' was coined. It should not surprise us that some young people, who mostly perceive the likelihood of acquiring an STI as remote, have taken the 'condom for safe sex' message as relating only to the prevention of unwanted pregnancy.

In addition, J.L. Smith and colleagues learned there is now, among some young men, a 'dismissive' discourse around STIs, linked to perceptions that STIs are not very serious and are curable: '[Y]ou can take antibiotics for a month and it will go away' (J.L. Smith *et al.*, 2012:491). The fact that HIV, once seen as a fatal threat, is now regarded as a chronic disease when treated with drugs may also feed this attitude.

There is, however, encouraging evidence that some young people do use dual methods of contraception, usually condoms and the pill, when having sex. As one 18-year-old in J.L. Smith and her colleagues' study said:

> You can never guarantee that a condom is not going to break. You can
> never guarantee that you're going to remember the pill. I mean if you're
> taking the pill your partner needs to be wearing condoms if you don't
> want to have a baby because it's just double insurance. (Female, 18 years)
>
> *(J.L. Smith et al., 2011:630)*

It is clear that, for this young woman, the insurance is about pregnancy, not
the risk of an STI. In other studies, it is difficult to tease out the reasons why
dual methods are used, but it is reassuring that more young people are being
doubly safe (Godeau *et al.*, 2008; Martinez *et al.*, 2011).

Why don't young people use contraception?

There are a number of reasons for contraceptive risk-taking among adolescents. They may be ignorant about the need for contraception, they may not
know how to use contraceptives, or they may be lacking in the skills necessary to go about the often embarrassing or difficult process of gaining access
to contraceptive advice and devices. Even with the appropriate knowledge
and skills, young people may not like the idea of using contraception or, at
best, feel ambivalent about this 'intrusion' into their sexual life. Finally, of
course, there may be overwhelming structural barriers to contraceptive use.
If access to contraception is difficult or if its cost is beyond the reach of the
adolescent then it is likely that, even with the best intentions, contraceptive
use will be minimal or absent.

Another factor that makes decisions about contraception difficult is the
frequently sporadic nature of adolescent sexual activity. Unlike most adult
sexual behaviour, adolescents' forays into sexual intercourse are likely to
be inconsistent and marked by long periods with no activity. This makes
the choice of contraceptive difficult, with 'female' options such as the pill
or intrauterine device (IUD) non-optimal, and the condom a more logical
option. But, as we shall see, there are barriers to making this apparently reasonable choice. Concerns about STIs add further complexity to the decision
about which contraceptive to use.

One way of understanding contraceptive behaviour in the light of the many
possible barriers to contraceptive use is to turn the problem on its head. What
factors must be present for adequate contraceptive behaviour to occur? How
knowledgeable are adolescents about their bodies and the reproductive process, and about the relationship between sexual activity and disease? What
evidence is there that this knowledge has an impact on adolescents' use of
contraceptives? The answer to the first question is encouraging. Many studies have shown that most adolescents, even young ones, have some understanding of conception and how their bodies work, they know that a girl can

become pregnant if she has intercourse, and the older adolescents are reasonably well-informed about contraception. STIs present a different picture. With the exception of HIV/AIDS, adolescents have surprisingly little knowledge of STIs, or of their methods of transmission and ways of avoiding infection. In the most recent study of Australian high school students (Mitchell *et al.*, 2014), knowledge about STIs was poor and there were many who held incorrect beliefs. For example, about 40 per cent did not know that chlamydia can affect both men and women or that it can lead to sterility. About one-third did not know that hepatitis C could be transmitted by sharing needles through injecting drug use or by tattooing and body piercing.

For those young people who lack the appropriate knowledge, the solution may appear simple. Contraceptive use and disease prevention can be increased with increased knowledge. But even when adolescents seem to have adequate knowledge it is clear that effective contraception does not always follow. Gendered perceptions of power play a prominent role in whether young people believe they can control their sexuality. Suffice to say here that many young women feel that they have little power to call the tune when it comes to sexual activity.

Somewhat related to this is the idea of self-efficacy, or confidence in dealing with contraception. For those adolescents who have little confidence in their ability to purchase condoms or go to the doctor for a prescription for the pill, contraception looms as an almost insurmountable hurdle to negotiate. Even in this enlightened age when condoms are advertised widely as an important means of avoiding HIV/AIDS and other STIs, and are readily available in vending machines, 40 per cent of adolescent respondents, both boys and girls, reported they did not use a condom in their last sexual encounter (Mitchell *et al.*, 2014). Not expecting sex, trusting a partner and/ or knowing their partner's history and not liking condoms were the most common reasons given for this potentially risky practice.

Among those adolescents for whom contraception is a perceived option, attitudes vary. For some, using contraception is inconsistent with a view that sex is, or should be, spontaneous and unpremeditated. For girls, even in today's more enlightened climate, there may still be a high psychological cost in acknowledging that they are prepared for casual sex (as might be assumed by the practice of ongoing contraception, such as taking the pill, or carrying around a condom 'in case'). Other young people find contraception to be 'messy' or 'unnatural'. Still others say that it interferes with the enjoyment of sex.

Safe sex

A number of studies have drawn attention to problems arising from the inconsistent contraceptive behaviour of male adolescents, their apparent lack of concern about contraception, and the tendency for some young girls to rely on the 'contraceptive vigilance' of their partners. Why are so many young people, especially males, resistant to contraception? When effective methods of contraception are readily available and the dangers of unprotected sex are known to adolescents, why are they so cavalier in their use of this technique?

Most negative attitudes are directed towards male contraceptive methods, an unfortunate view since condoms are an optimal method of pregnancy and disease prevention for adolescents, certainly at first intercourse. Although some enlightened boys today accept that the possible price for not using condoms is too high, for others the benefits do not outweigh the costs. This cost–benefit analysis has been shown to determine young boys' condom use. For example, if they believed that it was the male's responsibility to prevent pregnancy, young boys were more likely to use condoms. If they believed that their partner was on the pill, or that pleasure would be reduced, condom use was inhibited (Moore & Rosenthal, 2006).

Even if an adolescent wants to use contraception, that decision usually has to be negotiated with the sexual partner except in those cases where the female has made the decision to use the pill or other long-term devices such as an implant or IUD. Here it is essential that the couple have the social skills that will enable open communication of their wishes and needs. Studies of young people's communication about sexuality and contraception reveal that many adolescents fail to discuss these important issues during a sexual encounter (Mitchell *et al.*, 2014). Girls are particularly diffident about initiating contraception discussions, their lack of assertiveness leaving them vulnerable when their partner is resistant to the use of contraceptives. There is some evidence that girls are expected by boys to take the responsibility for contraception, an expectation that may be unrealistic when considered in the context of the difficulties girls face in asserting their sexual needs. Even when both partners have the best of intentions, there can be failure to contracept. Many adolescents report non-use of condoms during a specific sexual encounter, in spite of their previous intention to have 'safe' sex.

Why is this so? With increased exposure to messages about contraception; particularly condoms, in the media and through sexual health programmes in schools, and with increasingly easy access to contraceptives at point of sale and through family planning clinics, we might expect to see most young people acting responsibly in their contraceptive behaviour. Yet this is not the case. Everything we know tells us that much adolescent sex is unplanned and that explanations of adolescent sexual behaviour do not fit easily into rational decision-making or problem-solving models. At best these give an idealized and partial explanation of the behaviour in question. What needs to be taken into account is the situationally determined and urgent nature of adolescent sex. What sort of relationship does the adolescent have with his or her partner? Is it a 'long-standing' sexual relationship or a casual 'one-night-stand'? Do alcohol or drugs play a part in the encounter? How sexually aroused are the partners? To what extent are they able to control their sexual urges in the absence of contraception? All these questions and many more need to be asked and answered before we can understand why adolescents fail to take adequate precautions against pregnancy or disease.

Conclusion

Adolescent sexuality is subject to a complex web of influences, including the physical and psychological characteristics of the individual, the historical period and the ecological setting. The decisions that young people make about their sexuality, the behaviours in which they engage, the values and attitudes that they hold – all these are shaped by the particular context in which the adolescent lives his or her life. At any given time, choices about sexual behaviour will reflect the different physical, social, cultural and economic environments in which adolescents live and their personal qualities and life histories. Given the diversity of experiences that young people draw on, consciously or unconsciously, in determining their sexual behaviours, it is not surprising that we find a remarkable heterogeneity in those behaviours.

Because the choices made by adolescents flow on and affect their sexual wellbeing as adults, we need to understand the inconsistencies as well as the consistencies in young people's sexual behaviour, the commonalities as well as the differences, and the rational as well as the non-rational bases for that behaviour. Adolescents must make important decisions about sexuality that will reverberate throughout their lives. In this chapter we have considered several of those decisions: the decision whether or not to initiate sexual behaviour and, if sexually active, whether or not to use contraception; the decision about the timing and nature of relationships, and acceptable sexual practices. All these decisions are made in the context of what the adolescent feels is right and proper for him or her to endorse. For some adolescents, there is little difficulty in making these decisions. For others, the choices are hard to evaluate.

3

CHANGING BRAINS, CHANGING HORMONES, CHANGING BODIES

Most of this book is about psychosocial aspects of adolescent sexuality: how social context, family, culture, beliefs, personality and emotions affect the sexual behaviour of young people and how, in turn, young people's sexuality impacts on the world. Yet in essence, sex is a biological act; its evolutionary purpose is procreation. We are driven by ancient urges even if, as socialized human beings, we need not be slaves to the forces of nature. In this chapter we deviate from the social/psychological approach and present a description of the biological changes of adolescence, including recent research and theories about how those changes influence behaviour. Although biological development does not tell us everything about how and why we behave sexually, understanding of these processes is vital if the whole picture of sexual development is to emerge. This chapter thus focuses on changing brains, changing bodies and changing hormones. The interactions between biology and the social world are underscored in some of the topics discussed in this chapter, including the current high levels of body and appearance dissatisfaction among adolescents, the implications of very early puberty and the strange but pervasive fashion for hairless pudenda.

Boys or girls: what is the difference?

The early years

Adolescence has traditionally been considered to begin at puberty, a key stage in the development of adult sexual form and function. Yet puberty, though dramatic, is not a sudden change but a process for which biological preparations have been occurring since conception. The single cell that begins life and arises from the combination of mother's egg and father's sperm usually contains 23 pairs of chromosomes. One pair of chromosomes holds the determinants of genetic sex. This pair is usually either XX, denoting a female, or XY, denoting a male. Each of these genetic configurations provides a blueprint for sexual development of the male or female type but, particularly in the case of the male, does not guarantee this development. Certain conditions in the physiological environment of the uterus must prevail. After birth, although the die is usually cast in a biological sense, conditions of the psychological environment and their interactions with biological features of the individual can influence the ways in which maleness and femaleness are manifest. This influence extends, eventually, to how puberty is experienced and how adult sexuality takes shape. Some of the details of these complex interactions, which are not fully understood, are discussed in this chapter.

For the first six weeks of life, the human embryo is sexually undifferentiated. During the prenatal period, gonadotropin-releasing hormone (GnRH) is produced by specialized neurons in the brain. These neurons intermittently secrete pulses of hormone from nerve terminals in the hypothalamus, which in turn sends signals to the pituitary gland (a small organ at the base of the brain) to secrete the gonadotropic hormones responsible for sexual differentiation (Lee & Styne, 2013; Sisk & Foster, 2004). In the normal course of events, males develop testicles and, somewhat later, females develop ovaries. These structures, termed gonads, themselves produce hormones that further direct the development of male and female internal and external sex organs. Hormone secretion and balance is controlled by the reproductive endocrine system, involving interactions between the brain, the pituitary gland and the gonads. Both male and female reproductive systems produce androgen (the masculinizing hormone) and oestrogen (the feminizing hormone) but it is the concentration and balance of these hormones throughout life that determine male or female morphology and, to some extent, behaviour. In utero, testicles produce enough androgen to dominate the oestrogen in the male while ovaries produce enough oestrogen to dominate the androgen in the female. Once sexual differentiation has occurred, GnRH secretion declines and hormone pulsing rates decrease dramatically and remain that way from birth right through to the prepubertal period.

When babies are born, there is usually no ambiguity: the doctor or nurse says 'It's a boy!' or 'It's a girl!' It is only in rare cases, when sexual differentiation is incomplete due to some biological discordance in the chromosomes and/or gonads, that gender assignment is difficult. In the 1960s and 1970s, the common western social view that gender was a 'social construction' led to experiments in sexual reassignment of infants with undifferentiated or damaged external genitalia. These experiments were largely unsuccessful. Long-term follow-up of some of these sexually reassigned children reinforced the power of 'nature' as a force in determining sexual identity, sexual feelings and sexual behaviours (e.g. Colapinto, 2000; Diamond & Sigmundson, 1999). Today the notion that some individuals prefer to call themselves intersex or transgender, rather than be categorized as male or female, is much more widely accepted. For example, legal documents such as passports in some countries allow individuals the opportunity to characterize themselves as 'male', 'female' or 'other/non-specific' (Australian Department of Foreign Affairs and Trade, 2014). We use the term 'intersex' in reference to individuals whose chromosomes, gonads or genitals do not align with the categories of male or female; 'transgender' and 'transsexual' refer to individuals whose gender identity or gender expression does not match their biological sex at birth. These are uncommon conditions but they demonstrate the complex interplay between biology and cultural norms in shaping the expression of gender.

Whatever their gender, as children approach puberty there is once again an increase in the pulsatile release of GnRH, particularly during the early hours of sleep. Puberty begins when GnRH secretion gradually increases to a high enough level to stimulate gonadotropin hormone (luteinizing hormone (LH) and follicle stimulating hormone (FSH)) and steroid hormone (testosterone and oestrogen) secretion, resulting (eventually) in sexual maturation. At first these hormonal concentrations peak in the later hours of sleep but the concentrations increase throughout puberty, and by late puberty the diurnal variation is no longer present (Styne & Grumbach, 2011). There have been various theories about the 'trigger' for the increase in GnRH and so the onset of puberty, discussed later in the chapter. Recent research postulates that the intriguingly named kisspeptin – encoded by the gene called *KiSS-1* – is the major controller of GnRH function. Kisspeptins activate a 'puberty gene' (*GPR54*) that drives the neurological developments characteristic of the beginning of pubertal change (Seminara *et al.*, 2003; Sisk & Foster, 2004). The relationship between neural functioning and hormone secretion appears to be a two-way street. Not only does the brain have a role in triggering hormone release, but evidence is accumulating that hormones, in turn, affect brain structure and function (Blakemore & Choudhury, 2006; Raznahan *et al.*,

2010; Schultz, Molenda-Figueira & Sisk, 2009). These effects have the potential to give rise to differences between male and female brains.

Hormonal changes at puberty

Thus many of the gender differences in social behaviours, risk-taking and cognitive functioning at adolescence may be associated with hormone-driven changes in brain circuitry. Raznahan et al. (2010) point to adolescence as a time when young men die at disproportionate rates through accident, violence, suicide and substance abuse and young women become disproportionately prone to depression, anxiety and eating disorders. They also cite male–female differences in cognitive abilities at adolescence, with girls tending to be better at language tasks and boys at spatial abilities. There is plenty of controversy over whether these variations are largely a function of biological differences between the sexes ('nature') or dissimilarities in how families and the broader society treat girls and boys ('nurture'). Raznahan et al. (2010) argue the case for biological determinism, noting that stereotypic gender behaviours can be disrupted in medical conditions in which there are chromosomal and hormonal abnormalities, and that there is a 'longstanding recognition of the primacy of biological influences in shaping behavioral sex differences throughout the rest of animal kingdom' (Raznahan et al., 2010:16988). Indeed, new technologies and creative experimental methods are certainly demonstrating many links between brain structure and/or function and behaviour, including evidence pointing towards sex differences in behaviour that may be 'hard-wired' rather than a result of environmental influence (e.g. Ringli, Kurth, Huber & Jenni, 2013; Witt, 2007).

The outcome of this neurobiological research has been a de-emphasis on the effects of socialization on behaviour and a re-emphasis on the effects of biology, but there is still much research to be done and many controversies to be worked through. For example, magnetic resonance imaging (MRI) and electroencephalography (EEG) studies tend to be of a correlational nature, associating aspects of brain structure or function with behaviour. In many cases however, cause–effect pathways have not yet been demonstrated: variations in behaviour could shape brain development just as growth and change in the brain can influence behaviour. In addition, not all studies of brain structure or function among adolescents show significant differences between the sexes (e.g. Xie, Chen & DeBellis, 2012) and, given the complexity of the experimental methods, many studies access only small samples of participants. Like all nature–nurture controversies, the 'truth' is difficult to tease out and the attempt to do so is perhaps not even sensible as biological and social forces are so intertwined. Clearly, biological differences affect the way individuals respond to environmental stimuli. Equally clearly, environment can modify biology. Discussions about the origins of sex differences in behaviour and personality are often more motivated by political than scientific concerns. This may be due to awareness that an over-emphasis on biological explanations can be interpreted – incorrectly – as somehow implying the validity of rigid and unchanging sex role stereotyping.

Puberty triggers

The bodily changes associated with puberty occur both inside the body and externally. They begin when the hypothalamus signals the pituitary gland to release more intense concentrations and more frequent pulses of the gonadotropic hormones into the bloodstream. These hormones, the release of which precedes noticeable bodily changes by about a year, stimulate increased production of oestrogen and androgen by the ovaries in the girl and the testes in the boy. The ovaries increase their production of oestrogen sixfold in the girl's body, and the testes produce 20 times the amount of the androgen (testosterone) in the boy's body. Both sexes have male and female hormones circulating in the bloodstream but the balance is different. During adolescence a boy's androgen level becomes 20–60 per cent higher than that of a girl, while her oestrogen level becomes 20–30 per cent higher than his.

What triggers the gene-based messages and the chemical signals from the hypothalamus to the pituitary to begin the release of gonadotropins is still being debated. Sisk and Foster (2004) argue that, from an evolutionary perspective, the timing of puberty will be based on the organism being sufficiently physically developed, socially linked and in an optimal environment to begin the reproductive process. This evolutionary explanation of the onset of puberty is one that relies on signals to the brain from within the body and from the environment, that the individual is 'ready enough' to develop mature reproductive organs and so be in a position to reproduce. These researchers suggest that there are likely to be multiple triggers for puberty because of the number and complexity of the variables that determine reproductive success.

Age and genetics

Age alone does not qualify, as puberty begins at different times for different people, although most adolescents begin within the age range of 9–16 years.

Lee and Styne (2013) list heritable factors, ethnic differences, weight, environmental pollutants and stress as all being implicated as triggers or disruptors to puberty's onset. We consider each of these in turn.

Twin and familial studies indicate that between about 40 and 80 per cent of the variance in puberty timing in girls can be explained by heritable factors (e.g. Morris, Jones, Schoemaker, Ashworth & Swerdlow, 2011). There are few studies of the genetics of male puberty (given that boys do not have the clear puberty marker of menarche), but twin studies of boys' growth spurts suggest very high heritability (Silventoinen, Haukka, Dunkel, Tynelius & Rasmussen, 2008). Ethnic differences in timing of puberty are also likely to be steered at least in part by genetic factors. Wu, Mendola and Buck (2002) found such differences among a US sample of 1168 girls aged 10–16 years (330 non-Hispanic White, 419 non-Hispanic Black and 419 Mexican American) for whom menarche data were available. The mean age at onset of menarche was 12.1 years for African-American girls, 12.2 years for Mexican American girls and 12.7 years for White girls. These ethnic differences remained even after adjustment for current body mass index and several social and economic variables. A large study of US boys by Herman-Giddens *et al.* (2012) also demonstrated racial differences, with African-American boys showing significantly earlier mean ages for genital development, pubic hair and testicular volume than White and Hispanic boys.

Weight

For girls, a strong predictor for the onset of menarche is weight (Lee & Styne, 2013). Over 40 years ago, Frisch and Revelle (1970) presented the controversial hypothesis that attainment of a critical body weight (around 47 kg for White girls) and a related change in metabolic rate sets off the decrease in hypothalamic sensitivity to sex hormones which in turn leads to pituitary activation. More recent research suggests it is adiposity (fat deposits) rather than weight that is important, although as Lee and Styne (2013) point out, the association between pubertal advancement and higher adiposity does not prove a causal link. Although there is much research yet to be done, the hormone leptin, discovered in 1994, may provide the mechanism that links puberty and body fat. Puberty in mice can be advanced experimentally by increasing leptin levels (Chehab, Mounzik, Lu & Lim, 1997) and leptin-deficient children do not attain puberty until this hormone is replaced (Farooqi, 2002). Leptin is secreted in fatty (adipose) tissue, with more adipose tissue leading to more leptin, which in turn may be a signal to the body that sufficient somatic growth has been attained to support pregnancy. There is some controversy about whether leptin levels and weight gain are 'start' signals for puberty in boys (Ahmed *et al.*, 1999; Lee & Styne, 2013). It has been argued from the evolutionary viewpoint that the lack of a clear link between puberty and weight in males is perhaps because males do not have to develop the energy reserves to support pregnancy and lactation (Sisk & Foster, 2004).

Environmental pollutants

Various environmental pollutants, including lead, dioxins, fire retardants, DDT and other insecticides, have been implicated in delaying puberty, although the research is equivocal except for the case of lead. Higher blood concentrations of this element are associated with delayed puberty in both girls and boys (e.g. Denham *et al.*, 2005; Williams *et al.*, 2010). It has also been speculated that hormonal supplements (particularly oestrogen) given to animals farmed for food may raise the level of sex hormones in children, potentially leading to earlier puberty in girls and feminization in boys. Lee and Styne (2013) point out that although there is a plausible argument that supplements and man-made chemicals have the potential to disrupt the human endocrine system, the research to date has reported conflicting results, perhaps due to the small samples and varying methods used, making comparison of results difficult. In addition, most pollutants occur as mixtures so the active ingredient associated with any damage is hard to assess. Further, it is quite possible that disruption to puberty, fertility or other sexual functioning through environmental pollutants may occur at 'critical periods' in development so that the timing of exposure needs to be considered in well-designed studies, which for ethical reasons are usually opportunistic, rather than true experiments with planned treatments and control groups.

Social factors

Social stressors are also linked with early puberty. Effects are relatively weak but difficult to explain from a purely evolutionary viewpoint. For example, girls in father-absent families show a tendency to reach puberty earlier, as do girls in families where an adult male is present who is not the girl's father (Ellis & Garber, 2000). Research also suggests that poor father–daughter relationship and maternal mood disorders are associated with earlier menarche (Bourguignon & Parent, 2010). A study of 3311 Turkish adolescents (Semiz, Kurt, Kurt, Zencir & Sevinc, 2009) showed lower menarchal ages for girls who were overweight and obese and/or experienced in-family stress (parents' marital conflict, physical violence of father to mother or of mother to offspring), while Trickett, Noll and Putnam (2011) and Zabin, Emerson and Rowland (2005) demonstrated that the experience of childhood sexual abuse was a predictor of early puberty in girls. For boys, the role of stress is more equivocal. The Turkish study of Semiz *et al.* found that boys subjected to family stress, specifically parents' marital conflict or parental separation, were more likely to experience delayed puberty. Graber, however, argues in a review that 'family stress clearly does not predict [pubertal] timing in boys' (Graber, 2013:266).

Whether puberty is early, delayed or 'on-time', it signals extensive physiological changes in brain and body as the child transitions to an adult. The changes in form and function have significant impact on all bodily systems – appearance, strength, fertility, functionality, cognitions, feelings and behaviours.

The adolescent brain: a work in progress

Nowadays there is no need to wait until people are dead to examine their brains; the advent of non-invasive brain scanning technology allows scientists to monitor brain development. Old ideas that brain function peaked at late adolescence and it was downhill all the way from then on have been well and truly overturned.

In adolescence there are significant changes in the brain's grey matter and white matter, and these have implications for cognition and behaviour. Furthermore, different parts of the brain mature at different rates. Grey matter in the cortex increases in volume throughout childhood until early adolescence. MRI brain scans of adolescents suggest that the increased growth of brain cells in the grey matter and their connections (synapses) peak at around 11 years for girls and around 12 years for boys. This change is then followed by synaptic pruning, in which grey matter volume again declines to adult volumes around the mid-twenties (Blakemore, Burnett & Dahl, 2010; Petanjek *et al.*, 2011; Selemon, 2013). The pruning occurs differentially in different parts of the brain, with the pre-frontal cortex, the site of higher order thinking and executive functioning, last to be affected (Gogtay *et al.*, 2004). The early adolescent dendrite growth allows for many more brain pathways; in other words the capacity of the brain is markedly increased. Pruning then increases the efficiency of the neural pathways and is thought to represent learning, in that certain well-used neural pathways are strengthened and unused pathways drop out (Lindenberger & von Oertzen, 2006).

White matter volume increases steadily between childhood and adolescence; growth then slows and stabilizes into adulthood during the mid-twenties (Blakemore *et al.*, 2010; Selemon, 2013). Males show significantly steeper age-related growth in white matter volume than females

(Perrin *et al.*, 2008, 2009). Myelination and thickening of axons is thought to be the main reasons for the increase in white matter volume. Myelination and synaptic pruning together in the prefrontal cortex improve the efficiency of information processing, and neural connections between the prefrontal cortex and other regions of the brain are strengthened (Segalowitz & Davies, 2004).

The functional significance of the brain changes in adolescence is not fully understood, but research is accumulating.

Improvements in brain function and working memory

Change in brain volume during adolescence (specifically grey matter thinning in the frontal lobes) correlates with improved cognitive performance, including verbal and spatial memory (Sowell, Delis, Stiles & Jernigan, 2001).

General intelligence is linked with developmental changes in cortical grey matter. A study reported in *Nature* (Shaw *et al.*, 2006) demonstrated that young people with very high intelligence showed 'robust' early adolescent increases in grey matter followed by equally strong grey matter thinning (or pruning) in later adolescence.

Neuroscientists believe that the period of pruning in adolescence is as important as the period of neuronal growth in childhood, because it leads to a consolidation of learning. Giedd and colleagues (Giedd *et al.*, 1999; Giedd, 2008) in their classic studies argue for the importance of adolescents engaging in activities that stimulate and 'exercise' the brain connections important for cognitive and psychomotor skills in adulthood, such as those involved in playing sport, academic study and music.

Age, working memory capacity and reading ability are positively correlated with myelination and axonal thickness in the left temporal lobe in children and adolescents aged 8–18 years according to an MRI study by Nagy, Westerberg and Klingberg (2004). They and others have concluded that the white matter changes, especially in certain areas of the brain such as the frontal lobes, are important in brain maturation and the development of higher cognitive functions – reasoning, planning and rational thought.

Problems in development during the cortical pruning phase

Researchers are of the opinion that there is an optimal level of pruning of synapses. Shaw *et al.* (2009) associated attention deficit hyperactivity disorder (ADHD) with excessive cortical thinning; others have suggested that the pruning process can go astray, leading to the loss of important neural connections which may in turn lead to psychiatric disorders such as schizophrenia, although this hypothesis is not yet fully supported by evidence (Boksa, 2012).

Further, while waiting for these changes to occur, the adolescent brain is 'still under construction' (National Institute of Mental Health, 2011) with the potential for mismatches between physical, emotional and cognitive development. Although some brain changes are linked with puberty as described previously, others are more dependent on age and experience. There can be incongruities between the bodily changes of puberty (increase in bodily strength, sexual maturity, adult bodily appearance, increasing sex drive) and the brain development required for mature decision-making and self-regulation of behaviour and emotions. The 'executive functioning' area of the brain – the prefrontal cortex – is among the last areas of the brain to fully mature, usually sometime in the twenties (Petanjek *et al.*, 2011). Adolescence therefore becomes a time of diminished prefrontal cortical control, which has been used to account for the high rates of risk-taking and poor judgements among young people, especially those in 'reward-sensitive' environments where the temptations of drugs, alcohol, speed and sex are high. Although adolescents may know and understand the dangers of their actions, and even be able to quote verbatim how to avoid these dangers, in the heat of the moment this knowledge may not be processed by the young, 'plastic' brain with its over-abundance of 'unhelpful' connections.

Indeed, Dahl (2004), in his address to the American Psychological Association on this topic, quotes Shakespeare's *The Winter's Tale*, Act III:

I would that there were no age between 10 and 23, for there's nothing in between but getting wenches with child, wronging the ancientry, stealing, fighting.

(Dahl, 2004:5)

Dahl points out that although these adolescent tendencies towards irrationality, impulsivity and risk-taking have been noted for millennia, the neurobehavioural underpinnings are only just beginning to be understood. Giedd reminds us, however, that the adolescent brain is not 'a broken or defective adult brain' (Giedd, 2008:341), but a system of great plasticity in which increased connectivity and integration between different brain parts and brain functions is occurring, making adolescence a time of 'great risk and opportunity'. For example, researchers believe that young people are more susceptible to addiction to alcohol, cannabis, nicotine, cocaine and other mind-altering substances (Ehrlich, Sommer, Canas & Unterwald, 2002; Johnston, O'Malley, Bachman & Schulenberg, 2013), and indeed that adolescence may be a 'critical period' in relation to potential for addiction (Chambers, Taylor & Potenza, 2003). It is not only addiction but also brain damage that is at risk, with Selemon (2013) describing studies indicating that the detrimental effects of alcohol consumption seem to be magnified in adolescence and young adulthood, in comparison with adults in their late twenties.

The implication is that if experimentation with these substances is to occur, the longer it is delayed the better. This is a different conclusion from one once suggested to parents with respect to alcohol – that if young people try it early in the context of family, they will get used to it and learn to drink responsibly. The neuroscience of brain plasticity leads to the conclusion that it is better to delay until the brain circuitry is wired into its more mature adult form, and more capable of decision-making on the basis of knowledge, not just emotion.

Further, the adolescent brain is considered more responsive to stress than the adult brain and, as a consequence, is potentially more vulnerable to depression (Andersen & Teicher, 2008). The extreme stress of sexual abuse may well have different consequences for adolescents than for children, with a small study by Andersen et al. (2008) showing that sexual abuse is associated with different brain pathology depending on whether it occurs in childhood or adolescence. Prefrontal cortex grey matter volume deficits were more pronounced in adult subjects who experienced sexual abuse at ages 14–16 than among those for whom the abuse had occurred earlier.

Empathy may also be compromised during adolescence. A range of studies (Choudhury, Blakemore & Charman, 2006; McGivern, Andersen, Byrd, Mutter & Reilly, 2002) argue that the development of empathy or social perspective-taking undergoes changes during puberty in parallel with the discontinuous processes of brain maturation, in that the ability to take another's point of view may be affected during the period of synaptic thinning. McGivern et al. suggest that social insight requires a 'fully connected' frontal lobe, and adolescents are only 'partially connected'. His team examined the reaction times of 246 children (10–17 years) and 49 young adults (18–22 years) in response to emotionally related information. Correct identification of emotions was significantly faster at 10 years than at 11 and 12 years of age in girls and boys, the approximate ages of puberty onset. A peripubertal rise in reaction time declined slowly over the following 2–3 years and stabilized by 15 years of age. Blakemore (Blakemore, 2008; Blakemore & Choudhury, 2006) reviewed several studies relating to an interruption at puberty in the developmental course of face recognition and mental state attribution, and speculated that this setback in emotional growth relates to functional changes during adolescence of the 'social brain' – the medial prefrontal cortex and the superior temporal sulcus. These parts of the brain are apparently underdeveloped and underused by adolescents compared to adults, but as young people mature, they begin to use these regions more during decision-making, indicating that they increasingly consider others when making choices.

In summary, the adolescent brain is a 'work in progress'. As the body needs to be nourished, exercised and protected during its periods of growth and change, so too does the brain. Although to date there are few studies that tell us how this should occur, those that do exist, along with common sense and 'the wisdom of the ages' suggest that the best approaches are likely to involve avoidance/delay of addictive substances and unhealthy activities (e.g. gambling, viewing pornography) along with participation in exercise, learning, practice at judgement and problem-solving and continued education in social perspective-taking. Although we cannot put the lid on young people's burgeoning sexuality (nor would we wish to), there is a sense in which caution, protection and delay is warranted as an antidote to risky and unsafe behaviours and choices.

Adolescent bodies: sweat, pimples and beauty

More visibly, adolescence marks the final phase of physical growth, resulting in adult stature and physical sexual maturity. About one year after pubertal hormonal activity has been initiated, the adolescent growth spurt begins. This leads to an average increase in height for girls of 19.6 cm and for boys of 21.1 cm, although there is great individual variation. The growth spurt begins for girls any time between 9 years and 15 years, with the average age at about 10.5 years. The peak year of growth occurs at 12 years and the growth spurt is usually completed by age 14. For boys, the growth spurt generally starts later between 10 and 16 years, with the average age of commencement being 12.5, peak at age 14 and spurt completion at 16 or 17. The average duration of the growth spurt is 2.8 years for both sexes.

Growth in height is dramatic during this period. Much of this is in trunk length and the long bones of the legs, contributing to the stereotype of the gangly adolescent. Because of the delay in onset of the growth spurt among boys, 12-year-old girls are on average taller than boys, but this is reversed for all subsequent ages. Weight gains occur also, largely due to increases in muscle and fat, with increases in muscle size contributing to increased strength. Power, athletic skill and endurance all increase progressively and rapidly through adolescence with most boys surpassing most girls on these dimensions. Bodily proportions also alter. Children begin puberty with shoulders slightly broader than hips. For girls, the shoulder width/hip width ratio decreases throughout puberty whereas for boys this ratio increases.

Changes for girls

Sexual maturation for girls includes the growth of pubic and axillary hair, breast development and menarche. Girls' progress through puberty is generally assessed by the five Tanner stages of each of pubic hair and breast development (Marshall & Tanner, 1969). The study by Wu *et al.* (2002) of 10- to 16-year-old girls in the US showed the average age at onset of pubic hair and the beginning of breast development was about 9.5–10.5 years, with the mean age for menarche about 12.5 years, although there were significant ethnic differences as mentioned earlier. Rubin *et al.* (2009) charted puberty development in nearly 3000 8- to 13-year-old girls in the UK and found the estimated median ages of beginning breast and pubic hair development were 10.1 years and 10.9 years respectively. Only one girl had attained menarche by age 8; 60 per cent had done so by age 13, with the estimated median age being 12.9 years. This latter age, however, does not represent a mean age for attainment of menarche, as 40 per cent of the girls in the sample had not yet reached this milestone, for which the 'normal' age range in developed countries is between about 10 and 16 years.

The menstrual cycle introduces a pattern of hormonal variations associated with ovulation, building up of the uterine lining in preparation for fertilization, and the shedding of this lining via the menstrual period. Oestrogen and progesterone levels rise and fall in association with these events. The uterus, vagina, vulva, clitoris and other internal structures undergo growth and development so that the adolescent girl has a functional reproductive system about 12–18 months after the first menstrual period and is then physically capable of bearing children.

Changes for boys

Sexual maturation for boys involves increased growth of the testes, scrotum and penis, pubic, bodily and facial hair development, and maturation of the internal prostate gland and the seminal vesicles. The five Tanner stages of genital development and pubic hair development in boys have traditionally been used to measure progress through puberty (Marshall & Tanner, 1970), although today the most widely used indicator for puberty onset in boys is a testicular volume of >4 mL (Lee & Styne, 2013). In the study by Herman-Giddens *et al.* (2012), boys in the US reached this milestone on average at about age 11.5 years. The first ejaculation of seminal fluid is likely to occur about 2 years after the beginning of pubic hair growth – either as a spontaneous emission or the result of masturbation. The number and mobility of sperm present in the seminal fluid increases throughout puberty, with a corresponding increase in fertility. Other changes include an increase in the size of the larynx, leading to the voice changing to a deeper register and, for boys and girls alike, growth of the sweat glands with accompanying increases in body odour and enlargement of the pores on facial skin. This last change, accompanied by hormonal changes, leads to the increased likelihood of acne.

It would be surprising if these momentous changes came and went without impact. The alterations to appearance, sexualization of the body, increasing hormone concentrations and their effects on mood and libido, uneven growth rates and inevitable comparisons with one's peers must all be coped with and incorporated into a new, adult body image. Mood swings, embarrassment and self-consciousness are common at this age. Physical awkwardness often results from growth asynchronies. Arms that are 15 cm longer than they were a year ago are apt to knock things over. Adolescents often appear to others as 'all arms and legs'. Other potential embarrassments for the self-conscious teen include body odours and acne. Many young people worry whether their growth patterns are normal. The peer group can be relentless in its pressure for conformity so that being, or even feeling, different in terms of body shape or fitness can be stressful. As adults we may see the acne as temporary, the growth spurts and awkwardness as colt-like grace, the fitness and flexibility as enviable and the young firm bodies as beautiful, but what adolescents see in the mirror often falls short of their ideal. Accordingly, we now turn attention to the effects of pubertal change and timing on body image and adjustment.

Timing of puberty

Secular trend

The average age at onset of puberty has shown a trend towards earlier occurrence – 'the secular trend' – which cuts across geographic and ethnic lines. Lee and Styne (2013) cite copious research indicating that there has been a decline in the age of menarche of 1–4 months per decade in industrialized Europe and the US over the last 150 years. In eighteenth-century Europe, menarchal ages of 17–18 years were recorded, whereas current data indicates that the age of about 12.5 years is average among girls in developed nations. The decline in the age of puberty across the twentieth century is thought to be due to improvements in nutrition and living conditions and has been linked with diet and weight in early infancy and late childhood.

Herman-Giddens, Kaplowitz and Wasserman (2004) point out, however, that earlier puberty is not always indicative of optimal functioning. They note the association between being overweight and earlier puberty. Lee and Styne (2013) argue that the secular trend had plateaued in most industrialized countries by the 1960s, but stepped up again in the last two decades. In the twenty-first century, an increasing number of girls and boys in the US are beginning puberty earlier than documented in studies in the last half of the previous century (Herman-Giddens, 2007; Herman-Giddens *et al.*, 2012). For example, Herman-Giddens *et al.* (2012) in a large study of 4131 healthy boys aged 6–16 years showed that boys are entering puberty earlier than previously thought, providing a convincing demonstration that male puberty begins in the general population around 10–11 years of age, 6–24 months earlier than is understood from studies undertaken 40–50 years ago. Among girls, breast and pubic hair development is increasingly common in otherwise healthy girls as young as 6–8 years. Similar trends have been noted in other western countries, for example in the study by Rubin *et al.* (2009) of girls in the UK. Although the earlier trend was seen to be associated with better health and nutrition, these researchers argue that 'the recent secular trend towards early puberty parallels that of the obesity epidemic' (Rubin *et al.*, 2009:254).

Very early puberty

When the onset of puberty is earlier than 8 in girls or 9 in boys it is described as precocious puberty (Blakemore *et al.*, 2010), a condition that occurs 10 times more often in girls than boys. Roberts notes that 'puberty has long been seen as signaling the end of childhood, so its occurrence in middle childhood (6–8 years) disturbs our sense of the life course' (Roberts, 2013:140). Medical tests are usually performed to check for serious (but rare) conditions such as pituitary tumours, but if health is otherwise normal there are two potential courses of action: no intervention or medical suppression of puberty with long-acting injections of gonadotropin-releasing hormone analogues. These injections, although usually well tolerated, can be uncomfortable and cause side effects so that some parents (and children) choose not to undertake this. Nevertheless, numerous blogs, newspaper and magazine articles have in recent years commented on the anxiety felt by girls and their parents about precocious puberty.

In one article, Christopher (2013) interviewed early-maturing girls and their mothers. A parent whose daughter reached menarche at age 9 said,

> This is a little girl. We'd only just sorted out her wetting the bed and [she] went straight on to periods.
>
> *(Christopher, 2013:14)*

Another mother asked:

> How do I prepare a seven-year-old to get her period? I mean they're still babies at that age. They don't understand what's needed in terms of the hygiene if you're not with them.
>
> *(Christopher, 2013:13)*

As Roberts (2013) says, the worst fear of parents is that children who look like adolescents will be pressured to act like them; they will be the object of sexual attention well before they are ready to cope with it. One young woman summed up her feelings about being tall, large breasted and having her first period at age 10:

> Sexual attention from adult men really screws with your head when you're a child.
>
> *(Christopher, 2013:13)*

Psychological effects of early and late puberty

What are the psychological effects of non-normative pubertal timing? This is a topic that has been widely researched, first in the 1960s and 1970s and again in the last 20 years. The first major studies of early and late puberty – the Oakland Growth Study and the Berkeley Growth Study – found that during their adolescence, early-maturing boys had advantages over their late-maturing counterparts in self-assurance, poise, confidence, relaxation and popularity, in fact in a range of social and academic performance characteristics (Mussen & Jones, 1957; Peskin, 1967). The explanation given was that because of their more manly appearance, early developers were more likely to be chosen as leaders, to be popular with peers and to be given responsibility by adults. These are all situations that are likely to increase feelings of self-worth and self-esteem. More recent studies and reviews suggest that the social advantages bestowed on early-maturing boys may no longer be evident, and that results from studies conducted during the 1950s and 1960s cannot be generalized to the contemporary situation. Today, studies are indicating that early-maturing boys are more likely than their late-maturing counterparts to exhibit elevated internalizing and externalizing behaviours in early to mid-adolescence (e.g. Mendle & Ferrero, 2012; Negriff & Susman, 2011), such as attention deficit hyperactivity disorder, oppositional defiant disorder, conduct disorder, hostility, aggression and risk-taking behaviours, as well as higher levels of depression and anxiety. Although these effects are generally small, they certainly lead us to rethink the previously supposed advantages of early puberty for boys.

Differences between findings of studies conducted recently and in the mid-twentieth century may relate to variations in methodologies used. The California Growth Studies of the 1950s used projective measures of adjustment rather than today's more reliable clinical indicators. As well, a re-analysis of the data by Peskin (1967) showed that even in the 1950s study, the early-maturing boys had more mood disorders than their peers, including greater anxiety and more frequent temper tantrums. Finally, the age range used for defining an 'early maturer' (not specified in the 1950s studies) is likely to have lowered in this century because of the secular trend. The implication is that those who reach puberty earlier these days are now younger than their counterparts in the 1950s, and therefore less able to cope with the changes and expectations they are facing. Indeed, Ge, Conger and Elder (2001) argue that this is the case. Their study showed maladjustment associated with pubertal signs in Grade 7 boys (about age 12), but not Grade 8 boys.

Not surprisingly, boys who mature earlier tend to be sexually active at younger ages (Mendle & Ferrero, 2012) and are more likely than later developing peers to download internet pornography (Skoog, Stattin & Kerr, 2009). The higher levels of sexual activity for early-maturing boys appear to be associated with testosterone levels and have been replicated cross-culturally, for example in Zimbabwe (Campbell, Prossinger & Mbzivo, 2005), Sweden (Edgardh, 2002), the UK (Downing & Bellis, 2009) and Hong Kong (Lam *et al.*, 2002).

Late maturing in boys has also been associated with symptoms of depression and some externalizing behaviours during the adolescent period (Negriff & Susman, 2011) but findings are not so robust as for early-maturing boys. Follow-up studies of off-time developers are rare, but there is some suggestion that late maturation is a risk factor for conduct disorders and substance abuse in young adulthood (Graber, Seeley, Brooks-Gunn & Lewinsohn, 2004; Graber, 2013), whereas early maturation for boys is associated with fewer negative sequelae in adult life (Graber, 2013).

The outlook is far more positive for late-maturing girls, who tend to do better at school and show little psychological symptomatology in comparison with peers (Graber, 2013). On the other hand, across several cultural groups early maturing in girls is a risk factor for poor body image, depression, substance abuse, eating disorders and disruptive behaviour (e.g. Alcala-Herrera & Marvan, 2014; Copeland *et al.*, 2010; Graber, 2013; McCabe & Ricciardelli, 2004; Stice, Presnell & Bearman, 2001). Graber (2013) argues that in comparison with early-maturing boys, girls who reach puberty before their peers demonstrate greater severity in both internalizing and externalizing disorders. This is a clearly vulnerable group, at least during their adolescence. Copeland *et al.* (2010) found most problems dissipated by young adulthood, however the tendency towards depression remained, especially in young women who also had conduct problems during their teenage years. In addition, early-maturing girls had more sexual partners than their late-maturing counterparts, raising the possibility of unplanned pregnancy or the risk of sexually transmitted infections for this group.

Explanations for 'off-time' effects

The most common explanation given for the higher levels of maladjustment among early-maturing and to some extent late-maturing adolescents is that they are out of step with their peers at an age when peer acceptance is so important (the 'off-time' hypothesis). Because girls sexually mature about 2 years before boys, the off-time experience will be more intense for early-maturing girls (who might begin puberty at about 8 years of age) and late-maturing boys (whose puberty might not start until around 15 or 16). Early-maturing girls worry about their weight, may be embarrassed by their adult-like bodies when their friends are still children in appearance, and may feel pressured into sexual activity (or at least be subject of the 'sexual gaze') before they are ready to handle it. Parents and teachers may place higher expectations for the behaviours and performance of early maturers of both sexes, which can, of course, have either positive or negative effects depending on the child's own proclivities. Late-maturing boys are less likely to excel at sport or to be attractive to or interested in romantic partners during their adolescent years. Both these issues may affect popularity with peers which can, in turn, lead to acting out or internalizing. Late-maturing children may do well at school because they are less distracted by burgeoning sexuality, but this is only likely to happen in relatively protected environments where friendships and popularity are not overly compromised by a child-like appearance.

Although there may be currency to this social account, Graber (2013) argues for a more biological explanation of behavioural disorders among those with non-normative pubertal timing. In this scenario, hormonal changes at adolescence are hypothesized as vulnerabilities because of their effects on brain function. As discussed earlier in the chapter, the development of brain functions concerned with social information processing and reward sensitivity occurs earlier in adolescence than the more gradual development of the brain's cognitive control systems or 'executive functioning'. Graber postulates that there is a greater time lag in these different aspects of brain development for early maturers, leading to this group becoming more vulnerable to impulsive and risk-taking behaviours, and to heightened emotional arousal implicated in the development of psychopathologies such as depression. These young people will be more vulnerable to stresses from peers, school and family (and their vulnerabilities will last longer) than those with fewer asynchronies in their brain development. Using this model, problems faced by late-maturing adolescents are more difficult to explain but, as noted, research suggests these tend to be of smaller magnitude.

Adolescents: slaves to their hormones?

Although testosterone is termed the male sex hormone, it is present in females albeit in much lower concentrations. This hormone plays a key role in the development of the male reproductive system and secondary sex characteristics, and it is also associated with sexual arousal and behaviour. For example in one study, men who were exposed to scents of ovulating women maintained testosterone levels higher than those of men exposed to non-ovulation cues (Miller & Maner, 2010). Falling in love apparently decreases men's testosterone levels (Marazziti & Canale, 2004), as does becoming a father (Berg & Wynne-Edwards, 2001). Peper and Dahl (2013) reviewed studies to support the argument that increased testosterone leads to the adolescent brain becoming more sensitized to social rewards, which in turn can promote behaviour designed to raise status in the peer group, for example acting out, risk-taking or responding to peer pressure. Testosterone has been linked to higher rates of sexual activity, aggression and competitive behaviour, although not all studies show these relationships, as discussed below.

Oestrogen and progesterone drive female sexual development, and the concentrations of these hormones and associated neuropeptides in both females and males are related to behaviour and mood. Love and romantic feelings appear to be triggered by higher levels of the neuropeptide oxytocin (released in response to oestrogen), whereas vasopressin, the neuropeptide released in response to testosterone, is more strongly associated with sexual arousal (Hiller, 2005). But research on relationships between hormone levels and behaviours is often equivocal. For example, social mythology suggests that women fluctuate in their mood, interest in sex and self-esteem at different stages of the menstrual cycle. Although there is some research evidence to support this (e.g. Ziegler, 2007), not all studies show these effects. For example Schwartz, Romans, Meiyappan, De Souza and Einstein (2012) demonstrated that fluctuations in ovarian hormones (directly assessed through urine samples) did not contribute significantly to daily mood in healthy women.

Furthermore, similar levels of hormone concentration in different individuals do not necessarily lead to similar behaviours, and correlations between hormone levels and behavioural outcomes are typically weak (Halpern, 2003). Social circumstances have a tempering effect. For example, Rowe, Maughan, Worthman, Costello and Angold (2004) found that testosterone levels in adolescent boys were unrelated to the expression of aggression but did link to conduct disorder symptoms among boys with antisocial peers. However if the boys had non-deviant peers, their testosterone levels were associated with leadership abilities and behaviours. This study is one of several that suggests that the strength of association between hormones and behaviour will be modified by the social context in which the adolescent finds himself or herself, including internalized and externalized social sanctions and peer pressures.

Particularly relevant to adolescents is Buchanan, Eccles and Becker's (1992) proposal that changes in hormone levels within an individual – which come about during the developmental changes of puberty – require some adjustment. For example, although adult women may be accustomed to the effects of hormone level variations accompanying the menstrual cycle, early-adolescent girls may be highly responsive to these. High concentrations of certain hormones for one's age or rapid fluctuations of hormone levels may trigger more negative moods and greater mood variability. The important determiners of mood are not necessarily hormone levels per se, but the deviations in concentration from those with which the adolescent is familiar.

In summary, although sex hormones are enormously influential in growth and development, sexual maturity, sex drives, fertility and reproduction, their associations with behaviour are mediated and moderated by many factors, including individual differences, peer group influence and stresses within the family, school and wider social context. Although hormonal fluctuations may have a strong influence on susceptible individuals in vulnerable situations, most young people eventually learn to cope with changes in mood and motivation. A supportive environment along with clear expectations for, and encouragement of, socialized and mature behaviour are likely to help adolescents to manage their mood intensities. A higher degree of watchfulness from family and community organizations may be in order for those young people who are particularly at risk of internalizing or externalizing disorders because of their biological tendencies, environmental stresses or the interactions between these.

Body dissatisfaction: an epidemic of our times?

Sue Townsend's (1982) fictional adolescent, Adrian Mole, kept a diary full of fraught reflections on his growth spurt and the agonizingly (to him) slow growth of his 'thing' (penis):

> Tuesday September 8th Lousy stinking school on Thursday. I tried my old uniform on but I have outgrown it so badly that my father is being forced to buy me a new one tomorrow. He is going up the wall but I can't help it if my body is in a growth period can I? I am only five centimetres shorter than Pandora now. My thing remains static at twelve centimetres.

> Friday February 26th My thing is now thirteen centimetres long when it is extended. When it is contracted it is hardly worth measuring.
>
> *(Townsend, 1982:177)*

Such reflections are found not only among the fictional. Weinshenker (2010), writing online about young people and body image, quotes some real adolescents:

The best body is ribs, skin and bones, and that's the only thing I care about. (Female, 12 years)

I'm fat and ugly. I have to lose twenty pounds. I need a nose job, my hair is a mousy color; my lips are too thin and I could use lip injections. I exercised my stomach muscles and now they're hard, but I still have a belly. (Female, 15 years)

(Weinshenker, 2010)

It is true that one of the most compelling examples of the biological–social nexus comes from adolescents' concerns about their bodies. Early research addressed this by examining adolescents' feelings about their body image and the consequences of physical attractiveness. Most boys and men say that they want to be taller, more muscular and heavier. Many, if not most, young girls dislike their bodies, seeing themselves as fat or overweight when in fact they are either average or below average weight for their age and height.

Gender differences in body dissatisfaction

A robust finding in the research literature is that body image issues loom larger for girls. For example, Bucchianeri and colleagues (2012) in the US conducted a 10-year longitudinal, population-based study of 1902 participants, examining changes in their body dissatisfaction from adolescence to young adulthood. They found that body dissatisfaction was much higher for girls than boys; even the highest levels of males' dissatisfaction were, on average, lower than the lowest levels of females' dissatisfaction. A recent Finnish study of early to mid-adolescent girls and boys (Makinen, Puukko-Viertomies, Lindberg, Siimes & Aalberg, 2012) showed similar findings; girls' mean scores on a body dissatisfaction index were 30.6 compared to the boys' mean score of 18.9. Underweight girls were most satisfied with their bodies, but (on average) both normal weight and overweight girls were dissatisfied. This is not to say there are no body image pressures for boys and young men. The relatively new 'metrosexual' ideal for young men in cosmopolitan cities throughout the world involves careful attention to grooming, spending money on clothes and appearance, and developing a fit body, preferably with a 'six-pack'. Pressures to conform to these ideals have effects on behaviour and self-esteem.

Indeed, research indicates that body dissatisfaction has a range of negative health-related outcomes. It is linked with disordered eating patterns, including bulimia, fad dieting and weight gain (e.g. Ackard, Croll & Kearney-Cooke, 2002; Cooley & Toray, 2001; Neumark-Sztainer, Paxton, et al., 2006; Neumark-Sztainer, Wall, et al., 2006) and is a risk factor for depression and low self-esteem (e.g. Mond, van den Berg, Boutelle, Hannan & Neumark-Sztainer, 2011; Paxton, Neumark-Sztainer, Hannan & Eisenberg, 2006). An Australian longitudinal study (McCabe & Ricciardelli, 2004) of nearly 900 13-year-olds tested twice, eight months apart, showed that both girls and boys exhibited high levels of body dissatisfaction although the rates were greater for girls. In response to bodily concerns, boys were more likely to engage in strategies to increase muscle, such as participating in sport and using food supplements. Both of these strategies have the potential to be either healthy or unhealthy, the former when it involves exercise dependence, the latter when the supplements are dangerous for developing bodies, such as diuretics and steroids. The authors of this study found complex relationships between timing of puberty, extent of body satisfaction and healthy/ unhealthy outcomes for boys. For girls, the findings were more clear-cut. Both early- and late-maturing girls were at greater risk (than their on-time peers) of engaging in health risk behaviours in response to their body dissatisfaction. The strategies they used were focused on weight loss, and included disordered eating patterns and exercise dependence.

In the study by Bucchianeri *et al.* (2013), it was distressing to note that both sexes became more dissatisfied with their bodies as they moved through high school and into young adulthood. The dissatisfaction trend did not level off, as had been suggested by some previous cross-sectional research (e.g. Tiggemann & Lynch, 2001). The increase in body dissatisfaction over time was associated with a corresponding increase in body mass index (BMI). The researchers noted that a large proportion of their participants were categorized as overweight; this is likely to contribute to their continuing dissatisfaction, although it is not necessarily the sole cause. Indeed, given the relationships between body dissatisfaction and disordered eating, it is possible that dissatisfaction may contribute to weight gain through 'comfort eating', inappropriate dieting or bingeing as well as the reverse, setting up a vicious circle of discontent and weight gain in some young people, especially young women with their already high level of bodily discontent.

Body and identity

A recent phenomenon arising from the modern quest for the perfect (and for most people unattainable) body has been the rise in the number of adolescent girls and young adult women undergoing surgical procedures to control weight or to alter appearance. Monder (2007) discusses the increasing popularity of gastric bypass surgery for adolescents, raising questions about their psychological preparation for this major procedure and the long-term effects of limiting nutritional intake on still growing bodies. We hear of young women being offered breast augmentations or reductions as 18th or 21st birthday presents, or saving up for these operations because they believe that such body changes will somehow miraculously change their lives, even make them a different person. Monder (2007) notes the enormous increase in these kinds of elective surgeries over the past three or four decades despite the fact that in many cases the procedures are unnecessary for health and all carry some risk, even when performed by experts.

A different kind of body dissatisfaction is 'gender dysphoria' or 'gender identity disorder', terms describing dissatisfaction with one's assigned sex and its associated gender roles. Causes may be social/psychological or biological, for example, ambiguous genetic make-up or unusual prenatal hormone exposure, or a combination of both. One type of approach to these relatively uncommon conditions is to enable individuals to modify their bodies through hormone treatment and surgery so that their physical appearance more closely aligns with their gender identity. It is of interest that such sex reassignments are becoming much more frequent among young people. For example in one Australian children's hospital, demand for medical intervention for gender dysphoria increased 60-fold over 10 years (Stark, 2014). A non-medical approach to the distress of dysphoria, preferred by some transgender groups, involves a change of community attitudes, depathologizing gender variance and accepting multiple, rather than binary, categories of gender. Such an approach would reduce the stigma associated with the way of life practised by those who do not wish to characterize themselves as either male or female (Newman, 2002).

Why are adolescents more worried about their bodies than their minds?

This is something to ponder. There have been phases in history when youth worried about their immortal soul more than how they looked, so we are told, but the emphasis today, particularly for girls in western cultures, is on thinness. This is a standard of beauty which many young women aspire to but fail to live up to, usually because it is unrealistic for most.

'Ideal' body shapes

It appears that the more girls internalize a body shape ideal, the more dissatisfied they are with their own bodies. Clark and Tiggemann (2008), in an Australian study, investigated predictors of body image over one year, beginning when the girls studied were 9–12 years old. Poorer body image a year later was predicted by higher BMI, greater concern about appearance, higher internalization of appearance ideals and lower autonomy. Jones (2004) also investigated body image in somewhat older children (7th to 10th graders) over the course of a year, including both girls and boys in her research. For boys, commitment to internalized muscularity ideals was the clear significant predictor of body dissatisfaction one year later. For girls, the situation was more complex, with not only body shape ideals, but their own BMI, their social comparisons with friends and the extent they engaged in appearance conversations with their peer group also influencing dissatisfaction.

Attentional bias

For both girls and boys, 'attentional bias' towards idealized bodies gives a clue as to how internalizations of an ideal might occur. Cho and Lee (2012) investigated attentional biases of 39 young men and 41 young women with high and low body dissatisfaction, towards muscular male bodies and thin female bodies. An eye-tracker measured gaze durations and fixation frequencies while exposing participants to images of thin, normal, muscular and fat bodies of the same gender. Results revealed longer and more frequent attention towards muscular bodies in men who were more dissatisfied with their bodies, and towards thin bodies in high body dissatisfaction women. These groups also rated the muscular men and the thin women as more attractive than those who were satisfied with their own bodies.

Family influences

Families may be the key to why some young people focus more attention on the size and shape of their bodies. One US study investigated family weight talk, parent dieting and family weight teasing in the homes of adolescent girls at risk of obesity and disordered eating (Neumark-Sztainer et al., 2010). They found the girls' BMIs, body dissatisfaction, binge eating and unhealthy and extreme weight control measures were strongly associated with weight-related teasing. Maternal dieting and parent weight talk were associated with many disordered eating behaviours. The researchers point out that in no instances were family weight talk and dieting variables associated with better outcomes in the girls.

Weight teasing

Weight teasing is a common experience of both male and female adolescents and young adults. Eisenberg, Berge, Fulkerson and Neumark-Sztainer (2012) used survey data from a diverse sample of 2287 young adults, who participated in a 10-year longitudinal study of weight-related issues. Among this group, about one-third of females and one-fifth of males reported receiving hurtful weight-related comments by family members, with those who were over-weight or obese reporting the most teasing and weight-related criticism. Although parents may have been attempting to assist their adolescent to lose weight sensibly, findings of researchers such as the Neumark-Sztainer group suggest that negative comment is not an effective way to make a positive difference. In short, it seems that body dissatisfaction and disordered eating are more likely to occur in families where there is a preoccupation with appearance and weight. The self-consciousness of the developing adolescent is increased by the emphasis that others place on their bodily changes, espe-cially if that emphasis is of a critical nature.

Fashion

Fashion and the media play also a role in shaping our views of what con-stitutes the ideal body. There is copious research demonstrating this. Two examples indicate the range of media that may influence body image. First, a study by Ashikali, Dittmar and Ayers (2014) examined the role of reality television programmes that include cosmetic surgery. In these programmes, we typically see the 'before' – usually a sad-faced person with a slouched posture, no make-up, hair awry and baggy clothes. The 'after' shows us this same person post surgery (for example facial changes, breast implants, liposuction), extensive dental work, expensive clothes, professional make-up and hair styling. Ashikali et al. (2014) concluded that these programmes may have a damaging effect on adolescent girls' body image. They randomly assigned mid-adolescent girls to one of three conditions: watching a cosmetic surgery TV show which mentioned risks associated with surgery; watching a similar show which did not mention risks; or watching a home makeover programme (the control condition). Results showed that exposure to the cosmetic surgery programmes resulted in girls reporting more dissatisfac-tion with their weight and appearance although no changes were observed in attitudes towards cosmetic surgery. A second example was an investiga-tion of the relationships between body image and Facebook activity among adolescent girls (Meier & Gray, 2014). Among high school girls, elevated appearance exposure (sharing and looking at photos of self and friends on Facebook) was significantly correlated with weight dissatisfaction, drive for thinness, thin ideal internalization and self-objectification (emphasis on appearance as part of self-concept).

What is less clear from these and other studies is why social forces have developed which currently elevate the ideal of thinness above most, if not all, aspects of appearance for girls and women. Some theorists suggest that as economic conditions improve in any society, thinness and smaller waist-to-hip ratios are perceived as more attractive, whereas in cultures with limited economic opportunities and wealth, body fat, especially for women, is a sign of desirability (e.g. Pettijohn & Jungeberg, 2004). These researchers attempted, with moderate success, to correlate measures of economic 'hard times' in the US with various physical features of *Playboy*'s Playmate of the Year. The study was replicated by Webster in 2008 for the years 1967–2007, using a broader range of measures of perceived environmental security, including share price indices and assessments of existential threat (the Doomsday Clock). The evolutionary hypothesis was that in tougher, less secure times men would prefer larger women with greater waist-to-hip ratios. Results were so mixed as to be unconvincing support for the hypothesis.

Attitudes to genital development

Although many studies have been concerned with body image in adolescents, until recently few have asked young people about their responses to their developing genitals. Attitudes to genitals will begin to develop in childhood and be influenced by family attitudes, such as beliefs about modesty, cleanliness and sexuality. How do these attitudes affect young people's responses to the changes in their primary and secondary sex characteristics? From early infancy, parental ways of touching a child, holding him or her, expressing approval or disapproval, and reacting to children's activities in relation to bathing, handling of genitals, toilet training and masturbation help to shape the child's body image and beliefs about the 'goodness' and 'badness' or 'cleanness' and 'dirtiness' of various bodily parts. Children in most developed countries are socialized to believe that some bodily parts, notably the genitals, are not the subject of polite conversation nor are they to be viewed or touched publicly, although in these days of billboards showing advertisements for Viagra and fairly explicit television ads for tampons, social rules are far more liberal than they were even 10 years ago. Still, many a 2-year-old touching his or her genitals is told sharply to 'stop doing that', a command which must be confusing and anxiety-arousing given that the act was probably a pleasurable one. Within this social framework, it would not be surprising if genital growth was a source of adolescent anxiety.

Against this background of embarrassment and even shame about developing genitals and secondary sex characteristics, we paradoxically live in a society in which there is a great deal of bodily display. Entertainers gyrate on stage and in music videos, leaving little to the imagination. The women have large breasts and curvy bottoms; the men are muscular; both sexes are fit and toned. On porn sites, readily available to young people, 'idealized' genitalia are displayed – men have large, even 'supersized' penises and women have neat, hairless, 'clamshell' vulvas.

Surgical modification of the genitals

One possible outcome of this has been a trend towards surgical modification of the genital areas, particularly among young women. Liao and Creighton (2007) note that demand for cosmetic genitoplasty is increasing, pointing to television programmes and articles about 'designer vaginas', as well as to a survey by the British Association of Aesthetic Plastic Surgeons which reported a 31 per cent increase in the uptake of cosmetic surgery in the UK. Liao, Michala and Creighton (2010) further indicate that 'female genital cosmetic surgery is being mainstreamed in economically affluent nations' (Liao et al. 2010:20), with procedures including vaginal rejuvenation, designer vaginoplasty, G spot amplification and revirgination. They argue that this surgery carries risks and that alternative solutions to women's concerns about the appearance of their genitals should be developed.

In an article in the *Sydney Morning Herald*, Jacob (2013) writes that in Australia over the last 10 years medical rebates for labiaplasty (surgical reduction of the inner or outer labia) and vulvoplasty (surgical remodelling of the vulva) have almost tripled. She gives the example case study of 'Karissa':

> Karissa was 22 when she decided there was something wrong with the way she looked 'down there'. It was definitely not normal. How could it be? It had folds of skin that stuck out. Despite having never seen another woman's vulva, and with 'less consideration than buying a pair of shoes', she decided to have labiaplasty surgery.
>
> *(Jacob, 2013)*

And a young woman in a study by Howarth, Harding, Hayes, Simonis and Temple-Smith (under review) said, when asked about the ideal look for female genitalia:

> For women, it's more about, sort of, appearing discreet. Sort of having everything small, and neat and pink, and tucked away. (Adolescent female)
>
> *(Howarth et al., under review)*

Jacob argues that the trend has come about because young women are influenced by pornography, so readily available on the internet. They seem unaware that these images are usually airbrushed and modified with image-modifying software, sometimes as a result of censorship laws that do not allow depiction of the inner labia. The trend for complete removal of pubic hair makes women even more self-conscious that their labia are somehow 'imperfect' even though most women have no idea of the range of different sizes and shapes that comprise perfectly normal vulvae. Some feminists and women's health clinics are responding with coffee table books or websites showing a 'labia library'; a resource that may assist young women in removing the secrecy and mythology surrounding what is normal and counteracting the misguided search for an idealized vagina (e.g. Clark-Florey, 2013). Health practitioners also have limited education on this topic, and have called for such resources which offer information about normal variation to educate both themselves and young women who are seeking surgery (Harding, Hayes, Simonis & Temple-Smith, 2015; Howarth *et al.*, under review).

Pubic hair removal

Another fashion fad is the trend towards pubic hair removal, a fashion not restricted to the female gender. In order to evaluate the incidence, attitudes and practices of the removal of pubic hair as a body modification, Bercaw-Pratt *et al.* (2012) conducted a survey among 171 adolescents and young women aged 12–20 years who visited gynaecology clinics in Houston, Texas, USA. Over 70 per cent reported routinely removing their pubic hair. A much larger study of 1677 women in the US aged between 16 and 40 years found grooming of pubic hair was extremely common among women of varying demographics, the practice being correlated with being White, younger age and having five or more lifetime sexual partners. Shaving was the common method of hair removal in this sample, in contrast to a study by Tiggemann and Hodgson (2008) in which young Australian women favoured waxing. Major reasons given for pubic hair removal were that it was cleaner and neater and that pubic hair is unattractive. A study of 18- to 25-year-old Australian girls (Howarth *et al.*, under review) recorded comments aligning with the 'cleanliness' theme but also indicating peer pressure towards pubic hair removal.

> I think it's a good idea because I don't think having pubic hair is, first of all attractive, or hygienic. (Female, 18 years)
>
> When you have too much hair, it makes you look really manly, and like, really disgusting and gross. (Female, 21 years)
>
> All these girls were saying . . . it was a pool party or something . . . this was in Year 12. And, everyone said that they did or they were gonna get waxed or . . . they had . . . the laser hair removal, or . . . took care of it themselves, and one girl said she didn't. And . . . when she left, everyone was . . . 'Oh, like, that's weird'. (Female, 18 years)
>
> *(Howarth* et al., *under review)*

But underscoring the influence of fashion in these matters, the expensive and painful trend of pubic waxing may be coming to an end, as some celebrities begin to advocate a more natural approach to pubic hair (Stelio, 2014). Who knows what the next trend will be?

Historic and cultural practices

In fact, responses to developing genitalia are not restricted to individual preferences or the dictates of fashion. Throughout history and to the current day, some social groups have engaged in rituals and rites of passage that involve cutting and marking the genitals. Circumcision (trimming of the foreskin around the penis) occurs for new-born baby boys or as a pubertal 'rite of passage' in some religions and as a health and hygiene measure in some countries and cultures. There is currently much debate about the health benefits of circumcision and, although still common in the US, it is no longer routinely carried out among new-borns in maternity hospitals in Australia, the UK, Canada and New Zealand. It is interesting, however, that studies from developing countries and sexually transmitted disease clinics in developed countries show that male circumcision appears to be a protective factor against the risk of ulcerative-type sexually transmitted infections and also decreases the risk of HIV infection (Dave *et al.*, 2004).

There are, however, no known health benefits for the procedure of female circumcision, also known as female genital mutilation or female genital cutting, and defined by the World Health Organization (WHO) as all procedures that involve partial or total removal of the external female genitalia or other injury to the female genital organs for non-medical reasons (WHO, 2013a). These practices occur mostly in North and West African countries and are reported by UNESCO as having affected 125 million women and girls in those areas. The practices are considered by their proponents as important in reinforcing community values and rendering young women suitable for marriage. They tend to be carried out on girls between the ages of about 5 and 13 years by female tribal elders, without the use of anaesthetic. Their major purpose appears to be to keep women faithful and monogamous, as sex following most of these procedures is at best less pleasurable (when the clitoris is removed) and at worst extremely painful, when infibulation of the vaginal opening has occurred. Controversy about these practices is particularly fierce in western countries to which African immigrants have transported beliefs about their social necessity, beliefs in direct opposition to westernized views of women's rights and female equity.

Menstruation: curse, comfort or just inconvenient?

Menarche is often presented as marking the beginning of 'womanhood', and thus may be perceived as having great psychological as well as physical significance by girls and their parents. All the social meanings of being a woman are activated, such as ideas about sexiness, reproductive capacity, 'availability' and pressures towards stereotyping. Parents may feel ambivalent or negative about their child growing up, and being potentially sexually vulnerable. Given this confusion of potential responses, it would be surprising if some stresses did not ensue from achievement of this milestone in sexual maturation.

Earlier literature on menstruation suggested a high frequency of negative reactions. Women from past eras reported a lack of knowledge and preparedness, for example indicating that they were frightened by the blood, disturbed by the reactions of others or unsure about how to manage what has been termed a 'hygienic crisis'. Today's young women, we hope, are far more knowledgeable and better prepared. In a society that is more open about sexuality, we expect that girls will have learned about menstruation in a sex education class as well as discussed it with their mothers (or fathers) and girlfriends before their first period actually occurs.

Although this is true to some extent, even in today's sexually liberal environment there is still embarrassment and a sense of privacy associated with menstruation, reflecting ambivalent or negative social attitudes. Jackson and Falmagne (2013), in an interview study with thirteen 18- to 22-year-old young women, found they were conflicted about menstruation. The idea that menarche meant they had 'become a woman' was two-edged; on the one hand there was excitement and anticipation, on the other a reluctance to leave their girlhood behind. One said:

> I didn't like to tell my dad. I don't know, I just didn't want him to look at me differently.
>
> *(Jackson & Falmagne, 2013:387)*

And another:

> I was in seventh grade, and it's not like you're a *woman* in seventh grade.
>
> *(Jackson & Falmagne, 2013:387)*

These feelings are even more likely among those who experience puberty while they are still in primary school, an ever increasing number as we have seen earlier.

It appears also that girls do not know as much about menstruation as one would hope in this day and age. In White's (2013) US study, 11- to 15-year-old postmenarchal girls lacked accurate menstrual knowledge and felt unprepared for menarche. An open-ended question about why girls menstruate produced no response at all from 43 per cent of the girls. The remainder gave a range of responses, some accurate but others based on ideas of sin and punishment, for example:

> Girls get periods and cramps because God was mad that Eve made Adam eat the forbidden apple. So we have to pay for their sins.
>
> *(White, 2013:71)*

More than half the answers were negative in tone and included words like 'dirty', 'bad' and 'infected' to describe menstrual blood. Two decades ago an Australian study of Year 6 girls aged around 11 and 12 years (Moore, 1995) demonstrated that knowledge of menstrual changes was poor, with 60 per cent of girls uncertain about whether they could use tampons, most of the sample believing that mood changes were inevitable, and most also greatly overestimating the amount of blood loss to be expected in a typical period. One girl summed up the feelings of many in the following exchange:

> Interviewer: Why do you think girls get periods?
> Female, 11 years: I don't know. I don't know why we need this. Why don't boys get one?
>
> *(Moore, 1995:94)*

Menstruation is now much more openly referred to and reflected upon in media advertising, yet similar findings were found more recently by Fingerson (2006).

> It's messy and it's gross, and I don't want to have to deal with it. . . . You have to deal with stupid boys and physics class and algebra 2 and I don't want more things to deal with. (Female, 17 years)
>
> *(Fingerson, 2006:1)*

Continuing the theme of negative attitudes to menstruation, the young US women interviewed by Jackson and Falmagne (2013) still viewed menstruation as somehow dirty, shameful, needing to be kept secret and concealed. Several indicated their embarrassment at having to dispose of pads or tampons in school situations where there was some chance of this being noticed (for example disposal units outside the toilet cubicles). They, and the young women and girls in Burrows and Johnson's (2005) UK study, described in great detail their strategies for concealing and managing menstruation, including choice of clothing (not white), secretive ways to dispose of menstrual products, limiting activity to avoid possible 'leakage', carrying concealed sanitary protection 'just in case', and being careful about with whom they confided about this topic.

Attitudes to menstruation are even more adverse in some non-western cultures. Chinese premenarchal adolescents had largely negative expectations of menarche and their views were heavily influenced by indigenous cultural beliefs, for example that menstruation brings bad luck, that it is easier to get sick during menstruation, and that women should not wash their hair or eat raw or cold food during this time (Yeung, Tang & Lee, 2005). In some countries, menstruating girls are withdrawn from school or separated from others in their village (George, 2014). Several religions include rules and regulations about behaviours that may or may not occur when a woman is menstruating. But the many taboos and strictures surrounding this natural and healthy process are not confined to religious groups or third world nations, and their influence on young women underscores the need for accurate and unbiased education.

First ejaculation and wet dreams

There are hundreds, maybe thousands of websites about how to talk to boys about puberty but where is the research, or even the blogs or magazine articles, about what boys have to say about the changes they are going through? This does not seem to be a fashionable topic for research. Our knowledge of the psychological meaning of first ejaculation and 'wet dreams', a sign that fertility is developing in boys, is far less detailed than our knowledge of the effects of menstruation.

First ejaculations and wet dreams may be a source of guilt in boys if they are associated with masturbation (Halpern, Udry, Suchindran & Campbell, 2000) although the severe social condemnation of masturbation and its presumption as the cause of various health problems is largely a thing of the past as we have seen earlier. Back in 1985, Gaddis and Brooks-Gunn interviewed a small sample of adolescent boys about their emotional reactions to first ejaculation and found that two-thirds of the sample felt a little frightened by the experience although most had positive responses. Unlike girls, who had mostly discussed their first menstruation quite extensively with their mothers, none of the boys had discussed ejaculation with their peers and only one had mentioned the event to his father. Furthermore, the boys were extremely reluctant to engage in such discussions. In one of the few studies on this topic, conducted two decades ago, Stein and Reiser (1994) concluded from a small study of boys at a summer camp '[t]he 1st ejaculation, biologically significant in sexual and reproductive functioning, was found to be psychologically meaningful but socially invisible' (Stein & Reiser, 1994:373). Many of the boys felt unprepared for this experience, which had mostly occurred earlier than they expected and before they had heard about it in sex education classes. Common responses included surprise, curiosity, pleasure and confusion. Most of the boys did not tell anyone about the event and initially confused ejaculation and urination. The mean age of first ejaculation (semenarche) in this study was 12.9 years. This confusion is possibly exacerbated by the fact that some nocturnal emissions are known to follow non-sexual dreams. A Chinese study of 58 young men aged 19–24 years found that 80 per cent experienced wet dreams, although over 40 per cent reported having ejaculated following a dream devoid of sexual content (Yu & Fu, 2011). No participant experienced wet dreams more frequently than once per month.

A review of published literature on first nocturnal emission conducted in 2007 showed very little research on the topic has been conducted over the last 60 years. However studies in Asia, the US and Africa found the mean ages of the first wet dream to range from 13 to 16.5 years (Janssen, 2007).

The reluctance to talk about this topic is not confined to boys (or researchers). Frankel (2002) asked a small sample of parents of young adolescent boys whether they had communicated with their sons about first ejaculation, or whether they were intending to do so. Parents reported that they had rarely engaged in such communications, the majority (54 per cent) indicating 'I've never thought about it'.

Another issue of interest in the sexual maturation of boys involves the problems and difficulties they have in controlling erections – well documented in folklore but not in research. Such events may be embarrassing and humiliating or coped with readily via joking and humour. We do not really know from research how most young boys feel about untimely or unexpected erections, although this is not an unfamiliar topic of comedy sketches and movies. Further research on the psychological meaning of sexual maturation in adolescent boys is important to inform sex education, but difficult to carry out because boys are embarrassed to discuss these sexual topics in a serious way and adults, too, appear to find them embarrassing, an issue discussed further in the next chapter.

Conclusion

The biological and psychological changes of puberty, an increase in sex drive and the onset of sexual activity are key features of the transition from child to adult. As we have seen, there are substantial individual differences in the timing of puberty and young people's responses to it. Research suggests a greater likelihood of non-optimal outcomes for those experiencing early puberty than those who are on time or late, and this is particularly so for girls. The secular trend towards puberty occurring at younger and younger ages had plateaued but some commentators argue it has recommenced due to an 'obesity epidemic' in developed nations, although other causes have been mooted.

External bodily evidence of sexual maturation is not necessarily a marker of maturity in brain development, and indeed the adolescent brain has been described as 'a work in progress'. The asynchronies in brain development and sexual maturation among adolescents are particularly likely in those who physically mature at an earlier age. This mismatch in sexual capacity, cognitive development and emotional responsiveness can result in moodiness, impaired empathy, antisocial behaviour and poor decision-making, leaving young people vulnerable to impulsive behaviours that are not in their longer term best interests. The greater sexualization of modern culture along with changing social trends (such as the idealization of thin and hairless bodies) combine to make puberty even more difficult for some adolescents, although happily, most are resilient and manage the transition more or less adequately. Social environments in which there is tolerance for sexual and physical diversity, good sex education, protection from sexual pressure and family acceptance of children's developing sexual maturation are most likely to facilitate adaptive transitions.

4

THE SOCIAL CONTEXT

Parents and peers

> She [mother] said I'm not supposed to have sex until I'm fifty-one.
> *('Tweedy Bird' in Charmaraman & McKamey, 2011:257)*

> He's very open about it [sexuality]. He says that if there's anything that I
> want to know about something to do with that, he will tell me and he will
> explain. But usually I'm a bit embarrassed. . . . I'd rather not.
> *(Kirkman, Rosenthal & Feldman, 2005:56)*

In the next three chapters we examine the effects of some social influences on
adolescents' thinking about sex and their behaviours. These social factors shape
and interact with biology as young people learn how to interpret and act out
their sexual feelings on the basis of the social attitudes they extract from their
cultural contexts. These attitudes are initially formed at home, so that parental
models and teaching are important. But increasingly as children get older they
are influenced by the contexts provided by the peer group and the wider social
arena. In this chapter we describe parents' and peers' contributions to adolescent sexual behaviour. We focus on communication between parents and their
adolescents about sexual issues – how much and about what – as well as the
impediments to communication. The impact of the peer group's attitudes and
behaviours is examined, as well as the influence of age-discordant relationships.

Parents as influences

Education in sex hygiene is needed to establish better standards. . . .
The present unfortunate position, where so many gain their first

misinformation about sex from some precocious youngster and the furtiveness and indecency that surrounds the whole matter, should be forestalled. Parents may do much by answering truthfully the justifiable curiosity of the young child. The glib lies or stern reproofs, so often employed, are stupid and futile. The later instruction is deferred, the more difficult it is for parents to share the confidences of their young adolescents. Just when they might most help their growing boys and girls, who are just entering a new world of sex, their help is not sought.

(Sutton, 1944:558)

Has anything changed since this advice was given to parents over 70 years ago? The psychological literature assures us of the profound influence that parents have on the lives of their children. Parents are regarded as the primary socializers of their children, with influence over a variety of beliefs and behaviours. But when we turn to the domain of sexuality, we are dealing with an area of human functioning that has long been surrounded by guilt, mystery and controversy. How do parents translate their own feelings about sexuality into messages that they give their children? What influence do parents have on the sexual beliefs and behaviours of young people and how are these influences manifested?

Parents do have a special role in instructing their adolescents about sex. Among other opportunities, they have an emotional relationship with their child, they spend considerable time with them, often offering the opportunity for spontaneous talk, and they have a unique understanding of their child – their level of development as well as their personal qualities. Finally, parents have a vested interest in ensuring the health and wellbeing of their children, in the sexual domain among others.

Parental influences on sexuality and sexual wellbeing, however, are often coloured by parents' own experiences, cultural norms and the social mores of the time. For many parents, in the past at least, discussing sexual matters with their children was fraught with anxiety, embarrassment and a concern that doing so would encourage early sexual initiation.

Cultural beliefs about adolescent sexuality also play a significant role. As Amy Schalet in her study of American and Dutch families (2011) notes:

For American parents, teenage sex is something to be feared and forbidden: most would never consider allowing their children to have sex at home, and sex is a frequent source of family conflict. In the Netherlands, where teenage pregnancies are far less frequent than in the United States, parents aim above all for family cohesiveness, often permitting young couples to sleep together and providing them with contraceptives.

(Schalet, 2011:Preface)

My adolescent and your adolescent

Elliott (2010), in a fascinating article, writes of the 'sex panic' that continues to exists in the United States. She notes, quoting from an earlier study, that debates about teen sexuality 'reflect the twin assumptions that American teens are too innocent to know about sexuality and too sexual to be trusted with information' (Pascoe, 2007:29). In her study of parents of teenagers, Elliott concludes that they construct teen sexuality as a binary – their asexual teens vs. hypersexual other teens. She argues that parents think of their own adolescents as 'young, immature and naïve and, by association, sexually innocent' (Elliott, 2010:199). As one mother of a 16-year-old son said:

> When you look at your child, they're just so little and young. You just don't think of them ever even thinking about [sex]. It's hard to even think what you should be saying to kids. You don't think they are old enough when you think about those things.
>
> *(Elliott, 2010:199)*

Other parents thought of their teens in terms of 'being good'. Thus one mother, when told her 15-year-old son's girlfriend might be pregnant, was shocked because 'this is a really good solid kid' (Elliott, 2010:199). As Elliott notes, this mother's reluctance to conceive of her son as a sexual being because he is a good kid implies for her that sexuality is bad. In contrast, these parents seem to have no difficulty in describing other teenagers as highly sexual.

> The way teens are now, I know they're out there doing it [having sex]. [Teenagers and] . . . their cute little bodies and their raging hormones. They're like raring to go.
>
> *(Elliott, 2010:201)*

This optimistic view of parents' own adolescents and their sexual behaviours compared to those of other adolescents seems to have remained unchanged over the past two decades. In an early study of Australian parents, Rosenthal and Collis (1997) asked parents of 16-year-old teenagers for estimates about the level of sexual activity among 16-year-olds generally, and received answers reflecting current norms. The same parents, asked for their beliefs about their own teenager's sexual activities, were far more conservative in their estimates. In other words, parents found it hard to believe that their own children might have experienced intercourse even though they recognized that similarly aged teenagers were often sexually active. Moreover, parents held more optimistic beliefs than adolescents' teachers about adolescent condom use, knowledge and parent–child communication, and stronger beliefs in parental influence. The data from this study suggested that parents were seeing what they would like to see, rather than the reality.

Given the significance of parents in their adolescents' lives, it is important to know whether communication about sexual matters occurs and, if so, what topics are covered and does the communication influence behaviour.

Parents and adolescents do communicate – or do they?

Discussions about sex can be thought of as a form of sexual interaction and, in the family context, these discussions are often embarrassing even when both parents and adolescents have liberal attitudes and are comfortable talking about sexual matters. Furthermore, there may be some adaptive function in parents 'turning a blind eye' (even unconsciously) to adolescent sexual experimentation. Experimentation is one way in today's society for young people to gain a sense of independence from parents, to begin the process of growing up and the taking on of adult roles. Given that economic independence for adolescents is becoming less possible than it used to be, the move to independence through sexual expression may have healthy elements. Of course it has its risks as well. The concerned parent needs to tread the fine line between respecting an adolescent's privacy and providing information and a values framework to enable them to make sensible and well-informed decisions about sexual behaviour that also respect others' feelings and rights.

There is now considerable research to show that young people in western countries do access sexual health education from parents, although they are not the only or even the most common source (Mitchell, Patrick, Heywood, Blackman & Pitts, 2014; Planned Parenthood, 2012; Rothman, Miller, Terpeluk, Glauber & Randel, 2011; Secor-Turner, Sieving, Eisenberg & Skay, 2011).

Demonstrating that discussions with parents are not as frequent as we might like, in the most recent national survey of more than 2000 Australian students from Years 10, 11 and 12 (Mitchell *et al.*, 2014) only 27 per cent of male students and 43 per cent of female students reported using their mother as a source of information about sexual health. For fathers, these figures were lower; 23 per cent of sons and 16 per cent of daughters reported communication with fathers. School programmes, internet websites and female friends were more frequent sources for girls, reported by about half the female participants. Communication was less common for males but they used similar sources to those used by their female peers.

Regardless of the importance of parents in terms of providing information about sexual issues, there is another problem that has been identified in this communication process in many cultures. It seems that often parents and adolescents have very different perceptions about the frequency and content of any talk about sex. In general more parents think they have had 'the talk' about sexual health than adolescents do, with some parents admitting that they have never had this conversation with their offspring.

For example, a study of Hmong parent–daughter communication about sexual health showed that only a minority of young people recalled a conversation about sexual health, with much information being inaccurate (Meschke & Dettmeer, 2012). Communication was reported to be hindered by cultural traditions and thus comfort level in discussing such topics. In Tanzania, adolescents reported the little sexual communication that occurred was ambiguous and filled with warnings about sex (Kajula, Sheon, De Vries, Kaaya & Aarø, 2014), while Iranian and Chinese parents also only infrequently talked about sex to their adolescents (Merghati-Khoel, Abolghasemi & Smith, 2014; Zhang, Li, Shah, Baldwin & Stanton, 2007). Misinformation, myths and ignorance about sexuality development were common. Another issue arises for young people raised in immigrant families where a clash of cultures has been commonly documented by cross-cultural researchers. When parents come from a conservative, traditional culture, communication about sexual matters may become a challenge. In one study of Filipino-American families, the researchers found that discussion about sex was limited (Chung et al., 2005). This does open up the problem of how to encourage communication between traditional parents and their young people who have become acculturated to more liberal cultural norms.

Parents and their adolescents may also have misperceptions about each other that colour their willingness to talk about this sensitive issue. For example, parents may be uncertain and/or incorrect about whether or not their adolescent is sexually active. As mentioned previously, underestimates by parents of their adolescents' sexual experiences have been reported in several studies (see, for example, Liddon, Michael, Dittus & Markowitz, 2013). Many parents perceive talking about sex as posing particular challenges. Embarrassment and concerns about their adolescent's 'readiness' was reported as affecting sexual communication by over two-thirds of parents in one study (Jerman & Constantine, 2010), a finding confirmed in the study of mothers of teenagers by Elliott (2012). In another, fear and uncertainty marked the attitudes of parents when contemplating discussing sexuality with their adolescents, in part because of the silence around these matters when they themselves were young (Davis, Gahagan & George, 2013).

> I'm thinking 'Yah, who's really going to have these conversations?' Am I going to have that conversation with my daughter, and what is it that I say to her. You're always second-guessing yourself because, well, if no one taught you how to do it, then how do you know what you're doing is correct?
>
> (Davis et al., 2013:6)

Misperceptions in talking about sex: a two-sided effect

It's not only parents who feel uncomfortable talking about sex. A recent nationwide survey in the US showed that half of these adolescents feel uncomfortable talking about sex compared with 19 per cent of parents (Planned Parenthood, 2012). Furthermore, some young people may be reluctant to open a discussion because they believe their parents do not wish this to occur. There is evidence that many parents do not communicate about sex because they believe their adolescents do not wish to do so (Naik, 2008; NHS Bristol, 2009). A recent US study showed that mothers of adolescents perceive them, perhaps incorrectly, as highly resistant to these conversations. They also express ambivalence about when, what and how much to say to their children about this topic (Elliott, 2012).

This may well be compounded by adolescents misinterpreting the way in which parental messages are conveyed. Although parents may believe they are giving detailed, careful nuanced guidance, adolescents often say they hear a lecture, providing didactic, directive messages (Eastman, Corona & Schuster, 2006). As a result of their own anxiety, embarrassment and/or lack of knowledge, parents may communicate in a way that conveys disapproval of sexual activity (Davis et al., 2013). Further complicating the communication process is parents' failure or unwillingness to provide direct messages about sexuality and sexual health. Hyde et al. (2013) in an interview study, found that parents were more likely to communicate in a 'tacit manner through innuendo and intimation', believing that this constituted sex education. Given the likelihood of misperceptions occurring, it is questionable that the messages being delivered by parents are those received by their adolescents, an outcome not limited to western adolescents and parents. The Tanzanian study mentioned previously yielded similar findings. Although only some sexual communication was happening, adolescents reported that their conversations with parents were mostly ambiguous and filled with warnings about dangers (Kajula et al., 2014).

In an early study which matched parents' and adolescents' perceptions of parental contributions to the sex education of their children, Feldman and Rosenthal (2000) surveyed 209 10th graders, 156 mothers and 91 fathers. Parents evaluated themselves more highly as sex educators than did their adolescent children, with adolescents rating their parents as less comfortable with sexual communication, more controlling, more likely to bring up unwanted topics and more likely to avoid important issues than the parents rated themselves. Adolescents' evaluations of their parents' communications about sex were strongly related to ratings of their parents as communicators in general, but less so to frequency of sex-related communication. Quality rather than quantity of communication was an important variable in this study.

Jaccard, Dodge and Dittus (2002) reviewed a wide range of studies, concluding that about 70 per cent of parents say that they have talked with their adolescents about sex, whereas only about 50 per cent of their sons or daughters indicate that they have had discussions about sex with their parents. Perhaps parents believe they are making an impression because they have made a big effort to broach these topics, but they have not pitched their message to their child's needs, nor checked whether the message was communicated or understood. Jaccard and colleagues suggest that some parents raise the topic of sex education then do not continue because their adolescents tell them they already 'know'. However there may not be a follow-up check as to whether this is the case, given that the whole event may be shrouded in embarrassment with everyone keen to get it over quickly. Conversations may go along the lines of:

Son, I guess it's time we had a talk about . . . you know.
That's OK dad, we did it at school in biology.
You're sure? . . . your mother's worried you might get in with the wrong company.
No worries dad.
Great, I'm glad we had this chat.

Many adolescents worry about parents' reactions if they themselves talk about sexual health issues – in particular that parents will think they are having sex or are about to do so. In one study of Black families in Canada one young male said:

When we do talk about it, we kind of have to keep it like a joking topic because it's kind of weird if my mother and me, her son, talking about sex and all that. I just, some things where I think parents shouldn't touch down on. (Male)

(Davis et al., 2013:5)

For those young people who are sexually active, talking to their parents about sex can be especially difficult.

Many ignore the fact that you're having it, meaning that you can't talk to them about it or you know they will be disapproving so you have to be secretive about it.

(Sex Education Forum Survey, 2008)

What topics are covered?

Most parents are not trained as educators, let alone as biologists, sex educators or psychologists. Yet many feel that it is important that at least some sex education comes from the home, and try their best to impart information, attitudes and values. Sometimes too little can be offered too late, sometimes the content and timing is just right and sometimes what parents feel they have taught is not necessarily what is learned. One young study participant perceived it this way:

> Most parents give the 'birds and bees' talk when they feel ready not when the child is ready, which seems really weird and parents tend to get embarrassed and tend to give up!
>
> *(Sex Education Forum Survey, 2008)*

In the past, early parent–child discussions might have focused on the physiological aspects of sexuality, although not the sexual act itself (Angera, Brookins-Fisher & Inungu, 2008). We now recognize that it is important to go beyond this to encompass issues such as relationships, gender and values, and many parents now often see their role as dealing with the emotional aspects of sexuality rather than simply anatomy. Another participant said:

> Depends on parents. I was taught that sex is a very intimate expression of love that should only happen within a committed marriage relationship.
>
> *(Sex Education Forum Survey, 2008)*

While parents concern themselves with ensuring that their adolescents know about contraception, including the importance of condoms, and sexually transmitted infections, many also tackle more difficult topics such as intimacy, respect for others, setting the boundaries in relationships, including dating violence and how to deal with it (Rothman *et al.*, 2011).

Not surprisingly, cultural factors play a role in what is deemed by parents to be appropriate to discuss. A study of urban Thai families found that parents were more likely to talk about body changes and dating than sex-related issues and birth control (Rhucharoenpornpanich *et al.*, 2012). In contrast, de Looze, Constantine, Jerman, Vermeulen-Smit and Bogt (2014) found wide-ranging discussions had occurred between Dutch parents and their adolescents, covering anatomy, protection, contraception, relationships and rights. They interpret this in the context of open sexual communication characteristic of the Dutch culture, a conclusion that accords with that of Schalet (2011).

There is little research on the timing of communication, although there has been considerable airing of what is suitable at different developmental stages. In one longitudinal study of parents and their 13- to 17-year-old children (Beckett *et al.*, 2010) the researchers found that over half of the children had begun sexual activity (genital touching and oral sex) before topics such as birth control or resisting partner pressure for sex had been discussed, and more than 40 per cent had had intercourse before any discussion about STIs, birth control or condom use. Clearly parents need to be aware of the importance of addressing a variety of topics but also to do this at an early age. As any parent of an adolescent is aware, young people will not necessarily discuss their problems (including their concerns about sexuality) 'on cue'. If parents are perceived as available and ready to discuss issues according to the adolescent's emotional timetable, then opportunities for good communication are multiplied.

Do parents influence sexual behaviour?

We know, from a range of countries, that various aspects of parenting have an influence on adolescents' sexual behaviours such as delaying sexual initiation, number of partners and use of contraception (e.g. Aspy et al., 2007; Biddlecom, Awusabo-Asare & Bankole, 2009; de Looze et al., 2014; Deptula, Henry & Schoeny, 2010; Huebner & Howell, 2003; Karofsky, Zeng & Kosorok, 2001; Wang et al., 2013). Chief among these are parental involvement and connectedness, parental control or monitoring of adolescents' behaviour (de Looze et al., 2012) parental attitudes and values, including the setting of standards about children's sexual behaviour (Tsui-Sui & Manczak, 2013; Wight & Fullerton, 2013) and, not surprisingly, effective and open communication.

The importance of family connectedness and relationship quality, including in non-western cultures (see, for example, Abu & Akerle, 2006), has been well documented (e.g. Deptula et al., 2010; Guilamo-Ramos et al., 2006; Lenciauskiene & Zaborskis, 2008; Markham et al., 2010; Tsui-Sui & Manczak, 2013). Young people who perceive their parents to be warm, caring and interested in them and their activities are more likely to postpone initiation of sex, use contraception when they do become sexually active, and have fewer pregnancies.

Similarly, parental monitoring of young people's activities (e.g. supervision, knowing with whom and where they are going) is associated variously with delayed sexual initiation, fewer sexual partners, increased use of protection when having sex and reduced incidence of several STIs, in both western and non-western countries (Huebner & Howell, 2003; Longmore, Manning & Giordano, 2001; WHO, 2007a; Wight, Williamson & Henderson, 2006; Zimmer-Gembeck & Helfand, 2008). Biddlecom et al. (2009) found, in four African countries – Burkino Faso, Ghana, Malawi and Uganda – that parental monitoring influenced 12- to 19-year-olds' sexual activity, but not their contraceptive use. They concluded that a high level of perceived parental monitoring was the factor most strongly associated with reduced odds of adolescent sexual activity across all four countries for males and across three countries for females. . . . [but] parental monitoring had no significant association with adolescents' contraceptive use.

(Biddlecom et al., *2009:78)*

Studies that relate the initiation of early sexual activity to lack of family closeness and lack of parental support suggest that adolescents who seek independence early due to unsatisfactory family relationships regard sex as part of the expression of that independence. It is entirely possible, however, that the causal chain operates in the opposite way. Thus, an adolescent's sexual behaviour may lead to a withdrawal of closeness within a family. In a rare and early study of this causal chain, Feldman, Rosenthal, Brown and Canning (1995) investigated the possibility that parents influence their children's sexual expression indirectly, via the socialization of coping strategies and personality traits. They showed that learned restraint – incorporating the ability to delay gratification, inhibit aggression, exercise impulse control, be considerate of others and act responsibly – was a factor that mediated between family interaction patterns and adolescent sexual expression for boys. Family environment measures taken when the boys were in Grade 6 (aged 10–12) predicted with 70 per cent accuracy those boys who would be virgins or non-virgins 4 years later. Low-restraint boys were characterized by less supportive families, rejecting fathers, indulgent parents and a greater number of sexual partners at mid-adolescence. Although more research is needed in this area (for example, to investigate the role of restraint for girls), it is clear that the influence that parents have over their adolescents in the sexual domain is more likely to be indirect than a result of direct communications.

Although most studies show that self-rated open, skilled and comfortable discussions by parents about sexuality influence their adolescents' behaviour (e.g. Jerman & Constantine, 2010; Wang *et al.*, 2013), others have not. It seems that the impact of this type of communication is mediated by the nature of the messages and the quality of the parent–adolescent relationship. There is a suggestion that the meaning of 'openness' may differ among parents and thus in its influence on adolescent behaviours. An Australian study of parent–adolescent communication about sexuality revealed complex meanings in the understanding of 'openness' (Kirkman, Rosenthal & Feldman, 2005). As one mother said, 'I think it should be an open relationship and I think, well, I think mothers should be able to discuss everything, tell them everything, so they don't go out there in the real world naive' (Kirkman *et al.*, 2005:54). Another teenage girl described her parents as open in communicating about sexuality while at the same time declaring that they never discuss the subject. Her father echoed her views, saying, 'We don't really talk a great deal about it. I mean if they want to talk about it, I'm quite open' (Kirkman *et al.*, 2005:55). Even less communicative was this father when he said, 'We're pretty open. I sort of try and keep my mouth shut' (Kirkman *et al.*, 2005:55).

Although almost all used the term to describe good communication about sexuality, 'openness' was defined in different ways. These included willingness to answer questions while not keeping a spotlight on the topic; having an open-minded attitude; balancing openness with privacy; and being responsive to characteristics of the child. In examining the impact of 'open' communication we need to pay greater attention to these differences if we are to understand these conflicting outcomes.

Direct sex education/discussion is not the only way that adolescent sexuality can be shaped by parents. It may indeed have quite a small influence in relation to more indirect factors. Parents can influence adolescent sexual behaviour through transmission of attitudes (both directly and indirectly) and through their own behaviours. The marital and child-bearing behaviour of parents, including experiences with divorce, remarriage, living arrangements and apparent behaviours towards the opposite sex may provide and support role models for young people. Parents' discipline practices and parenting style will also shape young people's opportunities for and comfort with various sexual activities and the pace of the behavioural elements of their sexual developmental timetables.

Parental approval of adolescent sexual activity, traditionally low in earlier generations, remains so. Three decades ago, Darling and Hicks (1982) characterized the major parental communications about sex as reflecting these sentiments: 'Pregnancy before marriage can lead to terrible things'; 'No nice person has sex before marriage'; 'Petting can too easily lead to intercourse'; and – the one positive message – 'Sex is a good way of expressing your love for someone'. Have these attitudes changed? The generations of the 1980s and 1990s who embraced self- (and sexual-)fulfillment as a right are now parents of teenagers or young adults. These parents rebelled against the more traditional values of their post-war mothers and fathers, and might be expected to hold more liberal attitudes to their own adolescents' sexual activities. Indeed, parents and teenagers may now collude along the lines of 'Don't let your grandmother know you're on the pill'. However, as we have seen, this is not necessarily so.

Parental talk vs. parental behaviour

There is more than a little evidence that parent behaviour, of various sorts, has more influence on adolescents' sexual behaviour than parent talk.

If your parents are divorced or separated, and your mum or dad brings home different people on weekends and each night of the week and stuff, you sort of think that [having sex] is no big deal. It is not special or anything like that. But if your parents are married and stuff like that, you sort of see it as a big deal and should only share it if you love the person. (Female, 16 years)

(Moore & Rosenthal, 2006:101)

There is a strong relationship between a mother's own sexual experience as a teenager and that of her own adolescent daughter. Girls from single-parent families are more likely to become sexually active at an earlier age than those who grow up in two-parent families (Davis & Friel, 2001). There is considerable evidence that family structure is an important factor; the absence of one parent in the early teen years is linked to earlier sexual initiation and more partners several years later (Wight *et al.*, 2006; Zimmer-Gembeck & Helfand, 2008). A recent study of adolescent girls in Uganda (Pilgrim *et al.*, 2014) confirmed the effects of family structure in an African setting. Young women who lived with both biological parents had a lower risk of early sexual debut than those living in single-parent families, living with stepfathers, grandparents, other relatives or by themselves. The mechanisms underlying the effects of family structure are not clearly understood, however. They may be a function of role modelling, or they may reflect a lack of parental supervision, or they may in some way relate to paternal absence.

The range of studies reviewed here indicates that the generality of family atmosphere and the specifics of parental supervision practices have the potential to impact on adolescent sexual development. Parents, it seems, must find a balance in providing emotional support and healthy attitudes for the developing sexuality of their adolescent children, while also protecting them or limiting their opportunities for harmful (but not benign) sexual experimentation. Parents need also be aware of their role as models of behaviour. Given adolescents' finely tuned antennae for hypocrisy, they are unlikely to get away with a 'do as I say, not as I do' approach.

How do mothers communicate?

There are still relatively few studies that examine the specific aspects of parenting communication style. In several early studies, mothers' perceptions of the style, content and frequency of their communications with their adolescents about sex and sexuality were examined through analyses of semi-structured interviews with 16 mothers of 16-year-old sons and 14 mothers of similarly aged daughters (cited in Moore and Rosenthal, 2006). All the mothers assessed themselves to be effective communicators, but their styles differed greatly, in terms of who initiated and maintained the communication (mother or child), the comfort levels of the mother and teenager, the frequency of these communications, the contexts in which they took place and the topics discussed. The researchers isolated five styles of sexual communication: avoidant, reactive, opportunistic, child-initiated and mutually interactive. Avoidant styles were characterized by both the mothers and the adolescents being uncomfortable with discussing sexual topics, and these discussions being avoided, cut short or presented in generalized, non-personal terms when they did occur. Feelings and psychological issues were rarely discussed, the emphasis being on biological or factual material. Mothers using this style tended to reassure themselves that adequate sex education had occurred at school. A typical example:

> I think if he hasn't asked me now, he's probably not going to, so I would presume, you know, or else he's a bit embarrassed to talk about it. (Mother of son)
>
> *(Moore & Rosenthal, 2006:95)*

Reactive communicators were mothers who only reported one or two sex-related discussions with their teenager, and these were initiated when a pressing need was perceived on the basis of the child's behaviour, for example when the teenager appeared to be 'getting serious' with a romantic partner. Generally, the mothers did not feel particularly confident about these discussions; they feared alienating their teenager, but were concerned to get a message across. They tended to report that the discussions were mainly one-sided, but that this was characteristic of their discussions on a range of topics, not just sex.

> It's a bit hard sometimes to get conversation and things out of him, even just ordinary school work. (Mother of son)
>
> *(Moore & Rosenthal, 2006:96)*

Opportunistic communicators formed the largest category of mothers – they reported that they were willing to discuss sex-related topics with their adolescents, but did so infrequently. They sought shared occasions to initiate discussions, such as television programmes, family events and the stimulus of sex education occurring at school. They wove their communications in with other activities (such as preparing meals), bringing up issues almost as incidentals, as a way of dissipating anxiety and embarrassment. They talked about feelings as well as opinions, and covered a broad range of topics.

> It's not that we'll sit down and talk specifically about anything, it could just be something that we've seen on TV, something that perhaps they relate to what's happened around them and then we'll sort of have a discussion about it. (Mother of daughter)
>
> *(Moore & Rosenthal, 2006:96)*

Nevertheless these mothers, like the reactive communicators, did not get much response from their children and were largely unaware of what the adolescents were thinking about sexual issues.

Seven mothers were in the child-initiated communications group. These mothers were characterized by a communication style in which they waited until their adolescent brought up the topic before discussion. They believed that when the child was ready to engage in sex-related discussion, the conversations would be more fruitful than if they were parent-initiated.

> Yes, she would probably initiate it [from] something that might have happened at school or something. (Mother of daughter)
>
> *(Moore & Rosenthal, 2006:96)*

Or:

> He does it in layers sometimes. He'll ask a couple of questions and then perhaps go and stew about it and come back and ask some more. (Mother of son)
>
> *(Moore & Rosenthal, 2006:96)*

Finally, and perhaps most successfully, mothers in the mutually interactive group indicated that sex-related conversations could be initiated either by the adolescent or the parent, and both parties were comfortable about pursuing these conversations. Mother–child communications were generally characterized by openness, intimacy and emotionally based discussions. Mothers worked consciously to promote open communication and make time for their children to bring up issues and to be good listeners. They were comfortable about setting boundaries and respectful of the child's sensitivities. The authors of this study argued that mothers who were good communicators matched their message to the receptivity and needs of the listener, but also that there may be more than one optimal style for communication about sexual issues to teenagers. Some young people may be more concerned than others about privacy and intrusion into their personal lives as they struggle for autonomy and a sense of self. Some topics may be perceived as 'off limits' or overly invasive, such as discussions about masturbation.

Gender differences

Gender differences in parent–adolescent communication about sex are commonplace in research. Most commonly, fathers are far less likely than mothers to have engaged in any form of sex education with their children, especially with daughters. Same-sex communication is more common than opposite-sex, that is, fathers talk with sons, mothers talk with daughters (Davis *et al.*, 2013; NHS Bristol, 2009; Powell, 2008; Zhang *et al.*, 2007).

Why do fathers take very little part in the sex education of their children, particularly their daughters? The reasons appear to be complex and subtle. Kirkman, Rosenthal and Feldman (2002) interviewed mothers, fathers and young adolescents in 19 families in which the adolescents were in Year 8 of secondary school (aged about 13 years). Both parents acknowledged that sexuality was a difficult topic, but fathers felt these difficulties more keenly and tended to leave it to the mothers.

> My wife, she does a lot of talking . . . about life, sexuality. All sorts of things, all the time. Whereas I'm exactly the opposite. Not that I find – do I find it difficult? I don't know. I've never had to talk to my children . . . about these issues, because my wife's already done it. I feel almost guilty for not partaking. The other thing, of course, is I don't know how. It's not an excuse, it's a fact. I don't know how comfortable they would be, me trying to talk to them about these topics. . . . So I guess it's a bit of a coward's way out, to save embarrassment by both parties, that I'll just leave it to my wife.
>
> *(Kirkman* et al., *2002:60)*

They expressed puzzlement, confusion and disappointment at this state of affairs, overtly wishing in some cases that they could have overcome the barriers that had been present in communicating with their own fathers. The fathers in this study seemed to have strong, affectionate relationships with their children, but these relationships had been disrupted to some extent by the child's developing adolescence, as if the child's burgeoning sexuality was intruding into the relationship. Fathers felt awkward, nervous even about broaching sexual topics. One father said that trying to talk to his daughters was like 'talking to a tiger' (Kirkman *et al.*, 2005:62). The awkwardness was at least in part because the adolescents were embarrassed and often rejected or laughed off their fathers' conversational overtures.

Investigating merely how often communication occurs fails to take account of the tightrope some parents, especially fathers, feel themselves to be walking in trying to balance availability and reticence, overindulgence and taboo, affirmation and warning. One father said:

Don't put any limitations on them. Don't be afraid. I think that was a lot of problems with my parents. People are uncomfortable talking about sex, whereas really I like it. And it is one of the blessings of a good marriage. And you shouldn't be afraid of it and you shouldn't hide it. Neither should you flog it as it is today. I feel it's been so pushed out with advertising and in movies so much, people get a second-rate idea of it: that it's just a fly-by-night thing. Well it's not, I don't think. But it's not a taboo . . . it's somewhere in the middle.

(Kirkman et al., *2005:58)*

The researchers also found that although most families saw equal mother and father responsibility for communication about sex to adolescent children, in practice nearly all the talking was done by mother. This was recognized by all parties, and various explanations put forward such as 'women communicate better', and 'women are better at talking about emotional issues'. There was also an underlying tension about fathers communicating about sexuality, especially to their daughters. Kirkman *et al.* write 'the nature of male heterosexuality is that mothers are safer sexual communicators' (2002:71). In the families studied this was expressed by discussions of men outside the family as potentially dangerous and sexual predators. For example, one father said, 'I have talked to my daughters about the way a younger fit man is affected by sexual attraction and erections, and how good, common, normal sense can go out the window when he's rampant' (2002:71). Another commented, 'All they want to do is get in your pants and then they're gone . . . I'm a male and I know what mongrels males can be' (2002:71). Fathers also warned their sons of getting into 'bad company' with other males who might pressure women into having sex. Families in this study apparently bought into the 'male sex drive discourse', a powerful myth about masculinity that suggests men have inescapable sexual urges that they are unable to control or, at best, have great difficulty in doing so. The attribution of high power and sexual potency to men in general effectively prohibited men as fathers from taking a more caring, emotionally based role in family discussions about sexuality without metaphorically emasculating themselves.

The research literature is unclear as to whether these messages are relatively generalized or only evident among particular subgroups. What is clear, though, is that the attitudinal messages heard by children from their parents are somewhat different for daughters than for sons.

In one study (Elliott, 2010), both sons and daughters heard more cautionary messages about sex than positive ones from their parents, but the difference was greater for females and sons were far more likely than daughters to perceive liberal parental attitudes to sex. Elliott (2010) makes an interesting claim that

parents often reproduce and reinforce gender inequality in their lessons to their children about sexuality. . . . [P]arents try to protect their
daughters by stressing their sexual vulnerability and emphasizing the
dangers of sex, whereas sons are likely to be given parental leeway to
explore their sexuality.

(Elliott, 2010:192)

An earlier study by McNeely *et al.* (2002) provides some support for the
notion that the socialization process puts a brake on female sexuality, with
parents' rare discussions about sex with their children consisting for the most
part of warnings to their daughters. These warnings, implicitly or explicitly
emphasize the risks of sexuality. For example the poet Anne Sexton writes
to her 16-year-old daughter:

The right thing, the nice thing the kind-to-yourself [sic] thing is to
wait until it will be something special; not just fumbling on the grass or
on a couch or in a car. . . . I really think it's better to wait until you're
older and readier to handle it.

(Payne, 1983:36)

Some three decades later, the tone is different.

I go through her bag every night, and I saw condoms and I said, 'What
are these'. She said, 'Oh we got them in our class today'. I said 'OK.
I'll take them. I know you're not using them'.

(Davis et al., 2013:6)

Programmes for parents

In a review of programmes for parents, Kirby and Miller (2002) proposed
specific objectives, closely tied to aspects of sexuality and sexual wellbeing,
for interventions designed to assist parents to communicate more effectively
about sex to their adolescents. They suggest that good programmes will
(a) increase parents' knowledge about sexual issues and also about the sexual
behaviours of young people, (b) help parents understand that talking about
sex to adolescents is likely to have beneficial effects and is unlikely to increase
the chances that their adolescents will engage in sex, (c) help parents clar-
ify their own values about sex and express these in ways that do not 'turn
off' the adolescent, and thus foreclose further discussion possibilities, and
(d) improve parents' skills in talking about sexuality, through increasing their
comfort with the material, their listening skills and their skills in initiating

discussions. These authors argue that any good programme for parents will acknowledge that being uncomfortable with intergenerational family discussions about sex is normal and acceptable, because such discussions are always in danger of broaching taboo topics and privacy norms. They might also have added that, because of these taboos and norms, it may be appropriate for certain topics to be 'off limits'. Given that young people are frequently connected to social media and other technologies, parents may find it relatively easy to direct them to appropriate websites.

In the decade since Kirby and Miller reviewed parenting programmes, there have been many new initiatives designed to improve parents' willingness and ability to talk about sex to their adolescents. There is now a multitude of programmes designed to support parents in discussing sex with their children, young and old, although not all have been subjected to rigorous evaluation. In a recent and comprehensive review (of mostly US programmes), Wight and Fullerton (2013) identified 44 programmes from 1990 to 2009 that met standard evaluation criteria. Of these, some were school-based, some community-based and some were home-based audio or video programmes. They concluded that programmes with 'intensive' parental involvement could, indeed, modify adolescents' sexual behaviour. On the basis of their review, the authors provide the following recommendations for future programmes. Interestingly, these mirror elements of successful communication discussed above, focusing on: (a) developing greater parent–child attachment or connectedness; (b) improving parents' monitoring and regulation of behaviour; (c) helping parents communicate their values around sexual relationships; and (d) encouraging parents to model the behaviours they want their children to follow (Wight & Fullerton, 2013:21).

Another type of programme that appears to be effective is a workplace-based programme called Talking Parents, Healthy Teens (Eastman *et al.*, 2006). The authors suggest that the workplace setting makes attendance more convenient for many parents and may be a model worth pursuing. Each of the eight sessions in the programme provides parents with communication skills relevant to the topic under discussion, such as 'Building your relationship with your child', 'Listening skills for talking about sensitive topics'.

Finally, there is now a wide range of books and reports on children's and adolescents' sexuality and sexual health written specially for parents. We cite here one Australian government-funded initiative that was based on research, widely distributed and extremely well received. *Talk Soon. Talk Often* (Walsh, 2011) is a 70-page booklet, published by and available from the Western Australia Department of Health, written by a highly experienced sexual health community educator. It was developed after interviews with parents about the ways they currently approach educating their children about sex, reproduction, sexuality and relationships, and the kind of support needed to assist them to more effectively communicate with their children about these topics. Written in simple language and often using humour, the booklet covers not only a wide range of conventional subjects but also contemporary topics such as parenting in the digital age (how to deal with texts, tweets and Facebook), pornography and preventing child sexual abuse. *Talk Soon. Talk Often* provides parents with information about how to approach communication on a variety of topics, helpful tips for talking about sex, including what to do if children won't talk, how to talk to a gay adolescent and how to (and why) convey information about sexually transmitted infections. It ends with a useful list of excellent websites, books and other written resources. Highly recommended!

Peers

Although peer influence has little impact on young children relative to that of parents, there is a shift at adolescence, with peers becoming more important in forming young people's beliefs and regulating their behaviour. Peer influence is often cited as an important factor affecting adolescent sexual decisions, and this can operate in a number of ways. Young people can obtain information about sex from their friends, which may serve to guide decision-making about sex. This information is, of course, not always accurate, as reflected in long-standing myths about fertility such as 'You can't get pregnant the first time you have sex'. Second, adolescents can accept peer attitudes about sexuality. These can be implicitly reflected in peer behaviour which the adolescent may use as a model for his or her own behaviour, or they can be actively proselytized through discussion, questioning, teasing, dares, shaming and the like. The strong desire of many young people to be like their admired age-mates and part of a group can lead them to engage in the sexual behaviours and express the sexual attitudes that they perceive as characteristic of a particular 'hero' or group. It is well to remember that these peer influences are not always negative, as friends and adolescent groups may express and model healthy as well as unhealthy sexual attitudes and behaviours. This issue receives scant attention in current research, where the emphasis seems often to address only adult disapproval of peer influence on adolescent sexuality.

Peers vs. parents as sources of information

Earlier research about sources of sex information for adolescents showed that peers can be a major influence in this area (Davis & Harris, 1982; Dunne,

Donald, Lucke, Nilsson & Raphael, 1993; Thornburg, 1981). In this chapter we ignore the important and increasingly well-documented influence of peers via social media and the internet (discussed in Chapter 6) and focus here on face-to-face interactions.

In an early survey of undergraduate students aged 17–20 years (Moore & Rosenthal, 1991), we found that 69 per cent of sexually active young people felt they could discuss any concerns they had about sex with their friends, whereas only 33 and 15 per cent respectively felt this way about discussing sexual problems with their mother or father. In their study of high school students, Mitchell *et al.* (2014) found that there were interesting gender differences in sources of information about sexual health. Mothers were the most common source for males but female students were more likely to access information from female friends than anyone else. Fathers were one of the least likely sources of information for students of both sexes.

That young people feel more able to discuss concerns about sex with their friends than their parents has been confirmed in recent studies (e.g. Epstein & Ward, 2008; Secor-Turner *et al.*, 2011) although in some cases the differences are now less, possibly due to parents' greater willingness and ability to discuss these sensitive matters. This situation may vary across cultures. A study of 915 adolescents aged 14–18 years in Iran showed that mothers (51 per cent) followed by same-sex friends (40 per cent) were both the main and the preferred sources of sexual health information (Baheiraei, Khoori, Foroushani, Ahmadi & Ybarra, 2014). Here, however, the younger adolescents expressed a preference for parent-provided information whereas the older adolescents preferred their peers. A study of Nigerian female adolescents, however, has once again highlighted the importance of the cultural context, confirming the importance of peers given the relative absence of family participation in the provision of early sex education (Onyeonoro *et al.*, 2011).

What are the advantages and disadvantages of sexual information emerging from friends? Although it is certainly important for the young person who is establishing values and rehearsing for adult sexuality to have the sympathetic ear and counsel of friends, the sex education provided from this source can be limited when not supplemented by other sources. On its own, this can be a case of 'the blind leading the blind', with incomplete and wrong information being disseminated and with vital elements like the establishment of non-risky sexual behaviours neglected.

How is peer influence transmitted: attitudes or behaviour?

More commonly, it is young people's perceptions of what their peers think and do that influences behaviour (Lyons, Giordano, Manning & Longmore,

2011). Peer norms about sexuality appear to be a powerful influence. In one study, the initiation of sex was related to the perceived peer approval of sexual intercourse and to greater 'accumulation' of sexual partners over time (Coley, Lombardi, Lynch, Mahalik & Sims, 2013). Potard, Courtois and Rusch (2008) found that French high school students were more likely to be sexually active if their peers held permissive sexual norms, a finding confirming results from a study of American adolescents (Sieving, Eisenberg, Pettingell & Skay, 2006). Unfortunately among the French students this effect extended to risky sexual practices, with perceived permissiveness being associated with less use of contraception.

Not surprisingly, peer influence is relatively strong in traditional cultures where discussion of sex by parents is taboo or, at best, rarely occurs. Sychareun *et al.* (2013) explored predictors of premarital sex among unmarried young people in Vientiane, Laos and found peer influences were important factors, although they showed that parent–youth interactions, when they occurred, were also important. In a large study of Taiwanese young people, aged 20 years, Chiao and Yi (2011) found a strong influence of their perceptions of friends' behaviour on young people's premarital engagement in sex. The impact of peers' behaviour was even stronger among younger adolescents in a study conducted in the Philippines. Importantly, the more sexual behaviours (kissing, petting, having sex, etc.) peers were perceived to engage in, the more likely it was that young people had, themselves, engaged in these practices (Upadhyay & Hindin, 2006). This additive influence of peers' behaviour has also been shown among western adolescents (Ali & Dwyer, 2011; Miranda-Diaz & Corcoran, 2012). Miranda-Diaz and Corcoran capture the flavour of young people's perceptions in their title: 'All my friends are doing it', a fallacy we have heard, among similar others, from the early days of research.

Examining the longer term influence of peer attitudes, a US-based large-scale study of urban minority youth by O'Donnell and colleagues (2003) assessed 12-year-olds' (Year 7) attitudes to sex in terms of their beliefs about positive aspects of sexual initiation, for example the idea that sex 'proves you're a man/woman', or that it shows your partner how much you love him or her. In addition, the young people were asked to complete questionnaires about their attitudes to sexual responsibilities, and their 'sex refusal skills'. Finally, beliefs about how many of their peers had already had sex were sought, as was information on their own sexual behaviour. At Year 7, those reporting greater peer involvement in sex and more positive expectations for sex outcomes were more likely to have initiated sex at a very young age, that is, in their seventh year at school. Longitudinal follow-up of the study sample through to Year 10 (about age 16) showed that these variables were consistently associated with earlier sexual debut. Higher scores on sexual responsibility were associated with delayed timing of sexual intercourse, as were stronger refusal attitudes. In this study, the relationships between variables were similar for males and females, although sexual initiation was on the whole earlier for boys.

Gender differences

Halpern (2003), summarizing studies that assess the relative influences of hormonal and social factors on adolescent sexual behaviour, suggests that although both sexes are likely to have friends with similar levels of sexual experience, boys' experience with intercourse is more likely to be related to hormone levels than the influence of friends, while the opposite is true for girls. Several studies have indicated that girls whose best friends have had intercourse are more likely to also have had intercourse, while for boys, hormone concentration is a more powerful indicator of sexual experience (e.g. Udry, 1988, 2000). Widmer (1997) found a different pattern of influence for siblings however. He matched interview data from 183 pairs of cohabiting adolescent siblings from the Philadelphia Teen Study. After controlling for parental attitudes to young people's sex, he used logistic regression to provide evidence that older brothers had an influence on their younger siblings' sexual behaviour. He suggested that this effect acted primarily through a comparative process with older brothers' behaviour, such that both male and female adolescents in families with sexually active older boys were more likely to initiate their own sexual activity at an earlier age. This intriguing finding did not occur in the case of older sisters. Older brothers acted as role models, older sisters did not. Speculations about the processes by which this apparent sibling influence occurs need to be examined using both longitudinal and qualitative research.

Past research suggests that the messages that young girls receive from others about sex are more likely to be disapproving than the messages given to boys. This is particularly true about messages from parents, but also applies to attitudes expressed by friends. In this way the female peer network may, once again, act as a brake on early or deviant sexual activity, while among young boys this is less likely to be the case. Feldman et al. (1995), for example, showed in a longitudinal study of male adolescents that peer acceptance in Year 6 (ages 10–12 years) was related to having experienced multiple sexual partners by middle high school. They speculated that boys who were more popular had more chances to date, and therefore more chances to become sexually experienced. On the other hand, boys who were rejected by their peers in primary schools also showed higher levels of sexual experience in later adolescence, an association which Feldman and her colleagues linked to the low levels of self-restraint and general misconduct of these boys. These boys exhibited a pattern of 'acting out' of impulses, including sexual impulses. O'Donnell's (2003) study, discussed above, also showed that even among a highly sexually active and risk-taking group of urban minority adolescents, girls' attitudes to sex were more conservative than boys'. For example nearly 60 per cent of girls but only 44 per cent of boys disagreed with the statement 'A girl my age who has sex gets respect from other girls'. The same statement in relation to boys ('A boy my age who has sex gets respect from other boys') was, interestingly, only disagreed with by around one-third of both sexes. The impact of modern mores on these attitudes may lead to changes in such attitudes, but this is still to be determined.

An older partner?

One little studied aspect of peer influence on sexual development is the role of the sexual or romantic partner, 'date', boyfriend/girlfriend – whatever the prevailing terminology may be. Partners have the opportunity to have a strong influence on sexual initiation, on the risky elements of sexual behaviour such as contraceptive use, and on the emotions and future attitudes associated with sex. The evidence is that the age difference between partners is an important predictor of sexual behaviour. In one of the earliest studies of the impact of an older partner, Darroch, Landry and Oslak (1999) showed that although there were relatively few 15- to 17-year-old young women who had a much older partner, they had a low rate of contraceptive use and relatively high rates of pregnancy and birth. The older the partner, the more likely these outcomes occurred. Another early US-based study by Marin, Coyle, Gomez, Carvajal and Kirby (2000) of sixth graders (mean age 11.5 years) showed that having a boyfriend or girlfriend who was 2 or more years older was very strongly associated with having had sex, and with reporting more unwanted sexual advances. Kaestle, Morisky and Wiley (2002) in an analysis of nearly 2000 American girls found that those involved with an older partner were more likely to have had intercourse than girls with partners their own age, a finding that was stronger among the youngest females.

Young woman, older man

Demonstrating that age-discordant relationships are equally influential in other cultures, Wood, Hutchinson, Kahwa, Hewitt and Waldron (2011) conducted focus groups and individual interviews with 43 older adolescent girls (18–21 years old) in Kingston, Jamaica. They defined an age-discordant relationship as a sexual relationship between an adolescent female and a man who was 2 or more years older. These relationships were common and often began when girls were in early adolescence. Both adolescent girls with older partners and the older partners themselves tended to have multiple partners. Transactions of gifts, money or resources from an older partner were expected and common. Having an older male partner was strongly associated with unsafe sex practices among adolescent girls.

Studies conducted in several sub-Saharan African countries have revealed that girls engage in intergenerational sexual relationships without the protection of condoms, giving cause for concern about HIV transmission. Nkosana and Rosenthal (2007a) interviewed schoolgirls in Botswana investigating the dynamics of intergenerational sexual relationships. These relationships occurred for many reasons, often against the girl's will and for reasons associated with subsistence.

> He forced me to have sex with him and I was 16 years by then. He pressurized me and I felt obliged to obey, I just respected him and gave in. He was big enough to be my dad. What can you do? He did not use a condom. Although I did not fall pregnant I contracted an STD from him.
>
> *(Nkosana & Rosenthal, 2007a:186)*

However some young women did act as active social agents who engaged in intergenerational sexual exchanges oriented towards consumption.

> We are pushed into these relationships by material things like money, clothes, cell-phone, show off, posh cars and comfort. We are after a luxurious life.
>
> *(Nkosana & Rosenthal, 2007a:184)*

Interestingly, peer pressure also operated in some of these relationships but it was pressure felt from other girls – to keep up with them – that was the reason for this.

> Peer pressure, we compete with the type of cell phones we have, hair styles, type of vehicles our older boyfriends use and the amount of money we are given.
>
> *(Nkosana & Rosenthal, 2007a:184)*

In a culture where intergenerational sex is not uncommon, there were some girls who resisted (Nkosana & Rosenthal, 2007b). Personal factors that helped girls to resist these sexual relationships included a desire to maintain some power in decision-making, personal ambition, a sense of self-worth, acceptance of their economic circumstances, their knowledge of sexual risks and beliefs about virginity. Sociocultural themes that emerged included desire and respect for marriage, beliefs that older people should be as highly regarded as parents, social morals, especially about family breakdown, and respect for the experiences of close relatives. Finally, girls reported the importance of school connectedness and religious beliefs.

Group dynamics

We mention briefly here the impact of situations where groups of young people congregate for social interaction, often accompanied by drinking alcohol. Sexual pressure from peers under these circumstances may be direct or indirect, combined with considerable alcohol intake or not. In Australia, a 'rite of passage', Schoolies Week, has evolved over the past two to three decades. This is an event where young people at the end of their secondary schooling congregate at various locations, usually at the beach. Although there has been little research on the behaviours during this period, there is considerable anecdotal evidence that links the disinhibition that occurs as part of a large alcohol-fuelled fun-seeking group with regretted and/or unprotected sexual activity and sometimes, sexual violence.

The earliest study of this group activity was conducted by Smith and Rosenthal (1997). In a survey of 1796 young people at one popular site, about two-thirds of the young men and one-third of the young women expected to have sexual intercourse and of these, about 80 per cent expected to use condoms. Most expected to be drunk most nights or every night of their holidays and 27 per cent of young men and 17 per cent of young women expected to be 'stoned' most nights or every night. Most young men and a significant proportion of young women achieved these expectations. A more recent report found that one-third of males attending a Schoolies venue were expecting to have sex with multiple partners (Stark, 2011).

A similar rite of passage, Spring Break, occurs for college students in the US (and no doubt in other countries), with similar outcomes. Patrick, Morgan, Maggs and Lefkowitz (2011) found that college students, both male and female, had understandings with their friends about engaging in risky alcohol use and sexual behaviour during Spring Break. An understanding about getting drunk predicted a greater likelihood of binge drinking and alcohol-related consequences; an understanding of unsafe sex predicted not using condoms. In a later study, Lewis, Patrick, Mittmann and Kaysen (2014) showed the impact of normative perceptions of sex-related behaviours with a typical same-sex peer. Not surprisingly, those students who perceived their peers to have engaged in more sex with casual partners, more drinking prior to sex and a greater number of drinks prior to sex were more likely to engage in those behaviours themselves.

Clearly, at these events where large groups of young people interact, the possibilities for unsafe sexual behaviours are magnified. No doubt, the same might be said of the clubs, bars and other social venues frequented by young people, especially where alcohol is freely available. It has been suggested that greater police presence at these events, better regulation of sales of alcohol, and more involvement by parents and schools in the form of information and advice would reduce the extent of risky practices. Perhaps equally effective might be the suggestion by Lewis and colleagues (2014) that steps should be taken to correct young people's social norms about what might be happening at these events.

Conclusion

In summary, both parents and peers play a significant role in providing information about sex and sexuality or acting as role models. Parents can and do help their adolescents in learning about sex, although this is not universal. For some parents, opening the conversation is hampered by their own preconceptions and their concerns about introducing such a 'difficult' topic. Certainly, more fathers than mothers feel uncertain and even unable to enter into an exchange with their sons and, especially, their daughters. The role of peers in adolescent sex education is complex but more open. Peers talk to each other about sex but do not necessarily believe what they hear. There may be some sexual topics that can be more readily and confidently shared between peers, such as those related to emotional and relationship aspects of sexuality rather than topics where accurate information is required. Indeed, peers can act as important social supports for one another as they go through the highs and lows of romantic relationships and sexual awakening. Also important is that peers influence one another's sexual behaviour through the transmission of attitudes and through perceived sexual practices. Much of the 'peer pressure' described in relationship to adolescent sexuality seems to relate to beliefs about how others of the same age are behaving, and is more pronounced in situations where large numbers of young people gather for entertainment. The problem for young people is to balance wisely the information and advice they receive (if they do receive information) from parents with the potent force of the peer group in order to act in the best way possible to maintain their sexual wellbeing.

5

THE SOCIAL CONTEXT

Sex education, religion and the law

The teachers were very, very good teachers, they taught me a lot of things
I didn't know, they were AWESOME!

(Smith, Realini, Buzi & Martinez, 2011:270)

You have Sex Ed in high school. So you learn a bit from there, but I can't
really remember anything they taught us.

(Ewert, Collyer & Temple-Smith, under review)

We have seen in the previous chapter how parents and peers influence young
people in their sexual decision-making. We turn now to some of the other
factors that contribute to young people's sexual knowledge, practice and
attitudes. Where available, sex education programmes conducted in schools
are an important formal source of information, but there are also factors
that limit adolescents' sexual attitudes and choices. So while adolescents are
learning about sexual behaviour from a variety of sources, their views are also
shaped by the religious and cultural values and the legal constraints imposed
upon them by their society. In this chapter, we consider these more distal
influences of school, religion and the law on adolescent sexuality. A particular focus is on sex education, its goals, forms and effectiveness.

School-based sex education

Despite the fact that the availability and quality of school-based education
varies widely across the globe, school still provides an important opportunity

for delivering sex education. Schools are institutions regularly attended by young people and able to reach most adolescents. If sex education is implemented early enough, young people from diverse social backgrounds and with diverse needs can be reached, often before sexual activity has begun. With adequate resources and trusted personnel available to convey information to young people and to facilitate discussion, schools can provide 'a practical means of reaching large numbers of young people in ways that are replicable and sustainable' (Kirby, 2011:1), and potentially assessable in terms of impact. Importantly, the majority of young people and their parents support the idea of school-based education about sex and sexual health (Giordano & Ross, 2012; McKay & Bissell, 2010; Sherbet Research, 2009).

Approaches to school-based sex education: human rights or abstinence?

The approaches to school-based sex education have varied widely. Although many countries have adopted a broadly based human rights approach, which aims to give young people the knowledge, skills, attitudes and values they need to determine and enjoy their sexuality, others have limited either the availability or content of sex education for sociocultural, political and/or religious reasons. In the category of limited availability are many non-western countries in Africa, Asia and the Middle East (Croce-Galis, 2007; Mohktar, 2015; Roudsari, Javadnoori, Hasanpour, Hazavehei & Taghipour, 2013). In Malaysia, for example, parents' concern about their children accessing sex education and opposition from religious leaders as well as politicians has meant that school-based sex education is fragmentary and certainly not universal (Mohktar, 2015). Another example is the situation in Iran where sex education is minimal and delayed until beyond adolescence. A World Health Organization (WHO, 2007b) review of Iranian youths' sexual practices and knowledge revealed higher than expected sexual activity and poor knowledge about sexual and reproductive health. WHO concluded that 'adolescent sexual and reproductive health programmes are needed in the Islamic Republic of Iran to help adolescents acquire the information and skills they need to make informed decisions about safe sexual activity' (WHO, 2007b:3).

In the US, a religiously inspired 'abstinence-only' moral approach, while under challenge, remains a significant component of sexuality education (Peppard, 2008; Schaalma, Abraham, Gillmore & Kok, 2004). In addition, in a number of European countries such as Greece, Italy, Spain, the Baltic States (Lithuania and Latvia), Luxembourg and Poland, sexuality education is still controversial due to the levels of conservative religiosity (Parker, Wellings & Lazarus, 2009). Similarly, the functionalist approach, in which sexuality education is viewed through a biological and/or reproductive lens primarily as a risk-reduction rather than a health-enhancing strategy, is still predominant in European countries such as Austria, Italy and Poland (Parker *et al.*, 2009) and to a lesser extent in New Zealand (Sinkinson, 2009).

The controversial US-based abstinence education has been strongly endorsed by socially conservative politicians and religious groups. In the early 1980s, in a bid to reduce the high rates of teenage pregnancy, the Adolescent Family Life Act (AFLA) was passed in the US to subsidize sex education that promoted chastity and self-discipline. Increasingly, from that time, an abstinence-only curriculum was favoured and attracted large-scale federal funding. In many US school districts this was the only sex education option presented to young people, despite criticisms that over 80 per cent of programmes contained false, misleading or distorted information about reproductive health (Feijoo & Grayton, 2004). For example, as defined by the US government's Title V of the Social Security Act, the term 'abstinence education' includes eight principles that must be adhered to in abstinence programmes. These include teaching that abstinence from sexual activity is the only certain way to avoid out-of-wedlock pregnancy, sexually transmitted diseases and other associated health problems, that a mutually faithful monogamous relationship in the context of marriage is the culturally expected standard of sexual activity and that sexual activity outside the context of marriage is likely to have harmful psychological and physical side effects.

As a result of mounting criticism, in 2010, Congress eliminated two federal programmes that had funded abstinence-only education and initiated two new evidenced-based sex education programmes. Given the now considerable evidence (addressed in detail in Moore & Rosenthal, 2006, but see also Kirby, Rolleri & Wilson, 2007) that abstinence-only programmes have little positive impact on young people's sexual behaviours and understandings, it is not surprising that the US has joined most of the western world in moving to evidence-based programmes, although progress has been slow. Currently, 35 states and the District of Columbia require public schools to provide some form of sex or STI/HIV education (Guttmacher Institute, 2011). Most states specify how abstinence or contraception should be handled within schools in their jurisdiction, even if schools choose not to offer sex education. This guidance is still weighted towards stressing abstinence, with 19 states requiring that the emphasis be given to engaging in sex only within marriage. Although many states allow or even require that contraceptive information be covered, none require that it be stressed.

Compulsory or not?

In some countries, such as the Netherlands, France and Sweden, sex education in schools is mandatory (Bell, 2009). The UK, too, has recently mandated personal, social, health and economic education, which includes sexual health education, in primary and secondary schools (Formby *et al.*, 2011). Sex and relationship education is compulsory from age 11 onwards and involves teaching about reproduction, sexuality and sexual health. All schools must have a written policy on sex education. Some aspects of sex and relationship education form compulsory parts of the national curriculum for science, but parents can choose whether their children receive all other parts of sex and relationship education (UK Government, 2014).

In Australia, sex education is not compulsory but is widespread. In one recent study (Mitchell, Patrick, Heywood, Blackman & Pitts, 2014) most high school students (86 per cent) had received sex education at school with 37 per cent being taught first in Years 5 or 6. Moreover, the Australian government has funded the development of at least one sex education programme, Talking Sexual Health, which covers a wide range of topics in a value-free manner (Walsh, 2011). Like many other countries, Australia takes a comprehensive approach to school-based sex education, but has a particularly strong emphasis on diversity and respectful relationships (Bell, 2009; Ollis, 2014).

Although most sex education programmes encourage adolescents to delay their introduction to sexual activity, this is not their only aim. The philosophy of harm minimization acknowledges that many young people are sexually active, and thus they need know the risks and the best ways to reduce these.

What is taught?

Sex education can range from direct teaching about biological 'plumbing' through to decision-making and value-oriented approaches. The desired outcomes can be an increase in straightforward knowledge about bodily functions, improvements in sexually responsible behaviour or a combination of both to provide the adolescent with a script for dealing with sexual relationships.

The Netherlands' low rates of adolescent pregnancy and high rates of contraceptive use have often been attributed to comprehensive sex education (Ferguson, Vanwesenbeeck & Knijn, 2008). School-based sex education has been mandatory in the Netherlands for over 20 years, with the goal of empowering young people to set their own sexual boundaries. Students are provided with information about sexual development, reproduction, communication and assertiveness, pregnancy, sexually transmitted infections, contraception, sexual orientation and homophobia, the pleasure of sex, sexual values, respect for different attitudes regarding sex and sexuality, and skills for developing a healthy sexuality (Weaver, Smith & Kippax, 2005). Although sexuality education is still primarily focused on reducing risky sexual behaviour, topics are presented in a positive manner to normalize sexual feelings rather than inducing fear and shame in young people. This education is delivered in a context where access to sexual health services by adolescents is expected, and adolescent contraceptive behaviour is assumed to be the norm. The benefits of this education were highlighted in a comparison between Dutch and US adolescents which showed that although the proportions of adolescents who have had sexual intercourse in both countries is relatively similar, there are differences in reported contraceptive use. In both countries most participants reported condom use at first intercourse, although more Dutch adolescents reported using what they refer to as 'double Dutch' dual methods (condom and hormonal methods combined) at first intercourse. However, almost four times as many US than Dutch female adolescents reported no condom use at first sex (Ferguson *et al.*, 2008). Although proponents of sexuality education in the Netherlands acknowledge their programme is not perfect, they also recognize that its strength lies in the fact that its messages reflect prevailing community attitudes. The Netherlands' commitment to a rights-based approach to adolescent sexuality and sexual health clearly has had a beneficial outcome on the adolescent population.

An Australian programme gives parents a central role in sex education at their children's schools (Ollis & Harrison, in press). This 5-year project, now in its fourth year, is designed to implement a health-promoting and whole-school approach to sexuality education across a five-campus Preparatory to Year 12 college in a regional area. As a result of regular consultations with all constituents, sexuality education has become an important school policy: teachers and key support staff have engaged in professional learning; a mentor programme has been established; a community engagement/parent liaison position has been created; and parent forums have been conducted on all five campuses. The Health-Promoting School approach (Victorian Department of Education and Early Childhood Development, 2008) involves all stakeholders (students, teachers, parents, school authorities and student peers) in a holistic approach. Schools are regarded as only one facet of the environment in which students live, with parents, community groups and students themselves engaged in the creation of the programme. The impact on the knowledge, practices and attitudes of students of this innovative and intensive programme has not yet been evaluated. But the process of achieving delivery of this holistic approach has changed the local community, including school, students and parents and is an impressive model for implementation.

The commitment, ownership, motivation and pride of the teachers engaged in the development, planning and delivery of the classroom programme is evident and has supported their development as key change agents. This confirms the importance of ongoing professional learning, the provision of appropriate resources, time to plan and act, reflect and replan and the significance of public recognition and celebration. However, it also demonstrates the importance of a key feature of the Health-Promoting School model and that is the development of partnerships. The experience at 'Federation' College has shown the enabling effects of community support in developing the readiness for change in an environment often characterized by structures that make it impossible to undertake change without support, leadership and dedicated time (Ollis & Harrison, in press).

Unfortunately few programmes address the issues that cause significant HIV infection among adolescents in large parts of the world (i.e. Europe, Latin America and the Caribbean, and Asia). Those behaviours are unsafe injecting drug use, unsafe sexual activity in the context of sex work and unprotected (mainly anal) sexual intercourse between men. UNAIDS has reported that 60 per cent of young people aged 15–24 years are unable to identify correctly the ways to prevent HIV transmission, highlighting the need for early school-based education programmes, especially in those regions hardest hit by the virus (UNAIDS, 2008).

What young people want

Across the many different cultural settings of the world it appears that young people are united in their desire for sex education, broadly based and delivered in a safe and non-judgemental environment. For example, even though there are barriers to learning about sex in the classroom setting, such as embarrassment, concern about appearing 'too interested' in front of classmates and inappropriate timing for some individuals, young Australians nominate school programmes as one of the sources they most use for information on sex (Mitchell *et al.*, 2014). Recent research on young males found there is also a desire for regular sex education refreshers throughout the school years, as well as for those who go onto higher education (Ewert *et al.*, under review; Litras, Latreille & Temple-Smith, under review).

In one US study (P.B. Smith *et al.*, 2011), ninth-grade students were asked what they would like to learn about. The authors identified four major themes. Most common was a request for more information on STIs; next, students asked for information about 'anything' or 'everything', for example 'Everything I need to know so I could stay safe'. Others wanted to learn about sexual intercourse: 'What sex is all about and how it effects [sic] the teenager's life'; 'Not letting people pressure you to have sex'. Methods of reducing risk was a fourth theme: 'What should teens do besides abstain from sex to protect themselves'; 'Why birth control methods do not work sometimes' (P.B. Smith *et al.*, 2011:276).

Is factual information enough? A focus on factual rather than practical information was found in a US study (Boyar, Levine & Zensius, 2011) of 15- to 24-year-old students who had classes on anatomy, menstruation, pregnancy and STIs at some stage in their schooling. These young people were generally satisfied with the information they received, however some felt that they heard the same messages repeatedly (e.g. use a condom, practise abstinence) with little opportunity to raise new issues or explore complexities.

> I went to a bunch of classes, and after a while, you don't have to stress the point. (Adolescent male)
>
> *(Boyar et al., 2011:17)*

Although most young people surveyed by Mitchell and colleagues (2014) declared that the sex education they received was relevant, some noted absences.

> I think sex education should talk about homosexuality more. I was clueless and I don't think the word was even mentioned. . . . There were 180 people in my grade . . . we advertised and held a coming out of sexual preferences group purely so we could all have support and there were 19 gay/lesbian/bisexual kids there. That's 12%; at 12% of the grade population we have some right to education too.
>
> *(Sauers, 2007:110)*

> It was done through more of a biological lens and taught us about STI prevention and anatomy but did not include many topics that are very important, such as communication with partners, different relationship dynamics or unusual circumstances, actually getting pleasure from sex etc.
>
> *(Mitchell et al., 2014:74)*

Unfortunately (and not uncommonly) some students felt that their teachers were not suited to the task. Some tried to be funny in an inappropriate way, some were too authoritarian, and some were simply people to whom the students could not relate.

Preference for people other than school teachers to teach sex education is a common desire among students. Research in Australia showed that for two-thirds of young people in one study (Giordano & Ross, 2012) most preferred sexual health peer educators (i.e. trained young people) or sexual health educators from community organizations to deliver sex education in schools. Over three-quarters did not want faith-based organizations to deliver content and fewer than half supported the idea of science teachers delivering sexual health education. Young people in this study identified the following topics as those they wanted included in school-based sex education: information on STIs and contraception; gender and relationship issues; spiritual, ethical and moral considerations; legal issues; negotiation skills; body image; the impact of alcohol and other drugs on sexual behaviour; diversity in sexuality; and cultural considerations (Giordano & Ross, 2012:22). The need for education about sexual diversity was confirmed in a study by Hillier *et al.* (2010) in which about 40 per cent of young people wanted the sexuality education delivered by their school to be more inclusive of same-sex attraction and gender diversity.

Teaching about diversity

The International Technical Guidelines on Sexuality Education (UNESCO, 2009) encourage comprehensive sexuality education that includes a positive approach to gender and sexual diversity. However, given the vastly varying cultural beliefs about sexual diversity across the globe, it is not surprising to find that these issues are excluded in many countries. Significant legislative and cultural change would be required to achieve understanding and acceptance of sexual diversity within these communities. Without such attitudinal and legislative changes, it is difficult to see how sex education within schools could address these issues.

Globally, the needs of lesbian, gay, bisexual and transgender students are often overlooked in sex education. A national Australian survey of over 3000 young people aged 14–21 years found that one-third of participants were clear about their sexual identity prior to puberty (Jones & Hillier, 2012). Around 60 per cent had experienced verbal homophobic abuse and almost 20 per cent had experienced physical homophobic abuse, 80 per cent of this at school. However students who reported their school had policies against homophobia were more likely to state that they had received useful information from that school on discrimination, gay and lesbian relationships and safe sex, suggesting that visible school policies can not only protect students from homophobia but also result in the acceptance and inclusion of lesbian, gay, bisexual and transgender students. There were other strong associations with psychosocial measures that affirmed the value of policy-based protection. Fewer students who perceived their school had policy-based protection had thought about or engaged in self-harm or felt unsafe at school (Jones & Hillier, 2012).

Cultural issues

Where there is a range of cultural backgrounds among the students in a school, common issues of concern are that programmes may lack cultural sensitivity and/or the programmes fail to acknowledge differences in literacy, knowledge and language skills (Newton *et al.*, 2012).

The Norwegian experience is telling. The long-standing and highly regarded Norwegian sex education system commences at school entry and continues until the age of 16, with sex education integrated into many subjects from social science to religion (Bartz, 2007). The emphasis is on responsible decision-making and in early high school includes a day's visit to a local youth-based sexual health clinic to demonstrate contraception choices and STI testing. The challenge this poses for conservative students has recently been examined, particularly in light of the recent increasing ethnic diversity in Scandinavian countries. Sex education has been crit-icized for stressing Norwegian values in its curriculum, and not taking account of the needs of cultural minorities (Bartz, 2007). This is a prob-lem faced by many schools with multicultural student bodies and requires sensitive attention to parents' beliefs and traditions. Perhaps the type of programme initiated by Ollis and Harrison, described above, where parents form a critical part of the process of developing the programme, might be one way of overcoming problems of cultural sensitivity within multicul-tural classes. One review of parents conducted in the UK (Department of Education, UK Government, 2009) showed that these parents were keen supporters of comprehensive school-based sex education, regarding this as hugely important in their child's development. None believed that parents should have the option of removing their child from sex education classes; they did, however, make the point that they wanted to have better understanding of what was being taught so that they could feel reassured and informed.

The situation in many non-western countries is even more difficult for those wanting to encourage school-based sex education. As discussed previ-ously, in some countries, sex education is deemed unacceptable because of the strong religious and cultural prohibitions around sex, especially for girls. For example, schools play very little role in the delivery of sex education in Iran, although a recent study, one of the first of its kind in that country, sug-gested that young women are very keen to receive such information.

> It has been explained in the books but we cannot understand anything from the book. For instance, regarding fertilization, there is something in our textbook on biology, but we understand nothing from that chapter as it is so short and ambiguous. It's better to remove that chap-ter from the book! (Female, 16 years)
>
> *(Javadnoori, Roudsari, Hasanpour, Hazavehei &*
> *Taghipour, 2012:543)*

The students asked about its meaning and the teacher said that it's not the right time for you to know about that. I stand up and said but I assume it's the right time. We have no understanding about men's sexual issues and in the near future we have to live with a man under the same roof! (Female, 16 years)

(Javadnoori et al., 2012:542)

Nepal provides another example. There is recognition of the need for school-based sex education in this country. Students aged 14–16 are taught basic sex education using a chapter on reproductive health from a textbook, which covers a range of topics associated with reproductive health (Pokharel, Kulczycki & Shakyac, 2006). A study of over 450 students found that adolescents were not getting the information they needed from this approach. Many students felt uncomfortable with the topics, and did not feel their teachers were skilled enough to offer such instruction, or capable of providing a safe environment in which questions could be asked.

We have to obey the teachers in every respect. . . . They are like our parents not like our friends with whom we can discuss any issue. How can you imagine I can get answers to my questions on reproductive health and sex with them? To do that, I need to have a lot of courage and I also have to think about the consequences.

(Pokharel et al., 2006:59)

Thailand is typical of many countries in that the focus of sex education is largely on biological issues rather than practicalities (such as how to put on a condom), emotional issues or negotiation skills. Vuttanont, Greenhalgh, Griffin and Boynton (2006) surveyed over 2000 students in Thai schools and found that these young people demonstrated conflicting aspirations about sexual expression and sex education. While desiring modern western relationships that allowed public displays of affection and experimentation with sex, they also valued the traditional norms of modesty and virginity (in girls). A common query was around masturbation, which highlighted the mixed messages to which they are exposed. Traditional Thai culture views masturbation as a male activity which is sinful, dirty and unhealthy, whereas western culture sees masturbation as private but normal, harmless and useful in learning about the body, especially for females (Vuttanont *et al.*, 2006).

With sexual issues prominent in mass media, the rise of social media as a way of communicating about sex and trends towards increased sexual activity among young people, many of these countries may have to face the challenge of determining how to reduce sexual harm while respecting cultural and religious beliefs.

The timing of sex education

> I go to a catholic school, and we were taught to wait until marriage to lose our virginity, when half the school weren't virgins, which is pretty pointless . . . we weren't taught about sex until year 10, when I had already had sex. (Female, 17 years)
>
> *(Sauers, 2007:107)*

When is it acceptable and an appropriate time to provide sex education in schools? Recently there has been a recognized need to start sexuality education at a young age (Goldman, 2008; Kane, 2008; Kesterton & Coleman, 2010) and make it comprehensive within a broader health framework which includes social and gender/sexuality issues as well as reproduction (Mason, 2010; Walker & Milton, 2006). Nevertheless, just as many parents do not discuss sexuality with their children until they believe their child is in a relationship that might lead to sex (Eisenberg, Bernat, Bearinger & Resnick, 2008), in many countries, sex education is deferred, if it occurs at all, until secondary school, or the mid- to late teens. Unfortunately, for many students, as we have seen in earlier chapters, this may be too late to prevent sexual risk behaviours. Just as teaching about contraception needs to occur before many class members are sexually active, so too, the timing of puberty (now earlier than ever) means that teaching about menstruation is of little value if many of the female students already menstruate.

Criticisms of the late timing of school-based sex education have been made by a number of researchers. Thus, Boyar *et al.* (2011), in their US study of over 1500 young people, noted that school-based education was often mistimed. For example, teachers were still not talking about contraception to 16- to 18-year-old students even though the majority of the class was already sexually active. This is not an uncommon problem. A survey of over 1200 south-east Nigerian students aged 14–17 years and their teachers examined the association between class level at the time of receiving sex education at both home and school, and self-reported pregnancy in the last 3 years of school (Ochioga, Miettola, Ilika & Vaskilampi, 2011). Reported cases of unintended pregnancies were highest among the junior students, and about 40 per cent of the students did not use contraceptives for their first sexual experience. The authors suggest that sex education might have a stronger impact if provided before 14 years of age. Moreover, early sex education may lessen the need for this to continue in the later years of school. A report by Durex (2009) revealed that regardless of their nationality, the younger a person is when they initially receive sex and relationships education, the less likely they will feel the need for further sex education at later stages in their lives. The report concludes that universal access to formal sex and relationships education should be guaranteed to young people before the age of 12.

Scandinavian countries may be regarded as among the leaders in providing early sex education in schools. Traditionally held up as models of good practice, sex education in these countries is integrated throughout the school curriculum, from primary school through to the end of secondary school, with a focus in early adolescence (Weaver *et al.*, 2005). An even more comprehensive approach to early sex education is that of Ollis and Harrison in their Health-Promoting Schools project described above. In their wide-ranging research, they have shown that young children in Years 5 and 6 have a keen sense of what they want to learn about. They are not as concerned about the topic of reproduction (the physical mechanics, conception and pregnancy) as about love and being close. Girls and boys have different priorities. For example, boys want to know more about sex and sexual feelings, about masturbation and contraception and STIs than girls. Boys are most interested in discrimination and the law, and girls are most interested in knowing what to do (Ollis, Harrison & Richardson, 2012).

Regardless of when formal sex education starts in schools and how excellent the programme, its success stands or falls on the ability and commitment of those teaching it.

Teachers' perspectives

The quality of teaching in sex education courses has the potential to enhance or minimize its impact, as the comments from students earlier in this chapter highlighted. Effective sex educators need to be interested in teaching the subject, comfortable discussing sexuality, good communicators and skilled in the use of participatory learning (UNESCO, 2009). Traditionally, sexual health has not been taught by trained specialists. Home economics teachers, school nurses or physical education teachers (or some mix of all three) may be given this task, often with little preparation or support. Many teachers are not proficient at presenting sensitive and controversial topics, and may feel uncomfortable or anxious about doing so.

Indeed, research suggests that teachers in many countries feel ill-prepared to deliver sex education. In Spain, a study of almost 4000 teachers showed nearly half had no education at all in relation to sex and relationships (Martinez *et al.*, 2014). Elsewhere in Europe, less than one-third of Finnish teachers assigned to teach sex education had training to do so (Kontula, 2010),

106 The social context: sex education, religion and the law

and in Norway very few sex education teachers are trained, although school nurses have training to deliver sexual health education (Bartz, 2007).

A study of women teachers in rural Lesotho, Africa found that they struggled between a desire to protect their students' sexual innocence, and the need to deliver sex education as a teacher (Khau, 2014). In their villages, traditional values do not support sexuality education, and thus people who teach it are not respected. One way of addressing this, the author suggested, is to invite community members to teach traditional issues, such as circumcision and traditional contraception, alongside formal sex education (Khau, 2014).

In Australia, a survey of over 300 secondary school teachers found the most frequently taught topics were factual information on STIs, HIV/AIDS, safe sex practices, reproduction and birth control methods as well as managing peer pressure, relationships and feelings, alcohol and sexual activity, decision-making and dealing with emotions. Refraining from intercourse until feeling ready was a strong message. Sex education was most likely to be covered in Years 9 and 10 of secondary school, with puberty, reproduction and body image covered in earlier years. Sexual pleasure was discussed by less than half of respondents (A. Smith *et al.*, 2011). Although teachers generally felt sex education increased students' knowledge of sexuality and sexual health, they judged it to be less effective in helping young people explore feelings, values and attitudes, and in strengthening skills to sustain risk-reducing behaviour. Teachers were not comfortable with some aspects of the sex education curriculum. Many requested assistance to discuss the more sensitive topics such as sexual abuse and same-sex attraction. Almost 70 per cent stated they needed assistance teaching 'the impact of communication technology on sexuality and relationships', and more than half wanted help with 'the impact of media on sexuality and identity' (A. Smith *et al.*, 2011:30).

Although classroom teachers are part of the school structure and thus known and trusted by the community and students, the advantage of specialist sex education teachers is that they can be linked more readily to community-based reproductive health services. Although evaluations have demonstrated that programmes can be effectively delivered by both groups of educators, many students prefer external teachers for this role (Kirby, Obasi & Laris, 2006).

One of the key factors influencing teachers' attitudes and competence is the extent to which they are engaged in developing the sex education programme and trained to deliver it. Professional development of teachers prior to undertaking the delivery of the programme to students ensures that teachers feel confident and competent. Ollis and Harrison (in press) write that the commitment, ownership, motivation and pride of the teachers engaged in the development, planning and delivery of the classroom programme is evident and has supported their development as key change agents. This confirms the importance of on-going professional learning, the provision of appropriate resources, time to plan and act, reflect and replan and the significance of public recognition and celebration.

(Ollis & Harrison, in press)

Ollis, Harrison and Maharaj (2013) provide a comprehensive account of preparing teachers to teach sexuality education pre-service training, for those wishing to pursue this topic.

Evaluations of school-based sex education programmes

One of the most challenging aspects of sex education is determining whether or not it has been effective, and how effectiveness should be measured. Impact may be measured in terms of better knowledge, improved attitudes, lower sexual risk (e.g. use of contraceptives, delay of sexual initiation) and greater comfort in communicating about sexual issues. As might be expected, given the wide range and content of sex education programmes and the difficulties in effecting behaviour change, outcomes vary.

Several studies have concluded that providing young people with sex education does not lead to earlier or more frequent sexual activity, a concern commonly expressed in the past (McKay & Bissell, 2010).

In 2011, Kirby undertook a comprehensive review of 87 sex education programmes in a wide range of countries on behalf of UNESCO. He reported that of the 63 studies that measured initiation of sexual intercourse, one-third showed a delay of this and none showed hastening of sexual initiation. One-third led to a decrease in the frequency of sexual intercourse, 44 per cent led to a decrease in the number of sexual partners, and following 40 per cent of the programmes condom use or contraception was increased. Kirby concluded:

> The positive results on the three measures of sexual activity, condom and contraceptive use and sexual risk-taking, are essentially the same when the studies are restricted to large studies with rigorous experimental designs. Thus the evidence for the positive impacts is quite strong.
>
> *(Kirby, 2011:6)*

Nevertheless, Kirby points out that the effective programmes yielded only modest reductions in risky behaviours, although he concluded this can mean significant reductions in pregnancy and STI rates. Importantly, Kirby's review found that effective programmes were not limited to western countries but were found in many regions, including Asia, Africa, the US and Europe, and the UK. In Nigeria where there has been no mandatory sex education despite high rates of sex among school-aged adolescents, poor contraception and high rates of STIs, HIV, abortion and abortion-related mortality, a recent study found that a sex education intervention programme reduced at-risk sexual behaviours of school-going adolescents. These at-risk behaviours included multiple partnering and anal sex (Esere, 2008). Although this was a small study, it showed potential for broader population benefits if such a programme were to be introduced across Nigerian schools.

In another evaluation of UK programmes, the evidence was less clear-cut. Wight (2011) assessed three different sex education programmes and found only limited effects. All three programmes improved sexual health knowledge and had some positive impacts on attitudes, with peer educators having more success with modifying norms, and teachers having more success at improving knowledge. However, the programmes had very little impact on reported behaviour, suggesting that other factors such as community-based sexual health promotion and changing family attitudes may have already achieved most major behaviour changes, a point also made by Boonstra (2014). Wight concluded that, although important, sex education is probably most beneficial when it aligns with critical points in a young person's own sexual experience.

Overall, there is a large body of evidence that well-designed programmes do have a significant positive impact on sexual health behaviours. One US study of the association between formal sex education and sexual behaviours showed that sex education that includes instruction about both waiting to have sex and methods of birth control improved the health and well-being of adolescents and young adults (Lindberg & Maddow-Zimet, 2011). Abstinence-only programmes were less effective. Other evaluations of abstinence-only programmes have shown these programmes to be ineffective at stopping or even delaying sex (Kirby, 2008; Underhill, Montgomery & Operario, 2007). In fact there is some suggestion that virginity pledge programmes actually increased risk for STIs and pregnancy and participants were less likely to seek STI testing or to use contraception when they did have sex in comparison to non-pledge-takers (Brückner & Bearman, 2005).

In considering how to provide the best possible sex education programmes in schools it needs to be remembered that schools influence young people in ways over and above their formal educational role. Peer group influence is important, as discussed in the previous chapter, but there is also an 'informal' curriculum in relation to sexuality. Examples include school policies on sexual minorities and bullying, the level of support that sex education teachers experience from the principal and school community, ease of communication between students and teachers and even seemingly trivial issues like how graffiti is handled. This informal curriculum can give strong messages to young people as to what is acceptable sexually, what issues can be discussed and what issues are off limits. Charmaraman and McKamey (2011) take up this point in relation to what they call 'accidental' school influences. They argue that there are many opportunities for these influences to impact on young people, concluding that:

> local contextual factors, including school policies, norms about how and in what ways students and teachers relate to one another, and the neighbourhood in which schools were located were essential components of how students made meaning of sexuality, gender and relationships.
>
> *(Charmaraman & McKamey, 2011:16)*

Messages about healthy sexuality can also be learned from school subjects other than sex education, underlining the importance of a whole-school approach to supporting the sex education curriculum. Studying novels in which sexual decisions are made and their outcomes discussed, experiencing physical education classes in which value is placed on a healthy and well-functioning body or feeling comfortable to discuss a range of controversial issues in the classroom can all contribute to healthy sexual decision-making.

Best practice in sexuality education

Many countries have provided a framework for the development of a comprehensive sex education programme. In Canada, the Public Health Agency of Canada's (2008) Canadian Guidelines of Sexual Health Education has developed a framework based on information (providing relevant information), motivation (ensuring the motivation to use this information) and behavioural skills (skills to put the information into practice).

McKay and Bissell (2010) note 10 key ingredients of effective programmes, which include allowing a realistic allocation of time, providing teachers with appropriate training, using effective teaching methods, using research to determine students' needs, covering a wide range of issues (including activities that address the student's environment and social context), providing opportunities to practice (e.g. limit setting, negotiation), and, importantly, to evaluate programmes in order to assess strengths and weaknesses so that subsequent programmes can be improved.

In similar vein, Kirby and his colleagues (2007) describe 17 characteristics of sexual health education programmes, many of which are shared by a large majority of the successful programmes. These characteristics include methods of developing the curriculum, such as conducting a needs assessment of the target group, multidisciplinary consultation with sexual health experts, ensuring the programme is in keeping with community values, and pilot-testing the programme. In addition to specifying overarching curriculum goals, Kirby *et al.* also stress the importance of creating a safe space in which young people can participate (this is especially relevant for lesbian and gay young people) and interactive teaching methods. Finally, characteristics to enable successful implementation of sex education are outlined, including engagement with appropriate authorities, and training, monitoring, supervision and support of teaching staff. This study highlights the many shortcomings of current research into sexuality education, and points to the need for further work to determine which educational strategies and activities are most effective at changing behavioural factors both across and within cultures. Research into sexual health programmes for young people has shown that many evaluations are too complex, underfunded and rushed, which compromises recognition of the nuances of programmes. In addition, often evaluations are conducted over too short a timeframe to examine long-term change (Newton *et al.*, 2012).

Religion

We turn now to a broader aspect of the social context, namely religion. Most religions emphasize or even ordain sexual values that encourage conservatism and restraint, such as premarital chastity and marital fidelity. Some proscribe contraception, homosexuality and abortion. Today's powerful pressures towards adolescent sexual activity militate against their continued involvement in traditional religion, a situation that can leave young people in a spiritual vacuum in terms of developing values about sex and relationships. Values adopted by the popular media and the adolescent subculture may well fill this vacuum and, as we have seen, sex education can play a powerful role in providing positive, value-based learning. If religiosity is an important part of an adolescent's identity, negative views of sexuality from within their faith can have a profound impact on their own developing sexuality and for those whose sexuality falls outside traditional heterosexuality, this can be extremely challenging (Harris, 2009; Ward, 2005).

Religiosity, not religion

There is now considerable research indicating that it is not religion per se that directly influences sexual behaviour. Rather, it is the extent to which

a young person takes on religious beliefs and attachment to religious institutions, namely their religiosity. Not surprisingly, religiosity often develops within the family environment (Manlove, Logan, Moore & Ikramullah,
2008). Along with other researchers, Manlove *et al.* found that higher levels
of family religiosity were associated either directly or indirectly with less
risky sexual practices, a finding supported by research with African-American
adolescents (Landor, Simons, Simons, Brody & Gibbons, 2011). Multiple
dimensions of adolescent religiosity, for example, their levels of religious
belief, prayer and attendance at religious services, as well as their scores on
composite measures of religiosity, are associated with delayed sexual initiation (e.g., Adamczyk & Felson, 2006; Jones, Darroch & Singh, 2005).

Overall, it appears that adolescents with high levels of religiosity are
among those least likely to experience early sexual initiation or multiple partnering. However, sexual conservatism among religious adolescents
may not simply be the consequence of personal or religious values, as these
young people are also more likely to associate with other religious adolescents, and thus the norms of the most salient peer group enforce the values
of religion.

By decreasing the likelihood of premarital sex, religiosity is also associated with a lower number of sexual partners (M.A. Gold *et al.*, 2010; Landor
et al., 2011). A less healthy outcome suggested by some studies is a possible
relationship between religiosity and negative attitudes about sex, for example narrow views on appropriate sexual expression (Manlove *et al.*, 2008;
Rostosky, Regnerus & Wright, 2003). It also appears that although delaying
sexual initiation may be one outcome of religiosity, once sexual debut has
occurred there is little evidence that religiosity has an impact on condom
or contraceptive use (Nonnemaker, McNeely & Blum, 2003). One finding
of interest is that religiosity in adolescents may be protective against both
accidental and intentional pornography viewing (Hardy, Steelman, Coyne &
Ridge, 2013). Comparison of pornography users and non-users among
young men attending a religious US university showed users had lower levels
of past and recent individual and family religious practices (Nelson, Padilla-
Walker & Carroll, 2010).

Questions raised when examining the relationship between religiosity and sexual behaviour among western adolescents are complex and the
answers are likely to be different from those in countries with strong religious proscriptions regarding adolescent sexuality. We need to know more
about how these young people's sexual practices and beliefs are influenced
by their religions. It is clear from this brief review that religion is only one
of many factors influencing sexual attitudes and expression. As Rostosky,
Wilcox, Wright and Randall (2004) note in their comprehensive review of
the impact of religiosity on young people's sexual behaviour, account needs

to be taken of how other factors such as gender, ethnicity and relationships interact with this social construct.

The law

It would be impossible to review, for all states and nations, the laws that deal with adolescent sexual behaviour. Many countries have such laws, and they provide a broad framework for decisions about acceptable ways for adolescents to express their sexuality. Young people are included among the general population in the many laws relating to sexuality, including those concerning abortion and homosexuality. Some laws, however, are specifically designed to protect young people. These include laws about age of consent and privacy of medical consultations as well as laws relating to the use of new technologies for sexual purposes. We deal briefly with each of these in turn.

Age of consent

Age of consent laws specify an age below which it is illegal to engage in sexual intercourse. There is no standard international age of consent; this varies from country to country and often between states or territories within countries. In many places the legal age of consent is complex and may be different depending on circumstances such as gender, type of sexual practice, partner age difference, if a partner is in a position of authority, whether partners are married or unmarried, and the legality of homosexual sex.

For example, in England and Scotland, 16 is the age of consent for both girls and boys to have heterosexual or homosexual sex, while in Ireland this age is 17. Across the US, age of consent varies according to state, but generally varies between 16 and 18 years. In Nigeria and Argentina, sex for both males and females is legal at 13, and in Argentina this is also the case for homosexual sex, but in Nigeria homosexual sex is illegal. In China, the legal age of both heterosexual and homosexual consent is 14, and in the Sudan, it is legal for both men and women to have sex only within marriage, and homosexual sex is illegal (ChartsBin, 2011). Laws against homosexuality and laws about engaging in certain sexual acts such as sodomy or oral sex exist in some countries, or states within countries, and are policed with more or less enthusiasm, depending on the social climate of the region and the times.

Age of consent laws are a social expression of our beliefs that it is appropriate to protect young people against sexual involvement until they are emotionally and physically ready, and that too early sexual activity may be damaging to growth and development. Within such laws, it is often the case that the actions of an older person who has sex with a minor are viewed in a more serious light than, say, the situation in which two minors have sex with each other. In Australia, for example, consensual intercourse with a young girl under 16 years of age was once uniformly unlawful, irrespective of the age of the girl's partner. In two jurisdictions in Australia, Victoria and the Australian Capital Territory, the law has now been changed so that intercourse with a girl aged between 12 and 16 years may occur lawfully, provided that her partner is no more than 2 years older than she is.

Privacy of medical consultations

Another way in which the law regulates sexuality concerns an individual's right to be treated as medically adult. These laws deal with the rights of a young person to give consent to medical or surgical treatment without the consent of parents, and the requirement of professional confidentiality on the part of the medical profession. The law, through such acts, supports the theory of harm minimization, and tries to ensure that young people are kept safe through their ability to access contraception and safe abortion if necessary.

Of course, one difficulty in attempting to regulate sexuality is that these laws are often unenforced and unenforceable. It is one thing to make sexual intercourse between a 15-year-old girl and a 19-year-old boy illegal. It is another to convince the pair in question that they should cease what they are doing because it is against the law. Nevertheless, there is a sense in which such laws acknowledge the confusions and misperceptions of parents about their children's sexuality by relieving parents of the need to make decisions. Clearly, these laws are not without controversy. For example there have been a number of cases in both Britain and Australia of parents challenging the medical privacy laws for adolescents, whereby under 16-year-olds have the right to contraception and abortions without their parents' knowledge (e.g. Curtis, 2006).

What is important in considering the effects of any of these laws on adolescent sexuality is that although they govern behaviour through regulation and punishment, they also shape attitudes and are, in turn, shaped by the prevailing social mores. It may be said that the law reflects the overt but not necessarily the implicit sexual values of a society. The degree to which laws about sexual behaviour actually affect sexual practice has not been systematically studied. It seems likely, however, that laws that are too out of step with current thinking will be far less likely to be obeyed or to influence sexual decision-making.

Digital technologies

The need for constant review of the law is evident when considering the enormous impact of digital technology on every aspect of our lives. Sexting (discussed in Chapter 6) is one example where new technologies have affected young people's lives. Sexting has led to a legal grey area in countries that have strict anti-child pornography laws, such as the US. Some adolescents who have texted photographs of themselves, or of their friends or partners, have been charged with distribution of child pornography, while those who have received the images have been charged with possession of child pornography. In Canada, although the creation and sending of nude photos of young people under 18 years technically breaks child pornography laws, an exception is made if the taking and sending of nude photos occurs only between the original partners (Slane, 2009).

The UK laws deal more clearly with sexting. Indecent images of those under 18 years are illegal, although the definition of 'indecent' is unclear but includes images of genitals, sex acts, naked people or female breasts. It is illegal to take, possess or share indecent images of anyone under 18 even if you are the person in the picture. In Australia, in the state of Victoria, a recent enquiry into sexting resulted in law reform, the first of its kind globally (Parliament of Victoria, 2013). Sexting without consent is now an offence in Victoria, and anyone who maliciously or deliberately spreads sexually explicit images of another person, or threatens to do so, faces prosecution. These new laws also include exceptions to child pornography offences, so that adolescents under the age of 18 will no longer be prosecuted or placed on the sex offenders' register for consensual, non-exploitative sexting (Premier of Victoria, 2014).

Given the rapidly shifting changes to digital technologies, it is clear that law-makers will have to be nimble to maintain the sexual safety of young people today. Equally clear is that many countries have not yet found an appropriate way to deal with this new world of communication.

Conclusion

Formal sex education in schools takes many forms and provides a widely divergent array of content from 'abstinence-only' programmes to programmes that encompass topics related to healthy living generally, as well as sexuality and sexual health. These topics include relationships, respect, gender issues, sexual negotiation and many others. In the past and to some extent currently, sex education, if delivered in schools, tended to be directed at older teens. There is now convincing evidence that education of this sort should begin in primary school, not least because a substantial minority of young people have their first experience of sex in their early teens. It cannot be argued unequivocally that sex education in schools has a powerful impact on practices, knowledge and beliefs. Rather than attribute this to a generalized lack of effectiveness of these programmes, we have seen that their success is enhanced where the content is reinforced by the behaviours and attitudes in society. The type of programme and other contextual features also play a role in effectiveness.

One powerful environmental context is religion, measured as religiosity or the extent to which young people adopt the tenets and practices of their religion. It is a key factor in delaying young people's sexual initiation and in decreasing sexual risk practices. This effect is most apparent in conservative countries where the prevailing religion teaches that sex among unmarried young people is taboo. Another and different context is provided by the laws in each country which proclaim certain sex-related behaviours unlawful, thereby making young people liable to criminal prosecution. A difficulty for the law is in keeping pace both with the rapidly changing societal views of some sexual behaviours, for example western attitudes to homosexuality, and with the evolving digital technologies which provide previously unthought-of opportunities for sexual communication. In the next chapter, we discuss in detail this changing youth culture and the role of new technologies in young people's sexual expression.

6

THE SOCIAL CONTEXT
Impact of media and technology

> I do my homework on it, like research and everything like that. I talk to
> friends via MSN or Skype. I play games on it like Warcraft or Everquest
> 2 or something like that. . . . I go on YouTube and stuff like that and look
> at videos. I listen to music on it. . . . I couldn't really live without the com-
> puter to be honest. (Male, 15 years)
>
> *(Davies & Eynon, 2013:27)*

The social context in which they live plays a significant role in young people's
sexual beliefs and behaviour. In the previous two chapters we examined the
impact of parents and peers, sex education and the broader social context –
religion and the law. Here, the focus is on one element of that context – the
adolescent subculture and, in particular, the impact of media and modern
technologies. New and old media, and their effect on youth culture, are
the major issues covered in this chapter. Here we consider the positive and
negative effects of mass media and technological change – particularly the
internet and its various manifestations – on sexual mores. Topics include
sexting, dating 'apps', pornography online and the potential for the internet
to provide high-quality information about sexual health.

Young people live in a world where they are bombarded by media messages
about current (and often ephemeral) fashions. They are constantly 'attached' to
different forms of social media through their mobile phones, tablets or computers. They are tweeting, texting, checking their Facebook status, playing
games, sending 'selfies' and participating in the wide range of communication
activities available through the new technologies. At times it seems as if these

new forms of connection have almost displaced face-to-face contact. But as will be seen in this chapter, there are both positives and negatives arising from these forms of communication in their influence on adolescent sexuality.

The power of youth culture in shaping young people's opinions and behaviours can be recognized in the conformity of youths to current fashions in clothes, music and leisure activities. The area of sexuality is just as subject to this influence as any other. Adolescents derive much of their information about sexual mores and behaviours from this subculture, which extends beyond immediate peers, and purveys sets of beliefs about what adolescents should be and are doing, from the point of view of their age-mates. These beliefs are communicated via various media directly targeted at young people. Influences include 'old media' such as publications for adolescents, movies, television, music and video clips, as well as all the options available through 'new media' – social media, apps for meeting people, instant communications through texting and sending photos via mobile phones, to name a few. The power of these new communication tools is the speed with which they can spread a message; once posted, material can 'go viral', potentially with widespread repercussions to both the sender and receiver.

In subsequent sections we discuss the influence of different forms of media on youth culture, specifically in relation to sexual attitudes and behaviours.

Magazines, movies, media role models

> Movies like *American Pie* push me to have as much sex as I can. (Male, 18 years)

> Teen movies like *American Pie* where all the guys are on a quest to 'get laid' makes me think I should be having more sex. (Male, 18 years)
> *(Sauers, 2007:85)*

There is ample evidence that heavy exposure to sexual content in the media is associated with more rapid progression of sexual behaviour and earlier first sex (Bleakley, Hennessy, Fishbein & Jordan, 2008; Chandra *et al.*, 2008; Collins *et al.*, 2004). A US study, for example, found that the average teenager from a sample of over 3000 middle school adolescents had high media exposure and in a typical month watched television and listened to music on 30 days, read magazines on 4 days and watched movies on 2 days (L'Engle, Brown & Kenneavy, 2006). Those who perceived greater support from the media for adolescent sexual behaviour reported more sexual activity and greater intention to engage in sex in the near future.

In terms of how adolescents gain information about sex, the media rate highly, along with parents, teachers and friends. A survey of nearly 500

14- to 16-year-olds in the United States found 57 per cent of this group used the media as a source of sex education, with television and movies assessed as the most informative media, followed by the internet, magazines and music (Bleakley, Fishbein & Jordan, 2009). A recent survey of Australian high school students in Years 9–12 found that websites were the most common source of information about sex (Mitchell, Patrick, Heywood, Blackman & Pitts, 2014).

How do media influence sexual behaviour? Some examples

Although it is likely that for today's youth, online sources have taken over from 'old' media in providing sex education, it is clear that media in general, whatever the source, have a powerful impact. An example of this impact is the way in which the media shape beliefs about male and female behaviour in romantic relationships. The models depicted are not always healthy or adaptive. Brown and L'Engle (2009) found that early exposure, at around age 13 or earlier, to X-rated material was associated, for both sexes, with more stereotypic gender role attitudes, for example, believing that males should 'always be ready for sex'. For boys, this early exposure was also linked to a greater tendency to sexually harass others, for example by making negative comments about a schoolmate's body, weight or clothing, touching a schoolmate in a sexual way, or pressuring a schoolmate for a date.

Given this impact, it makes sense to ask what messages about sexuality are being conveyed and perceived. Some commentators have described the media as a 'superpeer', which constantly emphasizes that youthful sex is normative and risk free (Strasburger, Wilson & Jordan, 2009). Television shows geared towards adolescents actually have more sexual content than adult-oriented shows, yet there is rarely any reference to the need for contraception or for behaving in a sexually responsible manner (Kunkel, Eyal, Finnerty, Biely & Donnerstein, 2005). Movies, music and television are highly sexualized. Documentaries now on prime-time TV show how to improve your sex life and air issues such as transgender, cross-dressing, bondage and many other quite explicit aspects of sex and sexual performance. Although these programmes bring sex out in the open as a natural and healthy part of life and may have a positive impact on young people who feel concerned about their sexuality, they can also set a sexual agenda for young people that does not necessarily reflect their own desires.

A strong media message is about what counts as sexually attractive. Through the media, power is offered to those who are perceived to be beautiful. Many western societies are obsessed with body weight; media depictions of beauty stress youth and thinness. As we have seen in a previous chapter, these emphases can lead to unhealthy dieting, unnecessary cosmetic surgery, use of performance-enhancing or body-building drugs and obsession about appearance.

Magazines

Magazines aimed at adolescents provide an example. The paediatrician-sponsored website HealthyChildren.org (2013) argues that such magazines have not changed substantially over recent generations, and are effectively 'girls' magazines' as young men do not read them. They report 'On the whole, they still convey a two-dimensional impression of adolescent girls as boy-crazy clothes-horses who are obsessed with how they look.' There is an emphasis on articles such as 'How to look hot', 'How thin is too thin?' and 'How to win his heart'. Analysis of the content of these magazines reveals that they are designed primarily to tell girls that their most important function in life is to become sexually attractive enough to catch and hold on to a boyfriend (Brown, Steele & Walsh-Childers, 2002). Although teenage magazines have waned in popularity since the use of the internet became widespread, several points are worth making. First, these magazines are still of interest to younger girls aged in the 8–12 year age range, so their sexualizing influence is beginning earlier than for previous generations. Second, the types of content popular in the magazines, particularly advice about how to look sexy and be popular with boys, is still sought after by teenage girls, but now it is more likely to be accessed through the internet from platforms such as celebrity bloggers and YouTube sites (Carter, 2013). On the positive side, McKee (2011) argues that in Australia, teenage magazines and their online counterparts serve an important function in providing information about sex to young people, stepping in for parents who are failing in their responsibility to educate their children about sexual safety and healthy sexual development.

Movies

A specific illustration of how sex in the media may influence adolescents comes from a study of how exposure to movie content is associated with sexual behaviour in young people. O'Hara and his colleagues examined 684 top grossing movies from 1998 to 2004, coding the number of seconds that sexual content was shown (O'Hara, Gibbons, Gerrard, Li & Sargent, 2012). Most of the movies (over 80 per cent) had some sexual content and few mentioned safe sex or contraception. Researchers then recruited over 1000 young adolescents (12–14 years), who reported on their viewing of 50 of the (randomly selected) movies. Six years later these young people were resurveyed to assess their sexual behaviour. In short, the results showed that adolescents who were exposed to more sexual content in movies began sex at younger ages, had more sexual partners and were less likely to use condoms with casual partners, putting them at greater sexual risk. The researchers, although aware that correlation does not necessarily equate with causation, recommended that parents restrict the sexual content of movies to which younger teenagers are exposed.

YouTube

Another example of gender stereotyping comes through many of the videos and YouTube clips of popular singers and bands. These can give powerful messages about sexuality, not only in terms of their lyrics but also of their behaviour. Popular music and dancing has been likened to a mating ritual, in which rhythm and simulated sexual movements indicate attraction and provide sexual release. Of course, complaints about sexual explicitness in music and dancing have been made for many generations, sometimes in relation to activities that seem exceptionally tame by today's standards, in which depictions of sexual violence, misogyny and exploitation are all too common.

It is impossible to avoid sex in the media. What is portrayed are not only overt depictions of sexual acts but many subtle messages about sexuality and relationships. Not all of these are negative, by any means. For example several soap operas have had characters modelling 'safe sex' messages, and presenting discussion of difficult sexual issues, such as coping with homosexual feeling and identity, sexual harassment and non-consensual sex. Popular movies for children and adolescents have used strong female characters who are resourceful, problem-solving and effective, rather than the traditionally passive princess, saved by a knight on a white charger. In the next section, we consider the positive and negative aspects of the currently most ubiquitous of all media influences on young people, those offered through internet and cell phone technologies.

New technologies and youth culture

Almost all of the activities in which young people engage are now facilitated by the use of digital technologies. This is an era in which many young people seem more interested in their identity online than their existence offline. These technologies are available in varying levels across most countries of the world and to some extent have speeded up the globalization of youth culture. Even though the internet is censored or difficult to access in some places, once available, access to technology appears to be followed quickly by its use for sexual gratification. For example, a recent study showed 20 per cent of a large sample of high school students in Peru had been involved in 'sexting', that is, sending nude photos or sexually explicit messages via their mobile phones (West et al., 2014), and although laws about sending inappropriate content via mobile phone are stricter in Asian countries than in the west, reporters in Singapore (Koh, 2014a) and Hong Kong (Pittar, 2014) found the young women they interviewed readily admitted to sharing nude 'selfies' with their boyfriends. Nevertheless, most of the research on the impact of digital technologies on the sexual behaviour and habits of young people comes from the west, so this will be the major focus of this chapter.

Access to and use of technology

How readily are young people able to access cell phone and computer technologies? Cell phone ownership is common among adolescents. In 2013, mobile phones were owned by 75 per cent of US adolescents aged 12–17 years (Pew Consulting, 2013), 93 per cent of UK 12- to 17-year-olds (eMarketer, 2013), and 89 per cent of Australians aged 14–17 years (Raco, 2014). Of these phones owned by adolescents, 50 per cent (US), 81 per cent (UK) and 69 per cent (Australia) were smartphones, effectively multimedia recording devices that also offer all the benefits of a pocket-sized computer, allowing access to the internet almost anywhere and anytime (Pew Consulting, 2013; eMarketer, 2013; Raco, 2014, respectively). Although exactly comparable figures are difficult to obtain, studies in other countries affirm the high rates of access to technology for the adolescents of today. Market research in Asia has shown that among young people aged 15–19 years, smartphone ownership is very common, almost universal in some cities (e.g. Seoul and Hong Kong) (Hakuhodo Global Habitat, 2013). As far back as 2009, a cross-sectional survey study of 1328 adolescents aged 13–20 years in nine secondary schools in Madrid found almost all students (97 per cent) had their own cell phone (Sánchez-Martinez & Otero, 2009). In Africa, smartphone penetration across all age groups is lower, estimated to be around 15 per cent but increasing (Parr, 2013).

How often and in what ways do adolescents and young adults use the internet, interact with social media, text, send photos via mobile phone, play computer games or access any or all of the new communication options? In particular, how often are these new technologies used for sexual communication or in ways that relate to developing sexuality? Several studies have attempted to estimate the daily use of technology by adolescents but it has proved difficult for research to keep pace with rapid developments, each of which seems to herald increasing interaction by young people.

Texting

One clear trend in the west is that non-vocal communication has become a preferred form of interaction between young people, with two-thirds of youth preferring to text rather than talk to their friends (Pew Research Internet Project, 2010). Girls more often than boys text their friends, but interestingly, young people still telephone rather than text their parents. One US study found that one in three adolescents sends more than 100 text messages a day and 15 per cent send more than 200 a day, or 6000 a month (Lenhart, Ling, Campbell & Purcell, 2010).

Apps

In addition to texting, with every week that passes, new mobile phone/computer tablet applications ('apps') become available. Among other services, young people can now use mobile phone apps to count calories, monitor weight and exercise and estimate blood alcohol levels, as well as for sexuality-related purposes such as monitoring their menstrual cycle and contraceptive use, anonymously contacting past sexual partners if they are diagnosed with a sexually transmitted infection or arranging to meet new sexual or romantic partners.

Social media

Social media use is ubiquitous among adolescents. In the US in 2012, 90 per cent of young people aged 13–17 years had some form of online presence. Three out of four adolescents had a profile on a social networking site (such as Facebook), and one in five had a current Twitter account (Common Sense Media, 2012). Similar figures are evident in the UK, many European countries, Canada, New Zealand and Australia. Nine in ten Australian adolescents in a large survey reported viewing a social networking site at least daily and 80 per cent sent or received instant or other chat messages at least once a day (Mitchell *et al.*, 2014). In the world of adolescence, not having a social media profile has been anecdotally described as 'social death'. These profiles involve presenting oneself both visually through uploaded photographs and verbally through posting comments and commenting on the posts of others.

Sixteen-year-old Philippa, a British teenager, is typical of many adolescents of her age, and is described here in an article in *The Guardian* newspaper by journalist Jon Henley (2010):

> Philippa has 639 Facebook friends, and claims to know 'the vast majority' (though some, she admits, are 'quite far down the food chain'). 'I don't want to be bigheaded or anything, but I am quite popular,' she says. 'Only because I don't have a social life outside my bedroom, though.' When the journalist telephones her, 129 of her friends are online.
>
> Facebook rush-hour is straight after school, and around nine or 10 in the evening. 'You can have about 10 chats open at a time, then it gets a bit slow and you have to start deleting people,' Philippa says. The topics? 'General banter, light-hearted abuse. Lots of talk about parties and about photos of parties.' Cred-wise, it's important to have a good, active Facebook profile: lots of updates, lots of photos of you tagged.
>
> *(Henley, 2010)*

In short, young people are using new technologies to communicate, learn new things and present themselves to the world. In the next sections, we consider some of the implications of this for sexual development.

Social networking and sexuality: benefits and concerns

Benefits

Although over-use of social networks has been associated with depression, this is evident among only a very small per cent of users according to a recent review (Common Sense Media, 2012). Indeed, in terms of relationship development and learning about sexuality, there are benefits of the use of social media such as access to information about sex, links to sexual health services and facilitation of the maintenance and initiation of new partnerships. In general, improvements in wellbeing through the use of social media have been noted. For example, in a longitudinal study, Baker and Moore (2008) examined new MySpace users after two months, comparing those who blogged with non-bloggers. In comparison to non-bloggers, bloggers showed that aspects of their social support had improved, including satisfaction with their number of friends, confidence in others and social integration. In a subsequent study, these authors found further evidence that blogging and posting on social networks enabled links with like-minded and empathic people, leading to expanded social networks (Baker & Moore, 2010).

Benefits of blogging and other social media activities may be heightened for young people who feel some sense of social or sexual marginalization. An Australian survey of same-sex attracted and gender-questioning young people aged 14–21 years found that belonging to an internet site provided a positive experience for them, with 75 per cent feeling accepted on the site for who they were, enabling them to feel proud of their sexuality (Hillier et al., 2010). A specific example of such a site is Tumblr, a microblogging social networking platform where users can create a personalized blog about a topic of interest, utilizing the sharing of text and visual media. Hart and Third (2013) argue that such sites allow young people to experience deep and enduring forms of intimacy online, in spaces that are protected from the potential criticism of their 'real life' friends or family.

Concerns

As will be seen throughout the chapter, social media also poses dangers to wellbeing and reputation. Young people can receive unsupportive and unpleasant comments on their social media posts as well as supportive ones, or perhaps even worse, their posts may be ignored. Bullying of young people via Facebook and other social media has been well-documented. For example, Mitchell and her colleagues found that nasty messages, sent via texts or on the internet, had been received in the past couple of months by over 80 per cent of their high school sample. Over 50 per cent reported receiving a sexually explicit text message and 43 per cent had sent such messages. Over 25 per cent had sent a sexually explicit nude or nearly nude photo of themselves and 42 per cent had received such a photo of someone else. These figures were considerably higher among those students who were sexually active, and among this group 70 per cent had received a sexually explicit nude or nearly nude photo or video of someone else. Nearly half the boys and one-quarter of the girls had used a social media site for sexual reasons (Mitchell *et al.*, 2014).

Adolescents who impulsively post photos of themselves in compromising situations (or when the photos are posted by others) can find this material is rapidly circulated to those who were not meant to be the audience. As all online interactions are permanently recorded, there is a possibility that these photos may be a source of future regret. Additionally, with pornography readily available to young people on the internet, unhealthy addictions and/or distorted attitudes towards sex and intimacy can develop, for example beliefs that violence during sex is pleasurable and normative. Although it is gratifying that 'Teens are much more likely to report using social media has a positive impact on their social lives than a negative one' (Common Sense Media, 2012:10), these dangers are important to note in advising youth about cyber-safety, especially in the sensitive area of sexuality.

Use of technology to meet sexual partners

Soon after the World Wide Web was established, the first online dating websites appeared. Some offered a legitimate dating service based on personality characteristics and photographs, aimed at those over 18 years. Other dating sites soon sprang up, catering for specific audiences such as younger people, same-sex attracted or those with a sexually transmitted infection (STI). Nowadays there is a plethora of such sites alongside chat rooms for making sexual connections, which target those seeking transient or more long-lasting sexual relationships.

A further facilitation of such sexual relationships has been made possible by geo-social positioning where the location of the user is used to connect people to potential partners who are close by. These apps allow hookups between potentially anonymous sexual partners. The first of these was Grindr, launched in 2009 for male-to-male sex, which currently links more than six million users across 192 countries. In July 2013, Grindr had nearly three million registered users in the US alone. The communication between potential partners who use these apps needs only to be extremely brief before they decide to meet, making it easy to omit important discussion around safe sex and the possibility of STI transmission. Indeed, a US study showed that gay men who utilize these apps had higher rates of chlamydia and gonorrhoea than men who met in clubs or online (Beymer *et al.*, 2014). However, the geo-spatial positioning possibilities of the apps also offer the potential for sexual health promotion. Recently Grindr has been utilized to increase knowledge of local health services, and to manage a disease outbreak in gay men in Australia, by sending sexual health-related messages to users within specific geographical areas where infection rates were known to be high (Su *et al.*, 2014). This strategy could be used more widely by apps of this type to offer health messages, warnings and services that are geographically matched to the users.

Most dating websites and apps are only available for those aged 18 years and older. Tinder, however, is available from age 13 onwards. At the present time, it makes 10 million matches every day, and to date has resulted in two billion matches worldwide (Tinder, n.d.). It allows users to 'like' or 'pass' fellow users, based on their picture, with mutual 'likes' offered the opportunity to chat via the app. After receiving a like, an individual looks at the picture of the 'liker' and is offered the choice to 'Start chatting? Or keep playing?'

> It's basically a hot-or-not game. The hot get liked and the others get the flick. I use it to pick up. It's easier to click and type than it is to talk in a loud bar. It's the way society is going. (Male, 23 years)
>
> *(Reist, 2013:1)*

> I jumped on to see what all the fuss was about and it's an easy way to find a fuck. Sometimes I will have four or five dates lined up in one week, and when I say dates, I really mean fucks because, well, that's what it's all about. (Male, 22 years)
>
> *(Reist, 2013:6)*

Such apps reinforce the notion that people are judged by appearances only. It has been argued that the balance of power here is in men's favour, with young women seeking approval by posing for Facebook profiles in increasingly provocative ways. The online hook-up space bypasses traditional dating where individuals have the opportunity to get to know one another and gradually share expectations about their relationship. Instead, these apps encourage quick progression to sex, causing one author to argue that some young women using them have become 'sexual service stations' for men (Reist, 2013:1).

To protect younger users on Tinder, those aged 13–17 years can only contact others in the same age range. Tinder requires participants to have a Facebook profile to register, and in this way the organizers argue that they are able to monitor accounts to look for older people posing as adolescents. However little can be done to stop what is now termed as 'catfishing' – posing as someone else while seeking to sexually exploit another.

On the positive side, dating/meeting apps and websites are not all about quick casual sex and instant gratification. Finkel, Eastwich, Karney, Reis and Sprecher (2012) note that these online tools for meeting people enable access to a greater array of potential partners than would generally be available from face-to-face meetings, and there is the opportunity to screen candidates for compatibility. Potential partners can chat for as long as they wish before deciding to meet, and meetings can be arranged to allow a hasty and safe exit in case the 'date' is not who they appear to be online. Many satisfying matches, short and long term, have been facilitated through these online services, and e-matchmaking may become the preferred courtship way of the future, given the many claims that these sites have fundamentally altered the dating landscape for the better. For example Becca, who met her boyfriend on Tinder, says:

> Of course there's the risk of meeting creeps on dating sites, but there's that risk when you meet people offline too. If you're smart about it, I think it's a great way to get to know someone. I can't imagine not having met my boyfriend, and without Tinder, I never would have known he existed.
>
> *(Manrodt, 2014)*

Nevertheless the dangers of these apps are likely to be far greater for the naïve and unsophisticated. Adolescents and young adults alike need to be aware of online dating safety in relation to protecting their privacy, arranging first meetings and detecting scams. Websites such as Online Dating Safety Tips (n.d.) provide some of this material. However they do not address all of the issues raised above, particularly that some of these apps, in allowing easy rejections of individuals based on appearances alone, can both be damaging to self-esteem and promote unhealthy stereotypes.

Sexting

Sexting refers to the sending and receiving of sexually explicit material via the internet. Suggestive messages can be sexted but the term often refers to sending photos of individuals who are naked or in suggestive poses, or sending photos of genitals. The practice is considered by some as an extension of flirting and sexual exploration.

But although some young people sext to flirt, to begin or to maintain a relationship, sexts can be also passed on to friends as entertainment, or to bully or harass. Smartphone applications are often used for sexting because the transmitted images disappear from the recipient's phone after a short time, leading to the mistaken impression of many senders that the image is no longer available. However it is possible for receivers to make copies of the image, store it and/or distribute it further, activities that have led to embarrassment and more serious outcomes in some cases.

Whether sexting leads to changes in sexual behaviours is unclear. In one US study of over 3000 older adolescents (18–24 years) there was no differences between sexually active 'sexters' and non-sexters in number of sexual partners, or number of unprotected sex partners in the past 30 days. There was also no relationship between sexting and psychological wellbeing (Gordon-Messer, Bauermeister, Grodzinski & Zimmerman, 2013).

But there are many anecdotes of young people being shamed, excluded from friendship groups or even needing to move schools because an explicit photo of them has been circulated (O'Keefe & Clarke-Pearson, 2011). In extreme cases, suicide has been attempted or occurred because the emotional distress was so great (Chalfen, 2009). Teenagers as young as 14 years of age who have sexted an image can face the risk of criminal charges for the production and distribution of child pornography in some countries (Prince & Jordan, 2004; Weiss & Samenow, 2010). This could be interpreted as a case of the law not keeping pace with social mores and, as such, several jurisdictions have changed the laws to exempt sexting between teenagers (Reilly, 2014).

Determining accurately the prevalence of sexting has proved challenging. Reported rates of involvement vary from 4 per cent in the US (Lenhart, 2009) to 50 per cent in Australia (Yeung, Horyniak, Vella, Hellard & Lim, 2014), depending on the age of participants, the sampling method, country of origin, year of the study and the way sexting is defined. A study of 937 ethnically diverse high school students in Texas found that sexting was related to impulsivity and substance use, but not depression or anxiety (Temple *et al.*, 2014). An Australian study of almost 1400 16- to 29-year-olds attending a music festival found that nearly half the males and over one-third of the females had ever sent or received a sext, most commonly with a regular sexual partner (Yeung *et al.*, 2014). Lower levels of education, greater recreational spending, inconsistent condom use and risky alcohol consumption were all independently associated with sexting. Consensual sexting included flirting and sexual experimentation and appeared to be a common and normalized practice among this sample.

Interview studies highlight that the roles of young people involved in sexting are quite complex. There can be a different subject, producer, distributor and recipient of the image (Ryan, 2010), and some of these roles may be held by a single person. The 'victim' of the sext is not always the person sexually exposed, but can also be an unwilling receiver who did not want to see the image.

> I had people offer to send it to me and I was like, 'No, I'm fine, I don't really need that.' (Male, 18 years)

> If it's a mate's girlfriend you just go, 'What are you doing?' You just look at them and you just go, 'Oh, not cool.' (Male, 16 years)
>
> *(Walker, Sanci & Temple-Smith, 2013:700)*

These researchers also identify a 'requester' of the sexually explicit images, usually a male, who may use pressure or coercion to obtain the image.

> [T]hey do that, 'I thought you loved me' thing. I've seen that happen a lot at school . . . yeah it's almost a threat. 'If you don't send a photo, if you don't do this, if you don't.' (Male, 18 years)
>
> *(Walker, 2012:78).*

Sexually explicit images are much more likely to be of girls; most are reportedly sent to boys and most involve self-produced images. The Third Youth Internet Safety Survey (YISS-3) (Crimes Against Children Research Center, n.d.), involving 1560 US young people aged 10–17 years, reported the most common reasons for sexting were as part of an existing relationship, as pranks or jokes, or trying to start a new relationship. However, sometimes sexts were sent as revenge:

> The boy asks the girl to send him some images or videos or something and then – so she does that and he keeps them forever, you know, in case of blackmail or whatever he wants to do with the images. Then they have a fight – or they break up or something and then he thinks 'Well, she's no good anymore and let's embarrass her in the best way I can,' and sends it out. (Male, 17 years)
>
> *(Crimes Against Children Research Center, n.d.)*

Adolescents' attitudes towards sexting vary widely. On one end of the spectrum are young people who view sexting as a safer alternative to real life sexual activity, while at the other end are those concerned about legality and the potential release of the images (Lenhart, 2009). Whatever young people's views on sexting, there is no question that this form of sexual activity has the potential to cause real harm to participants. Worryingly, sexting has occurred alongside a massive increase in the viewing of pornography, now widely available because of technological advances. It is to discussion of the role of pornography in youth culture that we now turn.

Pornography

> I was on [app] for about a half an hour with some mates and we saw about 15 penises. People literally sit there, put the camera up to their genitals and just masturbate for other people to see. Yep. And they also like to request to see, I don't know, your breasts, or get involved and masturbate together. (Female, 16 years)
>
> *(Walker, 2012:73)*

This quote offers reasons for the fears of many adults about adolescents' potentially inappropriate use of digital technology. The harms associated with exposure to sexually explicit material have become an area of concern and wide public debate.

Exposure to pornography

Many studies have sought to quantify intended and unintended exposure to pornography by young people, and although comparison of results is hampered by the differing methodologies, it is clear that exposure is widespread. Research in countries as varied as Iceland (Kolbeins, 2006), Sweden (Johansson & Hammarén, 2007), Cambodia (Fordham, 2006), Italy (Bonino, Ciairano, Rabaglietti & Cattelino, 2006) and Taiwan (Chen, Leung, Chen & Yang, 2013) suggest that, world-wide, large numbers of young people, particularly boys, are growing up exposed to the presence of sexually explicit media. Typical of such studies are two US surveys, each of around 1000 adolescents (Bleakley *et al.*, 2009; Brown & L'Engle, 2009), both of which found that two-thirds of males and about one-third of females had seen at least one form of sexually explicit material in the past year. A similar European survey of 4600 young people aged 15–25 years found even higher rates; 88 per cent of young men and 45 per cent of young women had consumed sexually explicit material in the past 12 months (Hald, Kuyper, Adam & de Wit, 2013). Despite different ages and settings, these and other studies show that intended viewing of pornography is higher among boys than girls (Flood, 2007; Häggström-Nordin, Tydén, Hanson & Larsson, 2009; Lofgren-Mårtenson & Månsson, 2010; Ma & Shek, 2013). An Australian survey of almost 500 young people (average age 18 years) attending a music festival found that three-quarters had ever seen porn, and the median age of first viewing was 14 years. Most of the young men were watching porn at least once a week, and of these 80 per cent watched it alone (Lim, Villa & Hellard, 2014).

Some parents and educational institutions place filters on computers and smartphones to prevent young people's access to pornography. However, there is evidence that young people who are determined to view sexually explicit material will do it regardless of the filters in place.

> Honestly, it just takes a bit of determined research and you can get past that kind of stuff. There's so many ways you can get around that kind of stuff, routing stuff, rerouting, going through different servers, and even like government bans . . . it takes me five seconds to download a different router and go through a different country's server and then you get access to whatever it was you were trying to get. (Female, 18 years)
>
> *(Walker, 2012:92)*

Sexual harms of pornography

Little research has examined the issues around the increasingly violent nature of pornography. Once seen as a marginal genre of the pornography industry, 'gonzo' porn, which is free of any narrative and includes gratuitous violence towards women, has now become mainstream (Crabbe & Corlett, 2010; Papadopoulos, 2010). Content analysis of popular selling and free-to-download porn movies show that almost all scenes contained violent physical aggression while over half of all scenes contained verbal aggression. Perpetrators were overwhelmingly male and targets of aggression were almost all female. Of concern was that targets most often showed pleasure or responded neutrally to the aggression (Bridges, Wosnitzer, Scharrer, Sun & Liberman, 2010; Gorman, Monk-Turner & Fish, 2010). Dines (2010) has also noted the common depiction of highly risky practices that are likely to transmit infection.

The ubiquitous absence of condom use in pornography has resulted in a recent legislative attempt in California to ensure porn actors wear condoms. Although couched in terms of occupational health and safety for the actors, normalizing safe sex behaviour by modelling this in pornography could have public health benefits. A Swiss study of young males, aged 16–20 years, found that in comparison to those young men who had never viewed pornography, those who were intentional or unintentional viewers of pornography (approximately 80 per cent of the total sample) were more likely not to have used a condom at last intercourse, suggesting that they may have modelled their behaviour on pornography (Luder *et al.*, 2011). Similar findings been reported in other studies in the US and Australia (O'Sullivan, Udell, Montrose, Antoniello & Hoffman, 2010; Lim *et al.*, 2014).

Pornography alters expectations

There is a relentless focus on young women's bodies in pornography, which includes unrealistic body types and sexual responses. A Swedish focus group study of young people aged 16–19 years found that they recognized that porn portrayed a 'discriminatory sexuality', where the man was symbolized as a strong well-built 'Hercules' and the woman as an underweight large-breasted 'Barbie', who was always subordinate to the man (Mattebo, Larsson, Tyden, Olssen & Häggström-Nordin, 2012).

> Very large breasts, thin waist, and I think you get a very distorted aspect of what a natural look is. That becomes the ideal. (Female)
>
> *(Mattebo* et al.*, 2012:44)*

Perhaps more worrying is that pornography has created expectations among adolescents of their own and their partner's sexual behaviours. Studies generating these findings have been conducted in Sweden (Häggström-Nordin, Sandberg, Hanson & Tydén, 2006), Australia (Walker, Temple-Smith, Higgs & Sanci, 2015), the UK (Marston & Lewis, 2014) and the US (Hernandez, 2011; Hussen, Bowleg, Sangaramoorthy & Malebranche, 2012).

> If you see [pornography] too early you can get a distorted sexuality . . . that girls are always turned on, always ready, foreplay is not necessary. . . . You copy just like it. Not just a little of inspiration but you really try to copy.
>
> *(Mattebo* et al.*, 2012:45)*

In two recent qualitative studies of Australian 15- to 18-year-olds, young people voiced their concerns.

> The guys . . . do expect stuff and it gets to the point where some girls think 'Okay if I want a boyfriend that's what I'm going to have to do. I'm going to have to become that person so I can get that guy.' (Female, 15 years)
>
> *(Walker* et al.*, 2015)*

I thought sex is like the most intimate form of bonding between couples. It is . . . but the sex that's just rough, that you see in porn, is just not right. . . . Treat the girls mean and things like that. (Male, 17 years)
(Litras, Latreille & Temple-Smith, under review)

Given that in pornography sex is generally separated from intimacy, it is not surprising that there is concern that exposure may drive and sustain sexist and unhealthy notions of sexual practice. An online Dutch survey of 745 adolescents aged 13–18 years found that viewing porn was associated with lower levels of empathy and a higher likelihood of viewing sex simply as a physical act, and women as sex objects (Peter & Valkenburg, 2006). Several studies have shown a link between pornography and sexual violence, for example Italian research with male adolescents aged 14–19 years showed associations between pornography use and sexually harassing someone or forcing them to have sex (Bonino *et al.*, 2006).

A recent in-depth study of anal sex among 130 16- to 18-year-olds in the UK found young people cited pornography as one reason for anal sex (Marston & Lewis, 2014). This supports earlier findings from Swedish studies showing that young male pornography consumers were more likely to have had anal intercourse with a girl, or tried to perform acts they had seen on pornography (Häggström-Nordin, Hanson & Tyden, 2005; Rogala & Tyden, 2003; Tyden & Rogala, 2004; Tyden, Olssen & Häggström-Nordin, 2001).

Among the problematic outcomes of exposure to porn are addiction to porn, poor psychological wellbeing, including feelings of guilt, shame and anxiety (Bryant, 2009), poor relationship quality, lower sexual satisfaction and sexual dysfunction (Szymanski & Stewart-Richardson, 2014). It has been argued that the messages in porn promote gender inequality and women's subordination by men (Crabbe & Corlett, 2010; Grov, Gillespie, Royce & Lever, 2011; Weinberg, Williams, Kleiner & Irizarry, 2010) rather than demonstrating what women may find pleasurable. It is of concern that these messages are helping to shape young men's sexual identities and their developing masculinity (Dines, 2010).

Pornography: any redeeming features?

Does exposure to pornography have any redeeming features for the sexual health of the young? One view is that young people who view pornography are capable of selecting, filtering and challenging its meaning (Day, 2009; Štulhofer, Busko & Schmidt, 2012) and that by teaching about sexual practices, pornography is educational (Helsper, 2005; McKee, 2007). For many young same-sex couples, pornography is their only source of education, as models depicting same-sex sexuality are limited in the offline world (Hillier *et al.*, 2010), although it has also been argued that gay male pornography is unhealthy and perpetuates inequalities (Kendall, 2004).

Young heterosexual people in some studies have claimed pornography has had a positive effect on their lives. Hald and Malamuth (2008) found most participants in a large Danish study of 18- to 30-year-olds claimed that pornography improved their sexual knowledge, attitudes towards sex, attitudes towards and perception of the opposite sex, and their general quality of life (Hald & Malamuth, 2008). A study of Taiwanese young men found that those who intentionally viewed porn identified it as having a positive value in their lives (Chen *et al.*, 2013), and one-fifth of young people in an Australian study said that porn should be a source of sex and sexual health information (Giordano & Ross, 2012). On balance though, it seems that an intense diet of pornography, particularly when it includes violence, is a less than ideal way of learning about sexuality. It can promote unhealthy attitudes and distort the development of positive relationships; it undermines intimacy and can be disturbing and even frightening when viewed by young teenagers without sexual experience. Pornography has always been and always will be with us, but its current ease of access via the internet provides a challenge to sex educators and parents of young people to present more balanced views of sex as pleasurable, intimate and relationship-enhancing.

Sexual health promotion in the digital age

One benefit of the digital age is that it offers many more opportunities for sexual health promotion than were available for previous generations. Currently, sexual health interventions are possible through web-based sexual health information, STI screening, testing and management through websites, online counselling and support groups (Minichiello, Rahman, Dune, Scott & Dowsett, 2013). The internet, especially social media, is gaining recognition as a valid delivery platform for health education generally, as it can be both interactive and anonymous (Buhi, Daley, Furhmann & Smith, 2009). It also offers access to information and services for those in rural and remote areas.

A critical review of studies (Simon & Daneback, 2013) found adolescents consistently use the internet for sex education, seeking information on many topics including sexually transmitted infections, pregnancy, contraception, relationships and sexual pleasure. In the US as early as 2010, it was estimated that more than half of 7th–12th graders had accessed health information online (Rideout, Foehr & Roberts, 2010). Another US study, of 1500 adolescents aged 13–24 years, found topics such as contraception, menstruation, pregnancy and STIs were frequently explored online, with most young people having looked up one or more of these topics on the internet (Boyar *et al.*, 2011).

Sex education websites

An example of a site with a good reputation for accurate information is Your Sex Health (n.d.). This website was developed for middle to older adolescents and young adults. It provides information about reproductive and sexual health, including emotional, practical and relationship issues, exploring real-life dilemmas in a 'True stories' section designed to appeal to young people. One clear aim of the site is to help young people assess the potential impacts of their sexual health decisions. For younger children, a site like The Hormone Factory (n.d.) uses puzzles, quizzes and other novel formats to present sex information to young people and to answer frequently asked questions. The tone is friendly and humorous, as well as sensitive to the concern and anxiety often experienced by children and their parents over this topic. For example, the content includes the issues that arise from children developing at different rates and how one might respond to those differences.

Unfortunately, however, the websites adolescents turn to for sexual health information do not always contain accurate information. For example, of 177 sexual health websites examined in a recent study (Buhi et al., 2009), 46 per cent of those addressing contraception and 35 per cent of those addressing abortion contained inaccurate information. Although there has been a proliferation of websites offering sexual health promotion, these are largely unregulated, and can expose viewers to erroneous or poor-quality material (Weaver, Horyniak, Jenkinson, Dietze & Lim, 2013).

Therefore, although sexual health promotion material delivered online offers great scope, it is also important to ensure that information is accurate. The site described above, Your Sex Health, provides some guidelines for consumers to assess site credibility. These include checking who created the site, who sponsors it, whether the creators are experts in their field and whether the sponsors are likely to be unbiased in their message or are pushing an agenda, such as potential commercial gain or the promotion of ideological or religious beliefs. It is also of value to check whether the websites use reputable sources for their information and whether a range of viewpoints about controversial issues are included. Although young people may not carry out such due diligence, one valued feature of the web is that, when searching for information on a topic relating to sexual health, it is very clear that there are many sources available, readily allowing for fact checking. So, despite potential inaccuracies, the internet can often provide the first step to solving a problem, and there is an informality about it that apparently appeals to the young, as implied by this young man:

> I don't use technology to find information about sex. I just Google it and sh*t.
>
> *(Boyar et al., 2011:34)*

Boyar and colleagues suggested to web designers that in order to strengthen the value of their sites as information sources for young people it is important to protect privacy. These researchers recommended the development of programs that protect user anonymity through not leaving digital trails.

It seems that young people do recognize the strengths and limitations of internet-based sexual health information. When asked where they would go for sexual health information, these Australian girls said:

> umm, Google, and then for accurate advice, I'd go to a doctor. (Female, 21 years)
>
> *(Nandaweera, 2013:46)*

> I probably would avoid going on the internet because anyone can write stuff on the internet . . . and sometimes it's hard to tell the difference between opinion and fact. (Female, 21 years)
>
> *(Nandaweera, 2013:47)*

And in a US study, one participant articulated the power of the internet in providing access to doctors for sexual health advice:

> He's gone to one medical school, but if you go online you can get advice from all over the world.
>
> *(Boyar et al., 2011:17)*

Digital media as sexual communication aids

As well as providing information, the internet can aid communication between sexual partners. A US study of technology-based sexual communication between dating partners showed that of 176 high school students, almost half had utilized technology to facilitate discussion with their dating partners on a range of sexual health issues. African-American and Hispanic youth were more likely than White adolescents to discuss condoms, STIs, pregnancy and birth control. Not surprisingly, girls were more likely than boys to discuss pregnancy and sexual limits. Of adolescents who were sexually active in the six months prior to the study, half did not use condoms consistently. However, consistent condom use increased nearly threefold among those adolescents who had used technology to discuss condoms, birth control, pregnancy or sexual limits, suggesting that technology-based communication may provide a non-threatening way to broach topics important to sexual health (Widman, Neal, Choukas-Bradley & Prinstein 2013).

Communication about STIs can be embarrassing. The Australian website, Let Them Know, enables people to email or text past sexual partners, anonymously, to inform them they may have contracted an STI (Let Them Know, n.d.). The website also provides tips on telling partners, information about STIs, and a page for people who have been informed they may have an STI. A similar site in the US, Inspot (n.d.), offers an expanded service to Canada, Peru, Puerto Rico and American Samoa. There are also websites where it is possible for a person to check whether they may need to see a doctor about potential STI symptoms, for example Check Your Risk (n.d.).

Websites tend to be relatively static, although the STI ones listed above have an element of interactivity. There are newer forms of technology that have more personalized interactive elements, and these show great potential for sexual health education although as yet there are few evaluation studies. Cell phone applications (apps), internet-based simulation games about sexual issues (for example how to cope with being a gay youth), regular text messages to cell phones (for example reminders about health checks) or YouTube and video clips (for example what to do when a condom breaks) from health providers have been developed and, although not yet widely distributed, have already become popular (Boyar *et al.*, 2011).

Some innovative strategies

The feasibility and acceptability of sexual health promotion delivered via text messaging has been explored in Australia. Young people aged 16–20 years who were sent text messages about sexual health showed significant improvements in their knowledge of STIs and reported improved rates of STI testing (J. Gold *et al.*, 2010a). A follow-up study of participants showed that they were more likely to remember and share messages that were amusing, which rhymed and/or were linked with particular annual events (J. Gold *et al.*, 2010b). Examples of the text messages were:

> Change your clocks, change your smoke detector battery. Change your partner, get an STI test.
>
> Protect your or your partner's eggs this Easter with a condom. Chlamydia can cause infertility. Enjoy the long weekend!
>
> *(J. Gold* et al.*, 2010b:3)*

A subsequent Australian trial found that texting and email could be used to improve the sexual health knowledge of young people aged 16–29 years of both sexes, and STI testing in women. However, the texts had no impact on reported condom use (Lim *et al.*, 2012).

Sexual health promotion can be delivered via YouTube and Facebook. With many YouTube visitors accessing the site several times weekly, and the majority of Facebook users sharing YouTube videos, the potential for wide dissemination is excellent. Australia's Victorian AIDS Council, for example, launched an online soap opera titled *Being Brendo* in 2010, aimed at 16- to 29-year-olds. It follows the lives of five young gay housemates as they cope with issues such as homophobia and STIs, exploring options in ways that are designed to be entertaining as well as informative. *Being Brendo* is interactive in that it seeks to engage the audience in online discussion relating to sexual health, building relationships and self-esteem (*Being Brendo*, 2014).

Sexual health services via the internet

A further innovative development has been to use the capacities of social networking sites such as Facebook, MySpace and Twitter to connect young people to sexual health services, not just so they will access information, but to enable interactions in the form of advice, testing and even diagnoses and treatment. From a health service perspective, the benefits are many and include low cost, wide reach and anonymity of access for young people who may be embarrassed to seek advice face-to-face, or who may live in areas where such services are not easily accessible.

Given the difficulties faced by many young rural and isolated adolescents in accessing confidential sexual health care, a national online survey was conducted in Australia to seek the views of 16- to 24-year-olds about whether they would utilize a telephone or webcam consultation for sexual health. Participants were generally positive about using the telephone.

> Over the phone is far less embarrassing. (Female, 20 years)

> Telephone consults would help a lot, especially if there was a short waiting time. I hate GP waiting rooms. (Male, 21 years)
>   (*Garrett, Hocking, Chen, Fairley & Kirkman, 2011:6*)

But these researchers found that most young people were wary of webcam consultations because they had strong concerns about the inherent confidentiality and security of the resultant video images.

> I would be concerned about the retention of webcam data. The doctor would need to have a policy about this. . . . If enough of this data exists it is inevitable that some of it will be misplaced or stolen at some point. (Male, 23 years)
>   (*Garrett* et al., *2011:6*)

However certain subgroups – young men, respondents with same-sex partners and respondents with three or more sexual partners – reported finding webcam consultations more acceptable.

Apps can also deliver sexual health messages, for example information on common STIs, evaluation of risk factors and identification of nearby testing clinics. The increasing sophistication of technology is exemplified by an app, now available, that allows consumers to 'bump' smartphones to share sexual health history. This requires the cooperation of the consumers' health professionals who, after the clients have been tested, document on the app that the clients are free from STIs (MedXSafe, n.d.).

Such new digital media and technology provides a great opportunity to reach young people and play an important role in their sexual health. But how effective is it? International studies have examined the impact of digital media interventions on the sexual health knowledge, attitudes and/or behaviours of young people, and shown evidence that they increase knowledge of HIV, STIs and pregnancy, and delay initiation of sex (Guse *et al.*, 2012) as well as improve health and safety behaviours of young people (Hieftje, Edelman, Camenga & Fiellin, 2013).

Designers of these apps and websites need to talk to young people about what they want to know and how they would like this information to be presented. This was achieved through focus groups in designing the Your Sex Health website referred to previously. In one UK study young people were asked what elements of a sexual health website would appeal to them and engage them. They found young people wanted information about both health and pleasure, namely straightforward information on sexual pleasure, STIs and pregnancy, how to communicate with their partners, and how to develop skills in giving pleasure (McCarthy *et al.*, 2012).

Conclusion

Today's youth culture in the west, and to an increasing extent globally, is influenced by the mass media and especially by new digital technologies. With constant access to the internet for information and communication through social media to others, there is little reason to feel out of contact with the world. Yet the increasingly early sexualization of adolescents, the single-swipe acceptance or rejection from a potential hook-up and easy access to often violent and misogynist pornography have the potential to affect the development of healthy sexual relationships. There is concern that media and social networking sites are vehicles through which sexual harassment, pressure and coercion can be applied. On the other hand, the new media have positive potential to provide sex education, sexual health interventions, improve communication between sexual partners and facilitate new relationships.

7

GENDER, SEXUALITY AND ROMANCE

Interviewer:	*What does the word 'sex' mean to you?*
	Sex is like a need . . . it's sort of like water, and er, oxygen, no air and water. I mean it's sort of er physiological need, you know, if you like.
Interviewer:	*What do you think of sex?*
	It's kind of . . . your body wants sex, and it's sort of like wanting a glass of water.
Interviewer:	*Why do you have sex?*
	Because my spermatozoa accumulate in my testicles and it swells up . . .
	(Adolescent male)
	(Moore & Rosenthal, 2006:132)

Interviewer:	*What does the word 'sex' mean to you?*
	Some type of bonding, I suppose, or coming together as one.
Interviewer:	*Why do you have sex?*
	Um, I guess to express those emotions of caring for someone. (Adolescent female)
	(Moore & Rosenthal, 2006:132)

These quotes were collected a decade or more ago. In today's world of liberated and assertive young women, do these attitudinal stereotypes still hold? Is there any evidence for their generality? Petersen and Hyde note in their

2011 meta analysis of gender differences in sexuality that such differences 'are typically believed to be large, yet recent evidence suggests that some gender differences in sexuality are much smaller than common knowledge would suggest' (Petersen & Hyde, 2011:149). In this chapter, we explore some of these differences, with a focus on attitudinal and behavioural issues that impact not only on sexual expression but how this is framed through the lens of romance and intimacy.

Many books about adolescent and youth sexuality fail to address these more tender issues of love, intimacy and romance, but we see this as part of the adolescent sexual journey. We deal with these topics along with the debate about whether young men and young women really do differ in their sexual attitudes and desires. Does the double standard still exist? Do young men and young women have different motives for sex? Are men's sexual urges stronger than women's? These intriguing debates are aired in this chapter in the light of the latest social and biological research.

In earlier times, traditional gender roles for men were seen as worker, primary breadwinner and head of the household. Men were supposed to be assertive, confident, brave and independent. The female gender role was to bear and nurture children, run the household and care for people's feelings. Consequently, women were expected to be warm and expressive, tender and dependent. Sexually speaking, man was to be the 'hunter' and initiator of sexual activity, the one with the more powerful and demanding sex drive and the strong figure in a heterosexual relationship. The traditional woman played her role through being agreeable, cooperative, placating, flirtatious and attending to her appearance and the pleasure of the male, while retaining a respectable and ladylike demeanour in public. Today, life in developed countries is far less rigid in terms of the presentation of stereotypes and the pressure to conform. On the other hand, when it comes to sexuality, there are still different social expectations and taboos for young men and young women.

Are there gendered motives for sex?

Do gender differences include differences in motives expressed for having sex? Twenty-first century writers have pointed out a gender convergence towards expressed motives for sex and attitudes towards sexual encounters. Snapp, Cheney, Galiani and Lento (2012) surveyed 364 US undergraduates about their motivations for seeking a 'hook-up' – a sexual encounter that may or may not include intercourse. There were more gender similarities than differences. Young men and women were similarly motivated by desire for intimacy and closeness, self-affirmation and as a coping strategy.

Men endorsed enhancement (pleasure, feeling good) and peer pressure motives slightly more than women, but the gender differences were quite small overall.

In a study that examined the effects of both culture and gender on motives for sex, Tang, Bensman and Hatfield (2012) asked 277 Chinese and 266 US university students to rate the importance to them of four motives for sex. These were (a) to please a partner, (b) to maintain a relationship, (c) pleasure stimulation and (d) stress reduction. The first two were postulated to be more relevant to the collectivist Chinese culture and likely to be rated higher by females and Chinese students; the last two were proposed as more salient to the individualistic US culture and postulated to be more highly rated by males and US students. In fact, males rated all the motives significantly more highly than females, a finding which did not support sexual stereotypes. Although there were cultural differences as predicted for the individualistic motives, with US students scoring higher on these, both US and Chinese students rated pleasing a partner and maintaining their relationship equally strongly.

Woody, D'Souza and Russel (2003) used a different methodology to examine sexual motives by gender. They asked sexually experienced 19-year-olds to recall their emotions and motivations preceding first intercourse. The most common motives for boys were (in order): 'I was curious to see what it felt like' (curiosity), and 'I felt turned on sexually and wanted to do it for more pleasure' (pleasure). For girls, curiosity was also the highest rated motive although to a lesser extent than for boys. The second highest rating was for the statement 'I felt emotionally mature enough'. For both girls and boys, 'healthy' motives far outranked unhealthy ones such as 'I did it to escape from problems or bad feelings', or 'I did it because I was high on alcohol and drugs'.

These researchers also asked the young people about their feelings towards their partner. Here there were only a few gender differences. Attraction was the strongest feeling for both sexes, followed for boys by desire to please, being in love, and feeling safe and cared for by the partner. For girls, the order of ratings was slightly different, with feeling safe and cared for rated second highest, followed by 'in love' then wanting to please.

As with all studies in psychology, the outcomes depend on what you ask. Sprecher (2014) examined emotional reactions to first intercourse via US university students' self-reports of the anxiety, pleasure and guilt they felt after this milestone. Although not directly assessing motivations for sex, the study is important because Sprecher was able to access a sample of nearly 6000 students over a 23-year period (1990–2012), thus shedding light on changes across three decades. Overall, men reported more pleasure and anxiety than women and women reported more guilt. But in the most recent decade, the sexes had converged in their emotional experiences, with anxiety levels now similar. As well, women reported more pleasure and less guilt than in earlier years, but still found their first experience of intercourse less pleasurable and more guilt-inducing than men.

It would not be surprising to find there are cultural differences in this so-called gender divide. Schalet (2010) reports that Dutch girls are more likely than American girls to acknowledge feeling sexual pleasure and exercising sexual agency, and are less likely to feel guilty about masturbating. She also notes that sex education textbooks for young people in the Netherlands deal openly with issues of female pleasure, relationship competency and mutual respect between partners, the implication being that in more sexually open and less sex-conflicted societies, gender differences in attitudes to sex may be fewer.

McCabe (2005) reviewed literature from the 1970s to 2005 to address the issue: 'Boys want sex, girls want commitment: Does this trade-off still exist?' Like the researchers above, she concluded that in the 2000s there are more similarities than differences between girls and boys in the emphasis and value they place on intimacy and sex, particularly in committed relationships, and particularly among older adolescents.

Our own studies have shown that ideas of love and romance are impor-tant aspects of sex for both adolescent boys and girls, who expressed positive evaluations of these aspects of relationships (Moore & Rosenthal, 2006). 'Loving, caring and affection' were the primary motivations for having sex among most boys and girls in our middle-class Anglo-Australian samples. The desire to experience a loving relationship with 'the right person' is shown by their responses to the question 'What do the words "romantic love" mean to you?'

> I see romantic as roses, candlelit dinner, holding hands, walking down the beach – stuff like that. Someone to talk to, to love, basically. (Adolescent male)

> From movies and things, I see it everywhere. When you think you have the right person, and you have someone forever, and you don't want to break up. You love them and they love you, and you think there is nothing wrong and you are perfect for each other. (Adolescent female)

> When you are really involved with each other and you don't think about anything else except the other person and you are really close. (Adolescent female)

I think it is more when you have a strong friendship with someone like a girlfriend or your wife or your fiancée . . . it is much different to sex although there might be sex in it, it is different. Romantic love is more sensual and more deep; and it comes from deep inside, where[as] sex – you just want to get it done and it might be over, like a one-night stand. (Adolescent male)

(Moore & Rosenthal, 2006:208)

Interestingly, Snapp *et al.* (2012) point out that it is important to highlight gender similarities as well as differences in motivations for sexual encounters. Focusing on the male as predator (seeking only pleasure) and female as victim (seeking romance and intimacy) perpetuates gender inequities and traditional sexual scripts. Their arguments are consistent with the findings that both young men and young women are interested in relationship quality as part of their sexual experience, and that differences between the sexes in attitudes to sexual expression are decreasing over time (Petersen & Hyde, 2010). They underscore the idea that both sexes can benefit from the positive aspects of hook-ups and other youthful sexual encounters, and that both sexes can be vulnerable to hurt and disappointment when their expectations do not match their experiences.

Sex drive: urges, desires and restraint

In an extensive review of gender differences in sex drive (strength of sexual motivation), Baumeister, Catanese and Vohs (2001) concluded across many different studies and measures, men have shown

more frequent and more intense sexual drives than women, as reflected in spontaneous thoughts about sex, frequency and variety of sexual fantasies, desired frequency of intercourse, desired number of partners, masturbation, liking for various sexual practices, willingness to forego sex, making sacrifices for sex, and other measures.

(Baumeister et al., *2001:242)*

These evolutionary psychologists present compelling (although rather dated) evidence to support their conclusions, and indeed the idea that the sex drive is stronger for men than for women is the stuff of novels, magazines and the blogosphere. Why these differences? Are they a function of biology, social conditioning or both?

This is a controversial issue. Baumeister *et al.* (2001) point out that four leading textbooks on human sexuality either 'avoid the issue of gender differences or cautiously suggest that there is no difference' (Baumeister *et al.*, 2001:243). The reason behind this caution (and controversy) relates to the perceived role of social conditioning in shaping manifestations of sexual drive, including both behavioural and cognitive aspects. Those on the side of 'nature' present data on the role of male sex hormones in fuelling sex drives, and use evolutionary arguments for why species survival is favoured if males have stronger sexual urges and females are more selective with whom they mate. Protagonists of the 'nurture' argument point to the social pressures that shape gendered behaviour and suggest that as young women are granted more licence to express their sexuality, differences in sex drive will diminish.

Hormones and sexual arousal

Testosterone levels in boys and men are strongly associated with their sexual activities, including sex drive and masturbation. For example, men who have sexual encounters with casual or multiple partners experience large increases of testosterone the morning after (Hirschenhauser, Frigerio, Grammer & Magnusson, 2002). Another study found that testosterone increased in young heterosexual men in response to a brief conversation with a young woman, the increases apparently associated with whether the woman was deemed desirable (Roney, Mahler & Maestripieri, 2003). Testosterone concentrations in females are far lower than those in males (see Chapter 3). Nevertheless, women with higher baseline levels of testosterone demonstrate greater increases in sexual arousal. What is more, having sexual thoughts can play a role in raising the testosterone levels of both men and women (Goldey & van Anders, 2011).

Research on the role of neuropeptides (brain-affecting hormones) in arousal and sexual pleasure suggests the situation is more complex than some of these studies indicate. The neuropeptides oxytocin and vasopressin are secreted by the pituitary gland, their secretion regulated by the hormones oestrogen and testosterone respectively. Hiller (2004), reporting on laboratory investigations into hormonal release during human sexual activity, argues that oxytocin is associated with the experience of pleasure during arousal and orgasm in both sexes, whereas vasopressin is released only during male arousal. Feelings of love, attachment and protectiveness are also associated with oxytocin (a hormone associated with pregnancy and childbirth). This neuropeptide is secreted by both men and women during sexual activity, but more so by women, leading some theorists to argue that this is why the concepts of love and sex are more closely linked for women than men (Diamond, 2004).

Another hormone, vasopressin, has been associated with male craving, persistence and sexual assertiveness but there is speculation, based on animal studies, that an increase in this neuropeptide for women leads to a loss of sexual interest (Hiller, 2004). Further complexities are evident in the findings of Finkelstein et al. (2013) in their control group study comparing five groups of healthy men: four given gonadal steroid suppressants of varying strengths and the other a placebo. Although their major focus was on body mass and strength, the researchers also assessed sex drive and function. They found that the amount of testosterone required to maintain sexual function varied widely in men. Further, both testosterone deficiency AND oestrogen deficiency contributed to a decline in sexual function. This finding surprised researchers, who expected that testosterone alone was responsible for male sex drive. The role of oestrogen had not previously been recognized nor is it yet clearly understood.

Social factors and arousal

As well as the complexities in understanding the roles of male and female sex hormones, it is also difficult to disentangle the role of hormones from that of social factors in sexual arousal. Hormone levels clearly interact with social factors (such as perceived attractiveness of a potential partner) in the prediction of sexual thoughts, arousal and activities. Early studies (e.g. Udry, Talbert & Morris, 1986) showed that testosterone levels in girls are associated with sexual interests (masturbation, thinking about sex) but not necessarily with behaviours. We could infer from this that girls act out their libidinal wishes to a lesser extent than boys.

A related question is whether self-reports of sexual arousal/desire actually correspond to physiological measures. A meta-analysis by Chivers, Seto, Lalumière, Laan and Grimbos (2010) combined over 100 different studies to determine the correlation between self-report measures and laboratory measures of sexual arousal, finding that the correlations were much higher for men than for women. Why might this be so? Petersen and Hyde (2010) point out several possible explanations. One is that men have a direct visual image of their arousal though penile erection whereas for women, genital blood flow is less obvious. Another possibility is that men may be more experienced at recognizing their own arousal because of their greater engagement in masturbation and use of pornography. Finally, it is possible that women tend to underreport their degree of arousal because of a sexual double standard in which guilt and shame are attached to female sex drive. Whether such a double standard still exists is discussed at length later in the chapter.

Writers such as Deborah Tolman (2005) claim adolescent girls are wary about admitting to their sexual desire even in this day and age because of worries about reputation, and confusion about what they 'should' be feeling. In her book *Dilemmas of Desire* (2005), she describes the ambivalent cultural messages that girls and women receive about expressing their sexuality: 'Be sexy but not sexual. Don't be a prude but don't be a slut.' She argues that girls are consistently portrayed as the object or the victim of someone else's desire, but their own sexual feelings are not accepted or acknowledged. Feminist scholars such as Tolman (2005) and Fine (1988) have appropriated the word 'desire', with its overtones of longing and repression, as a word more descriptive and suitable for describing female sexual feelings than 'drive' with its overtones of agency and acting out.

Adolescent girls in an interview study by Bale (2011) illustrate some of the confusion they face in expressing themselves in a social milieu that is ambivalent about women's sexuality:

> What's really frustrating is . . . you have an image of yourself as liberated women, as like a sexual adventurer . . . like you can do what you want, and you want to really experience your life . . . . But at the same time, the second someone calls you 'easy', you immediately want to scrub it out. (Female, 18 years)
>
> *(Bale, 2011:309)*

A 17-year-old girl from the same study gave her impressions of the differences between men and women in relation to pressures towards the restraint of sexual expression.

> Like every time you sleep with another person, that goes on your clock like you're a car with a speedometer. It doesn't really happen to guys but it does happen to young women . . . and every guy (you sleep with) it goes up and the more miles it goes the less desirable you are in a way. (Female, 17 years)
>
> *(Bale, 2011:309)*

It is clear that, although young women may have more licence to express themselves sexually than they did 10 or 20 years ago, greater social disapproval still attaches to sexually adventurous females. To use a term currently in vogue, girls can still be 'slut shamed' if they deviate from traditional gender expectations in their dress or behaviour. So although women and girls may be more conscious of their desires, they recognize the dangers inherent in expressing them in non-sanctioned ways.

More research is needed to tease out the physiological predictors of sexual arousal among adolescents, and their interaction with social factors, to understand sexual desire and pleasure as well as sexual drives and actions. Baumeister *et al.* (2001) favour an interactionist approach and believe 'it is fair to assume that there has been a significant influence by culture and society aimed at suppressing female sexuality' (Baumeister *et al.*, 2001:269). Indeed it is likely that culture shapes how both men and women present themselves sexually in their attempts to fit in with the mostly unwritten rules about what is desirable and acceptable behaviour for one's gender, rules which differ markedly across cultures and historical time, and are changing as we write.

A classic study on sex drive

To illustrate changes over time, a classic social psychology field experiment of the 1980s, assessing male and female receptivity to sexual overtures, was recently replicated with the aim of comparing results across almost 25 years. Originally, Clark and Hatfield (1989) used college student confederates to approach fellow college students of the opposite gender and ask: (a) Would you go out with me tonight? (b) Would you come to my apartment tonight? and (c) Would you go to bed with me tonight? In 1989 and in several early replications, young men and women were equally receptive to the request for a date (about half said yes), but the second and third questions led to markedly different responses. Nearly 70 per cent of men agreed to the apartment visit compared with 6 per cent of women. Not one woman agreed to the invitation to have sex but three-quarters of the men said yes.

The results were viewed as supporting evolutionary theory that males are genetically preprogrammed to have sex as often and with as many women as they can in order to maximize their reproductive (and thus evolutionary) success, whereas women gain evolutionary and reproductive advantage by more careful selection of partners who can nurture and protect them during child-bearing and child-rearing (e.g. Buss and Schmitt's 'sexual strategies theory'; Buss and Schmitt, 1993). Of the many criticisms of this study, the strongest was perhaps of the interpretation, with many writers arguing that social forces, not evolution, explained the results. Young women may be just as interested in sex as young men but feel that to admit to this would not only be extremely damaging to their reputation in the situation posed in the study but also dangerous – a real threat to safety.

If social forces are the key here, then today's more liberal attitudes towards women's expression of sexuality should lead to different results when the study is replicated, especially if variables like confederate attractiveness, perceived safety, conversational preludes to the question, culture and age group are controlled. The replication (Tappé, Bensman, Hayashi & Hatfield, 2013) used a paper and pencil approach, enabling many more controls and study conditions but losing the 'real life' aspect of the original research.

By and large, young women were still significantly far less likely than young men to agree to, or consider, an offer of sex, although in these replications, some women – about 5 per cent – did say yes (or 'maybe' – a choice not offered originally). But most surprisingly, far fewer young men said yes in the replications than in the original study. Only about a quarter of young men in 2013, compared with three-quarters in 1989, said they would take up the offer of casual sex. Of course in 1989, the study participants were unaware that they were part of an experiment, a situation unlikely to be allowed by today's research ethics committees. The replication sample, knowing they were part of a paper and pencil-based experimental study, may have censored their answers, but it is interesting that it was the young men only who had changed in the direction of greater caution. Perhaps today's emphasis on greater sexual equality is allowing men more choices as well as women!

What can we conclude from the 25-year comparison? Clearly, men and women respond differently to overtures for casual sex, but the differences between them have reduced over the last couple of decades. The evidence from this and other studies suggests both biological and social forces are at play in behavioural manifestations of sex drive. Additionally, although we often consider that a major social change has been greater tolerance of women expressing their sexuality, we may also be witnessing the results of a greater tolerance towards men not always feeling the pressure to present as sexually eager and willing.

Implications of male sex drive supremacy beliefs

Greater acceptance of men not always choosing to be 'predator' is welcome, because one unfortunate consequence of male sex drive supremacy beliefs has too often been that hormones are used as an excuse for bad behaviour. Reasons men have used for forcing sex – 'She led me on' or 'If she didn't want sex she shouldn't have dressed like that' – imply that once aroused, men must be satisfied. This idea, which demeans men as well as women, is not yet a thing of the past, as is shown in newspaper stories (in Britain, the US and Australia), for example 'One in five say drunk women partly to blame for rape, survey finds' (Perkins, 2014).

In 2004, we noted the frequency of news stories about elite sportsmen accused of rape, gang rape and other sexual violations, not just once, but on several occasions (e.g. 'AFL [Australian Football League] standing still on spate of sex assaults', Symons, 2004a; 'Degrading culture knows no boundaries', Symons, 2004b), and in 2014, these stories have not disappeared (e.g. 'A star player accused, and a flawed rape investigation', Bogdanich, 2014). These young men at the peak of their physical fitness and energy can find themselves in situations where there is an explosive mix of free-flowing alcohol, peer (or team) pressure, and strong sexual temptation. The adulation of young women is flattering, and can lead to a sense of entitlement that any kind of sexual behaviour will be tolerated. Indeed, this attitude is widespread, as epitomized by a university official investigating rape allegations directed at football recruits at an American university. This investigator was quoted as saying about the alleged victims: 'The question I have for these ladies in this is why they are going to parties like this and drinking or taking drugs and putting themselves in a very threatening or serious position' (Rosenberg, 2004). The implication is that restraint and respect for women cannot be expected once the boys are aroused, and it is the responsibility of the girls to keep control. It is probably what many parents fear they must teach their daughters, despite the unfairness of such an attitude and the way it treats female desire as both an aberration and an excuse for punishment. Although it is hoped that these attitudes are waning there is still evidence, even in developed countries, that they have not been entirely relegated to an historical curiosity.

Is there still a sexual double standard?

Early studies

The sexual double standard refers to the belief that men are socially rewarded for sexual activity whereas women are derogated. Whether a sexual double standard still exists is a controversial question, like the one about sex drives. A review of 30 studies published between 1980 and 2002 found evidence of different standards of sexual permissiveness for men and women (Crawford & Popp, 2003) and can serve as a baseline for examining change. These writers reviewed studies that used a range of methodologies, including experimental studies (for example rating the behaviour of men and women in hypothetical sexual scenarios), ethnographic studies (for example, observing sex education classes in secondary schools) and interviews/focus groups with men and women. Most of these studies were conducted with young people in their middle or later teenage years. The authors commented on the continuing power of the epithet 'slut' as a way of controlling female sexuality. They noted that beliefs that the double standard would fade away as a result of the women's movement and the sexual revolution 'may have been overly optimistic' (Crawford & Popp, 2003:22).

Subsequently, Marks and Fraley (2005) conducted a large sample survey of undergraduates and individuals on the internet and did not find support for a double standard when participants were asked directly about it. However, in later studies, using experimental methodologies, they showed different results. In a 2006 study (Marks & Fraley, 2006), young people read vignettes about a target man or a woman that contained an equal number of positive and negative comments regarding the target's sexuality. Participants recalled more information consistent with the double standard than inconsistent with it. In 2007, these same researchers asked college student participants, both individually and in small collaborative groups, to evaluate a male or female target who had 1, 7 or 19 sex partners. A double standard did not emerge when individual participants made judgements about males or females with many sex partners, but when collaborative groups evaluated the targets, a double standard was more likely to emerge (Marks & Fraley, 2007). These studies taken together suggest that young people today may be reticent about admitting to holding double standards, but that they could still exist in some more subtle forms, and are more likely to be expressed in situations where there is peer pressure or support for such ideologies.

Recent research on the double standard

Two recent studies point to evolution rather than revolution in the nature of the double standard. In the first, by Allison and Risman (2013), over 24 000 US undergraduates from 22 different campuses were asked how much they agreed or disagreed with the following statement (asked separately for male and female targets): 'If men/women hook up or have sex with lots of people, I respect them less'. Most of the participants (66 per cent of men and 70 per cent of women) did NOT endorse a double standard. They fell into two groups – the 'egalitarian conservatives' who disapproved of promiscuity in either sex, and the 'egalitarian liberals' who said they would not lose respect for men or women who had many sex partners. More young women than young men were in the conservative group with the reverse true for the liberals. About one-third of participants, however, did endorse a double standard, but they did not all hold a 'traditional double standard'. About 25 per cent of men and 4 per cent of women said they would only lose respect for women who slept around, but 16 per cent of women and 6 per cent of men endorsed a 'reverse double standard', saying they would only lose respect for men with many sexual partners. It is interesting that both sexes were more judgemental towards the opposite sex than towards their own. However, the study could be criticized on the grounds that participants were asked to assess the behaviour of both sexes and were likely to be aware that a comparison would be made. Social desirability bias may have been at work here, or alternatively the participants may have responded in terms of what they thought 'should' be the case rather than what they believed actually occurs.

A different methodology, used by Sprecher, Treger and Sakuluk (2013), led to different conclusions. For nearly 25 years, Sprecher and her colleagues have been asking undergraduate students in their human sexuality classes at a US university the same set of questions about their perceptions of the acceptability of sexual intercourse in five different relationship contexts. These were first date, casual dating (together less than a month), serious dating (together for about a year), long term/pre-engaged, and engaged. Results from nearly 8000 students over two decades showed that although there was no double standard relating to sex in a committed relationship, both young men and young women considered casual sex more acceptable for men than for women. Although this double standard was endorsed by only a minority of young people, the rate of endorsement had hardly changed over 23 years, even though general approval of casual sex was higher than it had been in the earlier decades. As one writer summed it up, 'The bad news in these findings is that the double standard still exists on average. The good news is that most young people do not subscribe to it' (Vrangalova, 2014).

Why a double standard?

Various theories point to what lies behind this double standard. 'Female control theory' postulates that women are more responsible than men for curbing female sexuality, through strategies like gossip, social stigma and slights on reputation (Baumeister & Twenge, 2002). The theory is based on a sexual economics approach, suggesting that women act to protect the 'market value' of their sexual cooperation by refusing offers of casual sex and deterring other women from accepting them. This gives women more bargaining power in the sexual marketplace, where to improve the evolutionary advantages of their offspring, they exchange sexual favours for commitment and protection, preferably by a high status male. These are not considered to be conscious strategies, but part of our instinct for survival, 'hard-wired' into our DNA.

In contrast, Rudman, Fetterolf and Sanchez (2013) propose a 'male control theory', arguing that men are more punitive than women towards sexually adventurous women; they are more likely to treat them with disrespect or aggression, or to suggest that they are 'asking' to be raped (e.g. Rudman & Mescher, 2012). Rudman et al. (2013) also demonstrated in a study of undergraduates that although men were more approving than women of casual sex, their approval was only extended to their male friends, not their female friends or relatives, to whom they were actively discouraging about promiscuous behaviour. Men were also more likely to endorse the statement, 'In my opinion, the sexual double standard is good and should be maintained' (Rudman et al., 2013:254).

It seems clear that the kind of methodology used in studies of the sexual double standard will influence the study outcome, suggesting that the issue is a complex and subtle one. Perhaps what we are seeing in these studies is a reflection of (many) young people's desire that the double standard should not exist but a recognition that in reality it does, although the circumstances of its application may indeed have changed. Cultural differences are also relevant here, in that many cultural and religious groups clearly express a preference for different sexual standards for men and women, enforcing them through social pressure, religious doctrine and sometimes civil law. Martel, Hawk and Hatfield (2004), for example, write of sexually permissive and sexually restrictive societies, and report that the sexual double standard is clearly evident in most Asian and African nations. In developed countries with high migration intake, these differences in mores can lead to a great deal of misunderstanding, confusion and conflict for young people 'on the margin' between cultures.

Romantic relationships

Adolescent sexuality is not all bad news, inequality, risky behaviour and a war between the sexes. Young people can enjoy the awakening of desire, the fun of flirting and the fulfilment of relationships as part of their sexual development. One aspect of this is romance, a topic once neglected by psychologists but recently subject to a flurry of research (Collins, Welsh & Furman, 2009). Love, romance and courtship are rites of passage for young people in westernized societies, although the convergence of falling in love, having sex and getting married (or getting married and having sex) common to the mid-twentieth century may be unravelling as casual sex becomes more widespread (e.g. Kumar, 2013). In this section, we consider research on both the pitfalls and positive outcomes of adolescent romantic relationships, as well as studies that indicate different styles of romantic relating may be associated with personality characteristics, developmental experiences and cultural context.

Crushes, romance and identity development

Teen crushes are a common first step for many adolescents in the development of romantic relationships. The young person develops strong feelings towards a 'target', someone they admire without necessarily knowing very much about them, and without any indication that the feelings might be reciprocated. The target may never become aware of the crush. This is usually the case when young people develop strong feelings for public figures such as actors and pop stars, but can also be true for crushes on older students at school who may be 'hero-worshipped' because of their looks, sporting prowess or popularity. Despite being one-sided, crushes can serve positive developmental purposes, for example adolescents can model the leadership or sporting prowess of an admired figure, although of course the opposite can be true as well, when the object of the crush is admired because of his or her risk-taking or anti-social tendencies. When the crush includes infatuation as well as idealization, the adolescent has the opportunity to learn to manage romantic feelings in a non-threatening way. Girls especially can spend hours talking with each other about their latest crush, which can help to normalize romantic and sexual feelings, making them less overwhelming. Pickhardt (2012) notes that most adolescent crushes are short lived but involve intense feelings that can provoke a great deal of anxiety. In his words: 'Like flowers, crushes have a short blooming life and are easily bruised' (Pickhardt, 2013).

The pioneering lifespan developmental theorist Erik Erikson (1968) viewed crushes and youthful romance as ways of contributing to self-understanding and identity. He described adolescent 'falling in love' as 'projecting one's diffused self-image on another and seeing it thus reflected and gradually clarified' (Erikson, 1968:132). The endless talk that is often part of these early romances is a way of trying out different forms of 'self' and having them mirrored back by the other person. Erikson cautioned against putting pressure on young people to make permanent commitments too early in life, before an adequate sense of personal identity has been established. Dating, 'hanging out' or engaging in whatever form of social interaction allows young people to experience romantic relationships is viewed in this influential theoretical framework as beneficial to social and sexual development as it helps the young person discover who they are and what sort of person they want to be – a precursor to being able to make a genuine and long-term romantic commitment to another.

Prevalence of romantic relationships in adolescence

How prevalent are romantic relationships in adolescence and youth? One good source of data is the National Longitudinal Study of Adolescent Health (Add Health), an American study of thousands of school children aged 12–18 years (Carver, Joyner & Udry, 2003; Grieger, Kusunoki & Harding, 2014). Carver *et al.* (2003) found approximately 65 per cent of both boys and girls had experienced a romantic relationship. Many of the romantic relationships were long term, more than half being a year or more in duration. A small number of boys and girls (2.2 and 3.5 per cent, respectively) nominated same-sex romantic partners. More girls than boys reported having sexual intercourse with their romantic partner, reflecting the pattern of girls being more likely to have intercourse within what they perceive as a romantic context. The social connectedness of these adolescent relationships was indicated by data showing that parents had met the partners of approximately three-quarters of the romantically attached adolescents, and a similarly large percentage had told others 'they were a couple', and gone out together in a group. The number of adolescents in romantic relationships is even higher with more inclusive definitions of these relationships (e.g. dating, spending time with or going out with someone for a month or longer) (Furman & Hand, 2006) and when older age groups are examined. For example, Grieger *et al.* (2014) estimated that over 80 per cent of the 14- to 17-year-olds from the Add Health study had experienced at least one romantic relationship. Clearly, romantic relationships are the norm among adolescents.

It is also true that there are significant numbers of young people who have not yet experienced this type of relationship or who do not currently have a girlfriend or boyfriend, a situation that can be perceived as stressful (Headspace, 2012). Given that adolescence is a time when there is a great deal of pressure to 'fit in', young people who are not linking up romantically can feel lonely, out of step with their peers or wonder 'what's wrong with me?' For example, the following young woman posted this quote online, describing her feelings about not having a boyfriend and asking for advice:

> I'm 20 and I've never had a boyfriend. Sometimes it's good, other times I feel down about it. My friends have boyfriends and so I compare myself to them, like am I not as interesting or as pretty as them. Also seeing as I've never had a boyfriend I've never held hands with a guy, or kissed a guy, or gone all the way with a guy. My sex life is non-existent and my personal life apart from my normal friends is a bummer. (Female, 20 years)
>
> *(Experience Project, 2014)*

On a different advice site, this young man similarly bemoaned his lack of success with girls and his feeling of depression about not having a girlfriend:

> [I'm] currently in 2nd year of college, in first year of college I messed up with two girls I met due to lack of experience. One I knew was into me but I did not pursue hard enough and she lost interest, another I was too aggressive and tickled her which came off as creepy. So here I am, 19-year-old kid. I go to the movies alone, haven't ever really gone out with a girl before . . . it is just killing me. The lack of love in my life and I don't even know what to do about it . . . my situation I think is depressing. (Male, 19 years)
>
> *(Forum Bodybuilding, 2011)*

Pros and cons of adolescent romantic relationships

Adolescent romantic relationships have the potential to provide positive learning experiences about the self and how to relate intimately to others. They can contribute to overall self-esteem and to beliefs about attractiveness and self-worth (Zimmer-Gembeck, Siebenbruner & Collins, 2001, 2004). They can assist young people in renegotiating and developing more mature relationships with their parents, raise young people's status in the peer group, and offer a safe environment for learning about and experimenting with sexuality (Collins *et al.*, 2009). On the other hand romantic relationships can sometimes hinder identity development through closing off options (such as may occur with early parenthood) or through exposing the young person to abusive and violent interactions or unwanted or coerced sexual activity (Mulford & Giordano, 2008).

In addition, romantic break-ups among young people are often associated with depression (Davila, 2008; Welsh, Grello & Harper, 2003). Incongruence between relationship expectations and actual experiences (termed relationship inauthenticity by Soller, 2014) is positively associated with the risk of depression, suicide ideation and suicide attempts. Break-ups are, however, very common features of adolescent romantic relationships, and their impact is not always particularly severe or long lasting although some young people are more vulnerable than others. Illustrating this, in a study of Australian and Hong Kong students in their early twenties, 80 per cent of those young people who had ever been in a romantic relationship had experienced at least one break-up (Moore, Leung, Karnilowicz & Lung, 2012). As a result, 40 per cent of participants felt very hurt, even though the majority of the relationship dissolutions were self or mutually initiated. Partner initiation of the break-up was, however, the strongest indicator of being very hurt, along with the young person having a 'clingy' relationship style and a tendency towards higher levels of negative mood. But although often hurtful, break-ups can be growth promoting. Connolly and McIsaac (2009) researched Canadian school-based adolescents and found the majority described their break-ups as self-initiated (77 per cent). The most common reasons given for ending a relationship related to unmet affiliative, intimacy, sexual or interdependence needs. In other words, young people were 'moving on' when their relationships were not experienced as fulfilling, and in the process, hopefully learning more about themselves and others.

Attachment and romantic relationships

What is it about the desired state of being in love or romantically attached that can have so much potential for positive and negative outcomes? One answer revolves around characteristics of the individual in love, another to the nature of the relationship, and yet another to the ways we socially construct love and romance. At the individual level, various studies indicate that insecure attachment styles are implicated in less satisfactory romantic partnerships. What does this mean? Attachment theory suggests that infants form various kinds of bonds with their carers, and the quality of these bonds affects adult relationships, especially close or romantic relationships (Tracy, Shaver, Albino & Cooper, 2003). Securely attached people are 'good at' relationships; they learn to trust in others and to manage a healthy 'give and take' in their intimate associations. Insecurely attached individuals are either overly anxious and 'clingy' about their adult relationships (anxiously attached) or relatively indifferent to others (avoidantly attached). Bogaert and Sadava (2002), in a large-scale and oft-quoted Canadian study, found that anxiously attached young people saw themselves as less physically attractive, had an earlier first intercourse, more sexual partners and were more likely to be unfaithful than those with secure attachment styles. Interestingly, this anxious group was more likely than the securely attached to express very strong love towards their romantic partner, even though they were also more likely to be unfaithful. It has been suggested that infidelity in relationships is linked with discomfort about the desire for intimacy, particularly among the avoidantly attached (e.g. Mikulincer & Shaver, 2010).

Tracy *et al.* (2003) also found anxiously attached adolescents reported most instances of being in love. If they had sex, fear of losing their partner was more likely to be given as the motive than it was for secure young people. It has been suggested that anxiously attached individuals are ambivalent about commitment (Joel, MacDonald & Shimotomai, 2011). These researchers argue that dissatisfaction with their relationships and fear of negative evaluations by others push anxiously attached youth towards relationship-destructive behaviour (such as infidelity), whereas dependency on a partner motivates behaviours designed to maintain their relationships, such as close attention to a partner's needs.

Another example of the role of attachment comes from a study by Leung, Moore, Karnilowicz and Lung (2011). They showed that securely attached adolescents in both Hong Kong and Australia were less stressed, less likely to use avoidant and self-punishing coping styles and more resilient to relationship break-ups than those with insecure attachment styles. Finally, Pascuzzo, Cyr and Moss (2013) conducted an 8-year longitudinal study of Canadian young people across the ages 14–22 years, and found that those with more insecure attachment to parents and peers at age 14 were more likely to demonstrate insecure attachment styles with romantic partners at age 22.

Relationship characteristics

Relationship characteristics also impact on the outcomes of romantic relationships in adolescence. Welsh *et al.* (2003) list situations like unrequited love, infidelity of one's partner, sexual coercion and breaking up as potentially associated with depression in young people. In the case of unrequited love, fantasies about the other can be intense, sometimes leading to misinterpretations that the feelings are reciprocated. In extreme cases this may result in maladjusted acting out behaviours such as stalking (Leitz & Theriot, 2005), but usually the distress is turned inwards. Self-esteem can be damaged and would-be lovers may feel humiliated, unattractive and inferior.

Of more serious concern are adolescent relationships characterized by abuse, violence or conflict, a topic discussed in more detail in Chapter 11. Collins *et al.* (2009), in their review of adolescent romantic relationships, present evidence that aggression between romantic partners is common. Estimates vary greatly but the research suggests that between 10 and 48 per cent of young people in romantic relationships report experiencing physical aggression and 25–50 per cent report psychological aggression, including being sworn at, insulted and threatened. Boys are as likely to report abusive behaviour as girls. Several studies indicate that both victims and perpetrators of adolescent dating violence are more likely to have experienced childhood maltreatment and/or had substance abuse problems (Wekerle & Avgoustis, 2003).

Sociocultural attitudes to romance

Finally, social constructions of romance influence how young people feel about falling in and out of love, and how they act on those feelings. Although choosing a partner and partnering for love are regarded as a vital component of romantic love in the west, they may not be so important in all cultures. For example, in traditional Chinese society, some writers argue that romantic love is seen as subordinate to the needs of the group, typically the family (e.g. Li, Connolly, Jiang, Pepler & Craig, 2010). Love and romance are considered in the light of responsibility towards parents. Spontaneous expressions of love, especially in terms of non-marital sexual activities, are not regarded as appropriate. Youth from collectivist cultures generally appear to display more conservative attitudes to sexual expression and less commitment to romantic passion than is common in the west. For example, Li *et al.* (2010) compared 16- to 17-year-olds from China and Canada, and found that Chinese adolescents were less likely than the Canadians to have any form of romantic involvement, a finding also reflected in studies of Chinese and other Asian adolescents from immigrant families living in the west (Carver *et al.*, 2003; Connolly, Craig, Goldberg & Pepler, 2004). Similarly, among young people aged 18–26 years, Hong Kong Chinese youth were less likely than Anglo-Australians to have ever experienced a romantic relationship, and more likely to describe themselves as 'uninterested in relationships' (Moore *et al.*, 2012).

It has been argued that the west's focus on the significance of romantic relationships for young people as contributing to their sense of identity and self-worth is less likely to be shared in countries where there are higher levels of disadvantage and more emphasis on survival (Seiffge-Krenke *et al.*, 2010). A 17-nation study by Seiffge-Krenke and colleagues (2010) examined romantic stress among young people and compared it with stressors that were future-related (such as job training and potential unemployment) or self-related (such as managing moods and having friends). They postulated that romantic stress would be greater among young people in cultures that focus on individuality and free partner choice than among those in collectivist cultures, and that future oriented stressors would be perceived as greater than romantic stressors, especially in countries where there was more disadvantage and rapid changes in living conditions. The 17 countries were grouped into Middle Europe, North Europe, Eastern Europe, South America and the Middle East. Romantic stress was significantly higher among adolescents from Middle and Southern Europe, and for all country groups, future stressors were higher than romantic or self-oriented stressors. The authors suggest that romantic stress may be higher in the European nations because a romantic partner is a key to enabling separation and autonomy from one's family of origin, whereas financial and job success may be more important to this transition in some other countries. Love, they imply, may not be 'all you need'.

Falling in love and intimacy

We do not really need research to tell us that falling in love is an emotional experience and for adolescents these new feelings can be intense, frightening and hard to deal with even as they are, at the same time, miraculous and joyful. Nevertheless, some researchers have tried to examine this confusing state of being. In a fascinating study by Brand, Luethi, von Planta, Hatzinger and Holsboer-Trachsler (2007), newly 'in love' adolescents were compared with those who were single or in longer established relationships. The 'in love' group had increased scores on a measure of hypomania ('a mood state characterized by persistent disinhibition and pervasive elevated, euphoric or irritable mood, as well as thoughts and behaviors that are consistent with such a mood state') (Wikipedia, 2014) compared to the control group. Their diary entries indicated more positive morning and evening moods than among the controls, shorter sleep times but better quality sleep, lowered daytime sleepiness and better concentration during the day. No wonder some people become 'addicted to love'.

That 'first fine careless rapture' is, for many, an initial step in the development of intimacy, although we know from the examination of different cultural practices that intimate, committed and loving relationships need not always begin with an 'in love' stage. Erikson (1959, 1968) wrote that the development of the capacity for intimacy, and its culmination in the formation of a life partnership was a vital psychological task for young adults. He was referring to emotional as well as physical intimacy – the ability to share feelings with another, to self-disclose and to listen, to set mutual goals and to compromise individual desires in order to work towards 'couple' goals – as well as to share one's body in harmonious and mutually satisfying sexuality. Intimate relationships or expectations about their development are often initiated in the charged emotional climate of romantic relationships. Learning about the give and take of such relationships is part of the young person's journey towards maturity.

In developmental terms, general social competence is associated with participation in romantic relationships. Friendships offer a model for at least some aspects of romantic interactions, and friends also provide a sounding board and support for adolescents to discuss their romantic successes, failures and hopes. Having a large number of other-gender friends and being liked by many of one's peers in adolescence is correlated with current and future dating patterns (Collins *et al.*, 2009). A commonly held stereotype is that girls at adolescence may be better equipped to handle intimate relationships as a result of their experiences with same-sex friends, with girls' friendships characterized by more self-disclosure, discussion of problems, sharing of emotions and mutual support than boys' friendships. There is some research support for this stereotype, especially in relation to self-disclosure (Rose & Rudolph, 2006). In addition, Rose and Rudolph's review found evidence that girls tend to care more about dyadic friendships, are more likely to work towards group rather than individual goals in peer contexts and show greater empathy for others than boys, who tend to focus more on agentic goals, including their own dominance in the peer group. When romantic relationships begin, girls may have a head start on boys with respect to managing feelings and talking about emotions, whereas boys may be less able or willing to do so, leading to mismatches in communication and resultant misunderstandings. This has implications for relationship satisfaction, relationship maintenance and how and when sexual feelings will be expressed and acted on.

Romantic relationships change with age as well as showing gender differences. In Montgomery's study (2005) of nearly 500 young people aged 12 to 24 years, older adolescents indicated greater intimacy and more commitment-related romantic beliefs but less romantic idealization than younger ones. Thus, as young people mature in their relationships skills, they are less likely to idealize their partner and more likely to make commitments that are presumably characterized by a more realistic appreciation of what to expect from romantic relationships. With experience, love becomes a little less blind – which, of course, is not to say that it cannot make fools of us at any age.

Negotiating the sexual encounter

Communication difficulties

Negotiating the sexual encounter requires that partners are able to communicate with one another about sex. Sexual communication is vital because good communication can enhance people's sex lives by enabling them to understand each other's needs, to avoid misunderstandings – such as the idea that 'no' means 'yes' – and to talk to each other about precautions against pregnancy and sexually transmissible diseases. Such communication is not always straightforward. It can be undermined by embarrassment, defensiveness, fear of rejection, the desire to exploit or by simply misunderstanding one's partner.

In the area of self-confidence about sex, or sexual self-efficacy, gender differences have been noted, but not always consistently. Rostosky, Dekhtyar, Cupp and Anderman (2008) examined sexual self-concept (sexual esteem and sexual anxiety) and sexual self-efficacy among 388 US high school students. Boys reported lower sexual esteem, lower sexual self-efficacy and higher sexual anxiety than females. This certainly disrupts the stereotype of boys being sexually more confident, as does research by Giordano, Longmore and Manning (2006) whose findings, based on structured interviews with over 1300 US adolescents, provide in their words, a 'strong contrast to existing portraits'. Boys reported being just as emotionally engaged in their romantic relationships as girls, but they felt significantly less confident than girls about managing the various aspects of their relationships, and ascribed more relationship power to their female partners. Here we see a divergence from the research we described some 20 years ago. In Rosenthal, Moore and Flynn's (1991) Australian study, adolescent girls reported poorer sexual self-esteem than adolescent boys, and were less likely than boys to agree with statements such as 'I feel comfortable with my sexuality' or 'I am comfortable being affectionate with dating partners'.

There are other problems experienced in sexual communication, as these young girls' responses to the question 'Is it hard to say no to sex?' illustrate.

> When you are in that situation, I think it is hard to say it. I think you would have to. I wouldn't say it in words; but I would act it out, like move away or whatever. It is very difficult to say no, though. (Adolescent female)

> Yes. Because you are letting the guy down, you are showing him you don't want him as much as he thinks you do. You feel bad. (Adolescent female)

> *(Moore & Rosenthal, 2006:152)*

It is not clear whether girls are becoming more assertive or boys more diffident in their sexual communications, or indeed whether these findings are sample and measure dependent. What is important is for both sexes to learn to be more comfortable about sexual communication. Widman, Welsh, McNulty and Little (2006) noted that among adolescent dating couples, more open communication about sex from either male or female partners was associated with increased contraceptive use and greater relationship satisfaction.

Further, Mitchell and Wellings (2002) point out that lack of clear communication between young people puts them at risk of having sex that is 'unwanted, unanticipated or regretted' (Mitchell & Wellings, 2002:393). Following focus groups and semi-structured interviews with young people in Britain, they concluded that ambiguity was a key feature of sexual communication, and indeed served useful purposes. Ambivalent or ambiguous signals during flirting and in sexual contexts may protect individuals from the embarrassment of rejection, or guard against them making false assumptions about where the encounter is headed. For example, a young man may prefer not to directly ask a young woman if she is interested in having sex; rather, he may rely on her bodily signals to decide whether to proceed with the encounter. The young woman in the situation may not wish to have sex but may also be reluctant to reject the advances outright. She may wish for a continuing relationship, and want to take things more slowly. Or, like one young woman in the Mitchell and Wellings study (2002), she may want to protect her self-esteem, as in:

> You're not going to come out with . . . 'I'm not going to sleep with you tonight', because that makes him think you thought you could. (Adolescent female)

> *(Mitchell & Wellings, 2002:401)*

These defensive communications serve a purpose but they ultimately make negotiated sex extremely difficult. Both parties can readily misinterpret what is happening, due more to their hopes and fears than the reality of the situation.

Sex, lies and reputation

One element of relationships in which communication falls short of ideal is the maintenance of honesty about other partners. Men and women lie about their sexual lives. For example it is typically believed that men overestimate and women underestimate their sexual experience. One test of this belief is a recent study by Fisher (2013), who surveyed Ohio college students aged 18–25 about their sex lives under two different conditions. The first group was told their answers would be anonymous; the second group was wired to a lie detector machine (which was actually fake). The study found women admitted to significantly more sexual partners when they thought their answers were being monitored by a lie detector, but men's responses did not vary according to the condition. Fisher concluded that women lie about how many lovers they have had because they are sensitive about their reputation and being labelled as sluts.

Reputation is one reason, but not the only one, that people lie about their sex lives. As relationships develop there is a desire to present in the best possible light. If a new partner knows too much about your past (and concurrent) loves and sexual adventures, this idealized impression may be difficult to sustain. Attempts to maintain the illusion of the exclusivity may require subterfuge. But although non-disclosure of other partners may work for a time, keeping relationships happy in ignorance, there is great potential for strong negative emotions of jealousy, betrayal and hurt, not to mention implications for safe sex practice (no need for condoms if you believe you are the exclusive partner). For young people, these can be difficult life lessons to learn.

Research on the way adults talk to each other can enlighten us further on the difficulties that can occur in communication about the emotionally laden topic of sex. Tannen (2007) argues that men and women use conversation differently; men converse with a focus on achieving social status, whereas women talk to achieve personal connection and avoid social isolation. In short, she says 'men want to report', and 'women want rapport'. Women's talk is characterized as about negotiating closeness, giving and seeking confirmation, and working out ways to reach consensus. Men's talk on the other hand often has the goal of disguising feelings and vulnerabilities so that power, control and independence are conveyed. The sexes misunderstand each other's conversational motives, leading them to non-communicative strategies such as dismissing the talk of the other as trivial, not registering what has been said because it is couched in tentative terms, or interpreting the lack of talk about feelings as indicating a genuine lack of feelings rather than an inability to discuss them. Others who have studied male–female discussions note that men are more likely to set the topic of conversation, to interrupt, to ignore women's conversational initiatives and to make assertions. Women are more likely to defer to male conversational opening gambits, to work to keep the conversation going and to be tentative and questioning in their speech. If these difficulties and misinterpretations occur between adult males and females, how much more will they pose problems for adolescent male–female conversations? And if the misinterpretations occur around topics with low emotional load, such as how to spend a weekend or share a task, what is the potential for misinterpretations about whether, when and how to have sex?

In fact, there are few systematic studies of what young people say to one another during courting, sexual preliminaries or during sexual activity but it is an area ripe for research, with Facebook and online chat rooms good places to start (see Chapter 6). Understanding more fully the nature of sexual communication may help young people to explain to each other their points of view. Sex education in schools has a potential role to play here in the facilitation of discussions about sex in which girls and boys can share their values, misunderstandings and myths as well as learn about their sexual plumbing.

Conclusion

Gender differences in sexual attitudes and behaviours are decreasing over time, with young people leading the charge. Although males and females differ in the biological forces they experience, the interpretation of those forces is culturally influenced. Modern western beliefs in sexual equity highlight that women as well as men can be driven by sexual desire, and that it is a personal responsibility to control those desires, not the responsibility of women. Nevertheless, traces of the double standard still exist, probably in more subtle forms than their blatant expression in past centuries. In the long run, research indicates that both young men and young women are interested in relationship quality as part of their sexual experience, both sexes can enjoy casual and hook-up sex, and both sexes can be vulnerable to hurt and disappointment when their expectations do not match their experiences.

8

SEXUAL DIVERSITY

I don't have to be categorised as anything. I'm me. That's why when people go – even now – are you gay, are you a girl, or are you a boy? Some people reckon I'm a lesbian for some reason. I say to them no, I'm just me. At the end of the day, I do what I do. I wake up just like any other human being. Just because of what I like in the bedroom doesn't necessarily mean it makes me a different person. (Adolescent female)

(Robinson, Bansel, Denson, Ovenden & Davies, 2014:17)

In many western societies, recognition of the nature of homosexuality is gradually evolving from a past of myths and stigma towards understanding, support and acceptance. Although the origins of homosexuality are still poorly understood, most researchers and health professionals now agree that there is no evidence that homosexuality is pathological in nature but rather is a variation in human sexual behaviour. It is important that we distinguish homosexuality, that is, sexual interest in individuals of the same sex, from gender variance, which refers to expressions of gender that do not match an individual's biological sex, and includes people who identify as transsexual, gender queer or intersex (Riley, Sitharthan, Clemson & Diamond, 2011).

Over the past few decades public opinion of homosexuality has altered dramatically in many developed countries. An increasing number of people in the public eye have declared their homosexuality, and in many TV programmes and films gays or lesbians are key characters. These offer 'models of possibility' for young people through which they might form a sense of self identity and manage their coming out (Robinson et al., 2014).

Nevertheless, homosexuality is still regarded by some as unnatural, deviant and problematic, and so growing up with an awareness of an attraction to the same sex is an undeniable personal challenge in the face of pervasive social stigma. But although homosexual young people still face discrimination and abuse that can impact negatively on their physical and mental health, the picture is not as bleak as it was two decades ago. Increasingly, for many young people personal (and public) acceptance of a homosexual identity as positive and fulfilling is possible.

There has been an increase in the number of young people identifying as homosexual or bisexual. The dominant themes of adolescent homosexuality are explored in this chapter. We consider how homosexuality is defined and the prevalence of this sexual identity during adolescence. Theories about the development of homosexuality and issues relating to coming out and homophobia are discussed, as well as the impact of their sexual orientation on the physical and mental wellbeing of young people.

What is meant by 'homosexual'?

Homosexuality involves not just sexual contact with persons of the same sex but also romantic feelings, emotional attraction, fantasies and a sense of identity. It is interesting that dictionary definitions fail to take account of this complexity, focusing solely on 'physical attraction' (*Oxford English Dictionary*) or 'sexual desire' in one definition or 'sexual intercourse' in another (*Merriam-Webster*). Martin and Lyon (1972) provide a better definition. A homosexual person is an individual 'whose primary erotic, psychological and social interest is in a member of the same sex, even though that interest may not be overtly expressed' (Martin & Lyon, 1972:1). As we shall see, even this definition leaves out the key defining characteristic of homosexuality.

Sexual orientation, sexual identity and same-sex attraction

The overarching term 'sexual orientation' describes a person's underlying sexual preferences, whether heterosexual, bisexual or homosexual. Sexual orientation has been defined as a consistent pattern of sexual arousal towards persons of the same and/or opposite gender (Spitzer, 1981), encompassing fantasy, conscious attractions and emotional and romantic feelings (Klein, Sepekoff & Wolf, 1985). Sexual orientation has three different dimensions that may not be congruent and may vary over time. The affective dimension refers to the gender of attraction; the behavioural dimension refers to the gender of sexual partners; and the cognitive dimension refers to the individual's sexual identity (Laumann, Gagnon, Michael & Michaels, 1994).

Sexual identity – how one sees one's own sexual self and identifies this to others – may be understood as a continuum ranging from heterosexual to homosexual. Over the last few decades sexual identity labels have changed, and we now have much wider scope for including and recognizing the many and varied experiences and individuality of those identifying as non-heterosexual. While acknowledging that this variety exists, in this chapter, which is focused on providing an overview of issues relating to sexual identity, we will mostly use the words gay, lesbian, bisexual and homosexual, except when referring to research that has been conducted within a specifically targeted population, such as 'same-sex attracted'.

Sexual identity does not always correspond with behaviour and attraction, though they are correlated (Richters *et al.*, 2014). A person may have desires they have not acted upon, or they may have chosen either a heterosexual or homosexual identity after experimentation with partners of both sexes. Usually sexual identity will be an expression of a person's underlying sexual orientation. For example, a young woman is romantically and sexually attracted to women. For many years she experiences intimate friendships with other girls. Some of the friendships have become sexual at times and these experiences have been pleasurable and satisfying. Her experiences tell her that she is lesbian and she desires a long-term romantic and sexual relationship with another woman. Because she had always assumed she was heterosexual, these feelings for other women are in conflict with her heterosexual identity. Over time, she begins to describe herself as lesbian to herself and others. Through romantic and sexual experiences she comes to develop a lesbian sexual identity.

Another example is a young man who has grown up in a large family. All his siblings are married and he, too, desires a marriage and a family. This is how he has always planned his life. He believes, as his upbringing has taught him, that these are the experiences that will bring him happiness. Yet, throughout his adolescence he has had intense crushes on other boys at school, sometimes leading to sexual experimentation. Sexual experiences with girls lacked intensity, pleasure and romantic attraction. Though he is aware of his sexual attraction to men, he discounts this as a passing phase. The idea that he might be gay is abhorrent. Eventually he marries; the marriage is without passion and lacks sexual interest. Children add fulfilment to his desire for a family but he remains dissatisfied and troubled. He chooses to suppress his attraction to men and adopts a conventional heterosexual identity. Would we describe this young man as heterosexual, homosexual or bisexual? None of these categories is entirely satisfactory.

Sexual orientation is commonly viewed as an either/or choice – one is either heterosexual or homosexual. Yet, the sexual practices individuals engage in, as distinct from sexual identity, can be sexual acts with both opposite-sex and same-sex partners. This is particularly so in adolescence, when it is assumed that sexuality is fluid and there is considerable transient sexual experimentation.

Schoolgirl crushes on female teachers or senior students are not uncommon. A heterosexual girl who has an incidental sexual experience with another student may feel that this one act makes her homosexual. Because she equates having sex with another woman as being homosexual, she may wrongly think of herself as a lesbian, causing considerable distress. As the following discussion shows, homosexual activity, homosexual fantasies and confusion about sexual orientation are fairly common among adolescents. However, only a small minority of adolescents actually develop a sexual identity as gay or lesbian. Thus, although same-sex preference and activity may help predict who is gay or lesbian, it does not determine sexual identity. It appears that homosexual activity is integral, but not sufficient in itself, to the development of a homosexual identity.

As many adolescents questioning their sexual orientation wonder if they are bisexual or homosexual, it is important to understand that there is a difference between bisexuality and transitory homosexual experiences of the sort that may occur in single-sex boarding schools, in prisons and among male sex workers who work with both men and women.

Bisexuality

A person who identifies as bisexual is sexually and emotionally attracted to people of both sexes (Hillier *et al.*, 2010). They may or may not be sexually active with partners of both sexes at any time but continue to be attracted to both sexes. Very little attention has been paid to young people who are bisexual and this group has been referred to as an invisible minority (Diamond & Butterworth, 2008; Firestein, 2007; Purdie-Vaughns & Eiback, 2008). A study examining medical literature over two decades found that most research does not distinguish between bisexual and homosexual participants, and only one in six studies noted bisexuality as a legitimate identity (Kaestle & Ivory, 2012).

An Australian study of over 3100 same-sex attracted or gender-questioning young people aged 14–21 years (mean age 17 years) found that after gay/lesbian, bisexual was the most commonly cited identity of these young people with young women more likely to identify as bisexual (42 per cent) than lesbian (39 per cent) (Hillier *et al.*, 2010). Evidence suggests that for some young people, identifying as bisexual reflects a time of transition – a time when they realize they do not fit neatly into a 'heterosexual' or 'gay/lesbian' category.

The word bisexual became really important to me at about the age 13. I had always had a fascination with anything gay, it seemed only normal I would think about experimenting. However it soon became obvious to me that what I was feeling went way past experimenting. The older, and more sexual/romantic I got, the more I realised that I wanted to be with another girl, and another girl only. Lesbian is such a scary word, or at least that's what it felt like. (Female, 15 years)

(Hillier et al., 2010:27)

Bisexuality can also be perceived as a safer middle ground for some young people when either working their sexual identity out (whether they eventually identify as gay/lesbian or continue to identify a bisexual) or, if they are clear about their homosexual identity, coming to terms with telling others and seeking acceptance.

I did tell a few friends that I wasn't straight, and I felt that by telling them I was bisexual, I would be less likely to be marginalised and ostracized like the other lesbians in my year. I also felt that a bisexual label would make me appear less foreign to 13-year-olds and keep my femininity intact. (Female, 19 years)

I probably wouldn't really call myself bisexual, because I know that I'm still not sure, and don't think that I should really slap a label on it just to satisfy others' curiosity. Probably though, I would be leaning towards lesbian more so than anything else. (Female, 18 years)

(Hillier et al., 2010:30)

This study also found there were young people who were less concerned with gender when it came to being attracted to someone; other personal characteristics of individuals drove feelings of attraction. Some highlighted the spectrum of sexual attraction and identity by expressing themselves as bisexual, but with a preference for either men or women:

I think that personality and charisma and looks are more attractive than gender. (Female, 18 years)

Simple: bisexual, male preference. (Male, 14 years)

(Hillier et al., 2010:30)

The minority stress experienced by gays/lesbians is also experienced by bisexuals and, in addition, bisexual young people face challenges from the homosexual community over the validity of their identity (Israel & Mohr, 2004;

Meyer, 2003). It is intriguing that now tolerance of homosexuality is more common in many developed countries, gay culture itself has become less tolerant of bisexuality, viewing those who claim to be bisexual as being in some way inauthentic, or wanting the best of both worlds (Pallotta-Chiarolli & Lubowitz, 2003; Richters *et al.*, 2014).

> I would like to see a broadening view of the gay and lesbian commu-
> nity. The community is remarkably hostile towards . . . bisexual people
> [by ignoring or pressuring to 'make their minds up']. (Female, 20 years)
> *(Hillier* et al.*, 2010:98)*

An historical overview

Crime or mental illness?

For centuries, homosexual acts were regarded as criminal activities. For example, the English Act of 1533 made buggery (anal intercourse between men) punishable by death (Brown, 1989). Historically, what we call 'homo-sexuality' was not considered a unified set of acts, much less a set of qualities. As Weeks (1977:12) described it, 'There was no concept of the homosexual in law, and homosexuality was not regarded as a particular attribute of a certain type of person but as a potential in all sinful creatures'. Lesbian sex was largely seen as unimaginable. Most civil laws against same-sex relations were quite explicit about the acts committed by males but did not specifically mention women. Homosexuality, or at least male homosexuality, remains a crime within some jurisdictions. Within some Christian, Islamic and other religious frameworks, homosexuality was, and is still considered, a sin, a violation of God's law.

From early last century, homosexuality, then known as 'introversion', became increasingly regarded as a medical illness, to be investigated, treated and cured. With the early failure of biological explanations and cures for homosexuality, psychoanalytic and behavioural theories proliferated and homosexuality was classified as a psychiatric disorder. It was not until 1973 that, influenced by political pressure from the gay movement, the American Psychiatric Association removed homosexuality as a psychiatric disorder from its official register of psychopathology (APA Task Force on Appropriate Therapeutic Responses to Sexual Orientation, 2009).

In the last decades of the twentieth century, with more liberal social atti-tudes towards sexuality, homosexuality was widely decriminalized, openness about homosexuality increased, and gay and lesbian communities developed throughout urban western countries such as North America, Europe and Australia. These changes and the advent of HIV/AIDS greatly altered the social environment in which young people recognized their homosexuality and became open about this.

Search for a cause

The search for a physiological cause, beginning in the late nineteenth century, failed to pinpoint a congenital deficit or find physical differences between heterosexual and homosexual men. Nevertheless, medical treatments to 'cure' homosexuality abounded, including castration and vasectomy. Later, in the 1930s and 1940s, hormone therapy (consisting of androgen supplements) was used, without significant changes in sexual orientation (Money & Ehrhardt, 1972). Treatment of homosexuality with electroconvulsive therapy (ECT) persisted into the 1960s.

Hormones, brain structure and genes

There have been three competing theories of a biological cause of homosexuality: the role of 'sex' hormones, brain structure and genetic predisposition. Hormonal theories explain homosexuality in terms of underexposure to male hormones or overexposure to female hormones during development (Grimbos, Dhawood, Buriss, Zucker & Puts, 2010; Kangassalo, Pölkki & Rantala, 2011). Although some research has indicated that early sex hormone signaling affects sexual orientation in women (Grimbos *et al.*, 2010), the evidence is correlational and requires further study. The search for a hormonal basis for homosexuality continues, but the current evidence is scant and contradictory, and the studies have been widely criticized for methodological deficiencies.

The search for the gay brain was led by LeVay (1991) who claimed to have discovered a difference between homosexual and heterosexual brains by demonstrating that cells in the brain which participate in the regulation of typical male sexual behaviour are more densely clustered in homosexual men. Although recent developments in neuroscience have allowed the development of new explanations of various human behaviours, current consensus is that the neurobiological processes underlying sexual orientation are largely unknown. Studies have found that stronger brain activity occurs in parts of the brain when people see images of the types of people to whom they are attracted (Hu *et al.*, 2008; Kranz & Ishai, 2006; Paul *et al.*, 2008). Recently, structural and functional neuroimaging studies have found that cerebral hemispheric volume and amygdala connections are different for those attracted to women (heterosexual men and lesbians) in comparison to those attracted to men (homosexual men and heterosexual women) (Savic, Berglund & Lindstrom, 2005; Savic & Lindstrom, 2008). However, in a critical review of the literature, Erickson-Schroth (2010) concluded that although structural and functional neuroimaging hold great promise in understanding the influence of biology on sexual orientation, they have not yet delivered any clear findings.

The notion of a purely genetic cause for homosexuality is contentious. Although a study of identical twins in 1991 was inconclusive (Bailey & Pillard, 1991), a recent but as yet unpublished study of the DNA of 400 gay men has shown that sexual attraction is influenced by genes on at least two different chromosomes. These were described by one researcher as 'male-loving genes'. At one end of the mating preference continuum are gay men who are sexually attracted to other males, and at the opposite end of the continuum may be lesbian women who have no sexual attraction to males (Graves, 2014). Researchers are very clear that these genes alone would not result in homosexuality and that other factors, such as hormonal exposure, would be necessary for this gene expression.

Psychosocial explanations

A different approach to the origins of homosexuality adopts a range of psychosocial explanations. Based on the fact that sexual practices and customs vary from place to place and time to time, these theories look to different life experiences and societal factors for explanations of the origins of homosexuality. An early and mostly discredited approach was based on Freud's speculations about homosexuality. Freud (1924, 1935) maintained that the relationship with one's father and mother was a crucial factor. He believed humans to be innately bisexual, passing through a homoerotic phase in the process of establishing a heterosexual orientation. Fixating at this homoerotic phase could occur, especially if a male had a poor relationship with his father and an overly close and binding relationship with his mother.

Another influential approach is taken by social constructionists, who believe identity is not fixed. They argue that one's identity cannot be 'discovered' as it is created through social interaction (Wilton, 2000). Various versions of this model have been criticized for failing to explain the development of homosexuality where individuals have no access to other homosexuals. Other models have considered multifactorial influences on sexual identity. One has been proposed by Cass after revision of her staged theory of sexual identity. Termed the social constructionist psychology approach, this model argues that sexual identity is a product of the interaction of three equally important elements – biological capacities and experiences, psychological capacities and experiences, and sociocultural environment (Cass, 2006).

As can be seen from this brief account, despite a variety of explanations being offered, the origins of homosexuality are still poorly understood. What is more useful is to consider the impact of their sexual orientation on young people's lives.

What does the research tell us?

Non-heterosexual adolescents are still one of the most under-researched groups of adolescents and the most poorly understood in terms of sexuality.

As we noted earlier, researchers have used different terminology in describing their participants and in the questions they ask. Some researchers have carefully specified a focus on same-sex attraction, a broad descriptor often used by young people to avoid the discrimination attached to homosexuality (Hillier & Harrison, 2004; McNair, Prestage, Russell & Richters, 2014). Other research has focused on sexual identity, asking young people if they identify as gay, lesbian, bisexual, transgender or intersex (GLBTI). As highlighted earlier, although this chapter is focused on sexual identity, studies that have been conducted on same-sex attracted populations will be acknowledged and reported when this work is relevant to homosexual and bisexual identity.

Prevalence

The prevalence of homosexuality and bisexuality is difficult to determine, especially given variations in definition used in studies and also that young people are often fluid in their sexual orientation (Savin-Williams & Joyner, 2014).

In Australia, research over the last decade shows a marked increase in both the number of young men and women identifying as same-sex attracted, with 8 per cent of young women by their mid-twenties identifying in this way (Smith, 2007, cited in Giordano & Ross, 2012). The most recent census in Australia showed that 1.6 per cent of young people aged 15–24 years in couple relationships reported they were in a same-sex relationship (Australian Bureau of Statistics, 2013c). In a national survey of over 2000 Australian secondary school students, the majority (83 per cent of young men and 76 per cent of young women) reported sexual attraction exclusively to people of the opposite sex, however 8 per cent of young men and 4 per cent of young women reported an attraction only to people of the same sex. Five per cent of young men and 15 per cent of young women were attracted to people of both sexes, and about 5 per cent of both sexes were unsure of their sexual attraction (Mitchell, Patrick, Heywood, Blackman & Pitts, 2014).

A national study in the UK on sexual attitudes and lifestyles through the life course found that of those aged 16–24 years, most (97 per cent) identified as heterosexual/straight, 1.5 per cent identified as gay/lesbian, 1.5 per cent as bisexual and 0.3 per cent as other (Mercer et al., 2013).

> The proportion of women reporting sexual experience with same-sex partners now exceeds that of men, at least at younger ages, when the proportion describing themselves as bisexual is highest.
>
> *(Mercer* et al*., 2013:1791)*

Although it is acknowledged that estimates of the sexual behaviour of the population can vary, depending on definitions and survey methods used (Gates, 2011), data collected from a US national sample of 13 495 men and women aged 15–44 between 2006 and 2008 found that fewer than 2 per cent of young men aged 15–17 reported any same-sex sexual behaviour but five times this number of young women did so (Chandra, Mosher, Copen & Sionean, 2011). Of the individuals aged 18–19 years in this survey, fewer than 2 per cent of males and females identified as homosexual/gay/lesbian, and about 1 per cent of males and 6 per cent of females identified as bisexual. Similar figures were found in a US Youth Risk Behaviour Survey of over 156 000 public school students in Grades 9–12, between 2001 and 2009 (Kann et al., 2011).

A recent paper has alerted researchers to the fact that some statistics around prevalence of homosexuality may be subject to wide fluctuations, based on observations that some previously openly gay adolescents may hide their identity during their young adult years; that some heterosexual adolescents may be confused about the use of romantic attraction as a proxy for sexual orientation; and that some mischievous adolescents may report same-sex attraction when none was present (Savin-Williams & Joyner, 2014). Given these observations and the difficulties of comparing research using different definitions, it is a hard task to accurately determine the prevalence of homosexuality and bisexual identity among young people.

Homophobia and coming out

An important task for most young people who identify as gay or lesbian is the process of 'coming out'. Disclosure of a gay or lesbian identity to significant others, notably family and friends, is one aspect of the process; the other is self acceptance of that identity. Flowers and Buston (2001) describe how a young gay man's acceptance of himself was dependent on others' acceptance of him as a gay man.

> It was almost as if you'd actually accepted it yourself for the first time . . . when you actually said it. . . . I felt like saying 'No, shut up!' but once I'd told that one person, you know, a lot of weight, a sense of relief almost that somebody knew and she didn't think 'Oh my God, he's a leper' or something. (Male)
>
> *(Flowers & Buston, 2001:58)*

For others, acceptance of themselves precedes that of others.

> I felt like the lowest piece of dirt on the planet. It was just swept under the carpet and then excuses like 'You're too young to know' were pulled out. I finally accepted me and my family couldn't. I felt like jumping back into the closet and bolt[ing] it shut. (Female, 18 years)
>
> *(Sauers, 2007:77)*

Some gay and lesbian young people, not surprisingly, are fearful or anxious about the outcome of such disclosure in the face of stigma and discrimination and may attempt to conceal their sexual orientation, seeking to pass as heterosexual. Others may partially come out, selecting a set of trusted individuals with knowledge of their sexual orientation. Yet others are open to all, actively supporting reform to minimize discrimination.

Homophobic language

The pervasiveness of homophobic attitudes makes coming out a difficult experience. Homophobia can be expressed directly through physical harassment and assault, even murder, but verbal abuse is more common. An exploration of hate language gives us a window onto the experience of young homosexuals a decade ago, when there was considerable evidence that homophobic verbal abuse was widespread, particularly in schools (Thurlow, 2001). Thurlow found that terms like 'poof' or 'queer' accounted for 10 per cent of the 'taboo' words used by students, but homophobic verbal abuse was rated much less seriously than other abusive terms. He concluded:

> Sticks and stones may be more likely to break their bones but the relentless, careless use of homophobic pejoratives will most certainly continue to compromise the psychological health of young homosexual and bisexual people by insidiously constructing their sexuality as something wrong, dangerous or shameworthy.
>
> *(Thurlow, 2001:36)*

Plummer (2001) added to our understanding of the power of language in the coming out experience by unravelling the meanings attached to terms such as 'poofter' and 'faggot'. He concluded that initially these terms do not necessarily refer to homosexuality.

> The ones that weren't playing sport . . . [who were] more interested in collecting bugs, reading . . . the ones that weren't sort of in the 'in crowd' were [called poofters].
>
> If you really, really, really wanted to offend somebody you call them a poof.
>
> *(Plummer, 2001:19)*

It is only as children get older that sexual connotations are attached to these terms. The powerful effect of these precisely targeted homophobic terms, even if they have their beginnings in a non-sexual sense, provides a hostile context for the development of a homosexual identity.

In recent years the use of another homophobic phrase has become increasingly common. One US study of gay, lesbian and bisexual students found '84.9 per cent of students frequently or often heard "gay" used in a negative way (e.g., "That's so gay") at school, and 91.4 per cent reported that they felt distressed because of this language' (Kosciw, Greytak, Bartkiewicz, Boesen & Palmer, 2012:5).

Part of the problem is that expressions of this sort are deemed to be harmless and simply humorous. In challenging the use of the term 'That's so gay' among Australian youth, Witthaus (2010) outlined strategies for confronting and interrupting homophobic language that can be used by teachers, health professionals and young people themselves. Below is an example of a conversation between the author (Daniel Witthaus) and a teacher. The teacher is questioning whether 'That's so gay' is language worth challenging:

> Teacher: What harm could it do? . . . It's just a word, it's not like a gay kid has had his head kicked in or anything.
> Daniel: Are students in these situations using 'gay' in a derogatory way?
> Teacher: But they don't even mean it.
> Daniel: Are they associating the word 'gay' with something that is lame, crap or 'sh★t'?
> Teacher: Well, yes . . . But . . .
> Daniel: Would it be fair and reasonable to say that using the word 'gay' in this way is likely to make the school environment more hostile and unwelcoming for lesbian, gay, bisexual and transgender (LGBT) young people?
>
> *(Witthaus, 2014:1)*

Humour and casting the phrase in terms of other minorities are among the ways one can challenge the use of 'gay' in this way.

> Why is it that you say 'That's gay'? Would we let you say 'That's so wog, spastic, abo . . . ?' Would you be allowed to say these other words and not get pulled up?
>
> *(Witthaus, 2014:2)*

More subtle expression of homophobia is apparent in careful avoidance of any behaviour that might be perceived as homosexual. Friends of the same sex or family may refrain from spontaneous embraces, people may shun unfeminine or unmasculine clothing or a woman may decide not to support feminism because she fears being called lesbian. The effect of homophobia on the depth of intimacy in male friendships may be quite significant, although these attitudes can change over time. There has been at least one study that has shown that boys and younger students were less willing than girls and older students to remain friends or attend schools with gay or lesbian peers (Poteat, Espelage & Koenig, 2009).

So, for some young people, coming out can be a fraught experience – one that can bring danger, discrimination, rejection and hostility. It can also take time to be sure about one's sexual identity. Family and school are the two most important parts of the young homosexual's world, which he or she has to confront when informing others of a homosexual identity.

Family responses to coming out

The process of coming out often polarizes families, and young non-heterosexual people may experience widely differing levels of family support. Some families fully accept their son's or daughter's homosexuality and continue to have the same relationship as they had prior to the disclosure of the child's sexual preference. Indeed, in many cases, parents had long suspected that their child is gay or lesbian and the admission of this is a relief for all. Some families may offer limited acceptance of the young person's homosexuality but not acknowledge or allow partners of the same sex in the home. Other parents may reject their child's homosexuality, often with traumatic consequences. Not surprisingly, family rejection has been identified by young people as one of the main causes of psychological distress (Diamond & Butterworth, 2008; McNair *et al.*, 2014).

> 'No, you can't be gay, it's too hard a lifestyle to live in, just be straight, it's a lot easier, you're just going through a phase'. I said, 'Listen, this phase

is after lasting for 3 or 4 years at this stage' . . . and he was like, 'Oh god no, it's too hard to live with, you can't go doing it. (Gay male, 18 years)
(Mayock, Bryan, Carr & Kitching, 2008:58)

Where coming out is met with rejection by family members, the young person may be asked to leave home, or made to feel so bad that they choose to leave home.

Basically what they said was that they wouldn't be happy but they wouldn't kick me out of the house type thing over it. But that doesn't seem to me very accepting of it. Oh we'll tolerate you but we don't really like you, as if it was some kind of personal choice. (Gay male, 20 years)
(Mayock et al., *2008:58)*

Young gay men and women in this situation may then suffer all the negative health consequences that accompany being homeless (Durso & Gates, 2012). In contrast, support from parents and family can have a very strong positive impact on the process of coming out, allowing young gays and lesbians to feel comfortable with their homosexual identity even in the face of discrimination from other sources.

Peer and school responses

Difficult as it may be to come out to family, it can be equally difficult, if not more so, to reveal a homosexual identity at school and beyond, although happily attitudes are changing in some cases, especially in schools where an understanding of sexual diversity is part of comprehensive sex education classes.

In a recent study in the UK, when asked about sexual attitudes, almost half of young men and two-thirds of young women aged 16–24 years thought that male same-sex partnerships were not wrong at all. Similar data were found for female same-sex partnerships (Mercer *et al.*, 2013). Although these figures show a liberalizing trend, it is notable that about half the young men and one-third of their female peers did not share this opinion.

One of the many fears of coming out for young people is based on their observations of gay stereotypes that still exist within many schools and communities, and among many young people themselves. For example, male gay identity has been associated in the public eye with promiscuity, drug use, sexually transmitted infections and predatory sexual activity. In rural areas, these attitudes may be even more prevalent, and young same-sex attracted people may fear for their safety if they come out.

For young people who are perceived as different and somehow do not fit into the dominant cultures in a society, school can be a very marginalizing experience. Many school policies and practices do not take into account the needs of students who are homosexual or bisexual. Homophobia is common in schools across the world (Davies & McInnes, 2012; Robinson *et al.*, 2014), and indeed many youth consider schools are not a safe place for people to come out (Davies & McInnes, 2012; Galan, Puras & Riley, 2009) because of threats, harassment and sometimes violence.

An Australian study of over 1000 sexually and gender diverse young people found that of those who experienced school-based homophobia, one-third could not concentrate in class, and a quarter acknowledged their marks dropped. About one in five missed classes, skipped days and hid at recess or lunch times in order to avoid harassers. Almost one in ten felt that they could not use the toilets in their school for fear of harassment. Young people experiencing homophobia often disclosed that they could not use the changing rooms at school (Robinson *et al.*, 2014) but school-based homophobia can take many forms.

> In relation to school events, we were banned from taking someone of the same sex to the debs, and a group attempted to run an LGBT sexual health class one year but couldn't get around the 'Catholic ethos' of the school. . . . I lost a close friend to suicide earlier this year as he couldn't face coming out and the jeering he was getting for being suspected of being gay. Yet the school he was in did NOTHING in the way of policy afterwards so it could potentially, and probably will, be repeated. I was also sent to a counsellor in the hope it would 'talk me out of being bisexual' and got a warning that if I dated girls in college or had gay friends my parents will not pay for my education. (Bisexual female, 18 years)
>
> *(Mayock* et al.*, 2008:64)*

Although for some young people, typical reactions to homophobia in school are shame, humiliation and fear, there can be positive responses. In one study, 42 per cent of young Australians indicating they experienced homophobia at school stated that they did not believe that the experience had affected them at all (Robinson *et al.*, 2014). Approximately one-quarter said that the experience led to their becoming activists in the areas of anti-homophobia in the schools they attended.

> I say something to challenge a person's perceptions, if they say something homophobic. When I saw graffiti, which said 'Stand up against gay marriage' I crossed out 'gay marriage' and wrote 'homophobia', so that it now read 'Stand up against homophobia'.
>
> *(Robinson* et al.*, 2014:28)*

When it comes to combating bullying and harassment of homosexual and bisexual students in schools, comprehensive policies and laws that specify personal characteristics such as sexual orientation are said to be most effective. For example, in the US, fewer students in schools with comprehensive policies heard homophobic remarks (such as 'faggot' or 'dyke') often or frequently, compared to students in schools with generic, non-specific policies or no policy. When schools had comprehensive policies, staff were reported to intervene more often when hearing homophobic remarks (Kosciw *et al.*, 2012). Many schools, however, did not have such policies. And if they did have anti-bullying policies, these did not specify homosexual or bisexual students:

> I feel as if the school tries to seem like a safe place, but . . . the anti-bullying policy doesn't say a thing about LGBT youth. . . . It leaves me somewhat apprehensive that [reporting] will get turned right back on me.
>
> *(Kosciw* et al.*, 2012:19)*

Fortunately there are some enlightened teachers or other individuals who provide support to these homosexual or bisexual young people.

> I had a teacher who I could talk to about anything. I was in a class with her from Years 10–12; the class had a bad rep[utation] because it was mainly kids with attitude problems and family problems. But the teacher was set on making a difference; I know so many kids she's helped get through school and so many that wouldn't still be there if it weren't for her.
>
> *(Robinson* et al.*, 2014:28)*

The global picture

So far we have focused on homosexual or bisexual young people in developed countries. This is largely because information is more readily available than in countries where the stigma of being gay or lesbian is considerable and there are significant cultural impediments to coming out.

Unfortunately the changes in attitudes that we have seen in developed countries have been less apparent, even absent, in other parts of the world. For example, in a survey conducted by Pew Research of 39 countries and almost 38 000 people, broad acceptance of homosexuality was evident in North America, the European Union and the majority of Latin America (Pew Research, 2014). This contrasted with broad rejection of homosexuality in predominantly Muslim countries, in Africa, Russia and in parts of Asia. The researchers noted, although with some exceptions, that in countries where people consider religion to be very important, where they believe it is necessary to believe in God in order to be moral, and pray at least once a day, there is far less acceptance of homosexuality. These trends in attitudes may eventually be reversed, however, as today's young people age. Age differences in views towards homosexuality were particularly evident in South Korea, Japan and Brazil, where those younger than 30 were more accepting than those aged 30–49 who, in turn, were more accepting than those aged over 50.

Having said this, there are circumstances where anti-homosexual societal norms prevail and when gains are made in acceptance, these may be short lived or compounded by other cultural factors. In February 2014, *The Independent* newspaper reported that the Indian High Court's 2009 decriminalization of homosexuality had been reversed (Buncombe, 2014). Gay sex, once more, is a crime punishable by up to 10 years in jail, putting the well-being of many at risk. Even in countries where there are no legal or religious impediments around homosexuality it is hard to shift attitudes. In South Africa, where homosexual couples have been offered freedoms and rights for over 10 years, including marriage, one study showed that perceptions of homosexuality are still negative (Roberts & Reddy, 2008). A study of gay Asian Pacific Islander men found that many voiced concern about being unable to fulfil traditional family obligations to continue on the family name by fathering a child (Han, Operario & Chou, 2011).

Young Arabs have reported the need to hide their sexuality from family members for fear of violence and bringing shame on the family. Others have described that to accept their same-sex attraction would require breaking their relationship with their family, their community and their religion (Kassisieh, 2011).

Research on homosexuality within developing countries is largely absent. In many countries, management of predominantly heterosexual concerns such as contraception and reproductive health, and management of HIV take priority. Furthermore, as we have seen, in many countries homosexuality is either stigmatized or forbidden, making accurate data collection impossible. For example, a review of the literature and research on the sexual and reproductive health of Malaysian adolescents acknowledged that cultural and religious sensitivities preclude collection of data on such issues as premarital sex, abortion and homosexuality (WHO, 2005). Reviewing research on teenage sexual attitudes in China, Yu (2012) commented that Chinese traditional sexual values focus on reproduction and social stability, and that there is therefore disapproval of premarital and extramarital relationships, homosexuality and masturbation. In a rare study of sexual identity, 73 per cent of participants in a Turkish study indicated past or present same-sex attraction, despite identifying as heterosexual (Eskin, Kaynak-Demir & Demir, 2005), suggesting that this may be a ploy to avoid disapproval or worse in many of these traditional societies.

In the some countries in the Middle East, similar constraints apply to those in most Asian countries. The cultural and political line may be to deny the existence of homosexuality, and homosexual practices and cultures are labelled and understood very differently from western lesbian, gay and bisexual identities and cultures (Habib, 2011).

Coming out in an intimidating environment

A very small body of literature has focused on the impact of coming out within specific ethnic–cultural communities. For example, psychological distress has been linked to coming out in Chinese gay men in Hong Kong (Wong & Tang, 2004), and the management of stress has been examined in gay and lesbian youth coming out in South Africa (Butler & Astbury, 2008). Concern about disclosing their sexual orientation and weakening their relationship with parents is a shared concern among Hispanic, African-American and South Asian-Indian adolescents in the US (Potoczniak, Crosbie-Burnett & Saltzburg, 2009). Given that family and extended family are often symbolic of origin and central to ethnic–racial identity, coming out can threaten not only general parental social support, but also the source of identity within their ethnic community (Potoczniak *et al.*, 2009; Savin-Williams, 2003).

Although negative attitudes towards lesbians and gay men are prevalent in countries where religion prohibits the existence of homosexuality, there are exceptions. People within some of those countries who have a more active sex life and liberal attitudes towards premarital sex have been found to have a more positive attitude towards homosexuals. Actually knowing a person who is gay or lesbian is also associated with more positive attitudes towards homosexuals (Gelbal & Duyan, 2006). This latter finding suggests that if more young people came out as homosexual to their family and friends, there would be greater understanding, but the cost of doing this seems to be prohibitively high in many societies.

Health and wellbeing

Given that homosexuality is a marginalizing experience, it is no surprise that it can be associated with serious consequences for health. Homosexual and bisexual adolescents are more likely than heterosexual adolescents to attempt suicide, have problems with alcohol use (e.g. binge drinking) and to have ever tried marijuana, cocaine or heroin (Coker, Austin & Schuster, 2010; Kann *et al.*, 2011; Ritter, Matthew-Simmons & Carragher, 2012). Use of alcohol and illicit drugs is common among all young people, but it is of even greater concern for homosexual and bisexual young people as they are at a higher risk of diagnosis of alcohol or other drug use disorders (Kann *et al.*, 2012; Ritter *et al.*, 2012). Moreover, the fear and ignorance surrounding HIV combined with social attitudes towards homosexuals can mean that in some countries HIV-positive young gay men experience discrimination both due to their sexuality and their HIV status (Stutterheim, Bos & Schaalma, 2008).

Mental health

Internationally, mental health is an area in which homosexual and bisexual populations (both youth and adult) suffer to a greater extent than heterosexual populations. They are more than twice as likely to have anxiety disorders, with significantly more lesbian/bisexual women affected. Interestingly though, anxiety disorders may actually be less common for lesbian or bisexual women than heterosexual women (Ritter *et al.*, 2012). Research indicates higher rates of depression among homosexuals, particularly lesbians and bisexual women.

Homosexual and bisexual individuals are also at greater risk of suicide. More homosexual and bisexual individuals compared to heterosexuals have had suicidal thoughts, planned suicide, have attempted suicide (Ritter *et al.*, 2012; Robinson *et al.*, 2014) or committed suicide (Goodenow, Szalacha & Westheimer, 2006; Zhao, Montoro, Igartua & Thombs, 2010).

We also know these young people are over-represented among homeless populations. A US national survey of homeless youth organizations found that approximately 40 per cent of homeless youth accessing these agencies were lesbian, gay, bisexual or transgender, and around 30 per cent of homeless youth utilizing housing programmes identified in this way (Durso & Gates, 2012).

As discussed earlier, bullying (frequently in school), homophobia and victimization are frequent experiences for gay and lesbian young people and can lead to feelings of guilt, shame, depression and isolation which often has a negative impact on health (Kosciw *et al.*, 2012).

> I hate using the world depressed but I was really down for about two years over just different things. The underlying issue was I was gay and stuff and I didn't happen to know it. (Gay male, 20 years)

I started getting very anxious and depressed but I could never identify or speak to anyone about it because to be gay was like [pause], it's harsh coming out and it was a huge thing for me. (Gay male, 21 years)

(Mayock et al., 2008:73)

Sexual and reproductive health

Sexual and reproductive health is another area of concern for homosexual and bisexual youth. Kann *et al.*'s report of over 156 000 US public school students found more homosexual or bisexual than heterosexual adolescents had their first sexual intercourse before the age of 13 (Kann *et al.*, 2011). An Australian study of more than 3000 same-sex attracted and gender-questioning young people found they were less likely to use a condom, twice as likely to become pregnant and more likely to contract a sexually transmitted infection compared to their heterosexual peers (Hillier *et al.*, 2010). One US study of over 2600 young women aged 15–20 years found that the 6.8 per cent who identified as bisexual were at higher sexual and reproductive risk than those who identified as heterosexual or homosexual (fewer than 2 per cent). These young women reported earliest sexual debut, highest numbers of male partners, greatest use of emergency contraception and the highest frequency for terminating pregnancies (Tornello, Riskind & Patterson, 2014). This study also reported that lesbian young women were younger at sexual debut and had more sexual partners than their heterosexual peers.

Accessing health services

One factor that compounds the health problems encountered by homosexual or bisexual youth are the challenges they have accessing a health service. Those who have not come out may not feel comfortable discussing sexual health issues with a health practitioner and may choose not to disclose to the very people who may be able to offer confidential support. Many gay communities provide specialty health services which will aim to be youth-friendly, but young people who are new to sex and new to their homosexuality or bisexuality can find such services overwhelming. Telephone helplines can be helpful for young people in this situation.

I called Kids Helpline as a kid because I was being bullied at high school for kissing a girl. They were great. They gave me helpful advice and made me feel like I had someone on my side and I wasn't in the wrong.

It was just nice to know that if it got any worse, I could always ring and hear a friendly voice.

(Robinson et al., 2014:38)

Protective factors

Although the section above paints a sombre picture of the health challenges facing homosexual and bisexual youth, there are many factors that can protect them from poor health outcomes and harm (Saewyc *et al.*, 2009). Although it is likely that homosexual role models in the public eye, supportive parents and public support of homosexuality through public events such as Gay Mardi Gras all create a more positive environment in which young people can become open about their homosexuality, little research has explored this.

A strong sense of connectedness is important for all adolescents and especially so for sexual minority youth. This relates to connectedness with people (parents, family, other pro-social supportive adults), school and spirituality (Eisenberg & Resnick, 2006). When adolescents can draw upon such protective resources, it enhances their resilience to cope with adverse situations (Saewyc *et al.*, 2009).

> My Dad goes, 'Oh he's my son'. And at that point I realised that Dad did not have a problem like, he could say it to other people. . . . It meant quite a lot to me like, that he didn't care . . . he didn't have to think about it or anything. (Male, 17 years)
>
> *(Mayock* et al.*, 2008:21)*

A number of protective factors have been found to reduce the vulnerability of gay, lesbian and bisexual adolescents to poor outcomes. Hatzenbuehler (2011) demonstrated the importance of positive social environments, defined by factors such as gay–straight alliances and school policies to protect gay, lesbian and bisexual students. He found that the risk of attempting suicide was significantly greater for gay, lesbian and bisexual young people in negative social environments than for those in positive social environments. In addition, Ryan, Huebner, Diaz and Sanchez (2009) found that family acceptance had a positive impact on gay, lesbian and bisexual youth. Those who experienced severe family rejection were over eight times more likely to report attempts at suicide than their peers from families with little or no rejection. A study by Eisenberg and Resnick (2006) of over 2200 gay, lesbian and bisexual adolescents confirmed the importance of these factors. Family connectedness, the presence of other caring adults and safe schools provided significant protection against suicidal ideation and attempts among gay, lesbian and bisexual youth.

Creating change

Testimony to their resilience in the face of a hostile environment, most homosexuals do not abuse drugs nor do they attempt suicide or become depressed. In one study, 60 per cent said that they felt great or pretty good about their sexual feelings and only 10 per cent felt pretty bad or really bad (Hillier & Harrison, 2004). One strategy used by these young people is to 'find, subvert or create and inhabit safe spaces in which they feel comfortable' (Hillier & Harrison, 2004). Some attest to the internet as a safe space to work through issues related to a homosexual identity. Others find activities such as sports provide opportunities to test their sexuality safely. In a study of young women participating in women's football, one respondent commented:

> As soon [as] you start to meet more people that are like you . . . it gives you somewhere you can go where you can relax, you can be yourself you're not paranoid the whole time because, because people will look at you strangely or whatever. (Female, 20 years)
>
> *(Hillier, 2007:14)*

The ability to resist the negative discourses associated with homosexuality – as illness, as evil, as unnatural, as a phase rather than the real thing – is described in a fascinating paper by Hillier and Harrison (2004). They tell how young people report finding the fault lines in these discourses, positioning themselves as normal and healthy. So Sandy was able to co-opt thinking about the normalized practice (heterosexuality) and apply this to homosexuality, thereby exposing double standards.

> How many parents say to their straight children I think you should have sex with someone of the same sex before you decide that you are straight? I'd say none, but swap it around to being queer and all of a sudden you don't know your own mind and have to justify yourself constantly. (Female, 20 years)
>
> *(Hillier & Harrison, 2004:90)*

This change at the personal level is accompanied by the beginnings of structural change. In Australia, there has been a significant shift in attitudes to gay and lesbian youth among policy makers, professionals who work with young people, researchers and communities – from a moral issue to one of safety and rights. This was aided, in part, by concerns about young gay people's vulnerability to HIV at a time when there was widespread public education about safe sex. An Australian sex education curriculum, 'Talking Sexual Health', has been based on this framework. The curriculum, for secondary students, includes discussions of sexual diversity and homophobia and also provides opportunities for teacher education to reduce ignorance and fear of classroom discussion. In the UK, government policy has promoted 'Healthy Schools', recognizing the importance of good health and social behaviour as well as citizenship (including human rights), in achieving positive academic outcomes. As Warwick, Aggleton and Douglas (2001) note:

> These twin sources of impetus towards health and citizenship – towards on the one hand good physical and mental health, and on the other a respect for personal integrity and worth – offer encouragement for the future.
>
> *(Warwick* et al., *2001:139)*

Technology

> The Internet had tons of accurate information regarding sexuality, things that were neglected in my schooling. . . . It told me that I was not alone, and that I didn't have to act in a certain (stereotypical) way, that I just need to be the person who I've always been. (Male, 18 years)
>
> *(Hillier* et al., *2010:59)*

The internet can be an anonymous, safe and supportive space in which to explore sexuality and sexual identity (Harper, Bruce, Serrano & Jamil, 2009; Hillier *et al.*, 2010; Robinson *et al.*, 2014). In one study, over 75 per cent of 1000 homosexual or bisexual youth felt the internet was a place where they felt accepted. The vast majority (85 per cent) had used the internet to explore their identity, although some still felt isolated (Robinson *et al.*, 2014).

The internet is also useful for adolescents to source information and support before coming out.

> When I was first starting to come out, I searched a lot of official websites for information, but more importantly I went on various forums to ask people their personal stories. . . . I was getting first-hand advice from someone going through or who had gone through what I was about to.
>
> *(Robinson* et al., *2014:36)*

The internet also offers the opportunity to seek anonymous support for those who are troubled. One-quarter of participants in the same study had utilized the internet to access social support services. Research in the US that included over 10 000 lesbian, gay, bisexual and transgender youth aged 13–17 years found they were much more likely than heterosexual youth to report that they can be more honest about themselves online than offline (Human Rights Campaign, 2014).

As Hillier *et al.* (2010) state:

> Young people were most likely to feel accepted, find others like them-
> selves and feel proud of their sexuality when on the Internet. Because
> of discrimination and homophobia these often elude them in their
> offline lives. Around half felt safe online and were able to disclose their
> sexuality, something that is not always easy to do offline.
>
> *(Hillier* et al., *2010:60)*

Two of their respondents had this to say about the value of the internet.

> When I was first questioning my sexuality I was about 15 and didn't
> have anybody around me who I could talk things over with or ques-
> tion, so I joined 'community' groups on livejournal with like minded
> people. . . . I didn't have a face-to-face group . . . the people on these
> live journal communities were my support group and the support had
> a huge impact on me. (Female, 18 years)

> When I first started to think I might be gay or bisexual I used the
> Internet a lot to find out about how I was feeling and what it meant.
> (Male, 16 years)
>
> *(Hillier* et al., *2010:62,63)*

The internet can also offer therapeutic and counselling assistance to young
gay people, a service considered long overdue (Rozbroj, Lyons, Pitts,
Mitchell & Christensen, 2014). One example is Out & Online (n.d.), an
online cognitive behavioural therapy programme for anxiety and depressive
symptoms that is designed to be relevant to same-sex attracted young adults,
aged 18–25 years.

Another useful source of online information is Wikipedia. One Asian
student reported:

> I've actually looked up different rights in different countries as well. . . . I
> didn't think that somewhere like Asia would be so intolerant. It just
> made me feel a little bit more secure, being here in Australia, knowing
> that you do have so many rights.
>
> *(Robinson* et al., *2014:31)*

However, not all young people find support, acceptance and positive engagement online. Bullying and harassment still occur from other sexual minority
individuals, particularly around the notions of expressing and categorizing

identities (Richters et al., 2014). In the same way that positive messages can proliferate, so can negative messages.

> I actually remember reading stories . . . they all ended up essentially saying 'but then I realised I wasn't gay'. . . . It was completely unhelpful to read a site geared towards young people's mental health and getting the impression that being gay was something you got over.
>
> (Robinson et al., 2014:37)

A tool for activism

An important use of the internet is as a popular tool for activism. In Hillier et al.'s 2010 study of 3134 young people aged 14–21 years (average age 17 years) who identified as same-sex attracted or as uncertain of their sexuality, nearly half thought they could help others using the internet. About one-third thought the internet was a place they could advocate for change around homophobia. A young man and a young woman shared their thoughts on this:

> Share my passion for helping against homophobia and trying to meet others with this passion. (Male, 19 years)
>
> I read about how open people are and it makes me proud. (Female, 17 years)
>
> (Hillier et al., 2010:61)

Learning about sex and hooking up

There is another interesting and possibly unexpected use of the internet made by young gay men. There is no doubt that the proliferation of digital technology has increased accessibility to pornography. Although for the heterosexual population most people would see this as a poor training ground for good sexual interaction, some young gay men have said that, in the absence of any depictions of male to male sexual expression, this is the only place they can learn what is potentially involved in physical relationships between gay men (Crabbe & Corlett, 2011). Other reasons young gay, lesbian and bisexual people access sexually explicit material online include clarifying their attractions, and as a sexual outlet, either because they found it difficult to find a partner or to minimize risks they associate with actually having sex. Once again, participants in Hillier et al.'s study offered detailed responses.

> In regards to using the Internet to explore my sexuality, porn was definitely the best thing (as embarrassing as it is). It allows you to have a

look at what interests you within your own comfort zone so you don't go off and do something stupid in real life. (Female, 17 years)

In relation to how I have used the Internet to explore my sexual identity, I'd say porn – it helps you realize what you're attracted to. (Female, 15 years)

(Hillier et al., *2010:64)*

In addition to this, the internet facilitates the possibility of quick hook-ups. Bauermeister, Yeagley, Meanley and Pingel (2014) examined the partner-seeking behaviours of single young men who had sex with men in the US, using data from an online study of over 1500 of young men who have sex with men aged 18–24 years. Over 87 per cent reported they had engaged in some sort of sexting behaviour, with 76 per cent reporting to have both sent and received a sext. When compared with heterosexual samples (Benotsch, Snipes, Martin & Bull, 2013; Temple *et al.*, 2012), these participants reported a higher prevalence of lifetime sexting suggesting greater comfort in sharing texts or pictures with prospective partners through online technologies. This is supported by research showing that young men who have sex with men use online technologies to explore their sexuality and meet partners (Bauermeister, Leslie-Santana, Johns & Eisenburg, 2011; Mustanski, Lyons & Garcia, 2011).

The establishment of mobile-based geo-spatial (GPS) partner-seeking applications such as Grindr.com and ManJam.com facilitate young men's exchange of sexual messages or pictures with potential male partners through mobile technologies, an activity which potentially can also increase sexual risk by facilitating immediate anonymous sex. In Chapter 6 we discussed some of the dangers of sexting and partner-seeking applications.

Conclusion

People need to realise that just because we're a certain way doesn't make us any lesser of a man or woman or trans. . . . Just because I'm a gay, feminine male doesn't mean that I can't fix a car or mow the lawn or something like that. . . . We're very human.

(Robinson et al., *2014:18)*

Although there is greater recognition of homosexuality in developed countries in the last two decades, this is still an area in need of attention from researchers. Many studies have included measures of sexual behaviour, but have not explored sexual identity, leaving us with only part of the picture. Sexual diversity is almost completely unexplored in countries where there is religious or cultural intolerance of difference. It is evident that families, schools and communities play a critical role in offering support to young people who are exploring their sexual identity and we need to know more about the factors that protect these young people against negative outcomes, as well as how they function. The serious health consequences often associated with the stress of coming out demonstrate the significance of this particularly challenging transition to adulthood.

9

SEXUALLY TRANSMISSIBLE INFECTIONS

Management and consequences

> You hear about people getting STDs all the time and you never expect you to be that one. . . . You never expect to be the person that has something, because you expect somebody else to get [it]. You never expect to actually get it yourself and so I just cried.
>
> *(Porterfield, 2005:50)*

As presented in Chapter 1, sexual health is more than the absence of disease. The World Health Organization (WHO) working description of sexual health takes into account the qualities of healthy sexual relationships and access to pleasure, as well as absence of discomfort. In other chapters of this book we cover some of these broader aspects of the sexual heath of adolescents, including normative biological changes, romantic and sexual relationships, pregnancy, unwanted, forced or manipulative sex and healthy and unhealthy attitudes towards gender differences and sexual diversity.

In this chapter, our focus is on sexually transmissible infections (STIs) among adolescents, including their incidence, causes and treatment. We highlight issues associated with STIs in general, as well as the specific diseases of chlamydia, human immunodeficiency virus (HIV), human papillomavirus (HPV), herpes and gonorrhoea. Most importantly, we address adolescents' reactions to these infections and the barriers – psychological, social and economic – against their effective control and management. Given the extended period of adolescence in developed countries, the strength of adolescent sex drives and current relatively liberal attitudes to adolescent sexual experimentation, there is ample opportunity for an adolescent to be at risk for an infection spread by sexual contact with a person who has already acquired one. Adolescents of today are far more likely than their grandparents to have multiple sexual partners, to participate in casual sex, to experience oral sex and experiment with bisexuality, all activities that raise the risk of STIs if appropriate precautions are not in place.

Is there a problem?

There is. Globally the highest reported rates of STIs are found among young people aged 15–24 years. Up to 60 per cent of all newly acquired STIs, and nearly half of all the people worldwide living with HIV, are in this age group (Dehne & Reidner, 2005). It is estimated that one in four young US women aged 15–19 years has an STI (Centers for Disease Control and Prevention, 2009). Although rates are high in the US and other developed countries, the major burden of disease occurs in low- and middle-income countries in Latin America, sub-Saharan Africa and Southeast Asia, with more than 490 million new cases of curable STIs occurring throughout the world each year (WHO, 2012).

As well as pain, discomfort and reduced functionality in the short term, STIs have the potential to impact significantly on sexual and reproductive health in the longer term. Many of these diseases are readily treatable, but untreated can lead to infertility or higher rates of infant mortality, cervical cancer and increased risk of other STIs, especially HIV (Centers for Disease Control and Prevention, 2010). Untreated STIs are also associated with congenital and perinatal infections in neonates, particularly in countries where disease prevalence is high (WHO, 2012).

The list of diseases that are potentially transmissible by genital–genital, oral–genital or anal–genital contact is very long. Although most diseases are found in every country, both the incidence (the number of new cases in a period of time) and the prevalence (the number of cases which exist over a period of time) vary greatly, particularly between developed and developing nations. Even within countries, the rates of STIs may vary widely within communities. In common with many other infections, STIs are more often found among those who are unable to access health services or to afford diagnosis and treatment. For example, the STI donovanosis has been largely eradicated from every country in the world except Australia, where a handful of cases have been found in the last few years within remote Indigenous communities (Bowden, 2005). Even where treatments are readily accessible and affordable, however, rates are rising. This is due to several factors: the rise of viral, and thus incurable infections, the development of antibiotic-resistant strains of infection which are spread by ready availability of travel between countries, and increases in risky behaviour.

Factors other than exposure that can affect the likelihood of acquiring an STI include gender (girls are more vulnerable biologically to many STIs than boys), a person's immunological status and the infectiousness of the STI. Adolescents at highest risk of STIs include young sex workers and their clients, adolescent boys who have sex with men or other boys, street children and children in correctional homes (Dehne & Reidner, 2005). Young people affected by poverty and other forms of social exclusion are similarly vulnerable because of their higher likelihood of engaging in risky sex and lower likelihood of seeking treatment for symptoms (Wellings, 2008).

Many types, many issues

STIs can be transmitted by viruses, bacteria or parasites: some are common, some are rare. Viruses include herpes, HPV, HIV and hepatitis A, B and C. Bacterial STIs are chlamydia, gonorrhoea and syphilis. Parasites include pubic lice (now rarely seen because of pubic waxing), scabies and trichomoniasis. In this chapter, we discuss five of the most common or serious of these diseases (chlamydia, HIV, HPV, genital herpes and gonorrhoea), as well as present information on generic issues such as protection and screening that are relevant to all STIs.

Chlamydia

Chlamydia trachomatis continues to be the most frequently reported STI and a significant public health concern for young people in the UK, US, Canada and Australia (Centers for Disease Control and Prevention, 2013a; Government of Canada, 2013; Public Health England, 2014a; The Kirby Institute, 2013).

Chlamydia infections in women cause inflammation of the cervix, which may spread to the rest of the reproductive system. There may be no symptoms, or women may experience vaginal discharge, pain during sex, painful frequent urination or vague abdominal pain. In around 10 per cent of young women, untreated chlamydia will develop into pelvic inflammatory disease which causes severe pelvic pain and fever (Oakeshott *et al.*, 2010) and may also lead to infertility (Haggerty *et al.*, 2010; Peipert 2003). Chlamydia is the most common cause of inflammation of the urethra in men in many developed countries. It can cause frequent and sometimes painful urination, although the majority of men have no symptoms. Complications include severe pain and swelling of the scrotum.

Despite the ease of diagnosis using a urine sample (Morre *et al.*, 1999) and single-dose treatment (Magid, Douglas & Schwartz, 1996), the greatest burden of chlamydia infection in developed countries is among young people.

In the UK in 2012 for example, young heterosexual people under 25 years contributed 64 per cent of total chlamydia diagnoses. One reason for this is that over 80 per cent of cases are asymptomatic (Peipert, 2003), and thus most young people are unaware that they have this infection and that they are likely to be transmitting it to each new sexual partner. Re-infection by an untreated sexual partner is common.

Other factors associated with increased vulnerability to chlamydia include early loss of virginity, limited health literacy and health skills, barriers to service access and use, and men who have sex with men, whose ano-rectal chlamydia infections are frequently undetected (Aitken, 2014; Australian Government Department of Health and Ageing, 2010).

In developed countries, young people with an Indigenous background, lower socioeconomic status or from disadvantaged minority groups are often at increased risk of chlamydia. In the US, for example, chlamydia rates for young African-American women are nine times as high as rates for White youth (Boyar, Levine & Zensius, 2011), and Australian Indigenous populations have rates approximately 10 times that of the non-Indigenous population (The Kirby Institute, 2013).

More than two-thirds of new cases of chlamydia occur in the developing world, where diagnosis and treatment are difficult given the scarcity of services and the often asymptomatic nature of the infection (Gaydos, Theodore, Dalesio, Wood & Quinn, 2004; Patel *et al.*, 2010). A number of years ago, sub-Saharan Africa had the highest prevalence of chlamydia worldwide (Romoren *et al.*, 2007). This has not seen much improvement over time, since chlamydia is still problematic in Africa, along with other STIs (WHO, 2012). Unlike several developed countries, most countries in the developing world do not have national chlamydia screening programmes (Patel *et al.*, 2010).

For those fortunate enough to live in developed countries with access to good health care, diagnosis and treatment of chlamydia is much easier. Yet, the diagnosis can still have a strong emotional impact. A diagnosis of chlamydia led these young people to talk of shame, embarrassment and loss of reputation:

> I was horrified. I am still horrified. I never thought something like that would happen to me. (Female, 18 years)

> I wasn't really expecting it. I was shocked and upset. It's an embarrassing thing that I've caught something and I could have spread it on to someone else. (Female, 19 years)

> Ashamed. 'Cos nobody wants to know you've got a disease. It doesn't make your character look too good, you know. (Male, 21 years)
> *(Temple-Smith* et al., *2010:420)*

Once diagnosed, chlamydia is treated by a short course of antibiotics during which it is advisable to abstain from sexual contact to prevent spreading the infection to partners. As with other STIs, partners should be informed, tested and treated if infected. While this sounds simple, it raises many issues such as the difficulties of communicating with sexual partners, matters of trust and possibly fears of retribution, where the infection was acquired outside the relationship. Some of these are discussed later in the chapter.

Human immunodeficiency virus (HIV)

HIV is a retrovirus, which if left untreated leads to a depletion of immune function and a range of subsequent infections and cancers which together make up the acquired immune deficiency syndrome (AIDS). HIV infection was once almost always fatal, and although still incurable, most individuals who now acquire HIV can manage their condition effectively given access to medication. HIV medication usually involves a combination of three or more drugs taken regularly to prevent HIV replication, which allows the immune system some opportunity to recover (Aitken, 2014). Although the cost of medication is beyond the reach of many in developing countries, major inroads have been made. For example, South Africa has reduced the cost of antiretrovirals (ART) to US$113 per person, per year, the low-est price anywhere in the world (WHO, 2013b). Over a decade ago, only 50 000 people were receiving treatment for HIV in Africa. Now, more than 7.5 million people are receiving treatment, with progress being reported in every region (WHO, 2013b). This significant increase in access to treatment is multifaceted and reflects 'political commitment, community mobilization, technical innovation, domestic and international funding and other forms of support that have catalysed the global scaling up of ART' (WHO, 2013b:7). However, the costs of newer HIV medications are reported to be still too high and beyond reach of many of those living in developing countries (Médecins Sans Frontières, 2013).

One of the greatest successes in recent HIV prevention programmes has been the use of antiretroviral therapy to prevent mother-to-child transmission of HIV. Numerous studies have now demonstrated that reductions in viral load with ART during pregnancy and breastfeeding reduce mother-to-child transmission (Townsend *et al.*, 2008).

Prevalence of HIV among young people

There are more than five million young people worldwide living with HIV/ AIDS, and every day an additional 2400 acquire the infection (WHO, 2011). Young people aged 15–24 years accounted for 40 per cent of all new HIV infections among adults in 2009 (WHO, 2011). Most live in sub-Saharan

Africa where 3.6 million youth have acquired HIV, followed by Asia and the Pacific where there are an estimated 550 000 young people living with HIV (United Nations Youth, 2014).

In the UK, an estimated 98 400 people were reported to be living with HIV in 2012 (National AIDS Trust, n.d.), and young people (aged under 24 years) accounted for 4 per cent of those receiving HIV specialist care.

In the US, more than 1.1 million people are living with HIV infection (Centers for Disease Control and Prevention, 2013b), with gay, bisexual and men who have sex with men (MSM) of all races and ethnicities identified as most seriously affected. In 2011, 2293 young people aged 13–19 years were diagnosed with HIV. The highest diagnosis rate that year was for those aged 20–24 years, with over 8000 new diagnoses.

Countries differ significantly from each other in relation to HIV transmission. Heterosexual transmission and mother-to-child transmission through breastfeeding and birth trauma is of major concern in developing countries. Australia has a relatively low rate of HIV infection, with 80 per cent of those with HIV listing male-to-male sex as their risk factor (The Kirby Institute, 2011). Transmission by injecting drug use is more often the reason for acquisition in Southern Europe. Some Northern Europeans are less likely than their peers to acquire HIV, as their genetic make-up offers protection from susceptibility to the infection, as well as modifying the course of disease (Novembre, Galavani & Slatkin, 2005). In addition to differing acquisition routes, there are other factors that contribute to HIV vulnerability. Gender inequality is one example. Women are far more likely than men to be the target of forced sex with someone with the infection, as illustrated by the statistic that women who have experienced intimate partner violence are 50 per cent more likely to be living with HIV (UNAIDS, 2012).

Adolescent vulnerabilities or their own risky behaviours are not the only sources of HIV infection for young people. Some children acquire the infection at birth, or through childhood blood transfusions or other needle-borne routes. Qualitative research suggests that transitioning from childhood to adulthood with HIV offers many challenges for which both health practitioners and their adolescent patients are ill prepared. Two major issues – managing sexuality as an adolescent with HIV and moving from paediatric to adult health services – are often the focus for this concern. Nevertheless, as Persson and Newman (2012) point out, many young people growing up with HIV show resilience and develop life skills to manage their illness.

> I found out I was positive about a month ago by my 9 month old bf [boyfriend]. . . . I am only 22 and I know my life is just starting. Not in the best way but it was God's will and I accept it. (Adolescent female)

I felt I was a good person, so why was GOD punishing me? I cried a lot. There were dark clouds all around. But, I slowly began to get better, thanks to some new meds . . . And they helped me to claw my way back into Life again. (Adolescent female)

(Avert, n.d.)

Key issues for young people with HIV

A recent global analysis of HIV found that despite differences between countries and health systems, young people with HIV all had several factors in common. Key issues facing this cohort are adherence to medication, disclosure of HIV status to potential partners and the lack of support networks (Greifinger & Dick, 2009).

There are many reasons why adolescents may stop taking HIV medications, and these include side-effects, treatment fatigue, self-stigma, lack of community support, denial, fear and mistrust of the medical profession to name a few (e.g. Garvie, Wilkins & Young, 2010; Murphy *et al.*, 2005; Rudy, Murphy, Harris, Muenz & Ellen, 2009). However, maintaining adherence to HIV treatment is critical to optimize health outcomes for adolescents with HIV, as besides keeping the infection at bay it contributes to preventing further transmission.

One US study of 166 adolescents with HIV found their levels of psychological distress differed according to the way in which HIV had been acquired (Orban *et al.*, 2010). Adolescents who had acquired HIV via risky behaviours reported more disclosure-related stressors, whereas those who had acquired it perinatally reported more medication-related stressors. Social support was found to be an effective coping strategy, but such support was often unsought for fear of stigma. The authors concluded that interventions to foster more adaptive coping with HIV-specific stressors were needed, particularly those related to long-term adherence to antiretroviral medications (Orban *et al.*, 2010).

For adolescents with HIV the issue of coping with how, when and to whom to disclose their HIV status can lead to anxiety and depression. For those questioning their sexuality, the situation is even more difficult as they often face discrimination on account of this, as well as their HIV-positive status.

It is apparent that living with HIV as an adolescent complicates what is an already challenging period of life. Further studies investigating the needs and challenges of young people as they transition to maturity and adult care are needed, particularly in terms of how to negotiate their sexual lives through the often turbulent phase of adolescence.

Human papillomavirus (HPV) / genital warts

HPV is transmitted predominantly but not exclusively through penetrative intercourse. Most people acquire HPV on their genitals at some stage during their sexual life and this virus will remain present in small amounts in the skin, being transmitted to others with whom it comes in contact. HPV infection is often benign, with most people not knowing they even have it. The virus often clears up within a few months, however it can lead to genital warts and also has a significant role in many cancers. People who do not clear the virus are at risk of developing cancer at some point in the future (Pitts, 2003). HPVs are estimated to cause almost all cervical cancers, at least 80 per cent of anal cancer and at least 40–60 per cent of vulvar, vaginal and penile cancers (WHO, 2014b).

Young MSM are particularly vulnerable to HPV. In a recent study of 200 young MSM aged 16–20 years, it was evident that sexual transmission of HPV occurred on average 1.9 years following sexual initiation (Zou et al., 2014). The median number of receptive sexual partners was four. The presence of anal HPV ranged from 10 per cent in those reporting no prior anal sex to almost 50 per cent in those with more than four partners, demonstrating the HPV vaccination should be undertaken early, and prior to sexual initiation.

HPV infection rates are highest among young women and usually peak not long after they become sexually active (Dunne & Markowitz, 2006). In the US, approximately 14 million people acquire HPV each year (Centers for Disease Control and Prevention, 2013c). In 2008, there were more than 14 million new cases of HPV, 49 per cent of whom were aged 15–24 years, representing about 25 per cent of the sexually active population (Centers for Disease Control and Prevention, 2013d). In some studies, HPV prevalence among adolescent girls has been found to be as high as 64 per cent (Tarkowski et al., 2004), but a systematic review of many clinic-based prevalence US studies found this figure to more commonly sit around 30 per cent (Revzina & DiClemente, 2005).

According to a study by Clifford et al. (2005), HPV prevalence is five times higher in sub-Saharan Africa than in Europe (lowest in Spain and highest in Nigeria). Prevalence of HPV (with rates adjusted for differing age distributions in different countries) is 26 per cent in sub-Saharan Africa, compared with 14 per cent in South America, 9 per cent in Southeast Asia and 5 per cent in Europe. In Australia, it is estimated that 8–12 per cent of young women aged 18–24 years have the virus at any one time (Pitts, 2003).

Impact and management of HPV

There are now two vaccines available for HPV, which are designed for use prior to sexual initiation. Mostly these are offered to 10- to 14-year-old girls. In some countries, catch-up vaccination is offered to older female adolescents, and more recently, to young men. In addition to preventing cancer of the cervix, it is anticipated that population-level vaccination will have a major impact on rates of other HPV-related cancers in the future.

Despite the high rates of HPV infection in the US, HPV vaccine uptake has been relatively low. In 2012, a national survey found that although just over half the girls aged 13–17 years had received at least one dose of the HPV vaccine series, only one-third had received all three of the necessary doses (Centers for Disease Control and Prevention, 2013e). In addition, vaccine uptake has been very low among boys (Centers for Disease Control and Prevention, 2012a). England has reported a much higher uptake through their HPV national vaccination programme, with 86 per cent of their target group (12- to 13-year-old girls) receiving the full course of vaccinations (Public Health England, 2013). In Australia, where HPV is now on the adolescent immunization schedule, in one national study only half of young women in the final 3 years of school reported having received the immunization (Mitchell, Patrick, Heywood, Blackman & Pitts, 2014).

Little research has examined the impact of HPV diagnosis. The livOne study (Porterfield, 2005) explored the experiences of 15 women in the US aged 20–55 years, who had been diagnosed with HPV for more than one year.

> I was worried about him [boyfriend] and it was embarrassing. I didn't tell him for a long, long time. I mean I still feel guilty about that part. (Female)
>
> For guys . . . If they don't see it, they are like, I don't have anything . . . my roommate just found out that she has it. Even though she knows that it is a small per cent cervical cancer, she still hates that she has it. (Female)
>
> *(Porterfield, 2005:47,61)*

HPV is a disease that can lead to serious consequences for sexual health and fertility, but it is now almost totally avoidable if communities can be persuaded to adopt a vaccination regime for young men and women before they become sexually active. As with chlamydia, however, there are practical, social and personal barriers to be overcome before this simple solution is in place.

Herpes

Lots of people on the web ask 'Is herpes the same as HPV?' The answer is no, they are different viruses. Herpes is caused by the herpes simplex viruses, of which there are two. Herpes Simplex Virus, Type 1 (HSV-1) usually affects the mouth, nose and throat and commonly causes cold sores. Herpes Simplex Virus, Type 2 (HSV-2) is more successful at affecting the genitals, however each virus can affect either the oral or the anogenital site (Aitken, 2014). Genital herpes is diagnosed with increasing frequency in the developed world, with approximately one in four US women and one in five US men with HSV, an increase of about 30 per cent since the late 1970s (Owusu-Edusei *et al.*, 2013; Satterwhite *et al.*, 2013). Rates for Australian adults (aged 15 years and over) are not as high but nevertheless significant, with approximately 12 per cent of Australian adults carrying the virus, about twice as many women as men (Cunningham *et al.*, 2006). This is similar to the prevalence in Britain. Young people aged 20–24 years have the highest rates of new herpes infections worldwide.

Symptoms of genital herpes include often painful, itchy blisters on the genitals, tiredness and flu-like symptoms, but the infection can also be symptomless. For that reason, HSV-2 can be transmitted by people who are unaware that they have it, or by those whose symptoms are in remission, leading them to incorrectly believe they are not currently infectious. A serious consequence of genital herpes is the risk of transmission from mother to baby during birth, which can compromise the baby's life. There is no cure for herpes, but medication is available to reduce symptoms and make it less likely that it will be spread to a sex partner. Research has demonstrated that HSV-2 infection is a risk factor for HIV transmission (Freeman *et al.*, 2006), so it is important that more effective preventive measures are found. It is believed that HSV-1 produces antibodies that help protect against HSV-2. A recent study by Bradley, Markowitz, Gibson and McQuillan (2014) showed that fewer of today's US adolescents have been exposed in their childhood to cold sores caused by HSV-1 than US adolescents in previous years. Without these antibodies, young people may be more susceptible to HSV-2 when they become sexually active. Increasing rates of oral sex are also thought to be implicated in the spread of this virus.

Gonorrhoea

There is a worrying increase in the incidence of gonorrhoea in developed countries. In Australia, the incidence of gonorrhoea doubled in the 1990s and almost doubled again in the first decade of the new century (The Kirby Institute, 2011). Infections have also increased dramatically in the UK with a 25 per cent increase between 2011 and 2012 alone, following on from many years of rising infection rates (Boseley, 2012). And in the US, too, gonorrhoea is increasing, with predominantly the younger age groups (15–19 or 20–24 years) affected in the US, the UK and Australia. Gonorrhoea is of particular concern not just because of the rising incidence in the young population but because the antibiotic drugs used to treat it are losing their effect as more resistant strains of the bacteria develop. Like chlamydia, gonorrhoea affects the reproductive organs, can be asymptomatic, and increases the chances of contracting other infections. If untreated it can lead to infertility in both men and women.

How to avoid STIs

Mostly, sexual transmission of STIs can be avoided by consistent use of condoms every time a person has vaginal or anal sex. As well, a condom (over the penis) or a dam (over female genitals) should be used during oral sex, and sex toys should not be shared unless covered with a new condom or washed between uses. Because it is usually not possible to tell if a person is infected (and they may not know themselves), these levels of caution are recommended especially if an individual has more than one partner or, of course, if their partner has had (and may still have) several partners. Risks are markedly reduced in monogamous relationships where partners have both had their disease status checked before beginning their sexual relationship. Unfortunately, these 'idealized' conditions do not usually apply to adolescent sexual experimentation.

Non-sexual transmission is possible for some STIs, for example via transmission by an infected mother during the birth process. In the case of HPV, skin-to-skin contact with an infected person can spread the disease. Transmission of HIV can occur through sharing dirty needles with intravenous drug users, or by the transfusion of infected blood. Apart from needle sharing among recreational drug users, these non-sexual transmission routes can be managed and controlled by medical interventions and appropriate public health protocols.

In short, the risks of both sexual and non-sexual transmission can be reduced to almost zero through a combination of cautious individual behaviour during sex and intravenous drug use, and appropriate and timely medical and public health intervention. For a variety of social, economic and individual reasons however, STIs are, on the whole, not well controlled in either developed or developing countries. In the next section we discuss this social context of STI management and outline perceived barriers to sexual health.

The social and medical context of STI management

In the last two decades increasing control over STIs has been possible because of medical advances and attitude change. Better availability and acceptance of the need for condoms in most western countries has limited disease spread. Vaccination is available for some infections, and in countries rich enough to ensure treatment is offered, the risk of dying from AIDS has diminished. Many STIs are now more easily diagnosed, treated and controlled, although the fact that some may be symptomless continues to provide many challenges.

On the whole, sexual health presents with a number of issues that are not present for many other areas of health. Myths and misperceptions can drive sexual behaviour in dangerous directions, for example the idea that sex with a virgin can cure AIDS, or that people who look clean and attractive are unlikely to have an infection. As well, social norms that govern the expression of sexuality include morals and religious beliefs, many of which have established notions of the relationships in which sexual activity can occur. Sexual behaviour is mostly considered to be a private matter, but as it usually involves others there are many reasons for discomfort or fear around sexual activity or discussion of it. Those who feel sensitive about any aspect of their sexual behaviour may be very reluctant to discuss this with another, particularly if they perceive that they will be judged or punished. This reticence can apply to discussions with potential, current and past partners and also to health professionals in relation to safe/unsafe practices, troubling symptoms and past behaviours. Lack of communication can have serious consequences for the person with the STI (or suspected STI) and their partners, ranging from unsafe sex to perpetration of sexual violence.

Some kinds of sexual behaviour are stigmatized and others, in some places, are criminal offences. Such laws may have an impact on sexual activity between young people, but they can also hinder efforts by young men and young women to protect their sexual health. In parts of Indonesia, for example, possession of condoms is a criminal offence (Wellings, 2008). This contrasts dramatically with parts of Brazil, where public schools are the second most popular access points for condoms (AIDS in Brazil, 2012).

In developing and, to some extent, developed countries, the sexual health of young women may be compromised by the sexual double standard, whereby men's premarital sexual activity and multiple partners are tolerated or even applauded, while women are expected to be virgins until married.

Young women having sex with men older than themselves, whose status is higher, and who provide financial rewards, are particularly vulnerable to men's infidelity (Nkosana & Rosenthal, 2007a).

So given the wide variety of social contexts in which sexual activity occurs, what do we know about how sexual health is managed among adolescents and youth? What are the prevention strategies used by young people, and what obstacles limit their uptake?

Individual barriers to managing STIs

Although today's adolescents are far more likely than those 30 years ago to use a condom for their first sexual intercourse or with a new partner, they do not appear to have adopted the practice of safe sex reliably with subsequent sexual encounters (Mitchell *et al.*, 2014; Steinmetz, 2013). In countries where both condoms and information about safe sex are freely available, what barriers remain that limit safer sexual practices among adolescents and youth?

An individual's ability to manage sexual health is dependent on a range of factors that interact in unpredictable ways. An awareness of safer sex practices and the potential consequences of ignoring the guidelines for these is a first step. But knowledge does not always predict behaviour, especially when there are strong emotions or social pressures involved. For example a young woman may abandon condom use because of pressure from her partner, or because she wants to please him. Even when the intention to use a condom is there on the part of both partners, these intentions may not be followed through because of situational factors such as being intoxicated or lack of ready access to a condom at the time. There are many individual barriers to safe sex practices, and in this next section we review some of them, including knowledge about sexual disease transmission, the nature of the relationship, communication with a sexual partner, perceptions of personal vulnerability, the emotional context and attitudes to condoms.

Knowledge

How much do adolescents know about STIs and how to avoid them? Although young people in developed countries appear reasonably knowledgeable about HIV, it is clear that other STIs are not on their radar, with most knowing little or nothing about chlamydia, HPV or any other STI (Boyar *et al.*, 2011; Latreille, Collyer & Temple-Smith, 2014; Mitchell *et al.*, 2014). Add to this the focus of much sex education on HIV/AIDS, which can lead young people to believe that this is the only STI that 'counts'. For example, in one study of over 2000 senior secondary school students, half the young men and nearly 40 per cent of the young women thought that chlamydia only affects women; just under half of the total sample had never heard of HPV and most answered 'don't know' to a series of questions about it (Mitchell *et al.*, 2014).

Nevertheless there is a relatively high awareness, which comes from learning about HIV protection, that condom use is a key to safe sex. Between 80 and 90 per cent of the students in Mitchell *et al.*'s (2014) study understood that condoms used during sex can help protect against HIV and that the birth control pill does not offer this protection. If these young people acted in the light of this knowledge, they would also be reasonably well protected against other STIs. In addition, young people in a recent US focus group study (Boyar *et al.*, 2011) indicated that they were well aware of the importance of using condoms during their sexual activity. But to underscore a point we made earlier about knowledge being a necessary but not sufficient driver of behaviour change, these young people also acknowledged that despite knowing the recommendations about safe sex, either they or their friends often ignored them. Reasons could relate to alcohol or drug use or lack of good decision-making skills but one participant summed it up as a matter being driven by the moment.

> You know what you are doing, but you're stupid. (Adolescent male)
> *(Boyar* et al.*, 2011:13)*

Nature of the relationship

Pressure from a partner, subtle or overt, gentle or aggressive, can overturn intentions to use a condom. Young people on the margins of society such as the homeless and those who trade sex for money or security are most vulnerable, but so too are those who let their strong feelings for another blind them to the reality of risk. This has been called 'trusting to love'; the idea that condoms are unnecessary because a current relationship is monogamous and promises to be long term. Many studies have identified that young people 'trust in love' and are less likely to use condoms with regular than with casual partners. As Bauman and Berman (2005:218) note: 'With intimacy and time come familiarity and trust. As several adolescents described it, a person who you know and care for won't hurt you.' But as they also note, it is an illusion of safety, demonstrated aptly in these quotes from young men (who refer to their regular girlfriends as 'wifey').

> Girlfriend, condom. If you're messing around with a friend, condom. Wifey, most likely no condom, you don't wear a condom. (Adolescent male)

It depends. If you're messing, more than likely you'll use a condom because she could of messed with anybody, you could of messed with anybody so you don't want to catch anything. If you're dating you still use a condom. If you're with wifey, most people don't. (Adolescent male)

(Bauman & Berman, 2005:218)

The consistently lower levels of condom use with regular partners (e.g. Lescano *et al.*, 2006; Moore & Rosenthal, 2006) suggest that adolescents may have acknowledged the STI threat in casual encounters but have yet to realize that in the fickle world of adolescent relationships, sex with regular partners also may entail a high level of risk. It is clear that the meaning of a 'regular' relationship varies, both in terms of duration and fidelity. For some adolescents, serial monogamy – or a succession of 'permanent' relationships – is the norm; others may experiment with casual relationships but do not admit this to their regular partners. Additionally, what counts as 'casual' depends on interpretation of where a relationship is headed, how much commitment to fidelity is expected, and whether the young person sees himself or herself as the sort of person who has casual relationships. If partners differ in their expectations about the nature of their sexual relationship, condom use is more likely to be inconsistent (Rosengard, Adler, Gurvey & Ellen, 2005).

Communication with a partner

Another significant barrier is inability to communicate with a partner about his or her past sexual history and about using condoms. Such communication is not an easy task, especially for adolescents brought up in families or cultures where discussion of sexual matters is, or has been, taboo. Even in cultures when attitudes to sex are liberal and few topics seem off limits, it can feel embarrassing or 'uncool' to raise the topic of protection, with its implication that a potential partner might be infected (or worse, that you might be).

Asked about their willingness to discuss a partner's sexual history, these adolescents responded as follows:

If you have just met her that night, you don't want to say have you gone to the doctor or whatever before we have sex. It is a bit hard to say that sort of thing. (Male, 16 years)

(Moore & Rosenthal, 2006:191)

It is embarrassing. What do you say? Usually I sleep with people I know and I know they haven't got any diseases. (Female, 16 years)

(Moore & Rosenthal, 2006:192)

But it looks like the new media may be breaking down some of these barriers. A US study showed that sexually active high school teens who texted about condoms were three times more likely to use them than those who did not discuss birth control and protection online (Widman, Nesi, Choukas-Bradley & Prinstein, 2014). Use of mobile phone apps which promise 'a free way to find STD testing, get the results on your phone and share your verified STD status' may become the technique of the future for young people, given that they normalize testing for STIs and sharing the results, as well as providing a method of doing this that does not require much conversation (Saul, 2013).

Personalization of risk

Many adolescents have not personalized the risk of STIs, perceiving these infections as a threat to others, not themselves. Adolescents' belief that 'it can't happen to me' has been shown to influence risk-taking in a variety of health-related situations including smoking and contraceptive use. Two young men from Latreille *et al.*'s (2014) study illustrated these feelings with their comments about the risk of STI infection:

> I mean because young men think they're kind of bullet-proof and it won't happen to them. (Male, 20 years)

> I think that when you are younger you are more likely to take a risk and younger guys might think, I don't know, it might be cool to do it without protection. (Male, 21 years)

> *(Latreille* et al., *2014:61)*

The illusion of invulnerability may also be fostered by engaging in risky acts that have no (immediate) negative consequences. Thus adolescents who repeatedly engage in unsafe sex without becoming infected are more likely to deny the riskiness of that behaviour.

Adolescents' belief that they are not at risk may stem from another misconception – that 'you can tell by looking' whether or not people have an STI.

> Most people I know just say, if it looks alright, it's fine. (Male, 16 years)
> *(Latreille* et al., *2014:60)*

The physical and sexual appeal of a prospective partner has been shown to affect perceived STI susceptibility (Knauper, Kornik, Atkinson, Guberman & Aydin, 2005). Inferences about the likelihood of infection of a partner, based on that partner's healthy, clean and/or beautiful physical appearance, are not uncommon among young people. Mitchell and her colleagues (2014) found nearly 20 per cent of high schoolers thought that someone who looked very healthy could not pass on HIV infection. It may be that adolescents are drawing on the socially constructed equation of beauty with good health – a link reinforced endlessly by the media.

Even more disturbing is the research by Meertens, Brankovic, Ruiter, Lohstroh and Schaalma (2013) who found that perceived STI susceptibility was influenced by the cleanliness of the room in which sex took place. In scenario studies, university students were assigned to one of four conditions and asked to imagine having unprotected sex with someone they had just met: (a) in that person's apartment or (b) in a hotel room. The next day they wake up and notice the room is either (c) quite dirty or (d) very clean. Although the effect sizes were small, participants in both 'clean room' conditions rated their chances of becoming infected with an STI as significantly lower than those in the 'dirty room' conditions, and they were more likely to say they would act the same way again. It would not be surprising if these subtle influences on sexual decision-making were more likely to occur among the less sexually experienced and those more motivated by strong emotions.

Emotions

Several determinants of condom use arise out of the immediate context of a sexual encounter. As might be expected, high levels of sexual arousal at the time of the encounter seem to reduce the likelihood of using condoms.

> When they're in a hurry, they don't use them. . . . 'cause it might mess up the moment.
>
> Sometimes, if we was in the mood and we didn't have a condom, we would just do it.
>
> *(Bauman & Berman, 2005:217)*

It may be that sexual arousal operates in a similar fashion to the effects of arousal on other tasks. For highly aroused young people, the encounter becomes the focus and the issue of whether or not to use a condom receives little or no attention. Arousal may be exacerbated by the use of alcohol or drugs, or strong feelings of attraction, or being in love. Even if there has been an initial intention to use a condom, it is less likely to be carried through, unless using protection becomes habitual.

Attitudes to protection, testing and treatment

Negative attitudes to condoms, for example beliefs that they reduce sensation, are unromantic, unpleasant or embarrassing to use, will reduce the likelihood of their uptake. The attitudinal barrier is one that has been the target of several public health campaigns, but the deep-seated belief, especially among young men, that condoms reduce sensation means that unless there are also strong counter beliefs that STIs are a real risk that condom use can allay, then the negative is likely to outweigh the positive.

With HIV now manageable as a chronic disease rather than one that kills, the attitude of complacency may have taken over. Young people, perhaps unaware of the risks to their long-term health and fertility, do not fear STIs as once HIV was feared. One US public health official, commenting on gonorrhoea rates increasing by up to 40 per cent in recent years put it this way: 'People don't have the fear of death from sex like they had 15 years ago. For the teenagers, that fear is gone, and people are not practicing safe sex as much as they used to' (Steinmetz, 2013).

There are other attitudinal barriers to managing STIs, including those involved in accessing the health system to be checked and/or treated for STIs. In the next section, we discuss these issues of screening and treatment from both a community health and an individual perspective.

Screening, testing and treating STIs

Strategies to manage sexual health at the community health services level include effective diagnostic tests, treatments and preventive vaccines as well as processes in place to facilitate partner notification.

Screening/testing

In some countries or populations with high levels of STIs, regular screening for STIs is offered. For example, in an attempt to control the spread of chlamydia among young people, chlamydia screening programmes have been trialed in the UK (Health Do, 2009), the Netherlands (Van den Broek et al., 2012) and Australia (Hocking et al., n.d.). In order to be successful, screening programmes must be widely adopted, but even when readily available, they may be under-used by young people. One of the complicating factors militating against sexually active young people having regular sexual health checks is their lack of awareness that some STIs have no obvious symptoms. STI testing services may have a greater uptake if they were built in to regular medical check-ups, with general practitioners asking about sexual health as a matter of course and in a manner that is youth-friendly and non-judgemental.

In the UK, most STI testing under the national chlamydia screening programme takes place in community health services such as doctors' surgeries and community sexual health services such as family planning clinics. As in other western countries, testing also occurs in other settings including schools, colleges and youth centres. Some countries now offer self-testing services in which young people order test kits from a website, produce a urine sample or swab and return the samples by post for laboratory analysis. Such screening programmes benefit both patient and practitioner by offering a relatively depersonalized and anonymous context in which to focus on sexual health. It can be seen in the following quotes that the idea of being judged as sexually promiscuous is present for some young people:

> I'd be kind of shocked [if I was offered a test]. (Female, late teens)
> *(Balfe, Brugha, O'Donovan, O'Connell & Vaughan, 2010:3)*

> I would feel offended if I was singled out for testing. That seems ridiculous but I think I would honestly. It would be important to say that everyone's being tested. It would make it more normal, to say everyone's doing it. It's a bit more acceptable. (Female, late teens)
> *(Balfe et al., 2010:4)*

There is evidence that young women accept chlamydia testing if it is offered to them, as long as it is offered to all young women and is not based on a health professional's judgement of a girl as being at high risk because of her sexual history (Balfe *et al.*, 2010; Pavlin, Parker, Fairley, Gunn & Hocking, 2008). Screening programmes also benefit health professionals as they are provided with additional chlamydia education and protocols that assist with follow-up of positive cases.

Treatment

In many countries and communities the stigma and discomfort around sex continues to have an impact on attendance at health services by young people for sexual health issues. Even when people have made a decision to seek health care, there is often great concern that they are being observed by others in the clinic waiting room, or that they will be asked in a public situation the reason for their visit. Research in Ireland indicates that efforts need to be made to destigmatize the act of attending clinics for STI testing. The authors (Balfe & Brugha, 2011) suggest that the stigma barriers are reduced by placement of clinics away from busy thoroughfares, with discreet entrances, and waiting rooms with spaces where individuals can be relatively anonymous, for example do not have their name called out by a receptionist, and can sit well apart from other waiting patients.

Discussing sexuality and associated health risks is still a major taboo in many societies, and this is especially true for young people talking to adults.

Few young people are confident to initiate discussion with their doctor of a symptom related to sex, and many health professionals are also uncomfortable in this role. Sexual health issues are not equally well taught in medicine and nursing courses across the world, and may be seen by some as less important than other aspects of health. In any case, even with good sexual health knowledge, not all health professionals have the communication skills to deal with these sensitive issues, especially with adolescents. So the way in which to initiate such sensitive discussion is an ongoing challenge for health professionals. On a positive note, at least one study has suggested that young people are prepared to discuss sexual health if their health professional initiates the conversation.

> There would be ways they could bring it up so it would be OK. But if it's just randomly on the spot, you know if you're not ready for it, then you just probably wouldn't. You would just want to get out of there. (Male, 16 years)

> I reckon if they brought it up I might. But I don't think I could say it first . . . so if they brought it up first, I reckon that'd be a lot more comforting. . . . I don't want my parents finding out. That's probably the concern. (Male, 17 years)
>
> *(Latreille* et al., *2014:59)*

Confidentiality issues

Issues of confidentiality can be especially problematic in rural communities where a young person may fear their presence in a clinic could provoke a question from others known to them about why they are there, or where the health care practitioner may be the parent of a friend, or a neighbour.

> There's the worrying of what others will think if they found out. (Male, 19 years)

> There's the fear of being judged. (Male, 19 years)
>
> *(Ewert* et al., *under review)*

In Latreille *et al.*'s study of young men, most stated they would prefer to discuss sexual health with a male doctor, with some also expressing a preference for one who was young.

I wouldn't be able to talk to some old dude about it because that would just be creepy as. (Male, 17 years)

(Latreille et al.*, 2014:59)*

Similarly, Balfe *et al.* (2010) found that young women preferred to be offered chlamydia screening by a younger female doctor.

I just think it's a lot easier to talk to a woman when there's something wrong. Especially about women's stuff. They'd understand more. (Female, late teens)

You can connect with someone the same sex. (Female, early twenties)

(Balfe et al.*, 2010)*

The internet and new media have great potential to provide young people with information and support about STIs. There are interactive informational websites, online support groups for those living with STIs, mobile phone apps that remind people about check-ups or medications and a variety of other creative and helpful resources available. These resources do more than inform and support; in making this material so readily available they help to 'normalize' activities such as getting regular checks for STIs and talking to potential partners about protection. In this way they may help overcome some of the emotional barriers to conversations about safe behaviour, especially disclosure of infection status to sexual partners.

Disclosure to partners

To stem the spread of infection, it is obvious that once a person has received a diagnosis with a transmissible STI, their sexual partners should be notified. Past and current partners can then be tested and treated if need be, and appropriate protection put in place for future sexual encounters. In some cases this may involve abstaining from sex until a treatment course is completed. In all cases it is likely to involve some difficult conversations, ones that the faint-hearted or irresponsible may choose to avoid. As we have seen from this chapter, young people feel concern for their reputation, shame, embarrassment and a whole range of emotions. They can fear that a partner may react abusively or that an important relationship may be severed. There is a great deal of material available online which gives advice and options for ways to tell a partner; some medical clinics will assist in contacting previous partners. It is even possible to send anonymous emails or texts (with accompanying information about what needs to be done next) from websites designed for this purpose. However until these diseases lose their stigma, this is never going to be an easy task.

Conclusion

Adolescents who live in developed countries have increasing control over their own sexual health. Improvements in vaccines, screening and treatments mean that bacterial STIs are mostly curable, viral STIs are mostly manageable, and in countries where HIV/AIDS treatment is affordable, mortality is less likely than for previous generations. However, many adolescents fail to personalize the risk of STIs and the belief that 'it can't happen to me' is still prevalent. Although many recognize the need to have casual or first-time sex safely, there is evidence that subsequent sexual interactions between partners are not always protected.

Despite the increasing openness about sex in the developed world, many adolescents remain uninformed about STIs and feel embarrassed to discuss possible infection with a partner or seek a health practitioner for advice. The digital world offers a space for adolescents to easily, and confidentially if they wish, engage in issues related to their sexual health. The online domain provides fruitful avenues for research into the utilization and effectiveness of STI-related websites and apps.

10

ADOLESCENT PREGNANCY

Choices and outcomes

I don't really think there are any disadvantages in having a baby now, I am completely ready for this responsibility. (Female, 17 years, with previous pregnancy, but no children)

(Rosengard, Pollock, Weitzen, Meers & Phipps, 2006:507)

Adolescent pregnancy has long been of concern in developed countries. Although many of the reasons for this are longstanding and similar across cultures, others have altered with changing social attitudes and are context dependent. Typically, the negative consequences of young (and often single) motherhood for both mother and infant have been the focus of public and policy concerns, as have the outcomes for pregnant young women who choose alternative paths to that of motherhood, such as abortion or adoption. Given the significant numbers of adolescent pregnancies, and the care and cost of these, it is essential to understand the dynamics underlying early pregnancies as well as the outcomes of these pregnancies.

In this chapter, we consider whether there have been changes in the numbers of teenage pregnancies and births over the past 50 or so years, the choices available for young people in dealing with an unwanted pregnancy, and the protective and risk factors for young women becoming pregnant. Decisions made about the pregnancy – whether or not to keep the baby – are examined, especially in light of consequences for the young woman's health and wellbeing. Finally, we bring young fathers into the picture, by asking 'What about fathers?'

Facts and figures

Adolescent pregnancy emerged as a focus of attention in the 1960s and 1970s alongside the so-called sexual revolution. Although some writers questioned whether the perceived 'epidemic of teenage pregnancies', so named by the Alan Guttmacher Institute (1976), was a reality, a decade later the numbers of these pregnancies continued to fuel concern. For example in the 1980s, Trussell reported one out of every ten women aged 15–19 years became pregnant each year in the US. Of the pregnancies, five out of every six were unintended, and most were conceived premaritally (Trussell, 1988:262).

Today about 14–16 million births annually worldwide are to adolescent women aged 15–19 years, with the vast majority occurring in developing countries (Lyra & Medrado, 2014; WHO, 2014c). Over the last few decades, adolescent birth rates have fallen in most developed countries, although this downward trend has slowed since 2000. Sub-Saharan Africa has the highest adolescent birth rate, at 123 births per 1000 (UNICEF, 2012).

Among developed nations, the US continues to have one of the highest adolescent pregnancy and birth rates (Centers for Disease Control and Prevention, 2012; Hamilton, Martin & Ventura, 2013; Koh, 2014b). In 2012, there were 29.4 births per 1000 women aged 15–19 years (rates for younger adolescents aged 15–17 years were about half this), representing more than 305 000 American teenagers.

Young US women are 3–4 times more likely to become pregnant than their counterparts in Germany, France and the Netherlands. The fact that the US birth rate for this age group is nearly 4–8 times higher than in these countries suggests that young people in European countries, in spite of having similar rates of sexual activity, are less likely to maintain the pregnancy to birth (Advocates for Youth, 2011). The UK has one of the highest birth rates in the European Union for young women aged 15–17 years, with only Romania, Bulgaria, Slovakia and Hungary having higher rates. Despite this, the current estimated number of pregnancies to UK women in this age group (30.9 per 1000 women) is the lowest since records began (Office for National Statistics, 2013a; World Bank, 2013a).

In Australia the current adolescent birth rate accounts for just under 3.7 per cent of all Australian births (16 births per 1000, Australian Bureau of Statistics, 2013a), much lower than the US and UK and even New Zealand (25 births per 1000 in 2012), but similar to Canada (World Bank, 2013b).

However any comparison of reported figures for pregnancies needs to be considered in light of the limitations of the data. For example, pregnancy rates may or may not include pregnancies that terminate in abortion, and those rates that do include abortion do not distinguish between abortion and spontaneous miscarriage. Also these rates cannot tell us whether the pregnancies were wanted or unwanted or whether or not they occurred within a committed relationship. Some young people plan a pregnancy and are delighted with this outcome; some find the positive experiences of parenting present an opportunity for their own development.

Contextual factors

Although falling birth rates among adolescents in developed countries can be explained by decreasing birth rates more generally, there are other factors that have contributed. These include increased range, availability and use of contraception, better sex education, easier access to and greater acceptance of abortion, and socioeconomic changes that have improved women's educational and career aspirations (Slowinski & Hume, 2001). There are, however, many factors that impact on teenage pregnancy and birth rates more generally.

Marital status

Marital status is a key factor and it could be expected that this would differentiate between wanted and unwanted pregnancies. There are considerable differences in rates of marriage among adolescent girls in developed and developing countries. Although the marriage rate of Australian adolescent girls (aged over 16 years) is very low (3.3 per 1000 marriages; Australian Bureau of Statistics, 2013b), in the developing world nearly 25 per cent of adolescent girls aged 15–19 years are married or in a committed relationship, with the greatest proportion of these in South Asia and Africa (UNICEF, 2012). Almost 90 per cent of births to adolescents in developing countries occur within marriage, and in some countries, such as western Asia/northern Africa, central Asia, and south-central and southeastern Asia, this figure is close to 100 per cent (UNICEF, 2012; WHO, 2008). In developed countries, however, births to adolescents are far more likely to be unintended, many pregnancies outside marriage end in abortion, and few adolescents who become pregnant are married when they give birth (Klein, 2005).

Socioeconomic disadvantage

The association between socioeconomic disadvantage, adolescent pregnancy and pregnancy outcomes has long been noted (e.g. Browning, Leventhal & Brooks-Gunn, 2004; Mahavarkar, Madhu & Mule, 2008; Shearer, 2000; Smith & Elander, 2006; Turner, 2004). In the US, the highest rates of pregnancy and childbirth are found in socioeconomically disadvantaged youth of any race or ethnicity (Hamilton, Martin & Ventura, 2012).

In Australia, young women from low socioeconomic backgrounds who become pregnant are nearly eight times more likely to give birth than their more affluent peers (Australian Institute of Health & Welfare, 2011; Giordano & Ross, 2012). Adolescent pregnancy rates are also consistently higher in rural and remote Australia than those in metropolitan areas, where resources and services are more accessible (Lewis, Hickey, Doherty & Skinner, 2009; Robson, Cameron & Roberts, 2006). Adolescents living in very remote areas are five times more likely to become pregnant than those living in major urban centres (Australian Bureau of Statistics, 2010).

Those who are homeless are an important subset of socially and economically disadvantaged young people. Many young women become pregnant while homeless, again for multiple reasons – seeking love and/or a relationship, enduring sexual abuse, and contraception failure or non-use (Crawford, Trotter, Sittner Hartshorn & Whitbeck, 2011). Importantly, this group represents a high pregnancy risk, as some homeless women use alcohol, tobacco or drugs before they are aware they are pregnant or during pregnancy. Many may have mental health issues (Whitbeck, 2009; Whitbeck, Johnson, Hoyt & Cauce, 2004). Access to prenatal care is difficult, and nutrition may be an ongoing problem during the pregnancy (Whitbeck, Chen & Johnson, 2006). Babies who are born to mothers who are homeless are at a very high risk for low birth weight, medical complications and developmental problems (Chapman, Tarter, Kirisci & Cornelius, 2007; Little *et al.*, 2005; Stanwood & Levitt, 2004).

Racial or ethnic background

This is strongly implicated in pregnancy and birth figures among young women in developed countries. For example, in the US, the highest rates of pregnancy and childbirth are found in young people who are African-American, Hispanic/Latino and American Indian/Alaskan Native. Together, African-American and Hispanic youth made up 57 per cent of US adolescent births in 2011 (Hamilton *et al.*, 2012). Latina adolescents have a higher adolescent birth rate than African-American or non-Latina adolescents (Santelli, Abraido-Lanza & Melnikas, 2009). Latinas also have had the smallest recent declines in adolescent pregnancy and birth rates among ethnic groups in the US (Ventura, Curtin, Abma & Henshaw, 2012). Latina and African-American adolescent mothers are also more likely than non-Latina White adolescent mothers to have a second child during adolescence (Rosengard, 2009).

This trend is also seen in other countries. In New Zealand, the adolescent birth rate of Maori and Pacific Islanders is double that of the European population (Ministry of Social Development, 2010). In Australia, young Indigenous women are five times more likely to become young mothers than non-Indigenous young women (A. Smith *et al.*, 2011, in Giordano & Ross, 2012).

Not surprisingly, there are differences in pregnancy and birth rates as a function of age. Although the pattern of declining birth rates in recent years applies to all cohorts, there are more births to older than to younger adolescents (Ventura *et al.*, 2012; UNICEF, 2001). In Australia, the birth rate for young women aged 20–24 years was three times that for 15–19-year-olds (Australian Institute of Health and Welfare, 2011). In part, these differences can be accounted for by the greater proportion of pregnancy terminations in the younger group, an issue discussed later in this chapter. Of course older adolescents are more likely to be sexually active and thus have more opportunities to become pregnant. A recent US study found that pregnancy rates among very young adolescents are extremely low, and that sexual activity in these teenagers is both rare and mostly non-consensual (Finer & Philbin, 2013). In a recent survey of Australian secondary school students, 5 per cent of sexually active students reported that they had experienced sex that resulted in pregnancy (Mitchell, Patrick, Heywood, Blackman & Pitts, 2014).

Mother's age

Adolescent mothers' age is an important influence on pregnancy and personal outcomes, with research showing that young adolescents are likely to have worse outcomes than older women. Compared to a woman in her twenties, the risk of dying or complications arising from pregnancy is dramatically higher for girls under 15 (25 times more likely) and twice as high for girls aged 15–19 years (Lyra & Medrado, 2014). Younger women have a higher chance of premature delivery and 'small for dates' babies, and disruption to their schooling will reduce subsequent employment options (Bateson, 2014; Klein, 2005). For young Indigenous women, the risks are greater still. Indigenous adolescents who give birth are twice as likely as non-Indigenous adolescent mothers to experience preterm births, small for date and low birth-weight babies. Infant mortality rates are also higher than in the non-Indigenous population (Chan, Scheil, Scott, Nguyen & Sage, 2011).

We have described only a few of the contextual factors that can affect fertility rates. An Australian study offers a good example of the variety of factors that can have an impact on fertility. In an analysis of young women attending a family planning service, those who were at highest risk of unintended pregnancy were young women who had not attended university, had had more than one partner in the last three months, were dissatisfied with their current contraception, were feeling vulnerable to pregnancy and not confident in their contraceptive knowledge, and who admitted to being unable to stop to use contraception when aroused (Ong, Temple-Smith, Wong, McNamee & Fairley, 2012). Uptake of and access to contraception are key to reducing rates of adolescent pregnancy (Pitts & Emans, 2014).

Contraceptive practices

There is currently a wide variety of contraceptive choices available to young women in the developed world. Contraceptive choice is generally based on multiple factors including the young woman's medical history, her preferences and cost. Although effectiveness and side-effects are relevant to all women, other factors such as reversibility, the possibility of detection by others and non-contraceptive benefits such as management of acne or heavy menstruation may be of particular importance to some young women (Bateson, 2014).

Contraceptive choice

In addition to the male condom and the contraceptive pill, recent developments include long-acting reversible contraceptives (LARC). Once inserted into the body, these require no action from the user and are sometimes referred to as 'set and forget' methods. An example is a contraceptive implant injected into the young woman's arm, which maintains highly effective, low-cost and immediately reversible contraception with few contraindications for up to 3 years.

Despite a lack of comprehensive comparable data on contraceptive choice, surveys suggest that the contraceptive pill remains the most widely used method (Mazza et al., 2012; National Collaborating Centre for Women's and Children's Health, 2005; Richters et al., 2003; Trussell & Wynn, 2008; Yusuf & Siedlecky, 2007). In Australia, 78 per cent of adolescents and young women aged 12–24 years choose the contraceptive pill, compared to almost 12 per cent who choose LARC (Mazza et al., 2012).

Barriers to contraception

Pitts and Emans (2014) highlighted a range of issues that can affect young people's use of contraception. Given the high cost of medical care in America, US adolescents may struggle to access contraceptives if they are not insured. However if they are insured only under their parents' health plans, confidentiality may be an issue. Although this financial issue does not arise in all countries, adolescents in many countries are often very concerned about attending their family practitioner for contraception, due to cost, embarrassment or fear of lack of confidentiality.

Simply managing a contraceptive consistently over time can be challenging for young women. Manlove, Ryan and Franzetta (2004) found that a hormonal method of contraception was associated with increased consistency of use among females, and suggested that hormonal methods such as injectables may be the most effective methods for sexually active adolescents. Some newer contraceptives, with the help of modern technology, remind a young woman to take her pill. Fortunately in this new technological world there are mobile phone apps that can be accessed for reminders. Receiving a daily educational text message has been shown to improve continuing adherence to the contraceptive pill in young women under the age of 25 years (Castano, Bynum, Andres, Lara & Westhoff, 2012).

Whatever the contraceptive, it is important in these times of increasing rates of some sexually transmissible infections (STIs) that young people are aware that contraception is not disease prevention. Although condoms are increasingly employed to prevent infection with HIV or other STIs, the tendency for many young people is to discontinue condoms when other forms of contraception are being used, despite the recommendations for dual contraception to prevent the transmission of STIs (Ong *et al.*, 2012).

Dual contraception

Take-up of dual contraception methods is low among adolescents, particularly in the US where rates are lower than elsewhere in the developed world and dependent on a number of factors. In a recent study of over 2000 unmarried young women aged 15–24 years, 34 per cent used condoms alone the last time they had sex, compared to 29 per cent who chose hormonal contraception or intrauterine device alone, and 21 per cent who chose dual methods (Tyler *et al.*, 2014). Dual contraception/disease prevention use was highest among educated adolescents and young women with some college attendance or a college degree (27 per cent), and those who were 18 years at first sex (28 per cent), while the dual method was lowest among those without insurance coverage (10 per cent) and with a previous pregnancy (10 per cent) (Tyler *et al.*, 2014).

Emergency contraception

Often a last resort when unprotected sex has occurred, emergency contraception (EC) or the 'morning-after pill' as it is commonly called, has become increasingly available. EC has a very low failure rate when taken within 24 hours of conception, is simple to use and has relatively few side-effects (Fairley & Sawyer, 2003). Knowledge of EC among sexually active young people is good

(Hobbs *et al.*, 2011) with high levels of take-up by young people in countries where it is available over the counter at relatively low cost. This situation exists in countries such as Australia, the Netherlands and the UK, but not in the US.

A recent study of Australian women aged 16–35 years assessing knowledge about EC and barriers to its use (Hobbs *et al.*, 2011) found over one-quarter had used this method of contraception, with some resorting to it more than once. Of the 161 women surveyed, 27 per cent had used EC, of whom 69 per cent had used it once, 22 per cent twice and 8 per cent three or more times (Hobbs *et al.*, 2011).

Unlike in Australia, where access is legal and relatively easy, in the US young women have difficulties in obtaining EC. For example, there are multiple EC brands currently on the market that contain the same hormone and each has different dispensing regulations. Moreover, a recent study (Wilkinson, Vargas, Fahey, Suther & Silverstein, 2014) provided insight into the experiences of some American adolescents when phoning pharmacies to ask about EC. Female callers posing as 17-year-olds requested EC using standardized scripts to phone 943 pharmacies in five US cities. Adolescents often received explanations of pharmacy policies in ethics-laden terms, and confidentiality was not always guaranteed. Some were told of false barriers to EC access (e.g. that they had to be 18 years, and could not get someone else to collect the EC for them).

> We do not sell it at our pharmacy. This is a Catholic hospital. Sorry. Bye.

> Actually, I think the new law is that it's 17 and with an ID, but I'm not sure if it's in effect yet. That's what I mean when I said bring someone who is 18, like your boyfriend or something, because some of the older pharmacists might not sell it to you. I'm going to warn you, though, that it is expensive – it's like $35–$40.

> You actually need to be 18 or older to buy it. So if it is for you, you would need to come in with a parent or legal guardian.

> You can't have the guy pick it up for you – we assume that whoever buys it is the one taking it, so you can't have him come in and get it for you.

> *(Wilkinson* et al.*, 2014:16–17)*

Clearly there are both legal and attitudinal barriers along with young people's lack of knowledge of their rights that can interfere with the uptake of EC.

Why do adolescents become pregnant?

About half of all adults describe their pregnancies as being unintended. By contrast, in a study of 15- to 19-year-old Americans, 82 per cent describe their pregnancies this way (Finer & Zolna, 2011). This high rate of unintended pregnancies is said to be partly due to inconsistent or no use of contraceptives (Manlove *et al.*, 2004). It is clear, however, that some adolescents are motivated to become young mothers (Klein, 2005). Some adolescents plan a pregnancy. For these young women the decision to become a mother is often influenced by social factors such as having a mother who had her own first child earlier than average, having friends who are young mothers and being in a stable relationship – which may or may not be marriage – with a partner. Other young women seem to take a 'what will be, will be' approach to possible pregnancy. For example, one study which sought the views of young mothers (aged 16–19 years) experiencing a repeat pregnancy found that, 'although mothers did not intend to get pregnant, they also did not intend to prevent pregnancy' (Herrman, 2007:92).

One common explanation of adolescent pregnancy is that the pregnancy is planned as a deliberate manoeuvre to get some sort of financial benefit or material gain, such as welfare payments or subsidized housing. In the US, an extensive analysis of the effects of welfare payments was carried out by Ellwood and Bane, three decades ago. They found no evidence to support the belief that high benefit levels encouraged child-bearing among young White and non-White unmarried women aged 16–23 years (Ellwood & Bane, 1984). It appeared that benefits had no impact on pregnancy decisions among young unmarried women, which is not to say that these young women will not turn to these benefits for support if they carry the pregnancy to term. In addition, according to a report by the Australian Government Productivity Commission (2014), the Baby Bonus, a monetary incentive given to mothers in Australia, was not shown to cause significant increase in adolescent pregnancies. Studies in other countries have shown that birth rate increases occurring immediately after the introduction of financial incentives are not sustained (Grant *et al.*, 2006; Milligan, 2002).

Planning contraception?

A second explanation offered for adolescent pregnancy is that adolescents become pregnant accidentally because they are do not plan contraception adequately. Evidence suggests that this is an oversimplification of what occurs. Some young women may struggle to control contraception because, for example, their partner is uncooperative or abusive. Research has shown that both a history of physical abuse by a partner and current involvement in a physically abusive relationship were associated with reduced consistency of contraceptive use (Manlove *et al.*, 2004) and becoming pregnant (Roberts, Auinger & Klein, 2005). This was confirmed by a recent study in the US that found that adolescents who had been sexually abused, physically abused or neglected were twice as likely to get pregnant than their peers who had not experienced such maltreatment (Noll & Shenk, 2013).

For some young women, contraception is regarded as bringing with it a host of unwanted consequences, both physical and psychological.

> After aborting my pregnancy I refused the doctor's suggestions to go on the pill, having experienced depression, anxiety and weight gain.
>
> *(Dixon, Herbert, Loxton & Lucke, 2013:1)*

Other young women fail to use contraception for reasons that demonstrate a lack of maturity. Ashworth (2014) shared excerpts from a US adolescent's email which was sent to a teen advice website. The email was entitled 'Stupid reasons for teenagers to get pregnant and why teenage pregnancy is a dumb idea in general.' The reasons given by this teenage reader for not using contraception were as follows:

> The end of my junior year produced an unexpected baby boom in my high school. The reason behind the sudden rise is what I call 'pretty babies,' or getting pregnant by a guy because you think you'll have cute kids. . . . One of the pregnant girls in my senior class said that she got pregnant because 'he was way too sexy not to have a baby with.' . . . Other girls in my school have been getting pregnant because their best friend did. . . . Or they get pregnant for the classic reason, to keep a boyfriend. . . . Despite shows like MTV's '16 and Pregnant,' there's a glamour factor about teenage pregnancy, with girls not realizing what they're getting themselves into. . . . There are always those teens who think that their situation will be different, that they won't drop out of school or have to raise a child on their own.
>
> *(Ashworth, 2014)*

Some authors advocate that sex education programmes in high schools need to do more than just increase adolescents' knowledge of how to delay sexual activity and effectively use contraception. Teaching adolescents about the economic, emotional and legal realities of parenting would provide adolescents with more information to make informed family planning decisions and reduce pregnancy rates among teenagers (Noonan, 2012).

Whether adolescents ever or always use contraceptives may be dependent on their particular sexual relationships and the characteristics of their partners. For example, if an adolescent girl did not know her partner before dating him, she is less likely to use contraception, and the odds of an adolescent girl using contraception increase with the duration of the relationship. Girls who had discussed contraceptive use with their partner before having sex were more likely to ever or consistently use contraception (Manlove *et al.*, 2004).

Some factors associated with effective contraception

Research suggests that age at sexual initiation and knowledge of contraception are two key aspects of use of effective contraception (see Chapter 2). Age of sexual initiation was identified by researchers over a decade ago as a risk factor for adolescent pregnancy (Hockaday, Crase, Shelley & Stockdale, 2000; O'Donnell, O'Donnell & Stueve, 2001; Woodward, Fergusson & Horwood, 2001). The older the adolescent girl at the time of sexual initiation, the more likely she is to use contraception and to use it effectively. A recent US study confirmed that this is still the case, where '[c]ontraceptive uptake among girls as young as 15 is similar to that of their older counterparts, whereas girls who start having sex at 14 or younger are less likely to have used a method at first sex and take longer to begin using contraception' (Finer & Philbin, 2013:886).

When there is a stable and committed male–female relationship, contraceptives are more likely to be used than when there are no romantic ties between sexual partners. Although condom use tends to be more prevalent in casual or uncommitted relationships, as we discuss in Chapter 2, those adolescents in committed relationships are more likely to use the oral contraceptive pill.

Unfortunately, ignorance is a factor in effective use of contraception. Many young women appear to have strong views about acceptable contraception, views not always based on fact. Peers, often ill-informed, are a very strong influence on young women's contraceptive decision-making (Pitts & Emans, 2014). Lack of experience, under-appreciation of non-contraceptive benefits, uninformed concerns about side-effects and lack of anatomical knowledge are all issues that need to be taken into account when information about contraception is offered, so that young people can make an informed decision about contraceptive use (Merki-Feld & Gruber, 2014).

Resolution of adolescent pregnancies: 'making the choice'

Today's pregnant young women (and their partners) have available to them a number of possibilities. They may choose to continue the pregnancy or not. If they choose to keep the pregnancy, they may decide to keep the infant or they may choose to make an adoption plan. The ready availability of legal abortions has enabled more young people to choose termination of pregnancy as an option. Today, pregnant adolescent girls are more able than their peers of previous generation to make this choice. The social stigma associated with unmarried mothers is less so they may choose to keep their child and rear it either alone or with the support of their partner. Each of these choices depends on a variety of factors and each brings with it different consequences.

Abortion

A large number of adolescents opt for abortion following an unintended pregnancy. In earlier generations when safe abortion was less accessible, the shame of a pregnancy outside marriage drove many adolescent women to seek a 'backyard' abortion, usually provided by a non-medical practitioner. Nowadays the law permits abortion to save the life or preserve the health of a woman in many countries (Faundes & Alvarez, 2011). Almost half of these countries also permit abortion to preserve a woman's mental health. In 29 per cent of countries, representing 39.3 per cent of the world's population, an abortion is legal in the first 12 weeks for any reason (Faundes & Alvarez, 2011). Laws tend to be more restrictive in Africa and Latin America than elsewhere (Center for Reproductive Rights, 2007). This has consequences for the number of illegal abortions, which are generally performed under unsafe conditions.

Even if termination of pregnancy is legal, barriers can still be present which may discourage or prevent adolescents from accessing these services. In many countries, proponents of 'Right to Life' will challenge women entering abortion clinics with photos of fetuses and highly emotive slogans. The anti-abortion attitudes of some health practitioners on religious grounds or in rural areas can also prevent young people from making a truly independent decision.

It is estimated that about half the adolescent pregnancies in Australia and New Zealand are terminated by abortion (Ford, Nassar, Sullivan, Chambers & Lancaster, 2003; Statistics New Zealand, 2003), a somewhat larger percentage than in the US (Centers for Disease Control and Prevention, 2012b). In the only Australian state that collects abortion data, South Australia, in 2011, '871 teenage women had terminations of pregnancy, accounting for 17.2 per cent of terminations. In 2011, the proportion of "known" pregnancies terminated was 49 per cent for teenagers compared with 20 per cent for women of all ages' (Scheil, Scott, Catcheside, Sage & Kennare, 2013:10).

Adolescents who choose to have abortions are more likely than those who carry their pregnancies to full term to be contraceptive users, single, have high educational or occupational aspirations, and to be of higher socioeconomic status.

Why do young women make this choice? A review of literature from 1996 to 2008 found that although reasons for doing so were highly complex, abortion was chosen because women believed that continuing with the pregnancy would have adverse impact both on their own life and on that of significant others (Kirkman, Rosenthal, Mallett, Rowe & Hardiman, 2010). Women, although often ambivalent about abortion, recognized the need to take into account their own health and welfare, and their sense of responsibility to the potential child and the genetic father. Despite cultural and social differences, there was remarkable consistency with a review conducted almost 20 years ago (Bankole, Singh & Haas, 1998). Consistent over time was that the decision to terminate was prompted by the wish to be a good parent. Young women provide a range of reasons for terminating their pregnancy, but those under 20 years old stated, in order of frequency, that they were too young, not ready for motherhood, could not afford to have a baby and were unmarried or in an unstable relationship (Santelli, Speizer, Avery & Kendall, 2006). These results confirmed an earlier study that also cited economic hardship, being unmarried and interference with school or career as reasons for abortion (Finer, Frohwirth, Dauphinee, Singh & Moore, 2005).

One small Swedish study (Thorsen, Aneblom & Gemzell-Danielsson, 2006) offers interesting insights into the perceptions of 16 adolescent girls about contraception and abortion. Only one of these girls reported having had an abortion but all maintained the importance of a woman's right to an abortion. Although they agreed that abortion was 'a painful necessity', fear of psychological trauma and mental distress after an abortion were of concern. Acceptable reasons for an abortion included condom breakage, rape, young age and immaturity, as well as low income or unstable relationship.

> I don't want to have a child right now, maybe when I'm thirty-something. A child needs to grow up in a stable family. If you can't have an abortion, maybe it would be given to an orphanage or just be left behind, or you raise it in a completely wrong way.
>
> *(Thorsen et al., 2006:304)*

Other studies have yielded comments reflecting the ambivalence felt in making and carrying out the decision to have an abortion.

> When I found out, it was like so exciting, to be honest. It was just like, 'Whoa! Wow! This is amazing!' But then it's just like: reality check! How ridiculous it would be to go through with it, because I'm so young. (Adolescent female)
>
> *(Rosenthal, Rowe, Mallett, Hardiman & Kirkman, 2009:22)*

> I really regret having an abortion because I wanted my baby. . . . It
> hurts me that I killed my first child. . . . To my baby: I love you and I
> am very sorry you did not get to live your life because your momma
> did a terrible thing. (Female, 15 years)
>
> *(Rosetta Foundation, 2014a)*

On the other hand, for some young women, abortion brought with it no
feelings of regret.

> The relief that I felt once I woke up, after the abortion: it was amaz-
> ing. . . . It's like when you have all these debts and you finally pay it
> off, it's like, like your chest is, just empty, and you've got this weight
> literally lifted off your shoulders. (Female, 18 years)
>
> *(Rosenthal et al., 2009:21)*

Whatever the reasons for their decision, and even within a social context in
which abortion is seen as a legal option, there are grounds for concern about
the health consequences of this decision. Adolescents are less likely than older
women to obtain abortions in the safer, earlier months of pregnancy (Ralph,
Gould, Baker & Greene, 2014; Rowe, Kirkman, Hardiman, Mallett &
Rosenthal, 2009). In one US study of the adolescents aged 17 years or
younger who sought abortion care, most sought this in the first trimester, but
they were more likely than adult women to present in the second trimester
(Ralph *et al.*, 2014).

Risks of abortion

What are the consequences of the decision to terminate a pregnancy for
these young women? Although young women who have chosen to terminate their pregnancy do not, in general, appear to have a higher incidence of
negative health outcomes than do older women, there are some risks associated with abortion. These include haemorrhage, damage to the cervix and
damage to the uterus. Pelvic inflammatory disease can result from infection
following a termination of pregnancy and, if not treated promptly, can cause
infertility or increased likelihood of tubal pregnancy.

Few studies examine the psychological consequences of abortion for
young girls. There is something of a paradox in the situation where abortion is now readily available to most young women in most western countries but it still stirs strong negative feelings among adolescents. A small
Australian study found that young people (aged about 20) rate women who
want to have children more highly than women who do not want to have

children, whether they are heterosexual or lesbian (Rowlands & Lee, 2006). Complementing the emphasis on women's role as mothers is a change in the way the fetus is regarded by some. Possibly as a result of early fetal imaging (Layne, 2002) and the survival of increasingly premature babies, there is evidence that the status of the fetus – and hence its role in the abortion debate – has been subtly changing to that of patient (Williams, 2005), extending the construction of 'fetal personhood' (Layne, 2002) and adding another layer of complexity to a decision that is difficult for most women.

The link between abortion and subsequent mental health issues is unclear. Do women who become pregnant unintentionally experience greater mental health problems after an abortion? Or is their mental health better off after terminating an unwanted pregnancy? Two major reviews examining this topic, which were subject to extensive criticisms (Coleman, 2011; National Collaborating Centre for Mental Health, 2011), came to completely different conclusions. A third subsequent review and reappraisal of the evidence concluded that there is currently no evidence to indicate that abortion has positive consequences for mental health (Fergusson, Horwood & Boden, 2013). In fact, findings suggested that for women having an abortion, there existed slight increases in mental health problems such as alcohol and drug use, anxiety disorders and suicidal behaviours compared to women progressing with an unwanted or unintended pregnancy. However, because there was no separate examination of different age groups, we do not know whether this finding applies to adolescents.

There is evidence that adolescents voluntarily involve others in their decision-making regarding pregnancy, with mothers and male partners most often being the individuals to whom young women turn. Research suggests that these individuals are most often supportive of adolescents' decisions (Ralph *et al.*, 2014).

For young women who do choose abortion as the means of dealing with an unwanted pregnancy, access to good counselling support is essential so that the decision whether or not to abort can be made after a careful, informed and thoughtful appraisal of the situation. For some, the process is akin to one of mourning in which the natural stages of grief and loss must be worked through. The adolescent who chooses to terminate her pregnancy needs to feel that that decision is the right one for her.

Giving up the baby: choosing adoption

> When I was 19 I became pregnant for the first time. Our first thoughts were to have an abortion because of how scared we were at the thought of not being able to raise our child. We both researched options and

after could not decide to abort. We decided adoption would be the best. . . . Through Adoption Star we met the best couple in the world! They had been trying for years to start a family, and we knew right away that they would be able to love my son the way I would AND provide him with everything he needed. His adoptive parents keep in contact every month with letters and pictures. We are also going to get to see him next weekend and after if we choose. In retrospect, adoption is the hardest decision a mother can make, but it is also the best if you are not completely ready for motherhood.

(Rosetta Foundation, 2014b)

Changing views in society have reduced the number of children who are in need of adoption. Adoption was once considered to be a solution to the problem of illegitimacy and potential impoverishment of single mothers, as well as a means of assisting infertile couples (Kenny, Higgins, Soloff & Sweid, 2012). However, the increasing social acceptance of single parenthood and levels of support available to lone parents have reduced the pressure on unmarried women to make this choice for their child. Adoption has thus become rare in western countries. For example, the number of annual adoptions in Australia has fallen significantly during the last 25 years. In 1987–1988 there were 1494 finalized adoptions; in 2011–2012 there were only 333 finalized adoptions – a 78 per cent decline in less than 25 years, despite the increase in population over that time (Australian Institute of Health and Welfare, 2012). Similar declines in adoptions have been experienced in the UK and US although overall numbers of babies adopted in these countries are much higher. For example, in England and Wales in 1987, there were just over 7201 adoptions, and by 2012 that number had reduced to 5053 (Office for National Statistics, 2013b). In the US in 1999, there were over 15 700 adoptions, which reduced to just over 8660 in 2012 (Bureau of Consular Affairs, 2014).

Nowadays in many countries adoption is characterized by the open exchange of information between birth and adoptive families (Australian Institute of Health and Welfare, 2012), although little research has examined the long-term psychological consequences of this from the perspective of the relinquishing parent or the adopted child.

Keeping the baby

Why do some young women choose to continue with a pregnancy and to take on the responsibilities of parenthood, often without a partner to provide emotional and material support? Taking a broad sociological perspective, it could be argued that unwed parenthood is associated with changes in society that have led to the two-parent family becoming less important for the economic wellbeing of parents and children. Equally, changes in cultural norms have resulted in children born outside marriage – and their mothers – no longer being stigmatized, as they once were.

A US study of 130 adolescents, half of whom terminated their pregnancy and half of whom went on to deliver their baby, found that those teenagers who were more likely to choose to have the baby were less likely to be risk-takers and to have no desire to leave home (Coleman, 2006). Another study based on interviews with 12 adolescents aged 16–19 years who had experienced repeat pregnancies found that all participants had considered the option of abortion, but all had decided against it (Herrman, 2007). Some of the mothers discussed that abortion was not an option for them personally.

> I was gonna get an abortion with her even though I don't believe in abortions . . . and once I did my research on it . . . I had her. I did so many bad things in the beginning of my pregnancy and she was not going anywhere.

Family members also figured into the decision to not have an abortion.

> [M]y dad said . . . 'you not getting an abortion' . . . if I get an abortion I have to leave . . . he is really against abortions . . . so it's like I had no choice . . . but in the back of my head . . . I didn't want an abortion neither.

Several of the women's partners opposed the idea of abortion.

> He said . . . don't kill one of my kids . . . so that's why he has ten now.
> *(Herrman, 2007:92)*

There is also considerable research to suggest that race plays a significant role in an adolescent's decision to keep her child. In the US, the number of pregnant teenagers who keep their babies has always been high for Black and Hispanic adolescents, communities which do not always believe that early child-bearing leads to social disadvantage.

A study of 247 pregnant teenagers (12–19 years of age) who presented for initial prenatal care at a women's hospital in the US found that although most of those pregnancies were reported to be unintended, 23.5 per cent were intended. The study found those who had intended their pregnancies took the view that this choice would enhance their lives, and many were unable to articulate any disadvantages to adolescent pregnancy and mother-hood (Rosengard *et al.*, 2006). Younger women, 12–17 years, most often commented on the way in which the pregnancy would improve relation-ships, whereas older adolescents, 18–19 years, commented more often on general lifestyle considerations.

> [G]onna get your own family and stuff like that. (Hispanic female, 12 years, intended pregnancy, no previous pregnancy)
>
> An advantage is that I feel a baby will make me and my boyfriend's relationship closer. (Hispanic female, 14 years, unintended pregnancy, no previous pregnancy)
>
> I think that it will keep me away from doing bad things like drinking alcohol and/or doing drugs. It will make me be more responsible and I'll learn how to depend on myself more. (Non-Hispanic female, 18 years, unintended pregnancy, no previous pregnancy)
>
> *(Rosengard et al., 2006:506)*

Young girls give many reasons for keeping their babies. Becoming a mother may not be a real matter of choice. Some young girls fail to realize, perhaps because they have erratic periods, that they are pregnant until it is too late to do anything but have the baby. Some may deny the pregnancy in the hope that it will disappear if they do not acknowledge it. Others may be frightened to tell people until after the time when an abortion would be possible. For some young girls motherhood is seen as having positive, although possibly short-term, consequences for their lives. Apart from having an object to call their own and to love, for some a baby may be seen as a means of keeping a boyfriend's interest, of complying with his wishes to keep the baby, or of achieving status because of their new 'adult' role as mother.

Consequences of choosing parenthood

Although we have relatively little research to draw on in determining the consequences for adolescents of choosing abortion or adoption as the out-come of an unwanted pregnancy, the decision to keep the baby and the consequences of that decision have been the focus of considerable research.

There are reproductive health disadvantages for young mothers and babies. Stillbirths and neonatal deaths are higher for mothers aged under 20 years, compared to those aged 20–29 years; the younger the mother, the higher the risk. Rates of preterm birth, low birth weight and other problems arising from delivery are higher among babies born of adolescents and these conditions all increase the chance of future health problems for the baby (Chang, O'Brien, Nathanson, Mancini & Witter, 2003; WHO, 2014c). These problems include developmental delay, academic difficulties, behavioural disorders, substance abuse, early sexual activity, depression and becoming adolescent parents themselves (Klein, 2005).

Adolescent motherhood

In line with the negative view of young mothers' life chances that prevailed until relatively recently, Arthur Campbell, an influential expert of the time, asserted more than 40 years ago:

> The girl who has an illegitimate child at the age of 16 suddenly has 90 per cent of her life's script written for her. She will probably drop out of school; even if someone else in her family helps to take care of the baby, she will probably not be able to find a steady job that pays enough to provide for herself and her child; she may feel impelled to marry someone she might not otherwise have chosen. Her life choices are few and most of them are bad.
>
> *(Campbell, 1968:238)*

Effects on the mother

These dire predictions have not been strongly supported by subsequent research. Although younger mothers may suffer an increasing level of disadvantage and distress relative to their peers, the mental health of younger mothers has not been found to be any worse than other mothers in Australia (Lee & Gramotnev, 2006). Many studies have, in fact, shown positive outcomes for some young mothers (Fessler, 2003; Leadbeater, 2001; Swann, Bowe, McCormick & Kosmin, 2003). It appears that teenage pregnancy and motherhood are not in and of themselves as incapacitating as once thought. Rather, contextual factors such as socioeconomic status and social supports predicted wellbeing better among their pregnant and non-pregnant, parenting and non-parenting adolescents than did parenting status. The US reality TV show, *Unwed Mothers*, which follows the lives of young mothers throughout their pregnancy and the child's early years captures well the impact of these contextual factors.

Nevertheless, economic adversity and educational difficulties are perhaps the most common outcomes of becoming an adolescent parent. Adolescent mothers do find it difficult to re-enter school and to complete their education, despite the presence in some schools of crèches for babies of students

(Littlejohn, 1996; Milne-Holme, Power & Dennis, 1996; Moffitt & The E-Risk Study Team, 2002). Since education substantially influences later life chances through income and occupational opportunities, this is a particularly important issue. But impending or actual motherhood may not be the sole or critical factor operating here. There is now good evidence that pregnant teenagers have lower grades and lower school motivation *before* becoming pregnant than their non-pregnant peers. Some researchers have noted that some of the characteristics of teenage school drop-outs (such as being impulsive, lacking in long-term goals and coming from unhappy families) are similar to those that lead to becoming an unmarried adolescent mother.

There is no question that the interruption to schooling or termination of education that often follows pregnancy and early motherhood has implications for the economic wellbeing of these young women. Most studies show that adolescent mothers are less likely than older mothers to find stable and well-paid employment. But once again, we should be wary of assuming a direct link between early motherhood and poor job prospects. Several writers have pointed out that the employment of young women is just as dependent on the conditions of the labour market and personal characteristics as it is on high educational attainment. Nevertheless, it is true that adolescents who begin child-rearing at an early age are economically disadvantaged and more likely to be dependent on welfare. Although the differences in income between early and later child-rearing decrease over time, these young mothers are at greater risk of poverty throughout their lifetime.

It is for this reason that many developed countries now offer school-based crèches to encourage adolescent women to return to school as soon as possible following the birth of their baby. In Australia there are many 'back to school' programmes, mostly based in regional areas, where it is recognized that many young mothers are in a cycle of welfare dependency based on a lack of education (Bradbury 2006; Shacklock, 2007; The Smith Family, 2014). Many students will be the first in their family to complete school and go on to higher education. The difficulties experienced by these young women, who have to add school and studies to the day-to-day tasks of parenting, often alone, are amply captured in these quotes.

> It's exhausting but this is not just about my future, it's about the future for my children as well. I have to do something to make sure our future is the best it can be. (Female, 18 years, with a 2 and a 1 year old)

> She's not walking yet but she is at that age when she's into everything – the other day she tore up one of my practice tests. (Female, 19 years, 20 weeks pregnant, with a 1-year-old)

> I don't get any time to study when I'm at home but when I come here
> [to school] I get a break from my son and I can focus on my work.
> (Female, 19 years, with a 21-month-old)
>
> *(Browne, 2012:1)*

Although many of these women face hardship, both socially and physically, in returning to school, for others it is a relief from the tedium of motherhood.

> After my baby was born I got bored. Staying home every day is very
> boring. There wasn't a day care for him and it was hard for me to go
> anywhere 'cause I haven't got a car or anything. . . . I decided to give
> it a try 'cause it's not exactly a school, you don't have to wear uniform
> and you don't have classes every single lesson. . . . I should pass my
> subjects but I have some catch-up classes to do 'cause I have a lot of
> absences because of my son. (Female, 17 years, mother of a toddler)
>
> *(Shacklock, 2007:4)*

Children of adolescent mothers

The prevailing view is that children of adolescent mothers face a number of challenges due to the young mother's immaturity, lack of parenting skills and inadequate financial resources. However, there are also concerns about the prospects for the child.

> [T]hey have less supportive and stimulating home environments, poorer
> health, lower cognitive development, worse educational outcomes,
> more behavioural problems, and are more likely to become teen parents
> themselves.
>
> *(Kirby, 2001:3)*

Other research has found that these children are more likely to experience early school-leaving, homelessness, foster care, juvenile problem behaviour and incarceration (National Campaign to Prevent Teen and Unplanned Pregnancy, 2013).

A study utilizing data from the British Household Panel Survey has now demonstrated that being born of an adolescent mother is associated with worse outcomes for young adults. This study is important as it was able to examine diverse outcomes, including such issues as educational attainment, wages and smoking. It also included information on siblings, allowing consideration of previously unobserved additive effects shared by children of the same family. The findings showed that children of adolescent mothers achieve a lower standard of education and have a higher probability of having a low income than those born to mothers over the age of 24 years. These children also have a higher likelihood of becoming an adolescent parent themselves, confirming earlier observations (Haveman, Wolfe & Peterson, 1997; Kiernan, 1997; Manlove, 1997). The study findings concluded that children born to mothers aged 23 or younger are generally less successful than children of older mothers over a range of life activities (Francesconi, 2007).

However, despite these negative findings, to date it has been difficult to separate the impact of socioeconomic status and family-related factors from adolescent motherhood per se on the outcomes for the child.

What about the fathers?

There has been little focus on adolescent fatherhood, an issue that is poorly understood and infrequently researched (Mollborn & Lovegrove, 2011). It seems that fathers, young or old, have long been invisible participants in the act of procreation and parenthood.

Little is known of young men's attitudes towards pregnancy before they find themselves as potential fathers. One small qualitative Australian study reported that young men saw pregnancy prevention as a shared responsibility between both partners (Collyer, 2012).

> I don't think the responsibility should rest solely on either person. (Male, 21 years)
>
> *(Collyer, 2012:37)*

In this study contraception was nearly always discussed in reference to preventing pregnancy rather than STIs; pregnancy was more of a concern for most young men than infections.

> I'd be more worried by the child byproduct, but both are pretty scary. (Male, 21 years)
>
> *(Collyer, 2012:37)*

Not all young men respond this way. In a cohort study of almost 300 pregnant couples aged 14–21 years, pregnancy desire was individually ascertained for each person. The degree to which each partner desired the pregnancy and partners' perceptions of each other's views were explored, and showed that half of both young men and women reported wanting the pregnancy. Wanting the pregnancy was positively linked with satisfaction with life and with their relationship, particularly among young men (Sipsma *et al.*, 2012), but Lyra (2003) found some young fathers less positive.

> No, we never thought of getting rid of the child (having an abortion), because it was part of our plan to have a child. It just wasn't the right time, but since it came . . .
>
> *(Lyra, 2003:4)*

> When I got the news, it was a shock. A real shock. I kept thinking for months, I was paranoid, not knowing which way to turn in my life. . . . A new family, I couldn't even support myself, how was I going to support another person and a child?
>
> *(Lyra, 2003:5)*

The major social role ascribed to men in most countries of the world is to find work and produce income. Very young men who become fathers struggle to fulfil this role, as many are still in school, live at home and are not in a position to be able to offer much support to partner and child. Where the father lives at some distance from the mother and child, being able to visit the child after school may require an adult's assistance. Nevertheless, many of these fathers do make an effort to remain engaged. In the US in 2010, adolescent mothers living apart from the father of their child reported that half of the non-resident fathers met with their child in the past month and, among those who did, about half visited at least weekly (Ng & Kaye, 2012).

Even though pregnancy in adolescence is generally seen negatively, it is viewed by some young people as a much wanted transition to adulthood, an opportunity for reprioritizing aspects of life, and giving up past undesired activities. A very small study of young men aged 16–19 years, with two children each, found that the participants perceived themselves as mature, responsible and concerned about the best future for their children and themselves, although all regretted the loss of adolescent freedom (Carvalho, Merighi & Jesus, 2010).

US data suggest that 34 per cent of adolescent women who were unmarried at the time of their child's birth marry the father of their child. Conversely, of those who were married or cohabiting with their child's father at the time of the birth, 38 per cent of those married and 42 per cent of those cohabiting had separated by the time the child was 5 years old (Ng & Kaye, 2012).

Before condemning those young men who fail to support their partners, financially or emotionally, we need to acknowledge that mothers (and their parents) can function as gatekeepers. For some fathers, access to their infants and children may be restricted, thus limiting the degree of paternal involvement in infant and child care even when they keenly desire the opportunity to participate in child-rearing.

There are few intervention programmes in the field of sexual and reproductive health to address the needs and concerns of fathers (Lyra & Medrado, 2014), and many unanswered questions about the consequences of teenage fatherhood – for the young fathers themselves, for their partners and for their children. Why do some young fathers accept their family responsibilities and obligations? How effective are these young men as parents and as partners? What is the effect of these young fathers on their children's development? These and other questions need to be addressed before we can fully understand what it means to father a child while still a teenager.

Programmes to reduce adolescent pregnancy

Not surprisingly, in light of the concerns about the number of unintended adolescent pregnancies and the potential for negative outcomes for mother and child, increasing attention is being paid to this issue. Reducing the rate of adolescent pregnancy is a priority recognized in government policy in some countries, including the US and the UK (Holgate & Evans, 2006; Kirby, 2007).

There are many programmes in developed countries that aim to address adolescent pregnancy. For example, a recent trial of a teenage pregnancy prevention intervention for almost 450 at-risk 13- to 14-year-old girls in England comprised 18–20 weekly sessions in preschool nurseries. Although there was little evidence of improved contraception use or lowered expectations of becoming pregnant while a teenager, there were improvements in self-esteem, sexual health knowledge and ability to discuss the pill (Bonell et al., 2013).

In a similar vein, and attempting to identify protective strategies that might reduce pregnancy rates, in one study, 200 non-pregnant adolescents aged 14–19 years were interviewed every six months for 2 years. The researchers found that pregnancy desire was associated with older age, short relationship duration and greater perceived stress. After accounting for potential confounders, desire to become pregnant doubled the risk of this occurring over the 18-month follow-up period (Sipsma et al., 2011). Those who were not in school and who expressed a desire for pregnancy were particularly at increased risk of pregnancy, suggesting this group would be good to target for an intervention aimed at improving coping mechanisms.

There are many examples of interventions to address adolescent pregnancy, but there is very little evidence to suggest they have much impact in reducing adolescent pregnancy rates. A review conducted in 2009–2012 identified over 1000 potentially relevant research papers reporting on such programmes, but only 10 per cent of these were of high or moderate quality, and in only 31 cases was there evidence of programme impact studies. In summary, the review team found no programmes with evidence of sustained, full-sample impacts replicated across two or more high-quality studies (Mathematica Policy Research, 2012), so better evaluation of programmes is necessary to determine the most effective interventions.

It may be that we need to turn to more youth-friendly strategies to deliver educational programmes of this sort. Given the level of appeal of digital technologies to adolescents, there is hope that these can offer more effective programmes. This appears to have been used to good effect in the UK by delivering sexual health and contraceptive advice in a youth-friendly way. The Kent Community Health NHS Trust's C Card initiative is a community-based contraceptive scheme, utilizing an iPhone app and a website (Penfold, 2012). More than 45 000 young people have registered with the site since its launch in 2007. The iPhone app uses interactive maps to direct users to their nearest condom outlets, and provides information on sexual health, emergency contraception and treatment for STIs. According to Penfold (2012):

> the scheme offers free condoms and contraceptive advice. Condoms are available from sexual health clinics, pharmacies, youth schemes and school nurses. Once a teenager is registered, the card can be used up to 20 times, before an appointment is needed to re-register for a new card.
>
> *(Penfold, 2012:6)*

Although this is an encouraging development, it is essential that such programmes be adequately assessed in both the short and long term to ensure that they are achieving sustained success in reducing adolescent pregnancy.

Conclusion

Our discussion of adolescent pregnancy and parenthood has highlighted the variability of outcomes for those concerned. It is clear that, for some, pregnancy is unplanned and the baby unwanted. For others, the decision to have a baby at an early age has positive outcomes whereas for others it brings in its wake a series of negative consequences. Adolescent parenthood may prove to be a difficult and disruptive choice, resulting in serious and permanent limitations to life's opportunities. But not all adolescent parents, especially mothers, experience difficulties. A substantial number complete schooling, marry (and do not divorce), find rewarding employment and their children develop along patterns which are not different from those of children of older parents. In spite of the very serious hurdles that these young people encounter, they are able to realize their ambitions and life plans.

What are the factors that protect these successful young parents from difficulties and distress? The importance of adequate social support in mediating the stress for young mothers, whether this comes from the child's father, parents or other family members, has been well documented. Not surprisingly, socioeconomic level contributes substantially. To be poor and undereducated is likely to decrease significantly the likelihood of wellbeing for these young parents and their offspring. One factor to which we have not yet paid attention is the interpretation given to adolescent pregnancy within the society. Is this seen to be a normative phenomenon or is it assumed to be disruptive of young people's normal life trajectory? In some cultures, it is clear that parenting at a youthful age is accepted and incorporated into everyday life. The African-American culture in the US provides an example, among western countries, of this process. In many studies, we find that parenthood at an early age is less disruptive of their everyday lives for young Black women than for their White counterparts.

Often adolescent pregnancy and parenting is seen to require special programmes to assist these young parents and their children. Considerable funds are spent to prevent adolescent pregnancy and to provide services to ameliorate problems after conception occurs. These include provision of family planning services, antenatal care, health and parenting programmes and a variety of comprehensive care programmes. There are some programmes that have been directed to promoting educational or occupational opportunities, including the provision of alternative schooling for pregnant girls. It is not possible for us to outline in detail the variety of programmes designed to overcome the negative health, social and economic consequences of early child-rearing. Rather, the responses to adolescent pregnancy are, to some extent, culturally bound as well as dependent on individual characteristics.

What is striking about the research findings is that adolescent parents are not a homogeneous group. Clearly many of the problems that beset these young people are not a function of their premature parenthood but are often shared by their non-parenting peers. Moreover, we still know too little about the impact of early pregnancy and parenthood. In spite of the plethora of books dealing with adolescent pregnancy, contemporary researchers have neglected the phenomenology of early motherhood and fatherhood. We have little idea of what it actually feels like to become a mother or father when one is little more than a child. Adolescent pregnancy and/or parenthood may be a monumental handicap to wellbeing and achievement, but even so, many young women, while regretting lost opportunities, cannot imagine themselves without their children and are happy as parents. As the words of this young mother testify:

> [S]ometimes I say to myself I wish I never had her. Maybe I would probably have had a boyfriend. . . . Sometimes when I've got money problems I say to myself if I didn't have her I'd probably be well off now . . . but then when I think of her I say no. She's mine, and I'm happy she's here.
>
> *(Phoenix, 1991:242)*

Nearly two decades later, other young women share these views.

> I always wanted to be able to take care of myself and when Emily [her daughter] came around, it was just . . . her. I just wanted her to live a long, healthy, happy, successful life, and I wanted her to have what I never had.
>
> *(Mangino, 2008:95)*

> Being a single mom is what got me up in the morning. . . . When you hold your child in your arms for the first time, you know it's just this weird feeling inside of you. It's a very powerful feeling and you're, like, I'll do anything for this child. Everything I do is for my son and a little bit is for me.
>
> *(Mangino, 2008:102)*

11

SEXUAL ABUSE, UNWANTED SEX AND SEXUAL SAFETY

Scope out your surroundings during the day. Whether you're working in a new place or new to campus, make sure you learn the safest way to walk from place to place. This means staying under well-lit lights, walking in places where people tend to be around, and even being near blue light emergency call boxes, if your campus has them.

(WikiHow, n.d.)

I was raped by an acquaintance in [...] Dormitory on [...] College campus. Some nights I can still hear the sounds of his roommates on the other side of the door, unknowingly joking and talking as I was held down.

(Epifano, 2012)

These two quotes demonstrate the fear and the reality of sexual assault. Although it is attack by a stranger that is most feared, in fact most sexual assault is perpetrated by someone known to the victim.

In this chapter we take up the important issues of sexual abuse and sexual safety. Different types of sexual abuse are discussed: abuse by an adult (either known to the victim or a stranger), sexual exploitation, intimate partner and dating violence, sexual coercion and unwanted sex, sexual harassment and dangers associated with social media. Outcomes of sexual violence as well as strategies and resources for its prevention are discussed and some of the limited research available on perpetrators is presented.

Globally, the high attractiveness of youth coupled with their low power and status targets them as frequent victims of sexual violence and abuse. Young women are especially vulnerable, as are any group of adolescents with less power than their peers, for example, those with an intellectual disability or from cultural groups where women's activities are tightly controlled. Even in societies where women have had equal rights for generations, young women are warned to be constantly on the alert to avoid sexual violence, as shown in the quotes above.

Sexual abuse

Sexual abuse occurs when a person is forced, coerced or tricked into sexual acts against their will or without their consent, or if a child or young person under the age of consent is exposed to sexual activities. The way in which consent is conceptualized by the law differs in different jurisdictions (Fileborn, 2011), but in many western countries it is deemed to occur only when a person above a designated 'age of consent' *freely and voluntarily* agrees to sexual activity.

Sexual assault occurs when someone is unable and/or does not give consent to sexual activity. The definitions of the kinds of unwanted sexual activity that qualify for legal purposes as sexual assault vary. For example, in some jurisdictions it may include groping or forced kissing; in others it may only include forced penetration. An inability to give consent would occur if a person was asleep or unconscious, significantly intoxicated or affected by drugs, unable to understand what they are consenting to due to their age or intellectual capacity, intimidated, coerced or threatened, unlawfully detained or held against their will, or they submitted due to the perpetrator being in a position of trust (e.g. New South Wales Government, 2013).

Prevalence

Although it appears to be systematically underreported to the authorities, sexual abuse affects the lives of many young people and adults. Cross-cultural comparisons of prevalence of sexual abuse are challenging, given the wide variation in views about what it comprises. In addition to different definitions, the measures used to assess levels of abuse and the opportunities for those abused to seek redress vary across countries. In countries and cultural groups where girls and women are considered as property of men, consent to sexual activity is conceptualized in a different way, making abuse even more problematic to measure. Forced marriages of under-age girls, for example, may be illegal, but in some cultural groups, family and social pressures can be so intense as to leave girls with little option to comply with the wishes of their male relatives. Most accept their situation, because opportunities for complaint or redress are limited or non-existent, and punishment for non-compliance can be severe. Reports and studies of sexual abuse all acknowledge that its occurrence is likely to be grossly underestimated, so prevalence data should be read with this in mind.

Physical and sexual violence often go hand in hand. WHO (2013c) reports that the global lifetime prevalence of intimate partner violence for ever-partnered women aged 15–19 years is 29.4 per cent, marginally less than that for women aged 20–24 years (31.6 per cent). Sexual violence rates are also high. A recent interview study of 42 000 women across European Union members found 11 per cent had experienced some form of sexual violence since the age of 15, either by a partner or some other person (European Agency for Fundamental Human Rights, 2014). One in 20 had been raped. More than 1 in 5 women had experienced physical and/or sexual violence from a current or previous partner, and over 1 in 10 women had experienced some form of sexual violence by an adult before they were 15 years of age.

Interviews with over 16 000 adults (9000 women) in the US found 18.3 per cent of women and 1.4 per cent of men had been raped at some time in their lives, including completed forced penetration, attempted forced penetration or alcohol/drug facilitated completed penetration (Black *et al.*, 2011). Most women (80 per cent) who had experienced a completed rape were first raped before the age of 25; for almost half this occurred before the age of 18 years. Rates are similar in the UK, where 16.5 per cent of 11- to 17-year-olds reported sexual abuse by an adult or a peer (Brown, O'Donnell & Erooga, 2011).

Although not as common as sexual violence against women, rape and other forms of sexual coercion directed against young men occur in a variety of settings, including at home, the workplace, schools, on the streets, in the defence forces and during war, as well as in police custody and in prisons. Studies conducted mostly in developed countries indicate that 5–10 per cent of men report a history of childhood sexual abuse (Krug, Dahlberg, Mercy, Zwi & Lozano, 2002).

Abuse in the family

Most reporting of sexual abuse is by adults who experienced abuse for many years preceding their report, usually as a child or adolescent. Sexual abuse involving incest or with a known adult, such as a friend of the family or step-parent, generally starts before the child reaches puberty, at around the age of 9, according to Daugherty (2006). There is evidence that most sexual abuse is, in fact, committed by someone known to the victim and many cases involve incest or rape by a known and trusted adult. Incest is not confined to any cultural group, socioeconomic level or religion (Atwood, 2007), however the incest taboo is one of the most widespread of cultural taboos in both present and past societies and close relative incest is prohibited by the world's key religions.

For the victim, the feelings of violation and shame that can accompany incest are often even harder to deal with than sexual abuse by a stranger outside the home. The following quote from a survivor of adolescent incest poignantly illustrates the breach of trust experienced by this young woman and her feelings of self-blame.

> It was in the context of a loving, trusting relationship. My father was somebody who represented right and wrong to me, which is why it was so difficult to understand what was happening to me at that age. One grows up with the idea that male sexuality, male passion, is somehow a woman's fault, something you're responsible for. As a little girl, I can remember being taught not to sit in a certain way, not to stand in certain ways – and it's very complicated to learn all those things, because you're supposed to be sexy and attractive to men; at the same time you're not supposed to lead them on, you're supposed to know what the balance is. Of course, I now realise that men must take responsibility for their own sexual feelings.
>
> *(Payne, 1983:59)*

Although sexual abuse by a biological parent is uncommon, the risk increases in families where there is a single parent, a step-parent or foster parents (Ronken & Johnston, 2012). A young woman molested by her step-father expressed her anger and sense of powerlessness to be able to stop the abuse from happening:

> I was molested by my step-dad. If I keep it inside it eats me up. I don't know why he did what he did, but he told me because I wasn't his real daughter he could. He started when I was 10. He started touching me right after he married my Mom. I was asleep one day and he came into my bedroom and just started to touch me all over. I told him to stop but he still didn't. He hit me because I tried to stop him. It didn't hurt but I got the message. (Female, 16 years)
>
> *(Atwood, 2007:1)*

Victims feel they have no one to turn to and fear that they may not be believed – a fear often justified. They believe that they will cause family break-up or be rejected by other family members. In the case of sexual abuse by a parent or step-parent, victims may feel betrayed by their non-abusing parent, who may be perceived to be powerless as a protector, or even as colluding in the abuse.

Although abuse by a stranger is traumatic, it is a situation with which people close to the victim are more likely to empathize and offer support than in cases of incest. Stranger sexual abuse is also an event in which the victim can readily interpret the perpetrator as evil, hated and different from normal people. This interpretation is far more difficult, if not impossible, when the perpetrator is a family member or respected adult. Such cases leave the victim uncertain of whom they can trust, an insecurity that may remain with them for life. Indeed, among both children and adults, more severe post-trauma symptoms have been consistently associated with incest by a father compared with other perpetrators (Naar-King, Silvern, Ryan & Sebring, 2002).

Research examining the effects of sexual abuse suggests that both violent stranger rapes and long-term incest beginning in childhood have the most damaging effects on psychological functioning. Sexual abuse in childhood is associated with both negative short-term outcomes such as guilt and anxiety, and longer term effects including drug and alcohol abuse, somatic problems, depression, suicide and relationship problems in adulthood (Bergen, Martin, Richardson, Allison & Roeger, 2004; Naar-King *et al.*, 2002). Victims may experience symptoms of post-traumatic stress disorder, such as nightmares and other forms of re-experiencing, as in the following example.

> It wasn't the physical pain – I used to go to another place in my head – what I can't get rid of are the nightmares, the thoughts and pictures that just come into my head and the fact that I just sometimes freeze when my boyfriend wants to have sex; he says he understands but how can he? It's like part me died when I was six. (Female, 18 years)
>
> *(Brown et al., 2011:6)*

Institutionalized sexual exploitation

In recent years, many developed countries have commenced investigations into sexual abuse that had occurred while young people were in the care of adults who, through a position of authority, acted as substitute parents. For example, in 2014 the Australian Government began a Royal Commission into Child Sexual Abuse that included investigation of religious groups, schools, institutions such as care homes, orphanages and organizations for young people such as Scouts and Guides. The commission was instituted because of the large number of complaints from survivors of sexual abuse who, as adults, at last felt able to talk about what had happened to them. Some of this abuse involves fear, force and violence from the outset. In other cases young people are 'groomed'; their trust is gained and they are gradually led into cooperating in behaviours that exploit their youth and innocence and potentially damage their health and wellbeing. Attempts to stop the exploitation by the young person may be met with threats, blackmail or worse.

In Britain, a report from the UK Office of the Children's Commissioner found that a disproportionate number of children and young people who are sexually exploited are living in out-of-home care (Department of Education UK, 2012). Following this report, urgent reforms to protect children in residential care homes from sexual exploitation were announced. These involve more robust checks before children are placed in care homes and a review of all aspects of the quality and effectiveness of children's homes – including their management, ownership and staffing.

Similarly, a review of child protective services in Ireland in 2006 found that the majority of cases of underage sexual exploitation investigated by police involved children in the out-of-home care system (Department of Health, Social Services and Public Safety Northern Ireland, 2006), yet 7 years later no concerted action to remedy this situation had been taken, according to press reports of parliamentary debate on this matter (McAdam, 2013). The debate raised the point that all children, whether in care or living at home, need education about strategies to stay safe from adults who would groom them for sexual exploitation. It is worth pointing out that education is not always enough in situations where young people lack the power to act; they also need protection from such predators.

A disturbing aspect to these cases is the extent to which whole communities appear to have been 'in denial' about the extent of sexual abuse of children and adolescents. Young people were routinely not believed if they complained, often because of the high status or reputation of the abuser, or their valued position in the family or society in general. This has been underscored not only by the reports of institutional abuse described above, but by recent events in which several well-known and respected entertainers were charged with sexual abuse of children following complaints from their now adult alleged victims. First there is disbelief; then as more cases come forward, the full story emerges. Many children do not mention their abuse to anyone because they think no one will believe them. They also may be afraid of the abuser, or feel guilty, ashamed, or believe the abuse was their fault. The result of publicity around high-profile cases has raised community awareness in ways that will hopefully lead to improved protocols for child protection and improved sex education for both children and families. The danger is a backlash into moral panic in which all men are regarded with suspicion and the expression of intergenerational affection is marginalized as deviant.

Trafficking and sex tourism

Another crime that is hidden in many communities is the sexual exploitation of adolescents through human trafficking and sex tourism (McClain & Garrity,

2011; Pearce, Hynes & Bovarnick, 2013). The United Nations through their Optimal Protocol on the Sale of Children, Child Prostitution and Child Pornography (United Nations, 2000) prohibits such exploitation, as do the laws of most countries. Sexual exploitation of children has been defined by the International Labour Organization (n.d.) as including child prostitution, trafficking of young people for the sex trade, child sex tourism and the production, promotion and distribution of pornography involving children. UNICEF as long ago as 2006 estimated around two million children and adolescents are the victims of sexual trafficking, and this number is likely to be substantially higher today.

It is not only in 'third world' countries that these crimes occur. In the US, for example, cases of human trafficking have been reported in all 50 US states (US Department of State, 2009). Mitchell, Finkelhor and Wolak (2010) report that US adolescents aged 14–17 years represented the largest proportion of victims, and 11 per cent of those prostituting were under 14 years. Pearce *et al.* (2013) discuss some of the problems that occur in developed multicultural nations such as the UK when trying to tackle this crime. The extent of trafficking may be masked and children can slip through child protection safety nets because of language or communication problems, children's fears of retribution and/or authorities focusing on immigration issues to a greater extent than child welfare. What's more, the sexual and work-related exploitation of children – child slavery in many cases – is, according to Pearce *et al.*, 'the third most profitable organised criminal activity in the world, after weapons and narcotics' (Pearce *et al.*, 2013:2); thus greed and vested interests make its eradication a serious challenge.

Pearce *et al.* (2013) also consider the challenges of treating sexually exploited and trafficked young people, especially those who have been coerced into believing that their lifestyle is normal, or that it is they who are the criminals rather than their abusers. These writers warn against 'victim profiling' of particular cultures, noting that some trafficking within the UK is unnoticed because it arises from children being abused in family contexts or neglected when in residential care. They also note that boys as well as girls are vulnerable to such exploitation, particularly as they are more likely than girls to be homeless and 'on the streets'.

It is widely believed that the increased use of the internet has increased the incidence of child sex trafficking, because it is a resource for providing access to vulnerable women, girls and boys (for example through Facebook, dating sites and chat rooms). The unregulated nature of the internet also allows groups of paedophiles, pimps and the like to communicate with one another, share images and resources (for example through advertising child prostitutes to sex tourists) and generally avoid prosecution (e.g. Kunze, 2010).

How do young people become involved? Adolescents, made vulnerable by poverty, disadvantage or simply naiveté, can be lured into the sex industry through kindness and gifts, which can make them feel indebted or even believe that they are in a love relationship with their exploiter. Alternatively threats, intimidation, violence and even kidnapping may be used to ensnare the victim (Williamson & Prior, 2009). In other situations, adolescent and pre-adolescent children may be sold into prostitution or slavery by impoverished parents (e.g. Parry, 2014).

Child and adolescent sex tourism is another aspect of sexual exploitation and occurs when perpetrators travel, either within their own country or internationally, and engage in sexual acts with minors. These 'tourists', who are almost exclusively adult males, may be regular abusers or they may engage in such sexual acts as an opportunistic experiment. Being in a different (usually poorer) country or area, away from the socializing constraints of work and family, perpetrators may feel protected by their anonymity; they may believe they have licence to engage in unprotected and/or violent sexual practices without guilt. The organization End Child Prostitution and Trafficking (ECPAT, 2015) notes that 'those who exploit children when they travel may try to rationalise their actions by claiming sex with a child is culturally acceptable or that money or goods exchanged benefit the child and community, or by setting their own thresholds for defining who is a child'. Some countries have now made it illegal for their citizens to travel to other countries for the intent of engaging in sexual exploitation of children, but this is a difficult activity to police.

Research that is available indicates long-term consequences of sexual exploitation for both young women and young men (Carbone-Lopez, 2012). Adolescent victims of sexual exploitation and trafficking universally demonstrate many negative physical and mental outcomes related to the acts they are forced to perform, the fear they experience and the gross distortions of human sexual and affectionate feelings to which they are exposed. They are also often forced to perform sexual acts without protection, making them more vulnerable to pregnancy and sexually transmitted infections than their adolescent peers. Tragically, many victims do not seek rescue, as their lack of resources makes them dependent on their pimps or captors, a situation magnified for those who have been trafficked internationally. Young people who escape the control of pimps often have no other means of survival and fall back to prostitution (Williamson & Prior, 2009).

Sexual exploitation of young people, whether organized or opportunistic, is a serious crime requiring heavy-duty political and legal intervention. But sexual abuse and unwanted sex for young people more commonly occurs within the context of their peer group relationships, and in the following sections we discuss these issues.

Intimate partner abuse and dating violence

Forced or pressured sex in the context of dating is relatively common. A recent British study of over 15 000 people over the age of 13 years (average age of 18 years for women and 16 years for men) by Macdowall *et al.* (2013) found that 20 per cent of women and 5 per cent of men reported attempted non-volitional sex (sex against their will), and 10 per cent of women and 1.4 per cent of men reported experiencing completed non-volitional sex. Only 33 per cent of men told someone about it, compared to 42 per cent of women, and younger people rather than older people were more likely to tell someone.

One study found that up to 8 per cent of older adolescent girls (16–20 years of age) reported experiencing actual or attempted sex against their will. Associated with sexual victimization was substance abuse (such as binge drinking and marijuana use), health risk behaviours such as sex without birth control, and ever having been in a fight (Champion *et al.*, 2004). Similarly, another study described the role of alcohol in the experiences of forced or coerced sex against adolescent and young adult women, whereby perpetrators were reported to have consumed alcohol immediately prior to the assault, or victims were coerced to consume alcohol by their perpetrators. Self-blame about their exposure to unwanted sex was common, as was a reluctance to define those unwanted experiences as sexual assault or rape given the concomitant nature of the alcohol consumption (McCauley *et al.*, 2014). Mental health concerns and negative education outcomes were also associated with dating violence.

The US National Survey of Youth found that nearly 12 per cent of female students and 6 per cent of male students reported being forced to engage in intercourse at least once in the past year (Youth Risk Behavior Surveillances, 2004). Young men in particular may be reluctant to report due to both the stigma associated with forced male-to-male sexual contact and the high degree of shame for men in admitting victimization. Men who have sex with men are known to be vulnerable to sexual victimization (Macdowall *et al.*, 2013).

Correlates of dating violence

Those reporting a history of dating violence are more likely to have fewer close friends and be engaged in other serious health risk behaviours, such as substance abuse, unhealthy weight control and contemplation of or attempts at suicide (Banyard & Cross, 2008; Exner-Cortens, Eckenrode & Rothman, 2013; Foshee, McNaughton Reyes, Gottfredson, Chang & Ennett, 2013; Kim-Godwin, Clements, McCuiston & Fox, 2009). These behaviours may be a consequence of experiencing violence, especially if it occurs over a significant period of time; they may be risk factors for becoming involved with a violent partner, or the behaviours may be linked through a third factor such as poverty or family background. Longitudinal data suggest violence as a causative factor in other anti-social or self-destructive outcomes. For example recent findings from the National Longitudinal Study of Adolescent Health in the US confirm that, 'dating violence experienced during adolescence is related to adverse health outcomes in young adulthood' (Exner-Cortens *et al.*, 2013:71). Their study found that 5 years after being victimized by dating violence as adolescents, both young men and young women reported increased suicide ideation and a continuation of violence into their adulthood. Young men also reported increased anti-social behaviours and marijuana use, whereas young women reported increased heavy episodic drinking, depressive symptomatology and smoking.

Not surprisingly, having violence-supportive attitudes is a risk factor for sexual violence. In a national survey of 5000 young Australians aged 12–20 years, young men were more likely than young women to agree with pro-violence statements (National Crime Prevention, 2001). In response to the question 'Is it OK for a boy to make a girl have sex, if she has flirted with him or led him on?', 79 per cent of females and 52 per cent of males disagreed strongly and 12 per cent of males and 3 per cent of females agreed. A survey of over 1000 Japanese, Kuwaiti, Indian and US undergraduate students showed men in all four countries had more supportive attitudes towards violence than women (Nayak, Byrne, Martin & Abraham, 2003; Pulerwitz & Barker, 2008). Furthermore, a community sample of Brazilian men aged 15–24 years showed that young men with less support for gender equitable norms were more likely to report that they had perpetrated intimate partner violence than men with moderate or high support for equitable gender norms (Pulerwitz & Barker, 2008).

Coercive and non-consensual sex

Unwanted sex does not always involve violence, but it may nevertheless be non-consensual and lead to long-term negative effects on psychological health and relationships. It is clear a great deal of sexual activity occurs among young people that is not consensual, or where consent has been obtained through dishonest, manipulative or fear-arousing strategies.

Adams-Curtis and Forbes (2004) use the term 'sexual coercion', recommending this 'to describe any situation in which one party uses verbal or physical means (including administering drugs or alcohol to the other party either with or without their consent) to obtain sexual activity against freely given consent'. They differentiated seduction and coercion thus: 'wearing down an individual with repeated requests and entreaties would be coercive as consent would not be freely given. A seduction in which the person changes her mind regarding whether she wishes to engage in sexual behavior would not' (Adams-Curtis & Forbes, 2004:99).

In highlighting the complexity of issues around coercion and consent, Adams-Curtis and Forbes (2004) put it this way:

> [I]n a stranger rape involving overwhelming physical force or the surreptitious administration of a stupefying drug, there is no dispute about the presence of coercion or the lack of consent. However, unambiguous situations are the rare exception. In fact, the most common scenario involves persons who know each other . . . who have been drinking . . . who have history of consensual sexual activity . . . and who have been engaging in consensual sexually stimulating activities. . . . At some point the woman signals that she wants to go no further, a signal that is often not spoken but must be inferred from her nonverbal communication. . . . The man, who may or may not have perceived and may or may not have understood the signal, continues his sexual behavior. His continuation usually involves little, if any force. He simply continues doing what he was before the signal was given.
>
> *(Adams-Curtis & Forbes, 2004:99)*

Why do young women and men comply with unwanted sex?

People within a long-term sexual relationship may, on occasions, comply with unwanted sex as part of the give and take within that relationship. However there is evidence that many adolescents will comply with unwanted sex outside this situation. Reasons include that they are in a position where they believe they have left it too late to say no and cannot now refuse without losing face, they are afraid of violence or they are physically unable, following use of drugs or alcohol, to communicate their wishes.

A national survey of over 2000 Australian secondary students in Years 10, 11 and 12 from schools all over Australia found that of those reporting they were sexually active, one-quarter had experienced unwanted sex (Mitchell,

Patrick, Heywood, Blackman & Pitts, 2014). Eight per cent of females and 5 per cent of males reported unwanted sex at their most recent sexual encounter. Although young women were more likely than young men to have ever experienced unwanted sex (28 per cent vs. 20 per cent), 'the numbers of young men are notable' (Mitchell *et al.*, 2014:28).

Many of the factors that increase an adolescent's vulnerability to unwanted sex are not of their own making, nor are young people in the position to overcome these factors without support. Factors include poverty, lack of education, gender inequality and crime (ECPAT, 2015). Earlier in the chapter we discussed some of these issues in relation to sexual exploitation, sex trafficking and tourism and sexual abuse in families. Community education, law enforcement, social welfare and programmes to both educate young people and help them overcome poverty are the key to eradicating these systemic vulnerabilities in the lives of children and adolescents worldwide. Although there are some protective strategies they can learn, ultimately sexual exploitation of minors must be tackled at national, international and local levels by attitudinal, organizational and legal changes.

There are, however, some individual and peer group factors associated with unwanted sex, particularly in the dating and hook-up culture common in western nations. These are discussed below.

Alcohol, fear and peer pressure

Students in the Mitchell *et al.* (2014) study cited being too drunk (49 per cent), frightened (28 per cent) or pressured by their partner (53 per cent) as the most common reasons for having sex when they did not want to. Of the sexually active students, 17 per cent reported they were either drunk or high at their most recent sexual encounter. More young men than young women reported being influenced by their peers (22 per cent vs. 9 per cent), whereas more young women than young men reported having sex when they did not want to because they were frightened (34 per cent vs. 15 per cent) or influenced by their partner (61 per cent vs. 37 per cent).

Drink spiking

Drink spiking (when illicit drugs are added to a person's drink without their permission) is a special issue related to unwanted sexual activity that has been reported with increased frequency in recent years. The motive is often to obtain sex while the victim is in a confused or even comatose state. Drink spiking occurs not only in licensed venues, but also at private parties, with so-called 'date-rape drugs' such as Rohypnol producing symptoms mimicking over-indulgence in alcohol or drugs. Victims may have difficulty gaining assistance from others, who believe they are drunk.

Emotionally charged environments

It is not only artificial stimulants or drugs that are implicated in unwanted sex, but the very nature of much of adolescents' socializing and leisure. For young people, the dating or 'going out' encounter has been described by O'Sullivan (2005) as an 'intensified exchange' – a situation of high emotional charge. So too are other situations in which young men and women meet for the purposes of potential romantic or sexual relationships, for example, pubs and clubs. The intensity of this charge may of course be heightened by drugs and alcohol, but it is also affected by strategies that both sexes use to increase their attractiveness such as seductive dress, flirtatious presentation, and displays of status and confidence designed to mask any underlying insecurities. This heady cocktail of youth, hormones, needs and alcohol can be great fun, but there is potential for unwanted and unhealthy outcomes, such as forced and coerced sex.

Ambiguity

In sexual situations, the boundaries of what constitutes coercion are not always clear for the young people concerned. Sexual situations can provide high levels of ambiguity, as well as the potential for impulsive action that is later regretted. This is illustrated by responses in a focus group study of school-based and college students in Australia by Crowley, Moore and Winkler (2004). Adolescents discussed whether sexual activity with someone who was too drunk to make an informed decision could actually be called rape. Some young people clearly did not define it as such and were inclined to 'blame the victim'. For example:

> [I]f they're passed out or close to it, then, like, it wouldn't be really considered rape 'cause they're not sort of doing anything to stop it, but obviously alcohol has put them in that situation. (Adolescent male)
> *(Crowley et al., 2004:3)*

Double standards

Another worrying view expressed in the study was that that some young people (girls, in particular) 'deserve what they get' because they dress or behave provocatively, or are known to have a 'reputation'. Sexual coercion is then justified by the perpetrator through the rationalization that the girl is 'asking for it' through her non-verbal cues. The following quotes from adolescents illustrate these ideas and show that they are not confined to males.

> Yeah well I reckon, I mean if a girl wears a really short skirt and like, you know, a belly, a top that, you know, shows everything, um I reckon um you're a bit asking for it. (Male)
>
> *(Crowley* et al.*, 2004:26)*

> I've got that certain friend who's blonde, big tits and very extroverted and she does get drunk on occasions. She's just a really nice person, very extroverted, but she gets into situations where the other person thinks well, she likes me . . . so they just go for it. She's so lost that she doesn't know what she's doing. So I definitely think if you're out there, sending, you know, not negative messages, you're more likely to be noticed. (Female)
>
> *(Crowley* et al.*, 2004:28)*

It seems that the impression of sexual availability, through dress, appearance and behaviour can still, for young women, be dangerous to both reputation and indeed to safety. The impression may or may not relate to the young woman's sexual wishes and desires. It may be a reflection of male projection, or a flirtation tactic designed (sometimes unconsciously) to lead to greater closeness to a potential partner. It may even be for the benefit of the female peer group, in an effort to out-compete them. In Chapter 7 we discussed the sexual double standard and the socialization pressures limiting the ways women can express their sexuality. For young women it seems it is sometimes easier to abdicate responsibility for their desires and let the 'magic of the moment' take over. Sometimes the moment does not turn out to be magic – the encounter goes 'too far', the sex is cursory and unromantic, the priming with alcohol means things get out of control. But the lack of a (verbal) language for young women to express their sexual needs adds to the ambiguity of sexual encounters, increasing possibilities for unwanted outcomes. Communication issues between the sexes were also mentioned in Crowley's study as contributing to misunderstandings about expectations, which may then lead to unwanted and later regretted sexual activities.

> I've definitely been in a situation where a person's been saying no but eventually I talked to them afterwards and they said yeah, 'I didn't mean that', and that puts me in a bit of a weird situation where I don't know where to draw the line. Some people say no and mean it, some people say no and don't, so if you had 10 girls in a row who said no and they really want it, and you get the one girl off, I mean, it's just, I guess, experience and you need to try and read the calls, read the signs, and some people just read them wrong. (Adolescent male)
>
> *(Crowley* et al.*, 2004:28)*

Misinterpretations in communication

Additionally, in the high arousal states of a sexual encounter, the non-verbal aspects of sexual communication are easy to misinterpret when a decision has to be made about whether to proceed with sex or slow down. Couples often do not decide to have sex verbally, but through action. The ambiguity may be perceived as reducing embarrassment (and in some cases personal responsibility for the decision to go ahead) or heightening romance and spontaneity, thus legitimizing being 'carried away' or 'overcome by passion' (Schaalma, Abraham, Gillmore & Kok, 2004). The desire for such ambiguity, seen by some as part of the 'magic' of sex, may therefore militate against the more prosaic discussion of whether this encounter is really wanted by both parties. Being overt about the desire for sex and indeed planning for safe sex is not a skill easily learned by observing others, but requires experience (sometimes with adverse consequences) or guidance provided by health promotion programmes (Schaalma *et al.*, 2004).

Conflict over withdrawal of consent

A related issue is withdrawal of consent (O'Sullivan, 2005). Some incidents of reported sexual forcing or coercion occur when permission has been given (either overtly or tacitly) to begin a sexual encounter but one party has a change of mind. Usually the mind-changer is depicted as the female, but men can and do change their minds as well. Partners may reject this change of mind for a range of reasons. They may not understand the communication if it is not clear, they may interpret it as sex play, or they may become angry, either forcing the sex to continue or expressing their anger through physical or verbal violence. Teaching young people about sexual communication must include education about being clear about what is wanted and accepting the rights of a partner, including the right to a change of mind, even if these are very difficult things to do in some situations.

Role of the hook-up culture in unwanted or regretted sex

The 'hook-up' culture, as described in a previous chapter, is a new development, facilitated by social media, which may lead to further opportunities for sexual miscommunication. Hooking up often refers to brief uncommitted sexual encounters between individuals who are not romantic partners or dating each other (Bogle, 2007, 2008). This form of interaction between peers makes casual sex normative and as such also appears to normalize sexual pressure. In a study of US college students, many female students recalled consenting to unwanted sexual activity, feeling it was their only option in the social situations in which they found themselves, despite the absence of threat or physical coercion.

> I ended up giving him a blow job because he wouldn't leave me alone. (Adolescent female)
>
> *(Wade & Heldman, 2012:138)*

Women dislike feeling this pressure but there is evidence that many feel unable to resist it. Even when sex was consensual and desired, females often reported highly unsatisfying encounters:

> Having sex was entirely for his enjoyment, when he wanted it, where and how. (Adolescent female)
>
> *(Wade & Heldman, 2012:141)*

> The guy kind of expects to get off, while the girl doesn't expect anything. (Adolescent female)
>
> *(Wade & Heldman, 2012:141)*

Other studies also suggest that many hook-up encounters are unwanted. In a sample of almost 200 US college students, 78 per cent reported unwanted sex in a hook-up, compared with 14 per cent in an ongoing relationship and 8 per cent on a date (Flack *et al.*, 2007). Another US study of over 750 female students found almost 50 per cent had had at least one experience of unwanted sex, 70 per cent as part of a hook-up, and 57 per cent in a committed romantic relationship (Garcia, Reiber, Massey & Merriwether, 2012).

Although most studies on non-consensual sex focus on women, a recent study of almost 300 young men in the US found that 43 per cent had experienced sexual coercion, of which 95 per cent was by women. Men identified a range of levels of coercion from verbal pressure, peer pressure and feelings of obligation, to physical force and rape (French, Tilghman & Malebranche, 2014).

> If my girlfriend is sad about something whether it is concerning me or not she pressures me into having sexual intercourse with her.

> I was coerced into sleeping with an older [woman] because I was told it would make me a big boy. I was only 12 at the time; the girl was 18 I believe.

> I was pushed into a bathroom by a girl and she started kissing me until I made her stop and explained that I didn't like her like that.
>
> *(French* et al., *2014:6)*

In summary, adolescents can be pressured into unwanted sexual activity because of perceived norms of the social situation they are in, because they are alcohol or drug affected, because they do not know how to express their wishes or are frightened to do so, or because they or their partner hold attitudes and beliefs supporting the use of force/coercion in certain situations and with particular 'types' of people. These non-consensual sexual encounters are often unreported due to the stigma and shame attached, or because many young people do not have a strong understanding of what constitutes sexual assault or rape.

Sexual harassment

Sexual harassment may not seem as serious in its outcomes as some of the behaviours described in previous sections, but it is nevertheless unacceptable, and is being more widely recognized as such. Although sexual harassment is usually considered within the context of workplaces or educational institutions, any unwanted attention of a sexual nature that creates discomfort can be described in this way. An Australian Human Rights Commission (2008) report on sexual harassment presents a long list of behaviours potentially qualifying in this category, up to and including attempted or actual rape or sexual assault. Generally, however, sexual harassment is understood as involving behaviours that are less violent and intrusive than rape but are nonetheless disturbing to the victim.

Examples of sexual harassment can include unwelcome touching or groping, inappropriate staring or leering, repeated unwelcome invitations to go out on dates, intrusive and offensive questions about the victim's private life or physical appearance, sexually suggestive comments, jokes, gifts or workplace posters or continued and unwelcome requests or pressure for sex or other sexual acts. The internet and social media can exacerbate opportunities for harassment through enabling perpetrators to make repeated or inappropriate sexual advances or share unsolicited sexual images, via email, social networking websites or internet chat rooms. When there is a power differential between the victim and the perpetrator, for example in the case of a supervisor and a junior worker or a student and a university lecturer, the victim can experience a real or imagined threat of job loss or low grades. In the words of one young woman who was supporting herself through university with a casual restaurant job:

> I can't afford to lose this job, but he keeps coming up behind me and putting his sleazy hands on me. He's started waiting for me after my shift finishes and asking me where I'm going, who with, all with a leer on his face. I'm scared if I say something he'll see me as a trouble maker and give me the sack. (Female, personal communication)

Prevalence of sexual harassment

A survey of nearly 2000 US secondary school children by the American Association of University Women (Ramirez, 2011) found the following disturbing statistics. Nearly half the adolescents surveyed had experienced peer-to-peer sexual harassment, including being subjected to unwelcome comments or jokes, inappropriate touching or sexual intimidation. Thirty per cent reported online harassment – unwelcome comments, jokes or pictures via text, email, Facebook and other tools, or having sexual rumours, information or pictures spread about them. Outcomes of these experiences included staying away from school, problems studying, poor sleep and stomach aches. Both boys and girls reported harassment but the rates were higher for girls (56 per cent compared to 40 per cent).

Statistics on employer–employee or teacher–student sexual harassment, in which adolescents and young people are the victims, are harder to come by and often go unreported or, if reported, are difficult to prove. Case material suggests that this sort of bullying can have serious effects on a young person's mental health and/or their career prospects. Various websites offer advice to young people regarding how to cope with sexual harassment, with key messages including that they should make a clear statement to the harasser that their behaviour is unacceptable, be aware of the policies and procedures surrounding sexual harassment in their school or workplace, tell someone in authority about the problem, keep a diary of events, and seek advice and support from others. In some cases, the victim may be advised to make an official complaint. However, although there are laws against sexual harassment in many countries and policies against this behaviour in many workplaces, making an official complaint can be fraught with difficulties and may be beyond the emotional resources of many young victims.

Dangers associated with online interaction

The digital age appears to have exacerbated sexual risk. New communication technologies blur the boundaries between the public and the private and some young people do not fully understand that online activity may have real consequences offline. The anonymity of the internet offers easy access to potential perpetrators of sexual harm.

Grooming is one such danger that can be exacerbated through online contact. A predator can pretend to be a young person and link up with children or adolescents in chat rooms, via mobile phone apps, on Facebook or through some other platform. Paedophiles can gain a young person's trust by showing an interest in their problems and concerns and presenting themselves as a true friend. The young person may be persuaded to supply their personal contact details, send sexually explicit photos or arrange a meeting with the predator. In some cases, young people have had their images circulated among paedophile rings, been sexually abused, forced into child prostitution or sexual slavery and even murdered. Many nations have enacted laws to guard against cyber grooming, however they are difficult to police. Teaching young people about cyber safety has thus become particularly important.

'Sexting', or sending a sexually explicit photo of oneself or another through an internet platform (e.g. email, Facebook), presents another danger to young people. Sexting is easy to do as smartphones now enable photos to be taken or videos made and readily transmitted to others. It is also common. In an Australian study of over 2000 young people by Mitchell *et al.* (2014), 26 per cent of secondary students reported having sent a sexually explicit photo of themselves and 42 per cent had received such a photo of someone else. This was more common among students who were sexually active, 70 per cent of whom had received a sexually explicit nude or nearly nude photo or video of someone else. Fifty per cent had actually sent such a photo or video of themselves and 17 per cent had sent a sexually explicit image of someone else.

In a recent study by Walker, Sanci and Temple-Smith (2013), girls were more likely to 'sext' their explicit images to boys than vice versa. The practice of sexting (both photo and text messages) is common among middle school youth, and co-occurs with sexual behaviour. Adolescents who sexted have been found to be seven times more sexually active and nearly twice as likely to engage in unprotected sex than their peers (Temple *et al.*, 2012). Sending sexually explicit photos only has been found to be associated with higher rates of sexual activity than sending text messages only (Houck *et al.*, 2014). Girls who had sent naked photos of themselves had a higher chance of engaging in risky sex, including having multiple partners and using substances before sex (Temple *et al.*, 2012).

The ease by which these images can be dispersed is of concern, especially as people lack control over their own image once it is sent. In some cases, the images are taken without the permission of the subject; in others, what may have been believed to have been a private communication with a girlfriend or boyfriend is widely distributed. Young people who send explicit sexual images through the internet can be subject to bullying and harassment, blackmail or become the target of adult sex offenders. As one UK parenting site pointed out:

> You can see how it could happen. Most phones have cameras, so it's the work of a moment to take a picture and press 'send.' And young teenagers aren't brilliant at thinking through the consequences of their actions. One minute it's a private photo. The next, it's public.
>
> *(Kavanagh, n.d.)*

Indeed, posting videos or images online has had terrible consequences for some young people. A 15-year-old Canadian girl was lured by an adult male, posing as a young man, to expose her breasts on a webcam. The picture ended up on a Facebook page made by the stranger, to which her friends were added. She was repeatedly bullied, despite changing schools, and eventually detailed her harassment on a YouTube video 'My story: Struggling, bullying, suicide, self harm' (TheSomebodytoknow, 2012; Wolf, 2012). Sadly, this young girl committed suicide weeks after posting the video, which had by then been viewed more than nine million times.

While recognizing that it is important to educate young people about these dangers, another view is that we should not engage in catastrophizing. Anne Mitchell, lead author of the Mitchell *et al.* (2014) study, said in an interview for *The Times* newspaper:

> It's a social, online world kids live in and sending these images and messages is part of their sexual relationships so it's really a new form of courtship. It appears to be happening universally and, while we need to be aware of the harm that can come if those messages are sent out far and wide or misused, it doesn't appear to be doing harm for the majority of kids.
>
> *(Prynne, 2014)*

Mitchell argued that it is important for parents not to panic but rather to ensure that they talk to their children about relationships, treating others well, and the dangers of posting online when privacy cannot be guaranteed.

Outcomes of sexual abuse

The consequences of sexual abuse, whether online or in-person, can have lasting effects. The relationship between having been sexually abused and subsequent harm has been frequently observed. These outcomes range from low self-esteem and an inability to develop intimate relationships to the perpetration of violence.

Childhood sexual abuse is a risk factor for being a victim of adolescent and adult sexual assault (Krupnick *et al.*, 2004; Noll, 2005). Sexual maladjustment has also been shown to result from sexual abuse in childhood and adolescence. There is a greater likelihood of starting sex at a younger age, having multiple partners, engaging in risky or impulsive sex, exchanging sex for money and suffering sexual dysfunction in adulthood (French & Dishion, 2003; Walsh, Latzman & Latzman, 2014). Child sexual abuse has also been shown to diminish an individual's ability to develop and maintain committed adult intimate relationships (Carbone-Lopez, 2012).

In adolescence, abuse by an intimate partner is associated with risk behaviours such as substance use, anti-social behaviour, violent behaviour, depressed mood and suicidal behaviour (Banyard & Cross, 2008). Young people who have been 'subject to unwanted sexual intercourse [are] over eight times as likely to take part in dangerous sex than those who have not endured forced sex' (Elliot, Beech, Mandeville-Norden & Hayes, 2009:580).

Although there are many studies reporting the serious short- and long-term effects of sexual abuse, there is also evidence from clinical studies conducted at various times in different decades that suggests childhood incest victims are not always severely psychologically damaged in adulthood (Atwood, 2007). Similarly, adolescent sexual abuse does not always lead to long-term psychological maladjustment. There are protective factors in adolescents' lives that are associated with resilience, the ability to work through and eventually cope with trauma. For example, perceived social support (particularly for girls) has been reported to moderate the effects of dating violence (Banyard & Cross, 2008). Family connectedness, a sense of caring by other respected adults, and school safety have also been identified as protective factors for young people who have been sexually abused (Eisenberg, Ackard & Resnick, 2007).

In general, though, the effects of childhood and adolescent rape and sexual abuse can be devastating. Their consequences are costly for the community in terms of the health, social adjustment and relationship quality. There is both an economic and humanitarian argument for increasing the resources currently being devoted to victims of sexual violence and the training of those who work with them.

Staying safe

Education, information programmes and resources

Preventive efforts against sexual violence take several forms, for example provision of information to parents and teachers about how to help children and adolescents to stay safe, classes and information provision via websites and books for young people at various age levels, and work with at-risk youth who fit the profiles of potential victims or potential perpetrators. Examples include school-based programmes which alert children and adolescents to potential dangers, raise discussion of what is appropriate and inappropriate touching, teach respect for others' boundaries, and give young people techniques to enable them to seek help when it is needed. One of the aims of these programmes is often to provide a safe space for young people to air their concerns about their experiences, to let them know that they are not to blame for another's abusive behaviour. Such school-based programmes may be integrated with a more general and comprehensive sex education curriculum and ideally will be tailored to the child's age and developmental stage.

The internet, as well as being a source of potential danger, also offers young people a readily accessible source of information about how to stay safe from sexual assault, and how to say no to unwanted sex, as in the following example from an Australian government website.

> If you think there is a chance that you might find yourself in a situation where you could be pressured into sex with your partner but you're not feeling ready, practice saying NO to the person in your mind beforehand. Think through how you could respond to what they might say, and how to stay in control. Talk to your friends about successful experiences they might have had, and how they handled similar situations.
>
> *(Queensland Health, 2010)*

Another example of web-based material is the US-based Rape, Abuse and Incest National Network (n.d.), which offers advice to young people about topics such as avoiding sexually compromising situations, how to resist sexual pressure, and computer safety, and also has a section for parents titled 'How can I protect my child from sexual assault?' In the UK, the website Think U Know (n.d.), under the auspices of the National Crime Agency, provides detailed information about potential sexual exploitation and an opportunity to voice concerns about specific people. Whether such websites are used or valued by the young people to whom they are targeted is unknown, as reports of evaluations of such websites are rare.

Self-defence training has been offered in some countries to young women as a strategy to reduce sexual assault, and there is some evidence that young women who have undertaken self-defence classes are more confident in their ability to effectively resist assault (Hollander, 2014). However, better evaluation of this on a broader scale is needed (Gidycz & Dardis, 2014).

A further type of preventive effort targets education of those who are at risk of engaging in sexually abusive behaviours, most usually groups of young men such as sporting teams or college student collectives. We know that association with male groups with strong masculine ideologies is linked to violence-supportive attitudes, which in turn link to perpetration of sexual violence (Murnen & Kohlman, 2007). Social and bonding activities in these groups may provide opportunities for the objectification of women, hypermasculine ideals and excessive alcohol use. Educational interventions are usually designed to present messages about the inappropriateness (and criminality) of violating another's boundaries, and to change misogynist attitudes.

One example of a national effort in this direction is the Australian Football League's (AFL) Respect and Responsibility Policy which was launched in 2005 and publicly outlined on the AFL's website (Australian Football League, 2014). This policy reflects the AFL's 'commitment to addressing violence against women and to work towards creating safe, supportive and inclusive environments for women and girls across the football industry as well as the broader community' and aims to:

- Increase players' understanding of how sexual assault, violence, harassment and abuse can affect the lives of women and girls
- Provide practical information that assists players to understand the meaning of consent, and identify situations that have the potential to go wrong
- Provide players with information that may assist them to build and maintain social relationships with women that are healthy and respectful.

(Australian Football League, 2014)

Interventions such as this may also be targeted at the community in general, for example in media campaigns that remind us that 'no means no', or that children and young adolescents are not in the position to give informed consent to sex.

Although many such programmes have been provided in communities, schools and universities with the aim of raising awareness and preventing relationship violence, unfortunately there is little evidence regarding whether the programmes are effective (Fellmeth, Heffernan, Nurse, Habibula & Sethi, 2013). A review of the results of 38 studies showed no convincing evidence that a range of educational programmes decreased relationship violence, including sexual violence, or that they improved participants' attitudes, behaviours and skills related to relationship violence. Results showed that knowledge about relationships improved slightly following the programmes, but none of the studies looked at their effect on physical and mental health, or on long-term changes in attitudes or behaviours (Fellmeth *et al.*, 2013).

Peer strategies

It is clear that young people develop strategies of their own, particularly to be used at parties, clubs and in other situations when alcohol is freely flowing. These ways of staying sexually safe, developed from the 'ground up' rather than dictated 'top down' by adults, can often be highly effective because they are accepted by the peer group. They can be incorporated into education programmes that flexibly involve input from young people and do not rely solely on didactic content.

Take care of friends

The major strategy in the Crowley *et al.* (2004) study mentioned earlier could be summarized as 'watch out for your friends'. By this was meant socializing in groups and keeping an eye on any group member who seemed to be getting drunk or was in a sexually vulnerable situation. The strategy was seen as both a way of protecting yourself and a way of protecting your friends. The following example demonstrates that in certain groups watching out takes the form of a peer group norm that protects the young people who are too drunk to look after themselves:

> If they're just say, flat out on the floor, we try to push them away in the corner or something. It's not like someone will start jumping on them and make them do something they didn't want. . . . Amongst our friends it's sort of understood that if a girl's really drunk, and can't really make decisions and you get with her, you get a really bad reputation because you've taken advantage of someone who's drunk. So everyone sort of bags you. . . . I think a lot of guys would be scared to go any further than kissing a girl – if you kissed a girl fine, but if you did anything further then, it's just really really bad, everyone would really hate you and all the girls would hate you.
>
> *(Crowley* et al.*, 2004:30)*

Nominate a responsible person when partying

Another peer-related strategy was socializing with a non-drinking friend such as a 'designated driver'. This friend was seen as someone who might intervene, not necessarily in an assertive or protective way, but to break the nexus between drinking and getting into trouble through, for example, a suggestion that it was time to leave.

Watch alcohol intake

Maintaining control of potentially out-of-control situations through counting drinks, watching (or 'nursing') drinks to ensure they were not spiked, or only getting drunk in familiar environments (presumably therefore perceived as safe) were also mentioned. Boys particularly liked the idea of 'knowing your limits' while girls were concerned with keeping an eye on their drinks to ensure they were not tampered with.

Don't be an ambiguous communicator

Being clear about your intentions, expecting to have 'no' taken seriously, and not taking advantage of someone who was drunk were also mentioned relatively frequently by girls, but rarely if at all by boys.

> Regardless of what your friends do or what you think the acceptable practice when you go into a club is, if you're not comfortable with something, you know, no matter where you are, it's OK for you to say, 'No! I don't want you to do that'.
>
> *(Crowley* et al., *2004:31)*

Get educated

Boys and girls also mentioned social, educational and institutionalized means to minimize sexual risk. Approaches suggested included changes and improvements to school-based sex/relationship education, and improvements in the assistance available to young people through counselling and support services. In other research adolescents reported that their sex education did not prepare them to deal with unwanted sex and sexual assault, for example,

> No-one really addresses sexual assault while you're in high school and then by the time you get to university there's no sex education . . . unless you're taking a specific course. (Female, 21 years)
>
> *(Carmody, 2009:55)*

Carmody *et al.* (2009) also noted that many adolescents were unaware that sexual assault mostly occurs between people who are known to each other, believing instead that assault by a stranger is a more likely event. In addition, their knowledge of what constitutes assault was poor.

> Knowing what type of assault there is, because there's heaps of types of assaults . . . it doesn't actually mean that it's going to be a penis or anything; it could be a stick . . . that's a form of sexual assault, it's penetration . . . just things like that so they know in simple language. (Female, 19 years)
>
> *(Carmody, 2009:55)*

In summary, sexual coercion and unwanted sexual experience are widespread for girls and certainly not unknown for boys. They can and do occur through violence and forcing, but the more common scenario is through peer or relationship pressure and communication misinterpretations. Although young people have developed some risk-reduction strategies to avoid unwanted sex, they often lack the confidence to implement them. The sexual double standard, which devalues female sexual desire but valorizes it in males as a sign of masculinity, leads to communication difficulties when a decision is to be made about whether to go ahead or not go ahead with sex. The media presentation of sexuality as the basis to popularity and happiness adds further confusion for young people who need to negotiate ways to express themselves sexually that are healthy and growth promoting, rather than degrading, unpleasant and inimical to psychosocial health. This task has proven too great for the next group discussed – adolescent sex offenders.

Adolescent sex offenders

Many experts in sexual assault argue that the focus of prevention should not be on risk-reduction strategies for women (although these are clearly important), but on identifying and managing the perpetrators of sexual violence (Charles & McDonald, 2005). A review of the research literature revealed that, 'adolescent sex offenders account for a significant number of child sex abuse perpetrators' (Veneziano & Veneziano, 2002:247).

A combination of individual, community and societal factors contribute to the risk of becoming a perpetrator of sexual violence. At the individual level are factors such as alcohol and drug use, coercive sexual fantasies, impulsive and anti-social tendencies, hostility towards women, hypermasculinity and a childhood history of sexual and physical abuse. However both the community and society more generally contribute to the risk of sexual violence by tolerating norms that support male superiority and sexual entitlement.

Adolescent sex offenders are likely to be socially isolated, have problems with behaviour and academic performance and share a common background that includes serious family problems such as neglect, and physical and sexual abuse (Veneziano & Veneziano, 2002).

It has been suggested that adolescents who display sexually abusive behaviours might represent an early stage on the pathway towards sexual offending. Characteristics shared by these adolescents are high rates of removal from the family, experiences of physical and emotional abuse, learning and language difficulties, and social deficits (Withington, Ogilvie & Watt, 2013).

Offences range from obscene telephone calls, voyeurism, exhibitionism, indecent assault (sexual fondling or touching, usually short of penetration), through to rape. However there is evidence that adolescent sex offenders do not necessarily progress to adult sex crimes. In a rare study on this topic, Nisbet, Wilson and Smallbone (2004) followed up 303 males who had been assessed by the Sex Offender Program of the New South Wales Department of Juvenile Justice in Australia. All had either pleaded guilty to or had been found guilty of a sexual offence that occurred when they were between the ages of 11 and 17 years. First assessment was at 16 years with an average follow-up period of 7 years. About one-quarter of the young men received additional convictions for sexual offences before they were 18 years old, but only 5 per cent received convictions for sexual offences as adults (with a further 4 per cent charged but not convicted). The authors concluded that transition from adolescent to adult sexual offending is the exception rather than the rule, but it could also be argued that a longer time frame is needed to be confident of this prediction. One particularly interesting finding of this study was that non-sexual recidivism (that is, habitually relapsing into crime) was very high – more than 60 per cent of the young men received convictions for non-sexual offences as adults. In addition, having a prior non-sexual offence in adolescence was associated with almost a threefold increase in the odds of being charged with sexual offences as an adult. Both these findings indicate a strong element of anti-social behaviour (over and above, and possibly independent of, sexual deviance) associated with sex crimes.

Whatever the precursors of adult sexual offences, there is no doubt that treatment and management of adolescents who commit sex crimes is desirable, since this reduces the probability of re-offending, lessens the likelihood of escalation of crimes, and intervenes at a developmental period when anti-social behaviours may be less entrenched and more amenable to change. Edwards and Beech (2004) reviewed the effectiveness of treatment programmes for adolescents who commit sexual offences, focusing on drop-out and recidivism as their measures of effectiveness. They indicated that (a) the drop-out rates are very high, with often fewer than 50 per cent of adolescents completing the programmes, and (b) future offending is associated with drop-out, which in turn relates to older age and impulsivity. The implication was that current programmes are not meeting the needs of the adolescents who attend them. Edwards and Beech claimed that different personality subtypes showed different patterns of recidivism and that each subtype has correspondingly specialized treatment needs.

Carr and VanDeusen (2004) suggest four main risk factors for male sexual aggression. Although their research is confined to college campuses in the US (and thus a late adolescent–young adult population), these factors may also apply to younger adolescents. They are male sex role socialization, alcohol abuse, personality traits and child abuse and neglect. The role of male peer support in sexual coercion, forcing and violence has been noted in environments such as university campuses and sporting clubs, where sexual conquest of women can be valorized but attitudes towards women, particularly women who express their sexuality, are hostile. Farr, Brown and Beckett (2004) compared hypermasculinity levels of 44 male adolescent sex offenders with 57 non-offending adolescent males. They found the young offenders scored significantly higher than non-offending boys on two subscales of the hypermasculinity measure, 'Callous sexual attitudes towards females' and 'Adversarial attitudes towards females and sexual minorities,' but they did not differ on 'Violence as manly' or 'Danger as exciting'. This suggested to the authors that hypermasculinity per se may not be the culprit, but rather what characterized adolescent sexual offenders were their negative and hostile attitudes to women.

Alcohol use may be associated with personality characteristics and attitudes among certain types of perpetrators. For example, Gross, Bennett, Sloan, Marx and Juergens (2001) demonstrated that even with low doses of alcohol, men in an alcohol consumption condition rated a female in a hypothetical dating scenario as being more sexually aroused than their counterparts in a non-consumption condition. Zawacki, Abbey, Buck, McAuslan and Clinton-Sherrod (2003) compared the personality characteristics, attitudes and experiences of men who had not committed sexual assaults with those of men who had done so, either with or without the involvement of alcohol. Among their sample of male college students, 31 per cent reported they had verbally coerced a partner to have sexual intercourse, 9 per cent admitted to forced sexual contact short of intercourse, 4 per cent to attempted rape and 14 per cent to completed rape. About three-quarters of these men reported alcohol involvement, mostly of both victim and perpetrator. Compared to non-perpetrators, men who had sexually coerced were more likely to have a history of delinquency, exhibit aggressive and dominant personality traits, and have experienced incidents in which they misperceived a woman's friendliness as sexual interest. They also had stronger attitudes supporting violence towards women. Alcohol-involved perpetrators were more impulsive than the other two groups, and were more likely to believe that alcohol enhances sex drive and that women's drinking signifies sexual interest. The authors suggest these types of perpetrators would benefit from interventions that challenged and provided corrective feedback about the inaccuracy and potential destructiveness of such beliefs.

It is well known that those who engage in sexual abuse often avoid conviction because of the difficulties associated with proving, beyond reasonable doubt, that they have been guilty of an offence. Compounding the difficulty is the fact that many sexual crimes are unreported because of victims' fear and shame, and the further trauma that physical examination, questioning and court appearance involves for those who have been raped. The unfortunate (and still present) tendency for society towards victim-blaming in cases of rape can make court appearances even more traumatic for the assaulted person and render conviction of the assailant unlikely in the absence of overwhelming evidence. The attitude of some police and juries, that women who have been genuinely raped should have shown signs of a struggle, has been challenged by evidence that over 50 per cent of women experience tonic immobility (an involuntary component of the fear response characterized by freezing or immobility in situations involving extreme fear coupled with physical restraint) at the time of their assault. These women go on to report greater psychological impairment than those who do not experience tonic immobility (Heidt, Marx & Forsyth, 2005).

Society's readiness to endorse a position of blaming the victim arises from a complex rape mythology, an element of which is the belief that women with a sexually active history are always willing to consent to sex or that they forfeit their right of choice. Other pervasive beliefs are that women who dress in a so-called provocative way are sexually willing, that women enjoy men forcing them to have sex, and that when a woman says 'no' to sex, she means 'yes'.

Myths about rape, together with sexist attitudes and beliefs, provide a framework for justifications of sexual coercion and force. The belief that masculine biological urges are so strong that they must be satisfied at any cost, and that those who do not exhibit such strong sex drives are not 'real' men, puts pressure on men to display their masculinity by 'scoring' sexual conquests. This view encourages the interpretation of male–female encounters basically as sexual, precluding other options such as friendship or non-sexual intimacy. Young men who are socialized within this context and who find their sexual drives thwarted may feel justified in expressing anger and forcing their partners to engage in unwanted sexual behaviour.

A recent review of almost 200 studies examined risk and protective factors in the perpetration of sexual violence (Tharp *et al.*, 2013). It showed a range of community, relationship and individual level factors to be associated with sexual violence, highlighting the need for comprehensive prevention programmes that focus on multiple risk and protective factors. Two key areas were identified that were consistently and significantly associated with sexual violence but are not typically addressed in most prevention programmes: the presence and acceptance of violence, and unhealthy sexual behaviours, experiences or attitudes.

Conclusion

Sexual violence, abuse, exploitation or coercion do not happen to the majority of adolescents but nevertheless, young people are far too often the victims. The extent to which children and adolescents have been the targets of sexual abuse has been hidden for many decades, but more recently this shameful situation is being exposed. Although young people can learn strategies to protect themselves to some extent from predatory adults and violent peers, for the most part the response to childhood sexual abuse must be made at the national and international level, with changes to laws, social welfare and training of those who work with youth, accompanied by clear messages that sexual exploitation cannot be tolerated.

At the interpersonal level, the message to young men and women is that healthy sex is a shared experience in which both parties have equal rights. Peer norms which valorize men as sexual predators and women as their victims, or which give special status and admiration to male sexual drive and conquest but equate female sexuality with promiscuity and low reputation do not contribute to healthy sexuality. Yet these very values are entrenched in adult culture – and not just in countries where women do not have equal rights, but also in subgroups (such as some sporting clubs or college societies) within developed nations.

In many cases there appears to be a need to resocialize young men to think differently about sex, as shared experience rather than exploitation. Young women, too, need assistance in learning to express their sexual needs – whether this be for different forms of sexual activity or no sex at all – and in understanding the social forces which often place them in the role of sexual victim. There are programmes which have been effective in other areas and which could be adapted to resocializing young people's views of sex. These include work with families and school populations to reduce sex role stereotyping and assertion training for women and children, such as the protective behaviours programme in which children learn the difference between 'good' touching and 'bad' touching. More directly, interventions that encourage male perpetrators of sexual violence to relearn appropriate sexual relationship skills and to handle their violence more effectively are being carried out. However, as we know, regressing and drop-out rates from programmes suggest there is still much to learn about how to conduct such interventions.

Adolescent sex should be safe, pleasurable and a shared experience in which both parties have equal rights. In every society there are embedded attitudes that militate against healthy sexual relationships. Overcoming these attitudes requires political will as well as education and community support.

12

PERSPECTIVES ON ADOLESCENT SEXUALITY

Two decades of change

As long as teenagers can understand the realities and consequences of their actions, and know what they have to do to be safe and respectful, they can have sex at a young age and turn out just FINE. I'm living proof of that. (Male, 18 years)

(Sauers, 2007:125)

Living in an online world

If we had to point to the biggest recent change in the adolescent peer culture, it would have to be the explosion in the use of digital technologies. These technologies have had an influence on most people across the globe, but arguably the greatest impact has been on the adolescents of today, who have not experienced the world without them. Young people seem to be constantly attached to their mobile phones or tablets – texting, engaging in online chat, posting and commenting on Facebook, sharing photos, accessing information, playing games, meeting new people and interacting in various ways with others both inside and outside their face-to-face network. This change has had a significant impact on all aspects of their living including their sex lives, hence our subtitle to this edition of *Sexuality in Adolescence: The digital generation*.

Experimenting with sex online sounds less risky than 'real' sex but there are clear perils in this new mode of communication, as we have outlined throughout the book and especially in the chapter on the youth generation. Adolescent sexual experimentation occurs as it always has, but with sexting, online hook-ups, YouTube and the like it has the potential to come back to haunt young people. Meeting and chatting to people online can be a wonderful way to make new friends, explore one's sexuality and find sexual partners but the possibilities for sexual predators are multiplied. So too are pressures to conform to a particular body type and form of self-presentation.

Information about sex on the internet helps adolescents to privately unravel the mysteries of their changing bodies in a safe space as well as to learn about less risky sexual practices, but there is also misinformation and the distortions of readily accessible pornography to confuse and misrepresent the intimacy of sex. Education about safe use of the internet has become part of the armoury that young people need to negotiate the life transition through adolescence. Parents, too, need to become internet-savvy so they can advise and monitor younger teenagers about online safety.

Globalization of youth culture

The online world not only influences young people in developed nations. The sexualized culture of the west, including its fads and fashions, is rapidly spread through online and offline media. The west's more liberal attitudes to sexuality and adolescent sexual expression are conveyed worldwide through movies, music, television, the internet and, particularly, through social media. The notion of adolescence as a transitional period between childhood and adulthood – a 'moratorium' in Erikson's (1968) terms – is becoming a globalized one. It is an attitude that has led to changes in laws about age of consent in many countries. Most jurisdictions recognize that there should be an age enshrined in law below which it is not in the developmental interests of a young person to engage in sexual behaviours with another; children and adolescents need protection from those who are older and have more power. However many countries and states now recognize that sexual experimentation between teenage peers can be a benign developmental influence and certainly need not be harmful. In these jurisdictions, sex between young people of similar ages is not punishable or pathologized.

Further evidence for the globalization of youth culture comes both from published literature and young people's online activity. Both show increasing commonalities between adolescents from many nations and cultural groups in terms of the questions they ask about sex, the problems they experience, their sexual behaviours and their sexual attitudes. As the world gets smaller, westernized messages about sex and individualism are being communicated far more widely. Thus in this volume we have been able to report on research from many countries, including even the most sexually conservative, relating to the sexual behaviours, sexual health and sex education of young people.

Sexual inequities and exploitation

But despite increasing globalization, there is still enormous diversity across nations in economic and political circumstances, religious and cultural values, access to schooling and health care, and all those factors that ultimately influence sexuality. This diversity affects sexual health, behaviour, beliefs and attitudes. For example, ideas about gender are culturally specific and have a profound impact on young people's sexual lives. Gender inequalities make young women in many countries sexually vulnerable. We know that in many countries, young men are still seen to be sexual beings and young women are not. This belief is implicated in double standards regarding virginity and has important implications in regard to women's human rights.

Across the world, there are sexual inequities and there is sexual exploitation. There are horrifying statistics about the number of children who are exploited every year in the global commercial sex trade, and that sexual abuse and rape are experienced commonly by young and not-so-young women in many countries. In at least 76 countries, there are anti-homosexuality laws (Erasing 76 crimes, 2014) and in some cases the death penalty applies. Adolescents growing up in these communities do not have the same opportunities to express and develop their sexual natures in the relatively permissive and leisurely manner available to many young people in the west, and there is still much to be understood about how these differences influence adult sexual adjustment.

Another emergent change since the last revision of this book has been the widespread recognition that sexual abuse of children and adolescents is not a rare phenomenon. Issues such as sexual harassment, 'stalking' and predatory sexual behaviour in schools, at workplaces and on university campuses are being taken more seriously although there is still a long way to go. In several countries in the developed world, spurred on by adult survivors of abuse, large-scale investigations have been undertaken of organizations and institutions that have systematically sexually abused and exploited children and youths in their care. The scale of the abuse has shocked many, as has the extent to which the adult generation were in denial of its existence. Even when children and young people told parents, teachers or others in authority of what was happening to them, they were not believed. Only as adults have they been able to present their evidence, describe the devastating effects of the abuse on their psychological and sexual development and, in some cases, obtain redress or at least acknowledgement. As a result of these enquiries, there is more awareness and more help and protection available to young people who are at risk of being abused or already have been but this too comes at a cost. There is a danger that the panic that has arisen around sexual abuse will interfere with adults taking positive mentoring roles with young people. Already some men are diffident about expressing physical affection or talking about sex in an educative way to their children, lest these behaviours be misinterpreted.

Advances in research

It is not only changes in society that inspired this third revision of *Sexuality in Adolescence*. In the first edition, back in 1993, research and commentary on healthy adolescent sexual development was scant – now there is a flood. A plethora of innovative scientific methodologies has been employed with the effect of greatly increasing our understanding of adolescent development and experience, from biological, psychological, sociological and public health perspectives. Brain imaging and hormone analysis techniques have shed light on the triggers for and processes of puberty and the potential mismatches between physical and cognitive development during adolescence. Epidemiological studies have demonstrated further trends in early puberty, and there is still important work to be done in isolating environmental influences on this phenomenon. Social scientists who have worked in the adolescent sexuality field for 20 years or more are now presenting cohort comparisons, enabling us to examine the stability of sexual behaviours and attitudes, for example comparing adolescent dating patterns then and now or examining the nature and prevalence of the 'double standard'. The increase in cross-cultural studies mentioned previously also gives us clues as to which aspects of sexual expression are most influenced by social norms and which appear to be relatively stable across cultures and cohorts. As well, the creative use of qualitative methods has taken the study of adolescent sexuality far beyond an analysis of who does what to whom. It has enabled us to gain insights into what goes on in young people's heads as they make decisions about their sexual health and expression – an important understanding if we are to develop sex education and health promotion interventions that speak to young people in their own language and so have a chance of making a difference. Finally, the use of online and thus relatively anonymous data collection techniques has enabled the voices of marginalized and difficult-to-reach young people to be heard, and facilitated the growing practice of social researchers to include young people in the planning and design of research so that relevant questions are asked and issues canvassed.

But we need to know more

Nevertheless there is still much to be learned. There are still political impediments to sex research in western countries and even more strongly in some developing countries. Governments, funding agencies, schools and the like have set limits on what may and may not be asked of young people and what topics are off limits. Negative and derogatory attitudes on the part of politicians and policy makers have the potential to bring adolescent sex research to a standstill. There is an important role for researchers here in being able to demonstrate how the study of the sexual lives of young people is not about voyeurism or the encouragement of anti-social behaviour, but a reality check on what young people are actually doing and thinking – essential if there are to be improvements in adolescent sexual wellbeing through, for example, better health care, better education and ultimately better relationships.

Perhaps because of the cost and perhaps also because of the political wariness discussed above, longitudinal studies of sexual behaviour are still rare. We still know very little about sexual developmental pathways for young people. What are the factors that enhance or inhibit the capacity to achieve a fulfilling sexual life? We have not asked young people about their sexual histories and the meanings these have. We assume that the experience of having sex must influence subsequent experiences but we do not know much about how the accumulated knowledge, risks, practices and beliefs become incorporated into the sexual histories of young people, or how they relate to the strength of their adult relationships, their adult sexual adjustment or ultimately to their life satisfaction and fulfilment.

Adolescent sexuality in the twenty-first century

Sexual development is a lifelong process, not a task that begins at 12 and finishes at 20. This is true biologically as well as psychologically. Reproductive powers peak then fall away, sexual drives wax and wane, and social expectations shape how sexuality manifests itself at different ages and stages of life. Individuals learn through successes and mistakes to incorporate sexuality into their lives. There is time for adolescents to experiment and make mistakes, yet still get it right in the end. One relevant feature of the 1990s that has extended into the twenty-first century is a worldwide trend against marrying young. Except in some countries with strict traditions about marriage of child brides, there is now a chance for young people to learn more about themselves and others, to experiment sexually, and to be able to make more mature choices about whether to partner and with whom. Young adulthood is now a continuation of 'teenage-hood'; a time in which transitions of partnership and parenthood are postponed, and there is more time for exploration of different possibilities in love and work. But this opportunity also has its negative aspects. The risk of sexually transmitted infections is increased if experimentation is not accompanied by safe practice. High or even unrealistic expectations about a life partner and unwillingness to compromise individual goals for couple goals are other risks. So, while sexual development was once seen as culminating at the end of adolescence with marriage and child-bearing, today young people in their twenties and thirties may still have many sexual decisions to make before they choose a relatively stable path. Few studies examine how sexual beliefs and practices change between adolescence and emerging adulthood, and the relative influences of these life periods on relationship choices, sexual satisfaction and overall life adjustment.

Does the journey to sexual maturity have more pitfalls than it once did? Some of us grew up in an era characterized by repression, denial, shame and ignorance. Pregnant girls were spirited off somewhere for several months and came back sadder and without their babies, or they married in haste – what was called the 'shotgun wedding'. Sex talk was off limits, apart from dire warnings to girls and perhaps a nod and a wink to boys. Nowadays, contraception is readily available and there is more support for young mothers, whether they choose to keep or relinquish their babies. We have the language to talk about sex, there is greater tolerance, openness and debate, more acceptance that sex is a pleasurable activity and that sexual expression is part of a healthy life.

On the other hand, some might say we have gone too far in the sexualization of society – there is too much talk, too much graphic depiction. STIs are on the rise despite the availability of protection and treatment. Following a period when the threat of HIV/AIDS galvanized the sex education of young people in developed countries, the ability to manage this as a chronic disease has resulted in an emerging carelessness about STI prevention. Norms of appearance and behaviour are oppressively strict in the adolescent subculture, as they attempt to look 'hot' and act 'cool'. Sexual messages are ambiguous, particularly to young women, who must walk a tightrope between being seen as sexy but not sluttish. Clearly, in the domain of sexual mores, there are swings and roundabouts.

Nevertheless, sex in the twenty-first century remains a powerful force in the lives of young people. Adolescents still have crushes, fall in love, struggle to maintain or lose their virginity, desperately want to find a girlfriend or boyfriend, experience relationship break-ups, have fun with sex and agonize about it, depending on the day. Many parents still find it difficult to communicate with their adolescents about sex despite wishing otherwise. Along with adolescent idealism, hopes for commitment to another and moves towards sexual equality we still see evidence of sexual manipulation, coercion and the double standard. The power of the epithet 'slut' remains. Young people still get confused about the differing messages they receive from peers, home, school and, increasingly, the media. They want to know more about negotiating relationships, and struggle with those agonizing questions, 'Am I normal, and where do I fit in?'

In each edition of this book we have warned against overgeneralizing about adolescent sexual behaviour because of the wide range of differences between young people concerning what constitutes 'average' sexual behaviour. That warning still stands. The need for tolerance of difference remains today, as we have seen, with marginalized groups such as those who are gay and lesbian. The importance of sex education must still be stressed – young people do not know it all even in this era of such readily available knowledge. Indeed, they want *more* guidance as they reach each different milestone in the adolescent sexual journey. Finally, we have consistently emphasized the many positive outcomes of sexual activity for young people. Sex can enable people to feel lovable and provides an opportunity to express love, enhance closeness and sharing, and experience intimacy. Adolescent sexual experimentation has a role in contributing to mature development, as a step towards independence and a contribution to an individual's sense of self or identity.

REFERENCES

Abu, P.B. & Akerle, E.O. (2006). Parental influence on adolescents' sexual behaviour in Ibadan North Local Government Area of Oyo State, Nigeria. *International Journal of African & African American Studies, 5,* 41–56.

Ackard, D.M., Croll, J.K. & Kearney-Cooke, A. (2002). Dieting frequency among college females: Association with disordered eating, body image, and related psychological problems. *Journal of Psychosomatic Research, 52*(3), 129–136.

Adamczyk, A. & Felson, J. (2006). Friends' religiosity and first sex. *Social Science Research, 35,* 924–947.

Adams-Curtis, L.E. & Forbes, G.B. (2004). College women's experiences of sexual coercion: A review of cultural, perpetrator, victim, and situational variables. *Trauma, Violence, & Abuse, 5,* 91–122.

Advocates for Youth. (2011). Adolescent sexual health in Europe and the US. Retrieved from: http://www.advocatesforyouth.org/publications/419?task=view [Accessed 13 June 2014].

Ahmed, M.L., Ong, K.K., Morrell, D.J., Cox, L., Drayer, N., Perry, L., *et al.* (1999). Longitudinal study of leptin concentrations during puberty: Sex differences and relationship to changes in body composition. *The Journal of Clinical Endocrinology & Metabolism, 84,* 899–905.

AIDS in Brazil (2012). Department of STD, AIDS and Viral Hepatitis/SVS/MS. Retrieved from: http://www.aids.gov.br/sites/default/files/anexos/page/2011/49030/aids_in_brazil_2012_14442.pdf [Accessed 30 November 2012].

Aitken S. (2014). Sexually transmissible infections. In M. Temple-Smith (Ed.), *Sexual health: A multidisciplinary approach.* Melbourne: IP Communications.

Alan Guttmacher Institute. (1976). *Eleven million teenagers.* New York: Author.

Albert, B. (2007). *America's adults and teens sound off about teen pregnancy.* Washington, DC: National Campaign to Prevent Teen Pregnancy.

Alcala-Herrera, V. & Marvan, M.L. (2014). Early menarche, depressive symptoms and coping strategies. *Journal of Adolescence, 37,* 905–913.

Ali, M.M. & Dwyer, D.S. (2011). Estimating peer effects in sexual behavior among adolescents. *Journal of Adolescence, 34,* 183–190.

Allison, R. & Risman, B.J. (2013). A double standard for 'hooking up': How far have we come towards gender equality? *Social Science Research, 42*(5), 1191–1206.

Andersen, S.L. & Teicher, M.H. (2008). Stress, sensitive periods and maturational events in adolescent depression. *Trends in Neurosciences, 31*(4), 183–191.

Andersen, S.L., Tomada, A., Vincow, E.S., Valente, E., Polcari, A. & Teicher, M.H. (2008). Preliminary evidence for sensitive periods in the effect of childhood sexual abuse on regional brain development. *Journal of Clinical Neuropsychiatry, 20,* 292–301.

Angera, J.J., Brookins-Fisher, J. & Inungu, J.N. (2008). An investigation of parent/child communication about sexuality. *American Journal of Sexuality Education, 3,* 165–181.

APA Task Force on Appropriate Therapeutic Responses to Sexual Orientation. (2009). *Report of the task force on appropriate therapeutic responses to sexual orientation.* Washington, DC: American Psychological Association.

Arbes-Dupuy, V. (2000). *Dupes or collaborators? Young adults' sexual encounters.* (Doctoral dissertation). Melbourne: Australian Research Centre in Sex, Health & Society, La Trobe University. Retrieved from: http://nla.gov.au/anbd.bib-an24230605 [Accessed 31 December 2014].

Ashikali, E.-M., Dittmar, H. & Ayers, S. (2014). Adolescent girls' views on cosmetic surgery: A focus group study. *Journal of Health Psychology.* ePub ahead of print, 3 March.

Ashworth, H. (2014). Stupid reasons for teenagers to get pregnant and why teenage pregnancy is a dumb idea in general. Retrieved from: http://teenadvice.about.com/od/sex/a/stupid_causes_of_teenage_pregnancy.htm [Accessed 27 April 2014].

Aspy, C.B., Vesely, S.K., Oman, R.F., Rodine, S., Marshall, L. & McLeroy, K. (2007). Parental communication and youth sexual behaviour. *Journal of Adolescence, 30,* 449–466.

Atwood, J.D. (2007). When love hurts: Preadolescent girls' reports of incest. *American Journal of Family Therapy, 35,* 287–313.

Australian Bureau of Statistics. (2010). 4102.0 Australian social trends, Dec 2010. Retrieved from: http://www.abs.gov.au/AUSSTATS/abs@.nsf/Lookup/4102.0Main+Features10Dec+2010 [Accessed 23 May 2014].

Australian Bureau of Statistics. (2013a). 3301.0 Births, Australia, 2012. Retrieved from: http://www.abs.gov.au/AUSSTATS/abs@.nsf/allprimarymainfeatures/A627592148769660CA257D79001054D5?opendocument [Accessed 24th February 2014].

Australian Bureau of Statistics. (2013b). 3310.0 Marriages and divorces, Australia, 2012. Retrieved from: http://www.abs.gov.au/ausstats/abs@.nsf/Products/3310.0~2012~Chapter~Marriages?OpenDocument [Accessed 22 May 2014].

Australian Bureau of Statistics. (2013c). 4102.0 Australian social trends, July 2013. Same-sex couples. Retrieved from: http://www.abs.gov.au/AUSSTATS/abs@.nsf/Lookup/4102.0Main+Features10July+2013#age [Accessed 29 May 2014].

Australian Department of Foreign Affairs and Trade. (2014). *Sex and gender diverse passport applicants: Revised policy.* Department of Foreign Affairs and Trade.

Retrieved from: https://www.passports.gov.au/web/sexgenderapplicants.aspx [Accessed 31 December 2014].

Australian Football League. (2014). Respect and responsibility policy. Retrieved from: http://www.afl.com.au/news/game-development/respect-and-responsibility [Accessed 22 April 2014].

Australian Government Department of Health and Ageing. (2010). *Second National STI Strategy 2010–2013.* Canberra: Commonwealth of Australia.

Australian Government Productivity Commission. (2014). Has the baby bonus changed the patterns of birth by age? Retrieved from: http://www.pc.gov.au/research/completed/fertility-trends [Accessed 13 March 2014].

Australian Human Rights Commission (2008). *Sexual harassment: Serious business. Results of the 2008 Sexual Harassment National Telephone Survey.* Sydney, Australia: Human Rights and Equal Opportunities Commission.

Australian Institute of Health and Welfare. (2011). *Young Australians: Their health and wellbeing 2011.* Cat. no. PHE 140. Canberra: AIHW.

Australian Institute of Health and Welfare. (2012). *Adoptions Australia 2011–12.* Child Welfare Series no. 54. Cat. no. CWS 42. Canberra: AIHW.

Avert (n.d). Retrieved from: http://www.avert.org/stories/analisa and http://www.avert.org/stories/lisa-1 [Accessed 15 January 2014].

Baheiraei, A., Khoori, E., Foroushani, A.R., Ahmadi, F. & Ybarra, M. (2014). What sources do adolescents turn to for information about their health concerns? *International Journal of Adolescent Medicine and Health, 26*(1), 61–68.

Bailey, J.M. & Pillard, R.C. (1991). A genetic study of male sexual orientation. *Archives of General Psychiatry, 48,* 1089–1096.

Bajos, N., Bozon, M., Beltzer, N., Laborde, C., Andro, A., Ferrand, M. & Wellings, K. (2010). Changes in sexual behaviours: From secular trends to public health policies. *AIDS, 24*(8), 1185–1191.

Baker, J. & Moore, S. (2008). Blogging as a social tool: A psycho-social examination of the effects of blogging. *CyberPsychology and Behavior, 11,* 747–749.

Baker, J.R. & Moore, S.M. (2010). An opportunistic validation of studies on the psychosocial benefits of blogging. *CyberPsychology, Behavior and Social Networking, 14,* 387–390. doi:10.1089/cyber.2010.0202

Bale, C. (2011). Raunch or romance? Framing and interpreting the relationship between sexualized culture and young people's sexual health. *Sexuality, Society and Learning, 11*(3), 303–313.

Balfe, M. & Brugha, R. (2011).What concerns do young adults in Ireland have about attending health services for STD testing? *Deviant Behavior, 32,* 320–350.

Balfe, M., Brugha, R., O'Donovan, D., O'Connell, E. & Vaughan, D. (2010). Young women's decisions to accept Chlamydia screening: influences of stigma and doctor-patient interactions. *BMC Public Health, 10,* 425.

Bankole, A., Singh, S. & Haas, T. (1998). Reasons why women have induced abortions: Evidence from 27 countries. *International Family Planning Perspectives, 24*(3), 117–127, 152.

Banyard, V.L. & Cross, C. (2008). Consequences of teen dating violence: Understanding intervening variables in ecological context. *Violence Against Women, 9,* 998–1013.

Bartz, T. (2007). Sex education in multicultural Norway. *Sex Education: Sexuality, Society and Learning, 7,* 17–33.

Bateson, D. (2014). Contraception and unintended pregnancy options. In Temple-Smith, M. (Ed.), *Sexual health: A multidisciplinary approach*. Melbourne: IP Communications.

Bauermeister, J.A., Leslie-Santana, M., Johns, M.M. & Eisenburg, A. (2011). Mr. Right and Mr. Right Now: Romantic and casual partner-seeking online among young men who have sex with men. *AIDS and Behavior, 15*, 261–272.

Bauermeister, J.A., Yeagley, E., Meanley, S. & Pingel, E.S. (2014). Sexting among young men who have sex with men: Results from a national survey. *Journal of Adolescent Health, 54*, 606–611.

Bauman, L.J. & Berman, R. (2005). Adolescent relationships and condom use: Trust, love and commitment. *AIDS and Behavior, 9*(2), 211–222.

Baumeister, R.F., Catanese, K.R. & Vohs, K.D. (2001). Is there a gender difference in strength of sex drive? Theoretical views, conceptual distinctions, and a review of relevant evidence. *Personality and Social Psychology Review, 5*(3), 242–273.

Beckett, M.K., Elliott, M.N., Martino, S., Kanouse, D.E., Corona, R., Klein, D.J. & Schuster, M.A. (2010). Timing of parent and child communication about sexuality relative to children's sexual behaviors. *Pediatrics, 125*, 34–42.

Being Brendo. (2014). *Being Brendo* [video file]. Retrieved from: https://www.youtube.com/user/BeingBrendo [Accessed 5 July 2014].

Belgrave, F.Z. (2009). *African American girls: Reframing perceptions and changing experiences*. New York: Springer.

Bell, K.J. (2009). Wake up and smell the condoms: An analysis of sex education programs in the United States, the Netherlands, Sweden, Australia, France, and Germany. *Student Pulse, 1*(11), 1–3.

Benotsch, E.G., Snipes, D.J., Martin, A.M. & Bull, S.S. (2013). Sexting, substance use, and sexual risk behavior in young adults. *Journal of Adolescent Health, 52*, 307–313.

Bercaw-Pratt, J.L., Santos, X.M., Sanchez, J., Ayensu-Coker, L., Nebgen, D.R. & Dietrich, J.E. (2012). The incidence, attitudes and practices of the removal of pubic hair as a body modification. *Journal of Pediatric and Adolescent Gynecology, 25*(1), 12–14.

Berg, S.J. & Wynne-Edwards, K.E. (2001). Changes in testosterone, cortisol, and estradiol levels in men becoming fathers. *Mayo Clinic Proceedings, 76*(6), 582–592.

Bergen, H.A., Martin, G., Richardson, A.S., Allison, S. & Roeger, L. (2004). Sexual abuse, antisocial behaviour and substance use: Gender differences in young community adolescents. *Australian and New Zealand Journal of Psychiatry, 38*, 34–41.

Bettelheim, B. (1962). The problem of generation. *Daedalus, Winter*, 68–69.

Beymer, M.R., Weiss, R., Bolan, R.K., Rudy, E.T., Bourque, L.B., Rodriguez, J.P. & Morisky, D.E. (2014). Sex on demand: Geosocial networking phone apps and risk of sexually transmitted infections among a cross-sectional sample of men who have sex with men in Los Angeles county. *Sexually Transmitted Infections*, first published online 13 June 2014.

Biddlecom, A., Awusabo-Asare, K. & Bankole, A. (2009). Role of parents in adolescent sexual activity and contraceptive use in four African countries. *International Perspectives on Sexual and Reproductive Health, 35*(2), 72–81.

Black, M.C., Basile, K.C., Breiding, M.J., Smith, S.G., Walters, M.L., Merrick, M.T., et al. (2011). *The national intimate partner and sexual violence survey (NISVS): 2010 summary report*. Atlanta, GA: National Center for Injury Prevention and Control, Centers for Disease Control and Prevention. Retrieved from: http://www.

cdc.gov/violenceprevention/pdf/nisvs_executive_summary-a.pdf [Accessed 19 January 2015].

Blakemore, S.J. (2008). The social brain in adolescence. *Nature Reviews Neuroscience, 9*(4), 267–277.

Blakemore, S.J., Burnett, S. & Dahl, R.E. (2010). The role of puberty in the developing adolescent brain. *Human Brain Mapping, 31*(6), 926–933.

Blakemore, S.J. & Choudhury, S. (2006). Development of the adolescent brain: Implications for executive function and social cognition. *Journal of Child Psychology and Psychiatry, 47*(3–4), 296–312.

Bleakley, A., Fishbein, M. & Jordan, A. (2009). How sources of sexual information relate to adolescents' beliefs about sex. *American Journal of Health Behavior, 33,* 37–48.

Bleakley, A., Hennessy, M., Fishbein, M. & Jordan, A. (2008). It works both ways: The relationship between sexual content in the media and adolescent sexual behavior. *Media Psychology, 11*(4), 443–461.

Bogaert, A.F. & Sadava, S. (2002). Adult attachment and sexual behaviour. *Personal Relationships, 9*(2), 191–204.

Bogdanich, W. (2014, 16 April). A star player accused, and a flawed rape investigation. *The New York Times.* Retrieved from: http://www.nytimes.com/interactive/2014/04/16/sports/errors-in-inquiry-on-rape-allegations-against-fsu-jameis-winston.html?_r=0 [Accessed 23 April 2015].

Bogle, K.A. (2007). The shift from dating to hooking up in college: What scholars have missed. *Sociology Compass, 1*(2), 775–788.

Bogle, K.A. (2008). *Hooking up: Sex, dating and relationships on campus.* New York: New York University Press.

Boksa, P. (2012). Abnormal synaptic pruning in schizophrenia: Urban myth or reality? *Journal of Psychiatry and Neuroscience, 37*(2), 75–77.

Bonell, C., Maisey, R., Speight, S., Purdon, S., Keogh, P., Wollny, I., *et al.* (2013). Randomized controlled trial of 'teens and toddlers': A teenage pregnancy prevention intervention combining youth development and voluntary service in a nursery. *Journal of Adolescence, 36*(5), 859–870.

Bonino, S., Ciairano, S., Rabaglietti, E. & Cattelino, E. (2006). Use of pornography and self-reported engagement in sexual violence among adolescents. *European Journal of Developmental Psychology, 3*(3), 265–288.

Boonstra, H.D. (2014). What is behind the declines in teen pregnancy rates? *Guttmacher Policy Review, 17,* 15–21.

Boseley, S. (2012, 31 May). Sexually transmitted infection rates soar among the young. Retrieved from: http://www.theguardian.com/society/2012/may/31/sexually-transmitted-infection-rates-soar [Accessed 30 November 2012].

Boubli, M. & Elbez, J.C. (2010). Cited in *The Sex Educator 17* (2011, Spring). Retrieved from: http://publications.msss.gouv.qc.ca/acrobat/f/documentation/2011/11-314-01A.pdf [Accessed 31 December 2014].

Bourguignon, J.P. & Parent, A.S. (2010). Early homeostatic disturbances of human growth and maturation by endocrine disrupters. *Current Opinion in Pediatrics, 22*(4), 470–477.

Bowden, F. on behalf of the National Donovanosis Eradication Advisory Committee (2005). Donovanosis in Australia: going, going . . . *Sexually Transmitted Infections, 81*(5), 365–366.

Boyar, R., Levine, D. & Zensius, N. (2011). *TECHsexUSA: Youth sexuality and reproductive health in the digital age.* Oakland, CA: ISIS.

Bradbury, B. (2006). The impact of young motherhood. *Social Policy Research Centre Newsletter, 93,* July. Retrieved from: https://www.sprc.unsw.edu.au/media/SPRCFile/sprc_newsletter_93.pdf [Accessed 13 June 2014].

Bradley, H., Markowitz, L.E., Gibson, T. & McQuillan, G.M. (2014). Seroprevalence of herpes simplex virus types 1 and 2 – United States, 1999–2010. *Journal of Infectious Diseases, 209*(3), 325–333.

Brand, S., Luethi, M., von Planta, A., Hatzinger, M. & Holsboer-Trachsler, E. (2007). Romantic love, hypomania, and sleep pattern in adolescents. *Journal of Adolescent Health, 41*(1), 69–76.

Bridges, A., Wosnitzer, R., Scharrer, E., Sun, C. & Liberman, R. (2010). Aggression and sexual behavior in best-selling pornography videos: A content analysis update. *Violence Against Women, 16*(10), 1065–1085.

Brooks-Gunn, J. & Furstenberg, F.F.J. (1989). Adolescent sexual behavior. *American Psychologist, 44,* 249–257.

Brown, J., O'Donnell, T. & Erooga, M. (2011). *Sexual abuse: A public health challenge.* London: National Society for the Prevention of Cruelty to Children.

Brown, J.C. (1989). Lesbian sexuality in medieval and early modern Europe. In M.B. Dubermann, M. Vicinus & Chauncey Jr. (Eds.), *Hidden from history: Reclaiming the gay and lesbian past.* New York: Penguin.

Brown, J.D. & l'Engle, K.L. (2009). X-rated: Sexual attitudes and behaviors associated with US early adolescents' exposure to sexually explicit media. *Communication Research, 36*(1), 129–151.

Brown, J.D., Steele, J.R. & Walsh-Childers, K. (2002). Introduction and overview. In J.D. Brown, J.R. Steele & K. Walsh-Childers (Eds.), *Sexual teens, sexual media: Investigating media's influence on adolescent sexuality.* Mahwah, NJ: Lawrence Erlbaum Associates, pp. 1–24.

Browne, R. (2012). Back to school for teen mothers juggling babies and the HSC. *Sydney Morning Herald.* Retrieved from: http://www.smh.com.au/national/education/back-to-school-for-teen-mothers-juggling-babies-and-the-hsc-20121013-27jns.html [Accessed 22 May 2014].

Browning, C.R., Leventhal, T. & Brooks-Gunn, J. (2004). Neighbourhood context and racial differences in early adolescent sexual activity. *Demography, 41,* 697–720.

Brückner, H. & Bearman, P. (2005). After the promise: The STD consequences of adolescent virginity pledges. *Journal of Adolescent Health, 36,* 271–278.

Bryant, C. (2009). Adolescence, pornography and harm. *Trends & Issues in Crime and Criminal Justice, 368,* 1–6.

Bucchianeri, M.M., Arikian, A.J., Hannan, P.J., Eisenberg, M.E. & Neumark-Sztainer, D. (2012). Body dissatisfaction from adolescence to young adulthood: Findings from a 10-year longitudinal study. *Body Image, 10*(1), 1–7.

Buchanan, C.M., Eccles, J.S. & Becker, J.B. (1992). Are adolescents the victims of raging hormones: Evidence for activational effects of hormones on moods and behavior at adolescence. *Psychological Bulletin, 111*(1), 62–107.

Buhi, E.R., Daley, E.M., Furhmann, H.J. & Smith, S.A. (2009). An observational study of how young people search for online sexual health information. *American College Health, 58*(2), 101–111.

Buncombe A. (2014, 23 February). India's gay community scrambling after court decision recriminalises homosexuality. Retrieved from: http://www.independent.co.uk/news/world/asia/indias-gay-community-scrambling-after-court-decision-recriminalises-homosexuality-9146244.html [Accessed 9 April 2015].

Bureau of Consular Affairs, U.S. Department of State. (2014). Intercountry adoption: Statistics. Retrieved from: http://adoption.state.gov/about_us/statistics.php [Accessed 3 April 2014].

Burrows, A. & Johnson, S. (2005). Girls' experiences of menarche and menstruation. *Journal of Reproductive and Infant Psychology, 23*(3), 235–249.

Buss, D.M. & Schmitt, D.P. (1993). Sexual strategies theory: An evolutionary perspective on human mating. *Psychological Review, 100*(2), 204–232.

Butler, A.H. & Astbury, G. (2008). The use of defence mechanisms as precursors to coming out in post-apartheid South Africa: A gay and lesbian youth perspective. *Journal of Homosexuality, 55*(2), 223–244.

Campbell, A.A. (1968). The role of family planning in the reduction of poverty. *Journal of Marriage and the Family, 30,* 236–245.

Campbell, B.C., Prossinger, H. & Mbzivo, M. (2005). Timing of pubertal maturation and the onset of sexual behavior among Zimbabwe school boys. *Archives of Sexual Behavior, 34*(5), 506–515.

Carbone-Lopez, K. (2012). The life course consequences of childhood sexual assault: Effects on relationship formation and intimate violence across relationships. In L.M. Carpenter & J. DeLamater (Eds.), *Sex for life: From virginity to Viagra, how sexuality changes throughout our lives.* New York: New York University Press, pp. 88–108.

Carmody, M. (2009). *Sex and ethics: Young people and ethical sex.* South Yarra: Palgrave Macmillan.

Carr, J.L. & VanDeusen, K.M. (2004). Risk factors for male sexual aggression on college campuses. *Journal of Family Violence, 19,* 279–289.

Carter, M. (2013, 14 May). Teen mags: Still a girl's best friend? Retrieved from: http://www.independent.co.uk/life-style/health-and-families/features/teen-mags-still-a-girls-best-friend-8614418.html [Accessed 17 November 2014].

Carvalho, G.M., Merighi, M.A.B. & Jesus, M.C.P. (2010). The experience of repeated fatherhood during adolescence. *Midwifery, 26,* 469–474.

Carver, K., Joyner, K. & Udry, J.R. (2003). National estimates of adolescent romantic relationships. In P. Florsheim (Ed.), *Adolescent romantic relations and sexual behavior: Theory, research and practical implications.* Mahwah, NJ: Lawrence Erlbaum Associates, pp. 23–56.

Cass, V. (2006) Sexual orientation and the place of psychology: Side-lined, side-tracked or should that be side-swiped? *Gay and Lesbian Issues and Psychology Review, 2*(1), 27–37.

Castano, P.M., Bynum, J.Y., Andres, R., Lara, M. & Westhoff, C. (2012). Effect of daily text messages on oral contraceptive continuation: A randomized controlled trial. *Obstetrics and Gynecology, 119,* 14–20.

Center for Reproductive Rights. (2007). *The world's abortion laws.* Retrieved from: http://worldabortionlaws.com/map [Accessed 9 February 2014].

Centers for Disease Control and Prevention. (2009). *Sexually transmitted disease surveillance, 2008.* Atlanta, GA: U.S. Department of Health and Human Services.

Centers for Disease Control and Prevention. (2010). Sexually transmitted diseases guidelines. *Morbidity and Mortality Weekly Report, 59*, 1–109.

Centers for Disease Control and Prevention. (2012a). National and state vaccination coverage among adolescents aged 13–17 years – United States, 2011. *Morbidity and Mortality Weekly Report, 61*, 671–677.

Centers for Disease Control and Prevention. (2012b). *Teen pregnancy: About teen pregnancy.* Retrieved from: http://www.cdc.gov/teenpregnancy/aboutteenpreg. htm#a [Accessed 12 December 2012].

Centers for Disease Control and Prevention. (2013a). *Chlamydia.* Retrieved from: http://www.cdc.gov/std/chlamydia/default.htm [Accessed 4 July 2014].

Centers for Disease Control and Prevention. (2013b). *HIV in the United States: At a glance.* Retrieved from: http://www.cdc.gov/hiv/statistics/basics/ataglance.html [Accessed 10 February 2014].

Centers for Disease Control and Prevention. (2013c). *Sexually transmitted diseases: Genital HPV infection – fact sheet.* Retrieved from: http://www.cdc.gov/std/ HPV/STDFact-HPV.htm [Accessed 15 February 2014].

Centers for Disease Control and Prevention. (2013d). *CDC fact sheet: Incidence, prevalence, and cost of sexually transmitted infections in the United States.* Retrieved from: http://www.cdc.gov/std/stats/STI-Estimates-Fact-Sheet-Feb-2013.pdf [Accessed 15 February 2014].

Centers for Disease Control and Prevention. (2013e). *2012 Sexually transmitted diseases surveillance.* Retrieved from: http://www.cdc.gov/sTd/stats12/other. htm#hpv [Accessed 15 February 2014].

Chalfen, R. (2009). 'It's only a picture': Sexting, 'smutty' snapshots and felony charges. *Visual Studies, 24*(3), 258–268.

Chambers, R.A., Taylor, J.R. & Potenza, M.N. (2003). Developmental neurocircuitry of motivation in adolescence: A critical period of addiction vulnerability. *The American Journal of Psychiatry, 160*(6), 1041–1052.

Champion, H.L.O., Foley, K.L., Durant, R.H., Hensberry, R., Altman, D. & Wolfson, M. (2004). Adolescent sexual victimization, use of alcohol and other substances, and other health risk behaviors. *Journal of Adolescent Health, 35*(4), 321–328.

Chan, A., Scheil, W., Scott, J., Nguyen, A-M. & Sage, L. (2011). *Pregnancy outcome in South Australia 2009.* Adelaide: Pregnancy Outcome Unit, SA Health, Government of South Australia.

Chandra, A., Martino, S.C., Collins, R.L., Elliott, M.N., Berry, S.H., Kanouse, D.E. & Miu, A. (2008). Does watching sex on television predict teen pregnancy? Findings from a National Longitudinal Survey of Youth. *Pediatrics, 122*(5), 1047–1054.

Chandra, A., Mosher, W.D., Copen, C. & Sionean, C. (2011). *Sexual behavior, sexual attraction, and sexual identity in the United States: Data from the 2006–2008 National Survey of Family Growth.* National Health Statistics Reports No. 36. Hyattsville, MD: National Center for Health Statistics.

Chang, S.C., O'Brien, K.O., Nathanson, M.S., Mancini, J. & Witter, F.R. (2003). Characteristics and risk factors for adverse birth outcomes in pregnant and black adolescents. *Journal of Pediatrics, 143*, 250–257.

Chapman, K., Tarter, R.E., Kirisci, L. & Cornelius, M.D. (2007). Childhood neurobehavior disinhibition amplifies risk of substance use disorder: Interaction of parental history and prenatal alcohol exposure. *Journal of Developmental and Behavioral Pediatrics, 28,* 219–224.

Charles, G. & McDonald, M. (2005). Adolescent sexual offenders: An overview. *Online Journal of the International Child and Youth Network (CYC-Net), 80.* Retrieved from: http://www.cyc-net.org/cyc-online/cycol-0905-charles.html [Accessed 25 January 2014].

Charmaraman, L. & McKamey, C. (2011). Urban early adolescent narratives on sexuality: Accidental and intentional influences of family, peers, and the media. *Sexuality Research and Social Policy, 8*(4), 253–266.

ChartsBin 2011. (2011). *Minimum legal age of consent.* Retrieved from: http://chartsbin.com/view/03a [Accessed 5 November 2014].

Check Your Risk (n.d.). Retrieved from: http://www.checkyourrisk.org.au [Accessed 27 December 2014].

Chehab, F.F., Mounzik, K., Lu, R. & Lim, M.E. (1997). Early onset of reproductive function in normal female mice treated with leptin. *Science, 275,* 88–90.

Chen, A-S., Leung, M., Chen, C-H. & Yang, S.C. (2013). Exposure to internet pornography among Taiwanese adolescents. *Social Behavior & Personality, 41*(1), 157–164.

Chiao, C. & Yi, C-C. (2011). Adolescent premarital sex and health outcomes among Taiwanese youth: Perceptions of best friends' sexual behavior and the contextual effect. *AIDS Care, 23,* 1083–1092.

Chivers, M.L., Seto, M.C., Lalumière, M.L., Laan, E. & Grimbos, T. (2010). Agreement of self-reported and genital measures of sexual arousal in men and women: A meta-analysis. *Archives of Sexual Behavior, 39*(1), 5–56.

Cho, A. & Lee, J.-H. (2012). Body dissatisfaction levels and gender differences in attentional biases towards idealized bodies. *Body Image, 10*(1), 95–102.

Choudhury, S., Blakemore, S.J. & Charman, T. (2006). Social cognitive development during adolescence. *Social Cognitive and Affective Neuroscience, 1*(3), 165–174.

Christopher, L. (2013, 7 September). Puberty blues. Puberty is tough enough at the best of times, but even more so when it strikes early, *The Sydney Morning Herald.* Retrieved from: http://www.smh.com.au/lifestyle/life/puberty-blues-20130902-2szij.html [Accessed 19 January 2015].

Chung, P.J., Borneo, H., Kilpatrick, S.D., Lopez, D.M., Travis, R., Lui, C. & Schuster, M.A. (2005). Parent-adolescent communication about sex in Filipino American families: A demonstration of community-based participatory research. Ambulatory. *Pediatrics, 5,* 50–55.

Clark, L. & Tiggemann, M. (2008). Sociocultural and individual psychological predictors of body image in young girls: A prospective study. *Developmental Psychology, 44*(4), 1124–1134.

Clark, R.D. & Hatfield, E. (1989). Gender differences in receptivity to sexual offers. *Journal of Psychology & Human Sexuality, 2*(1), 39–55.

Clark-Florey, T. (2013, 17 February). The 'labia pride' movement. *Salon*.com. Retrieved from: http://www.salon.com/2013/02/17/the_labia_pride_movement [Accessed 19 January 2015].

Clifford, G.M., Gallus, S., Herrero, R., Munoz, N., Snijders, P.J., Vaccarella, S., *et al.,* IARC HPV Prevalence Surveys Study Group. (2005). Worldwide distribution of human papillomavirus types in cytologically normal women in the

International Agency for Research on Cancer HPV prevalence surveys: A pooled analysis. *Lancet, 366,* 991–998.

Coker, T.R., Austin, S.B. & Schuster, M.A. (2010). The health and health care of lesbian, gay, and bisexual adolescents. *Annual Review of Public Health, 31,* 457–477.

Colapinto, J. (2000). *As nature made him: The boy who was raised as a girl.* New York: Harper Perennial.

Coleman, P.K. (2006). Resolution of unwanted pregnancy during adolescence through abortion versus childbirth: Individual and family predictors and psychological consequences. *Journal of Youth Adolescence, 35*(6), 903–911.

Coleman, P.K. (2011). Abortion and mental health: Quantitative synthesis and analysis of research published, 1995–2009. *British Journal of Psychiatry, 199,* 180–186.

Coley, R.L., Lombardi, C.M., Lynch, A.D., Mahalik, J.R. & Sims, J. (2013). Sexual partner accumulation from adolescence through early adulthood: The role of family, peer, and school social norms. *Journal of Adolescent Health, 53,* 91–97.

Collins, R.L., Elliott, M.N., Berry, S.H., Kanouse, D.E., Kunkel, D., Hunter, S.B. & Miu, A. (2004). Watching sex on television predicts adolescent initiation of sexual behavior. *Pediatrics, 114*(3), e280–e289.

Collins, W.A., Welsh, D.P. & Furman, W. (2009). Adolescent romantic relationships. *Annual Review of Psychology, 60,* 631.

Collyer, A. (2012). *The unsafe sex? Young men's perception and understandings of contraception.* Unpublished Honours thesis. Melbourne: University of Melbourne.

Common Sense Media. (2012). *Social media, social life: How teens view their digital lives.* San Francisco: Common Sense Media. Retrieved from: https://www.common sensemedia.org/research/social-media-social-life-how-teens-view-their-digital-lives [Accessed 17 November 2014].

Connolly, J. & McIsaac, C. (2009). Adolescents' explanations for romantic dissolutions: A developmental perspective. *Journal of Adolescence, 32*(5), 1209–1223.

Connolly, J., Craig, W., Goldberg, A. & Pepler, D. (2004). Mixed-gender groups, dating, and romantic relationships in early adolescence. *Journal of Research on Adolescence, 14*(2), 185–207.

Cooley, E. & Toray, T. (2001). Body image and personality predictors of eating disorder symptoms during the college years. *The International Journal of Eating Disorders, 30*(1), 28–36.

Copeland, W., Shanahan, L., Miller, S., Costello, J., Angold, A. & Maughan, B. (2010). Do the negative effects of early pubertal timing on adolescent girls continue into young adulthood? *The American Journal of Psychiatry, 167*(10), 1218–1225.

Crabbe, M. & Corlett, D. (2010). Eroticising inequality. *Domestic Violence Resource Centre Victoria (DVRCV), 3(Spring),* 1–6.

Crabbe, M. & Corlett, D. (2011). Eroticising inequality: Technology, pornography and young people [online]. *Redress, 20*(1), 11–15.

Crawford, D.M., Trotter, E.C., Sittner Hartshorn, K.J. & Whitbeck, L.B. (2011). Pregnancy and mental health of young homeless women. *American Journal of Orthopsychiatry, 81,* 173–183.

Crawford, M. & Popp, D. (2003). Sexual double standards: A review and methodological critique of two decades of research. *The Journal of Sex Research, 40,* 13–26.

Crimes Against Children Research Center (n.d.). *Third Youth Internet Safety Survey (YISS-3)*. Retrieved from: http://www.unh.edu/ccrc/projects/yiss3.html [Accessed 12 November 2014].

Croce-Galis, M. (2007). *Earlier and more detailed sex education needed in Africa*. New York: The Guttmacher Institute.

Crowley, A., Moore, S. & Winkler, R. (2004). *Unwanted sexual activity among young people in the City of Boroondara: The role of alcohol and drugs. Report to City of Boroondara*. Melbourne: Swinburne University.

Cunningham, A.L., Taylor, R., Taylor, J., Marks, C., Shaw, J. & Mindel, A. (2006). Prevalence of infection with herpes simplex virus types 1 and 2 in Australia: A nationwide population based survey. *Sexually Transmissible Infections, 82,* 164–168.

Curtis, P. (2006, 23 January). High court to rule on parental consent for abortions. *The Guardian*. Retrieved from: http://www.theguardian.com/uk/2006/jan/23/health.healthandwellbeing [Accessed 16 December 2014].

Dahl, R.E. (2004). Adolescent brain development: A period of vulnerabilities and opportunities. *Annals of the New York Academy of Science, 1021,* 1–22.

Darling, C.A. & Hicks, M.W. (1982). Parental influence on adolescent sexuality: Implications for parents as educators. *Journal of Youth and Adolescence, 11,* 231–245.

Darling, C.A., Kallen, D.J. & VanDusen, J.E. (1984). Sex in transition, 1900–1980. *Journal of Youth & Adolescence, 13,* 385–399.

Darroch, J.E., Landry, D.J. & Oslak, S. (1999). Age differences between sexual partners in the United States. *Family Planning Perspectives, 31,* 160–167.

Daugherty, L. (2006). *Why me? Help for victims of child sexual abuse* (4th edn). Roswell, NM: Cleanan Press.

Dave, S.S., Johnson, A.M., Fenton, K.A., Mercer, C.H., Erens, B. & Wellings, K. (2004). Male circumcision in Britain: Findings from a national probability sample survey. *Sexually Transmitted Infections, 79*(6), 499–500.

Davies, C. & Eynon, R. (2013). *Teenagers and technology*. Hove, UK: Routledge.

Davies, C. & McInnes, D. (2012). Speaking violence: Homophobia and the production of injurious speech in schooling cultures. In S. Saltmarsh, K. Robinson & C. Davies (Eds.), *Rethinking school violence: Theory, gender, context*. New York: Palgrave.

Davila, J. (2008). Depressive symptoms and adolescent romance: Theory, research, and implications. *Child Development and Personality, 2*(1), 26–31.

Davis, A.N., Gahagan, J.C. & George, C. (2013). 'Everyone just keeps their eyes closed and their fingers crossed': Sexual health communication among black parents and children in Nova Scotia, Canada. *International Journal for Equity in Health, 12,* 55–66.

Davis, E.C. & Friel, L.V. (2001). Adolescent sexuality: Disentangling the effects of family structure and family context. *Journal of Marriage and Family, 63,* 669–681.

Davis, S.M. & Harris, M.B. (1982). Sexual knowledge, sexual interests, and sources of information of rural and urban adolescents from three cultures. *Adolescence, 17,* 471–492.

Day, W. (2009). A qualitative study of male youth experiences of viewing pornography. *Journal of Youth Studies, 12*(2), 163–173.

de Graaf, H., Meijer, S., Poelman, J. & Vanwesenbeeck, I. (2005). Cited in Schalet, A., 2010. Sexual subjectivity revisited: The significance of relationships in Dutch and American girls' experiences of sexuality. *Gender and Society, 24,* 304–329.

de Looze, M., Constantine, N., Jerman, P., Vermeulen-Smit, E. & Bogt, T.T. (2014). Parent–adolescent sexual communication and its association with adolescent sexual behaviors: A nationally representative analysis in the Netherlands. *Journal of Sex Research, 10,* 1–12.

de Looze, M., Harakeh, Z., van Dorsselaer, S.A.F.M., Raaijmakers, Q.A.W., Vollebergh, W.A.M. & ter Bogt, T.F.M. (2012). Explaining educational differences in adolescent substance use and early sexual debut: The role of parents and peers. *Journal of Adolescence, 35,* 1035–1044.

Dehne, K.L. & Reidner, G. (2005). *Sexually transmitted infections among adolescents: The need for adequate health services.* Geneva: World Health Organization.

Denham, M., Schell, L.M., Deane, G., Gallo, M.V., Ravenscroft, J., DeCaprio, A.P. & Akwesasne Task Force on the Environment. (2005). Relationship of lead, mercury, mirex, dichlorodiphenyldichloroethylene, hexachlorobenzene, and polychlorinated biphenyls to timing of menarche among Akwesasne Mohawk girls. *Pediatrics, 115,* 127–134.

Department of Education, UK Government. (2009). *Customer voice research: Sex and relationships education.* London: Sherbet Research.

Department of Education, UK. (2012, 3 July). Urgent reforms to protect children in residential care from sexual exploitation. Retrieved from: https://www.gov.uk/government/news/urgent-reforms-to-protect-children-in-residential-care-from-sexual-exploitation [Accessed 20 January 2015].

Department of Health, Social Services and Public Safety, Northern Ireland (2006). *Our children and young people – Our shared responsibility: Inspection of Child Protection Services in Northern Ireland.* Retrieved from: http://www.dhsspsni.gov.uk/oss-child-protection-overview.pdf [Accessed 20 January 2015].

Deptula, D.P., Henry, D.B. & Schoeny, M.E. (2010). How can parents make a difference? Longitudinal associations with adolescent sexual behavior. *Journal of Family Psychology, 24,* 731–739.

Diamond, L. (2004). Emerging perspectives on distinctions between romantic love and sexual desire. *Current Directions in Psychological Science, 13*(3), 116–119.

Diamond, L. & Butterworth, M. (2008). Questioning gender and sexual identity: Dynamic links over time. *Sex Roles, 59*(5/6), 365–376.

Diamond, M. & Sigmundson, G.K. (1999). Sex reassignment at birth. In S.J. Ceci, W.M. Williams & M.A. Malden (Eds.), *Nature–nurture debate: The essential readings.* Oxford: Blackwell Publishers, pp. 55–75.

Dines, G. (2010). *Pornland: How porn has hijacked our sexuality.* Boston: Beacon Press.

Dixon, S., Herbert, D., Loxton, D. & Lucke, J. (2013). 'As many options as there are, there are just not enough for me': A qualitative analysis of contraceptive use and barriers to access among Australian women [Abstract of Poster Presentation]. *European Journal of Contraception and Reproductive Health Care, 18*(Suppl 1), S136.

Doskoch, P. (2014, 1 September). The safest sex [Web log post]. Retrieved from: http://www.psychologytoday.com/articles/200910/the-safest-sex [Accessed 31 December 2014].

Downing, J. & Bellis, M. (2009). Early pubertal onset and its relationship with sexual risk taking, substance use and anti-social behaviour: A preliminary cross-sectional study. *BMC Public Health, 9*(1), 446.

Dunne, E.F. & Markowitz, L.E. (2006). Genital human papillomavirus infection. *Clinical Infectious Diseases, 43,* 624–629.

Dunne, M., Donald, M., Lucke, J., Nilsson, R. & Raphael, B. (1993). *National HIV/ AIDS Evaluation 1992 HIV Risk and Sexual Behaviour Survey in Australian Secondary Schools: Final Report.* Canberra, Australia: Commonwealth Department of Health and Community Services.

Durex. (2009). *Sex and relationships education: Assessing the gaps for Eastern European youth. The face of global sex report.* Retrieved from: http://www.gbcimpact.org/ files/Durex%20Network%20-%20Face%20of%20Global%20Sex%202009.pdf [Accessed 30 December 2014].

Durso, L.E. & Gates, G.J. (2012). *Serving our youth: Findings from a national survey of service providers working with lesbian, gay, bisexual, and transgender youth who are home-less or at risk of becoming homeless.* Los Angeles, CA: The Williams Institute with True Colors Fund and the Palette Fund.

Eastman, K.L., Corona, R. & Schuster, M.D. (2006). Talking parents, healthy teens: A worksite-based program for parents to promote adolescent sexual health. *Preventing Chronic Disease [serial online].* Retrieved from: http://www.cdc.gov/ pcd/issues/2006/oct/06_0012.htm [Accessed 19 January 2015].

Eaton, L., Flisher, A.J. & Aaro, L.E. (2003). Unsafe sexual behaviour in South African youth. *Social Science & Medicine, 56*(1), 149–165.

Edgardh, K. (2002). Sexual behaviour and early coitarche in a national sample of 17-year-old Swedish boys. *Acta Paediatrica, 91*(9), 985–991.

Edwards, R. & Beech, A. (2004). Treatment programmes for adolescents who commit sexual offences: Dropout and recidivism. *Journal of Sexual Aggression, 10,* 101–116.

Ehrlich, M.E., Sommer, J., Canas, E. & Unterwald, E.M. (2002). Periadolescent mice show enhanced DeltaFosB upregulation in response to cocaine and amphet-amine. *The Journal of Neuroscience, 22*(21), 9155–9159.

Eisenberg, M.E., Ackard, D.M. & Resnick, M.D. (2007). Protective factors and suicide risk in adolescents with a history of sexual abuse. *Journal of Pediatrics, 151,* 482–487.

Eisenberg, M.E., Berge, J., Fulkerson, J. & Neumark-Sztainer, D. (2012). Associations between hurtful weight-related comments by family and significant other and the development of disordered eating behaviors in young adults. *Journal of Behavioral Medicine, 35*(5), 500–508.

Eisenberg, M.E., Bernat, D.H., Bearinger, L.H. & Resnick, M.D. (2008). Support for comprehensive sexuality education: Perspectives from parents of school-age youth. *Journal of Adolescent Health, 42,* 352–359.

Eisenberg, M.E. & Resnick, M.D. (2006). Suicidality among gay, lesbian and bisexual youth: The role of protective factors. *Journal of Adolescent Health, 39*(5), 662–668.

Elliot, I.A., Beech, A.R., Mandeville-Norden, R. & Hayes, E. (2009). Psychological profiles of internet sexual offenders: comparisons with contact sexual offenders. *Sexual Abuse: A Journal of Review and Treatment, 21,* 76–92.

Elliott, S. (2010). Parents' constructions of teen sexuality: Sex panics, contradictory discourses, and social inequality. *Symbolic Interaction, 33,* 191–212.

Elliott, S. (2012). Talking to teens about sex: Mothers negotiate resistance, discom-fort, and ambivalence. *Sexuality Research and Social Policy, 7,* 310–322.

Ellis, B.J. & Garber, J. (2000). Psychosocial antecedents of variation in girls' pubertal timing: Maternal depression, stepfather presence, and marital and family stress. *Child Development, 71*(2), 485–501.

Ellwood, D.T. & Bane, M.J. (1984). *The impact of AFDC on family structure and living arrangements*. Report prepared for the U.S. Department of Health and Human Services, grant no. 92A-82. John F. Kennedy School of Government, Harvard University.

eMarketer. (2013). UK teens far outshine US counterparts in smartphone usage. Retrieved from: http://www.emarketer.com/Article/UK-Teens-Far-Outshine-US-Counterparts-Smartphone-Usage/1009837 [Accessed 25 September 2014].

End Child Prostitution and Trafficking (ECPAT) (2015). Retrieved from: http://www.ecpat.net/end-child-sex-tourism [Accessed 29 April 2015].

Epifano, A. (2012). An account of sexual assault at Amherst College, The Amherst Student, Opinion. Retrieved from: http://amherststudent.amherst.edu/?q=article/2012/10/17/account-sexual-assault-amherst-college [Accessed 15 November 2014].

Epstein, M. & Ward, L. (2008). 'Always use protection': Communication boys receive about sex from parents, peers, and the media. *Journal of Youth and Adolescence, 37*, 113–126.

Erasing 76 crimes (2014, 16 October). 79 countries where homosexuality is illegal. Retrieved from: http://76crimes.com/76-countries-where-homosexuality-is-illegal [Accessed 5 January 2015].

Erickson-Schroth, L. (2010). The neurobiology of sex/gender-based attraction. *Journal of Gay & Lesbian Mental Health, 14*, 56–69.

Erikson, E. (1959). *Identity and the life cycle: Selected papers* (Vol. 1). New York: International Universities Press.

Erikson, E. (1968). *Identity, youth and crisis*. New York: Norton.

Esere, M.O. (2008). Effects of sex education programme on at-risk sexual behavior of school-going adolescents in Ilorin, Nigeria. *African Health Science, 8*, 120–125.

Eskin, M., Kaynak-Demir, H. & Demir, S. (2005). Same-sex sexual orientation, childhood sexual abuse, and suicidal behavior in university students in Turkey. *Archives of Sexual Behavior, 34*, 185–195.

European Agency for Fundamental Human Rights. (2014). *Violence against women: An EU wide survey*. Vienna: EAFHR.

Ewert, C., Collier, A. & Temple-Smith, M. (under review). 'Young men think you have to be naked in front of the GP': Young men's perceptions of sexual health care.

Exner-Cortens, D., Eckenrode, J. & Rothman, E. (2013). Longitudinal associations between teen dating violence victimization and adverse health outcomes. *Pediatrics, 71*, 71–78.

Experience Project (2014). I have never had a boyfriend. Retrieved from: http://www.experienceproject.com/stories/Have-Never-Had-A-Boyfriend/4701328 [Accessed 15 January 2014].

Fairley, C.K. & Sawyer, S. (2003). What is all the fuss about? Arguments for and against making Emergency Contraception available over the counter. *Vicdoc, July*, 8–9.

Farahani, K.A.F., Cleland, J. & Mehryar, A.H. (2011). Associations between family factors and premarital heterosexual relationships among female college students in Tehran. *International Perspectives in Sexual and Reproductive Health, 37*(1), 30–39.

Farooqi, I.S. (2002). Leptin and the onset of puberty: Insights from rodent and human genetics. *Seminars in Reproductive Medicine, 20,* 139–144.

Farr, C., Brown, J. & Beckett, R. (2004). Ability to empathise and masculinity levels: Comparing male adolescent sex offenders with a normative sample of non-offending adolescents. *Psychology, Crime & Law, 10,* 155–168.

Faundes, A. & Alvarez, F. (2011). Abortion. In P. Van Look (Ed.), *Sexual and reproductive health: A public health perspective*. San Diego, CA: Academic Press.

Feijoo, A.N. & Grayton, C. (2004). *Trends in sexual risk behaviors among high school students: United States, 1991 to 1997 and 1999 to 2003. [The Facts]*. Washington, DC: Advocates for Youth.

Feldman, S.S. & Rosenthal, D.A. (2000). The effect of communication characteristics on family members' perceptions of parents as sex educators. *Journal of Research on Adolescence, 10,* 119–150.

Feldman, S.S., Rosenthal, D.A., Brown, N.L. & Canning, R.D. (1995). Predicting sexual experience in adolescent boys from peer acceptance and rejection during childhood. *Journal of Research on Adolescence, 5,* 387–412.

Fellmeth, G.L.T., Heffernan, C., Nurse, J., Habibula, S. & Sethi, D. (2013). Educational and skills-based interventions for preventing relationship and dating violence in adolescents and young adults. *Cochrane Database of Systematic Reviews,* Issue 6.

Ferguson, R.M., Vanwesenbeeck, I. & Knijn, T. (2008). A matter of facts . . . and more: An exploratory analysis of the content of sexuality education in the Netherlands. *Sex Education, 8,* 93–106.

Fergusson, D.M., Horwood, L.J. & Boden, J.M. (2013). Does abortion reduce the mental health risks of unwanted or unintended pregnancy? A re-appraisal of the evidence. *Australian and New Zealand Journal of Psychiatry, 47*(9), 819–827.

Fessler, K.B. (2003). Social outcomes of early childbearing: Important considerations for the provision of clinical care. *Journal of Midwifery and Women's Health, 48*(3), 178–185.

Fileborn, B. (2011). Sexual assault laws in Australia (ACSSA Resource Sheet). Melbourne: Australian Institute of Family Studies.

Fine, M. (1988). Sexuality, schooling, and adolescent females: The missing discourse of desire. *Harvard Educational Review, 58*(1), 29–53.

Finer, L.B., Frohwirth, L.F., Dauphinee, L.A., Singh, S. & Moore, A.M. (2005). Reasons U.S. women have abortions: Quantitative and qualitative perspectives. *Perspectives on Sexual & Reproductive Health, 37,* 110–118.

Finer, L.B. & Philbin, J.M. (2013). Sexual initiation, contraceptive use, and pregnancy among young adolescents. *Pediatrics, 131*(5), 886–891.

Finer, L.B. & Zolna, M.R. (2011). Unintended pregnancy in the United States: Incidence and disparities, 2006. *Contraception, 84,* 478–485.

Fingerson, L. (2006). *Girls in power*. Albany, NY: State University of New York Press.

Finkel, E., Eastwich, P.W., Karney, B., Reis, H.T. & Sprecher, S. (2012). Online dating: A critical analysis from the perspective of psychological science. *Psychological Science in the Public Interest, 13,* 3–66.

Finkelstein, J.S., Lee, H., Burnett-Bowie, S.M., Pallais, J.C., Yu, E.W., Borges, L.F., *et al.* (2013). Gonadal steroids and body composition, strength, and sexual function in men. *New England Journal of Medicine, 369*(11), 1011–1022.

Firestein, B.A. (2007). *Becoming visible: Counseling bisexuals across the lifespan.* New York: Columbia University Press.

Fisher, T. (2013). Gender roles and pressure to be truthful: The bogus pipeline modifies gender differences in sexual but not non-sexual behavior. *Sex Roles, 68*(7), 401–414.

Flack, W.F., Daubman, K.A., Caron, M.L., Asadorian, J.A., D'Aureli, N.R., Gigliotti, S.N. & Stine, E.R. (2007). Risk factors and consequences of unwanted sex among university students: Hooking up, alcohol, and stress response. *Journal of Interpersonal Violence, 22,* 139–157.

Flood, M. (2007). Exposure to pornography among youth in Australia. *Journal of Sociology, 43*(1), 45–60.

Flowers, P. & Buston, K. (2001). 'I was terrified of being different': Exploring gay men's accounts of growing-up in a heterosexist society. *Journal of Adolescence, 24*(1), 51–66.

Ford, J., Nassar, N., Sullivan, E.A., Chambers, G. & Lancaster, P. (2003). *Reproductive health indicators Australia 2002.* AIHW Cat No. PER20. Canberra: AIHW NPSU.

Fordham, G. (2006). *'As if they were watching my body': Pornography and the development of attitudes towards sex and sexual behaviour among Cambodian youth.* Phnom Penh: World Vision Cambodia.

Formby, E., Coldwell, M., Stiell, B., Demack, S., Stevens, A., Shipton, L., *et al.* (2011). *Personal, social, health, and economic education: A mapping study of the prevalent models of delivery and their effectiveness. Research Report DFE-RR080.* London: Department of Education.

Forum Bodybuilding. (2011). 'No girlfriend or first kiss, anyone been in this situation at my age?' Retrieved from: http://forum.bodybuilding.com/showthread. php?t=137840563 [Accessed 15 January 2015].

Foshee, V.A., McNaughton Reyes, H.L., Gottfredson, N.C., Chang, L-Y. & Ennett, S.T. (2013). A longitudinal examination of psychological, behavioral, academic, and relationship consequences of dating abuse victimization among a primarily rural sample of adolescents. *Journal of Adolescent Health, 53*(6), 723–729.

Francesconi, M. (2007). Adult outcomes for children of teenage mothers. Discussion Paper 2778. Bonn: Institute for the Study of Labor.

Frankel, L. (2002). 'I've never thought about it': Contradictions and taboos surrounding American males' experiences of first ejaculation (semenarche). *Journal of Men's Studies, 11,* 37–54.

Freeman, E.E., Weiss, H.A., Glynn, J.R., Cross, P.L., Whitworth, J.A. & Hayes, R.J. (2006). Herpes simplex virus 2 infection increases HIV acquisition in men and women: Systematic review and meta-analysis of longitudinal studies. *AIDS, 20,* 73–83.

French, B.H., Tilghman, J.D. & Malebranche, D.A. (2014, 17 March). Sexual coercion, context and psychosocial correlates among diverse males. *Psychology of Men & Masculinity* [Advance online publication]. Retrieved from: http://dx.doi. org/10.1037/a0035915 [Accessed 25 January 2015].

French, D.C. & Dishion, T. (2003). Predictors of early initiation of sexual intercourse among high-risk adolescents. *Journal of Early Adolescence, 23,* 295–315.

Freud, S. (1924). The passing of the Oedipal complex. In *Collected papers* (Vol. 2). London: Hogarth.

Freud, S. (1935). *A general introduction to psychoanalysis.* New York: Liveright.

Frisch, R. & Revelle, R. (1970). Height and weight at menarche and a hypothesis of critical body weights and adolescent events. *Science, 169,* 397–399.

Furman, W. & Hand, L.S. (2006). The slippery nature of romantic relationships: Issues in definition and differentiation. In A. Crouter & A. Booth (Eds.), *Romance and sex in adolescence and emerging adulthood: Risks and opportunities* (Vol. xi). Mahwah, NJ: Lawrence Erlbaum Associates, pp. 171–178.

Gaddis, A. & Brooks-Gunn, J. (1985). The male experience of pubertal change. *Journal of Youth and Adolescence, 14,* 61–69.

Galan, J.I.P., Puras, B.M. & Riley, R.L. (2009). Achieving real equality: A work in progress for LGBT youth in Spain. *Journal of Lesbian, Gay, Bisexual and Transgender Youth, 6*(2–3), 272–287.

Garcia, J.R., Reiber, C., Massey, S. & Merriwether, A. (2012). Sexual hookup culture: A review. *Review of General Psychology, 16*(2), 161–176.

Garrett, C.C., Hocking, J., Chen, M., Fairley, C. & Kirkman, M. (2011). Young people's views on the potential use of telemedicine consultations for sexual health: Results of a national survey. *Sexual Health, 9,* 192–193.

Garvie, P.A., Wilkins, M.L. & Young, J.C. (2010). Medication adherence in adolescents with behaviorally-acquired HIV: Evidence for using a multimethod assessment protocol. *Journal of Adolescent Health, 47*(5), 504–511.

Gates, G.J. (2011). *How many people are lesbian, gay, bisexual, and transgender?* Los Angeles, CA: The Williams Institute, UCLA School of Law.

Gaydos, C.A., Theodore, M., Dalesio, N., Wood, B.J. & Quinn, T.C. (2004). Expert review on: Comparison of three nucleic acid amplification tests for detection of *Chlamydia trachomatis* in urine specimens. *Journal f Clinical Microbiology, 42,* 3041–3045.

Ge, X., Conger, R.D. & Elder, J.G.H. (2001). The relation between puberty and psychological distress in adolescent boys. *Journal of Research on Adolescence, 11*(1), 49–70.

Gelbal, S. & Duyan, V. (2006). Attitudes of university students towards lesbians and gay men in Turkey. *Sex Roles, 55*(7–8), 573–579.

George, R. (2014). Blood speaks. *Mosaic Science.* Retrieved from: http://mosaicscience.com/story/blood-speaks [Accessed 31 December 2014].

Gidycz, C. & Dardis, C.M. (2014). Feminist self-defense and resistance training for college students. *Trauma Violence Abuse, 15*(4), 322–333.

Giedd, J.N. (2008). The teen brain: Insights from neuroimaging. *Journal of Adolescent Health, 42*(4), 335–343.

Giedd, J.N., Blumenthal, J., Jeffries, N.O., Castellanos, F.X., Liu, H., Zijdenbos, A., *et al.* (1999). Brain development during childhood and adolescence: A longitudinal MRI study. *Nature Neuroscience, 2*(10), 861–863.

Giordano, M. & Ross, A. (2012). *Let's talk about sex: Young people's views on sex and sexual health information in Australia.* Melbourne: Australian Youth Affairs Coalition and Youth Empowerment Against HIV/AIDS.

Giordano, P.C., Longmore, M.A. & Manning, W.D. (2006). Gender and the meanings of adolescent romantic relationships: A focus on boys. *American Sociological Review, 71*(2), 260–287.

Godeau, E., Nic Gabhainn, S., Vignes, C., Ross, J., Boyce, W. & Todd, J. (2008). Contraceptive use by 15-year-old students at their last sexual intercourse: Results from 24 countries. *Archives of Pediatrics & Adolescent Medicine, 162*(1), 66–73.

Gogtay, N., Giedd, J.N., Lusk, L., Hayashi, K.M., Greenstein, D., Vaituzis, A.C., *et al.* (2004). Dynamic mapping of human cortical development during childhood through early adulthood. *Proceedings of the National Academy of Science, USA, 101*(21), 8174–8179.

Gold, J., Lim, M., Hocking, J., Keogh, L., Spelman, T. & Hellard, M. (2010a). Determining the impact of text messaging for sexual health promotion to young people. *Sexually Transmissible Diseases, 38*(4), 247–252.

Gold, J., Lim, M., Hellard, M., Hocking, J. & Keogh, L. (2010b). What's in a message? Delivering sexual health promotion to young people in Australia via text messaging. *BMC Public Health, 10,* 792–803.

Gold, M.A., Sheftel, A.V., Chiappetta, L., Young, A.J., Zuckoff, A., DiClemente, C.C. & Primack, B.A. (2010). Associations between religiosity and sexual and contraceptive behaviors. *Journal of Adolescent Gynaecology, 23,* 290–297.

Goldey, K.L. & van Anders, S.M. (2011). Sexy thoughts: Effects of sexual cognitions on testosterone, cortisol, and arousal in women. *Hormones and Behavior, 59*(5), 754–764.

Goldman, J. (2008). Responding to parental objections to school sexuality education: A selection of 12 objections. *Sex Education, 8,* 415–438.

Goodenow, C., Szalacha L. & Westheimer, K. (2006). School support groups, other school factors, and the safety of sexual minority adolescents. *Psychology in the Schools, 43,* 573–589.

Gordon-Messer, D., Bauermeister, J.A., Grodzinski, A. & Zimmerman, M. (2013). Sexting among young adults, *Journal of Adolescent Health, 52,* 301–306.

Gorman, S., Monk-Turner, E. & Fish, J.N. (2010). Free adult internet web sites: How prevalent are degrading acts? *Gender Issues, 27*(3–4), 131–145.

Government of Canada. (2013). Chlamydia. Retrieved from: http://healthycanadians. gc.ca/health-sante/sexual-sexuelle/chlamyd-eng.php [Accessed 4 July 2014].

Graber, J.A. (2013). Pubertal timing and the development of psychopathology in adolescence and beyond. *Hormones and Behaviour, 64*(2), 262–269.

Graber, J.A., Seeley, J.R., Brooks-Gunn, J. & Lewinsohn, P.M. (2004). Is pubertal timing associated with psychopathology in young adulthood? *Journal of the American Academy of Child and Adolescent Psychiatry, 43*(6), 718–726.

Grant, J., Hoorens, S., Sivadasan, S., Loo, M.V., Davanzo, J., Hale, L. & Butz, W. (2006). Trends in European fertility: Should Europe try to increase its fertility rate, or just manage the consequences? *International Journal of Andrology, 29,* 17–24.

Graves, J. (2014). Born this way? An evolutionary view of 'gay genes'. In *The conversation.* Retrieved from: http://theconversation.com/born-this-way-an-evolutionary-view-of-gay-genes-26051 [Accessed 29 December 2014].

Greifinger, R. & Dick, B. (2009). *A qualitative review of psychosocial support interventions for young people living with HIV.* Geneva: WHO. Retrieved from: https://

www.k4health.org/sites/default/files/Psychosocial%20support.pdf [Accessed 24 November 2014].

Grieger, L.D., Kusunoki, Y. & Harding, D.J. (2014). The social contexts of adolescent romantic relationships. *Focus, 31*(1), 15–17.

Grimbos, T., Dhawood, K., Buriss, R.P., Zucker, K.J. & Puts, D.A. (2010). Sexual orientation and the second to fourth finger length ratio: A meta-analysis in men and women. *Behavioral Neuroscience, 124,* 278–287.

Gross, A., Bennett, T., Sloan, L., Marx, B.P. & Juergens, J. (2001). The impact of alcohol and alcohol expectancies on male perception of female sexual arousal in a date rape analogue. *Experimental and Clinical Psychopharmacology, 9,* 380–388.

Grov, C., Gillespie, B.J., Royce, T. & Lever, J. (2011). Perceived consequences of casual online sexual activities on heterosexual relationships: A U.S. online survey. *Archives of Sexual Behavior, 40,* 429–439.

Guilamo-Ramos, V., Dittus, P., Jaccard, J., Goldberg, V., Casillas, E. & Bouris, A. (2006). The content and process of mother-adolescent communication about sex in Latino families. *Social Work Research, 30,* 169–181.

Gupta, N. & Mahy, M. (2003). Sexual initiation among adolescent girls and boys: Trends and differentials in sub-Saharan Africa. *Archives of Sexual Behavior, 32*(1), 41–53.

Guse, K., Levine, D., Martins, S., Lira, A., Gaarde, J., Westmorland, W. & Gilliam, M. (2012). Interventions using new digital media to improve adolescent sexual health: A systematic review. *Journal of Adolescent Health, 51*(6), 535–543.

Guttmacher Institute. (2011). *State policies in brief: Sex and HIV education*. Retrieved from: http://www.guttmacher.org/statecenter/spibs/spib_SE.pdf [Accessed 3 November 2014].

Guttmacher Institute. (2014, May). *American teens' sexual and reproductive health. [Fact sheet]*. Retrieved from: http://www.guttmacher.org/pubs/FB-ATSRH. html [Accessed 31 December 2014].

Gyarmathy, V.A., Thomas, R.P., Mikl, J., McNutt, L.A., Morse, D.L., DeHovitz, J. & Szamado, S. (2002). Sexual activity and condom use among Eastern European adolescents: The study of Hungarian adolescent risk behaviours. *International Journal of STD & AIDS, 13*(6), 399–405.

Habib, S. (2011). Deconstructing sexuality in the Middle East (review). *Journal of Middle East Women's Studies, 7*(3), 113–115.

Haggerty, C.L., Gottlieb, S.L., Taylor, B.D., Low, N., Xu, F. & Ness, R.B. (2010). Risk of sequelae after Chlamydia trachomatis genital infection in women. *Journal of Infectious Diseases, 201*(Suppl 2), S134–155.

Häggström-Nordin, E., Borneskog, C., Eriksson, M. & Tyden, T. (2011). Sexual behaviour and contraceptive use among Swedish high school students in two cities: Comparisons between genders, study programmes, and over time. *European Journal of Contraception and Reproductive Health Care, 16*(1), 36–46.

Häggström-Nordin, E., Hanson, U. & Tyden, T. (2005). Associations between pornography consumption and sexual practices among adolescents in Sweden. *International Journal of STD & AIDS, 16,* 102–107.

Häggström-Nordin, E., Sandberg, J., Hanson, U. & Tydén, T. (2006). 'It's everywhere!' Young Swedish people's thoughts and reflections about pornography. *Scandinavian Journal of Caring Sciences, 20*(4), 386–393.

Häggström-Nordin, E., Tydén, T., Hanson, U. & Larsson, M. (2009). Experiences of and attitudes towards pornography among a group of Swedish high school students. *European Journal of Contraception & Reproductive Health Care, 14*(4), 277–284.

Hakuhodo Global Habitat. (2013, 9 August). Use of smartphone in 14 Asian cities. *Hakuhodo, 9*. Retrieved from: http://www.hakuhodo.jp/pdf/2013/20130809_2.pdf [Accessed 4 October 2014].

Hald, G.M., Kuyper, L., Adam, P.C.G. & de Wit, J.B.F. (2013). Does viewing explain doing? Assessing the association between sexually explicit materials use and sexual behaviours in a large sample of Dutch adolescents and young adults. *Journal of Sexual Medicine, 10*(12), 2986–2995.

Hald, G.M. & Malamuth, N.M. (2008). Self-perceived effects of pornography consumption. *Archives of Sexual Behavior, 37*(4), 614–625.

Halpern, C.J.T., Udry, J.R., Suchindran, C. & Campbell, B. (2000). Adolescent males' willingness to report masturbation. *Journal of Sex Research, 37*(4), 327–332.

Halpern, C.T. (2003). Biological influences on adolescent romantic and sexual behavior. In P. Florsheim (Ed.), *Adolescent romantic relations and sexual behavior*. Mahwah, NJ: Lawrence Erlbaum Associates, pp. 57–84.

Halpern, C.T. & Haydon, A.A. (2012). Sexual timetables for oral-genital, vaginal, and anal intercourse: Sociodemographic comparisons in a nationally representative sample of adolescents. *American Journal of Public Health, 102*(6), 1221–1228.

Halpern-Felsher, B.L., Cornell, J.L., Kropp, R.Y. & Tschann, J.M. (2005). Oral versus vaginal sex among adolescents: Perceptions, attitudes, and behavior. *Pediatrics, 115*(4), 845–851.

Hamilton, B.E, Martin, J.A. & Ventura, S.J. (2012). Births: Preliminary data for 2011. *National Vital Statistics Reports, 61*(5). Table 2.

Hamilton, B.E., Martin, J.A. & Ventura, S.J. (2013). Births: Preliminary data for 2012. *National Vital Statistics Reports, 62*(3). Retrieved from: http://www.cdc.gov/nchs/data/nvsr/nvsr62/nvsr62_03.pdf [Accessed 24 February 2014].

Han, C., Operario, D. & Chou, K.H. (2011). 'If I was infected with HIV, I would be letting my family down': Family influences on risk and protective factors for unsafe sex among gay Asian Pacific Islander men. *Health Risk & Society, 13*, 373–388.

Harding, T., Hayes, J., Simonis, M. & Temple-Smith, M. (2015). Female genital cosmetic surgery: What every Australian general practitioner needs to know. *Australian Family Physician*.

Hardy, S.A., Steelman, M.A., Coyne, S.M. & Ridge, R.D. (2013). Adolescent religiousness as a protective factor against pornography use. *Journal of Applied Developmental Psychology, 34*, 131–139.

Harper, G., Bruce, D., Serrano, P. & Jamil, O. (2009). The role of the Internet in the sexual identity development of gay and bisexual male adolescents. In P. Hammack & B. Cohler (Eds.), *The story of sexual identity*. New York: Oxford University Press, pp. 297–327.

Harris, A.O., Atwood, K.A., Kennedy, S.B., Taylor, C.H., Tegli, J.K., Barbu, E.M. & Shamblen, S.R. (2014). Correlates of condom use with 'main' and 'concurrent' sex partners among urban youth in post-conflict Liberia. *Vulnerable Children and Youth Studies, 9*(1), 86–96.

Harris, K.M. (2009). *The national longitudinal study of adolescent health (Add Health), Waves I & II, 1994–1996; Wave III, 2001–2002; Wave IV, 2007–2009.* Chapel Hill, NC: Carolina Population Center, University of North Carolina at Chapel Hill.

Hart, M. & Third, A. (2013, 8 November). Why Tumblr fosters deep and enduring forms of intimacy online. *On Line Opinion.* Retrieved from: http://www. onlineopinion.com.au/view.asp?article=15666 [Accessed 4 October 2014].

Hatzenbuehler, M. (2011). The social environment and suicide attempts in lesbian, gay and bisexual youth. *Pediatrics, 127*(5), 896–903.

Haveman, R., Wolfe, B. & Peterson, E. (1997). Outcomes for teens and young adults of adolescent parents. In R. Maynard (Ed.), *Kids having kids: Economic costs and social consequences of teen pregnancy.* Washington, DC: Urban Institute Press.

Headspace. (2012). *Adolescent romantic relationships – Why are they important? And should they be encouraged or avoided?* Melbourne: Orygen Youth Health Research Centre, National Youth Mental Health Foundation. Retrieved from: http://www. headspace.org.au/media/326676/romanticrelationships_adolescent_romantic_ relationships_why_are_they_important_headspace_evsum.pdf [Accessed 19 January 2015].

Health Do. (2009). *Young people's sexual health: The National Chlamydia Screening Programme.* London: National Audit Office.

HealthyChildren.org (2013). Teen magazines and their effect on girls. Retrieved from: http://www.healthychildren.org/English/family-life/Media/Pages/Teen-Magazines-and-Their-Effect-on-Girls.aspx [Accessed 17 November 2014].

Heidt, J.M., Marx, B. & Forsyth, J.P. (2005). Tonic immobility and childhood sexual abuse: A preliminary report evaluating the sequela of rape-induced paralysis. *Behaviour Research and Therapy, 43,* 1157–1171.

Helsper, E. (2005). *R18 material: Its potential impact on people under 18 – An overview of the available literature.* Research review conducted by London School of Economics for Ofcom. Retrieved from: http://stakeholders.ofcom.org.uk/ binaries/research/radio-research/r18.pdf [Accessed 23 April 2015].

Henley, J. (2010, 27 July). Teenagers and technology: 'I'd rather give up my kidney than my phone'. *The Guardian.* Retrieved from: http://www.theguardian. com/lifeandstyle/2010/jul/16/teenagers-mobiles-facebook-social-networking [Accessed 1 October 2014].

Herman-Giddens, M.E. (2007). The decline in the age of menarche in the United States: Should we be concerned? *Journal of Adolescent Health, 40*(3), 201–203.

Herman-Giddens, M.E., Kaplowitz, P.B. & Wasserman, R. (2004). Navigating the recent articles on girls' puberty in pediatrics: What do we know and where do we go from here? *Pediatrics, 113,* 911–917.

Herman-Giddens, M.E., Steffes, J., Harris, D., Slora, E., Hussey, M., Dowshen, S.A., *et al.* (2012). Secondary sexual characteristics in boys: Data from the pediatric research in office settings network. *Pediatrics, 130,* 1058–1068.

Hernandez, D. (2011). The effects of consuming pornography: Men's attitudes towards violence against women, dominance over and objectification of women, and sexual expectations of women. *Perspectives (University of New Hampshire), Spring,* 116–123.

Herrman, J.W. (2007). Repeat pregnancy in adolescence: Intentions and decision making. *American Journal of Maternal Child Nursing, 32*(2), 89–94.

Hieftje, K., Edelman, E.J., Camenga, D.R. & Fiellin, L.E. (2013). Electronic media-based health interventions promoting behavior change in youth: A systematic review. *Journal of the American Medical Association Pediatrics, 167*(6), 574–580.

Hiller, J. (2004). Speculations on the links between feelings, emotions and sexual behaviour: Are vasopressin and oxytocin involved? *Sexual and Relationship Therapy, 19,* 393–412.

Hiller, J. (2005). Gender differences in sexual motivation. *Journal of Men's Health and Gender, 2,* 339–345.

Hillier, L. (2007). Safe spaces: The upside of the image problem for same sex attracted young women playing Australian Rules football. *Journal of the Football Studies Group, 8*(2), 1–24.

Hillier, L. & Harrison, L. (2004). Homophobia and the production of shame: young people and same sex attraction. *Culture, Health and Sexuality, 6,* 79–94.

Hillier, L., Jones, T., Monagle, M., Overton, N., Gahan, L., Blackman, J. & Mitchell, A. (2010). *Writing Themselves In 3 (WTi3): The third national study on the sexual health and wellbeing of same sex attracted and gender questioning young people.* Melbourne: Australian Research Centre in Sex, Health and Society, La Trobe University.

Hirschenhauser, K., Frigerio, D., Grammer, K. & Magnusson, M.S. (2002). Monthly patterns of testosterone and behavior in prospective fathers. *Hormones and Behavior, 42*(2), 172–181.

Hobbs, M., Taft, A.J., Amir, L.H., Stewart, K., Shelley, J.M., Smith, A.M.A., *et al.* (2011). Pharmacy access to the emergency contraceptive pill: A national survey of a random sample of Australian women. *Contraception, 83,* 151–158.

Hockaday, C.M., Crase, S.J., Shelley, M.C. & Stockdale, D.F. (2000). A prospective study of teen pregnancy. *Journal of Adolescence, 23,* 423–438.

Hock-Long, L., Henry-Moss, D., Carter, M., Hatfield-Timajchy, K., Erickson, P.I., Cassidy, A. & Chittams, J. (2013). Condom use with serious and casual heterosexual partners: Findings from a community venue-based survey of young adults. *AIDS and Behavior, 17*(3), 900–913.

Hocking, J., Low, N., Guy, R., Law, M., Donovan, B., Kaldor, J., *et al.* (n.d.). 12 PRT 09010: Australian Chlamydia Control Effectiveness Pilot (ACCEPt): A cluster randomised controlled trial of chlamydia testing in general practice. ACTRN1260000297022. Retrieved from: http://www.thelancet.com/protocol-reviews/12PRT09010 [Accessed 23 April 2015].

Hogarth, H. & Ingham, R. (2009). Masturbation among young women and associations with sexual health: An exploratory study. *Journal of Sex Research, 46,* 558–567.

Holgate, H. & Evans, R. (2006). Sexuality and young motherhood: Discourses and definitions. In Holgate, H., Evans, R. & Yuen, F.K.O. (Eds.), *Teenage pregnancy and parenthood: Global perspectives, issues and interventions.* Abingdon: Routledge.

Hollander, J.A. (2014). Does self-defense training prevent sexual violence against women? *Violence Against Women, 20*(3), 252–269.

Hoque, M.E. (2011). Reported risky sexual practices amongst female undergraduate students in KwaZulu-Natal, South Africa. *African Journal of Primary Health Care &*

Family Medicine, 3(1), 6 pp. Retrieved from: http://www.phcfm.org/index.php/phcfm/article/view/281 [Accessed 30 December 2014].

Houck, C.D., Barker, D., Rizzo, C., Hancock, E., Norton, A. & Brown, L.K. (2014). Sexting and sexual behavior in at-risk adolescents. *Pediatrics, 133,* 1–7.

Houston, A.M., Fang, J.Y., Husman, C. & Peralta, L. (2007). More than just vaginal intercourse: Anal intercourse and condom use patterns in the context of 'main' and 'casual' sexual relationships among urban minority adolescent females. *Journal of Pediatric and Adolescent Gynecology, 20*(5), 299–304.

Howarth, C., Hayes, J., Simonis, M. & Temple-Smith, M. (under review). 'Everything's neatly tucked away'. Young women's views on desirable genital anatomy: A qualitative analysis.

Hu, S.H, Wei, N., Wang, Q.D, Yan, L.Q., Wei, E.Q., Zhang, M.M., *et al.* (2008). Patterns of brain activation during visually evoked sexual arousal differ between homosexual and heterosexual men. *American Journal of Neuroradiology, 29,* 1890–1896.

Huebner, A.J. & Howell, L.W. (2003). Examining the relationship between adolescent sexual risk-taking and perceptions of monitoring, communication, and parenting styles. *Journal of Adolescent Health, 33,* 71–78.

Human Rights Campaign. (2014). Growing up LGBT in America. Retrieved from: http://www.hrc.org/youth [Accessed 29 May 2014].

Hussen, S.A., Bowleg, L., Sangaramoorthy, T. & Malebranche, D. (2012). Parents, peers and pornography: The influence of formative sexual scripts on adult HIV sexual risk behaviour among Black men in the USA. *Culture, Health & Sexuality, 14*(8), 863–877.

Hyde, A., Drennan, J., Butler, M., Howlett, E., Carney, M. & Lohan, M. (2013). Parents' constructions of communication with their children about safer sex. *Journal of Clinical Nursing, 22,* 3438–3446.

Inspot. (n.d.). Retrieved from: http://www.inspot.org [Accessed 27 December 2014].

International Labour Organization (n.d.). *Commercial sexual exploitation of children.* Retrieved from: http://www.ilo.org/ipec/areas/CSEC/lang--en/index.htm [Accessed 20 January 2015].

Israel, T. & Mohr, J.J. (2004). Attitudes towards bisexual women and men: Current research, future directions. *Journal of Bisexuality, 4,* 117–134.

Jaccard, J., Dodge, T. & Dittus, P. (2002). Parent-adolescent communication about sex and birth control: A conceptual framework. In S.S. Feldman & D.A. Rosenthal (Eds.), *Talking sexuality: Parent–adolescent communication.* San Francisco, CA: Jossey-Bass, pp. 9–42.

Jackson, T.E. & Falmagne, R.J. (2013). Women wearing white: Discourses of menstruation and the experience of menarche. *Feminism & Psychology, 23*(3), 379–398.

Jacob, M. (2013, 17 November). Labiaplasty surgery on the rise in Australia but a backlash looms. *The Sydney Morning Herald.* Retrieved from: http://m.smh.com.au/health-and-fitness/dl-wellbeing/labiaplasty-surgery-on-the-rise-in-australia-but-a-backlash-looms-20131115-2xldg.html [Accessed 31 December 2014].

Janssen, D.F. (2007). First stirrings: Cultural notes on orgasm, ejaculation, and wet dreams. *Journal of Sex Research, 44,* 122–134.

Javadnoori, M., Roudsari, R.L., Hasanpour, M., Hazavehei, S.M.M. & Taghipour, A. (2012). Female adolescents' experiences and perceptions regarding sexual health education in Iranian schools: A qualitative content analysis. *Iranian Journal of Nursing and Midwifery Research, 17*(7), 539–546.

Jerman, P. & Constantine, N.A. (2010). Demographic and psychological predictors of parent-adolescent communication about sex: A representative statewide analysis. *Journal of Youth and Adolescence, 39,* 1164–1174.

Jewkes, R.K., Levin, J.B. & Penn-Kekana, L.A. (2003). Gender inequalities, intimate partner violence and HIV preventive practices: Findings of a South African cross-sectional study. *Social Science & Medicine, 56*(1), 125–134.

Joel, S., MacDonald, G. & Shimotomai, A. (2011). Conflicting pressures on romantic relationship commitment for anxiously attached individuals. *Journal of Personality, 79*(1), 51–74.

Johansson, T. & Hammarén, N. (2007). Hegemonic masculinity and pornography: Young people's attitudes towards and relations to pornography. *Journal of Men's Studies, 15,* 57–70.

Johnston, L.D., O'Malley, P.M., Bachman, J.G. & Schulenberg, J.E. (2013). *Monitoring the future, national survey results on drug use, 1975–2012,* Vol. 1: *Secondary school students.* NIH Pub. No. 06-5883. Institute for Social Research, the University of Michigan, under Research Grant No. R01 DA 01411 from the National Institute on Drug Abuse.

Jones, D.C. (2004). Body image among adolescent girls and boys: A longitudinal study. *Developmental Psychology, 40*(5), 823–835.

Jones, R.K., Darroch, J.E. & Singh, S. (2005). Religious differentials in the sexual and reproductive behaviors of young women in the United States. *Journal of Adolescent Health, 36,* 279–288.

Jones, T.M. & Hillier, L. (2012). Sexuality education school policy for Australian GLBTIQ students. *Sex Education, 12,* 437–454.

Kaestle, C.E. & Ivory, A.H. (2012). A forgotten sexuality: Content analysis of bisexuality in the medical literature over two decades. *Journal of Bisexuality, 12*(1), 35–48.

Kaestle, C.E., Morisky, D.E. & Wiley, D.J. (2002). Sexual intercourse and the age difference between adolescent females and their romantic partners. *Perspectives in Sex and Reproductive Health, 34,* 304–309.

Kahr, B. (2008). Cited in *The Sex Educator* 17 (2011, Spring). Retrieved from: http://publications.msss.gouv.qc.ca/acrobat/f/documentation/2011/11-314-01A.pdf [Accessed 31 December 2014].

Kajula, L.J., Sheon, N., De Vries, H., Kaaya, S.F. & Aarø, L.E. (2014). Dynamics of parent-adolescent communication on sexual health and HIV/AIDS in Tanzania. *AIDS and Behavior, 18*(Suppl 1), S69–74.

Kane, R. (2008). Editorial – Sex and relationship education: Bridging the gap between research and practice. *Health Education, 108,* 5–9.

Kangassalo, K., Pölkki, M. & Rantala, M.J. (2011). Prenatal influences on sexual orientation: Digit ratio (2D:4D) and number of older siblings. *Evolutionary Psychology, 9,* 496–508.

Kann, L., Olson, E.O., McManus, T., Kinchen, S., Chyen, D., Harris, W.A. & Wechsler, H. (2011). Sexual identity, sex of sexual contacts, and health-risk behaviors among students in grades 9–12 – Youth Risk Behavior Surveillance,

Selected Sites, United States, 2001–2009. *Surveillance summaries: MMWR, 60*(SS07). Adolescent and School Health, National Center for Chronic Disease Prevention and Health Promotion, CDC. Retrieved from: http://www.cdc.gov/mmwr/preview/mmwrhtml/ss6007a1.htm [Accessed 30 May 2014].

Karofsky, P.S., Zeng, L. & Kosorok, M.R. (2001). Relationship between adolescent-parental communication and initiation of first intercourse by adolescents. *Journal of Adolescent Health, 28,* 41–45.

Kassisieh, G. (2011). *'We're family too': The effects of homophobia in Arabic-speaking communities in New South Wales.* Sydney, New South Wales: ACON, Lesbian and Gay Anti-Violence Project.

Katchadourian, H. (1990). Sexuality. In S.S. Feldman & G.R. Elliot (Eds.), *At the threshold: The developing adolescent.* Cambridge, MA: Harvard University Press, pp. 330–351.

Kavanagh, M. (n.d.). The dangers of teens texting. *Parentdish.* Retrieved from: http://www.parentdish.co.uk/teen/the-dangers-of-teenage-sexting-advice-guidance-parents [Accessed 5 January 2014].

Kendall, C.N. (2004). *Gay male pornography: An issue of sex discrimination.* Vancouver, BC: University of British Columbia Press.

Kenny, P., Higgins, D., Soloff, C. & Sweid, R. (2012). *Past adoption experiences: National research study on the service response to past adoption practices* (Research Report No. 21). Melbourne: Australian Institute of Family Studies.

Kesterton, D. & Coleman, L. (2010). Speakeasy: A UK-wide initiative raising parents' confidence and ability to talk about sex and relationships with their children. *Sex Education, 10,* 437–448.

Khau, M. (2014). Sexuality education in rural Lesotho schools: Challenges and possibilities. *Sex Education, 12,* 411–423.

Kiernan, K.E. (1997). Becoming a young parent: A longitudinal study of associated factors. *British Journal of Sociology, 48,* 406–428.

Kim-Godwin, Y.S., Clements, C., McCuiston, A.M. & Fox, J.A. (2009). Dating violence among high school students in southeastern North Carolina. *Journal of School Nursing, 25*(2), 141–151.

Kinsey, A.C., Martin, C.E., Pomeroy, W.B. & Gregg, A. (1948). *Sexual behavior in the male.* Bloomington, IN: Indiana University Press.

Kirby, D. (2001). *Emerging answers: Research findings on programs to reduce teen pregnancy.* Washington, DC: National Campaign to Prevent Teen Pregnancy.

Kirby, D. (2007). *Emerging answers 2007: Research finding on programs to reduce teen pregnancy and sexually transmitted diseases.* Washington, DC: National Campaign to Prevent Teen and Unplanned Pregnancy.

Kirby, D. & Miller, B.C. (2002). Interventions designed to promote parent-teen communications about sexuality. In S.S. Feldman & D.A. Rosenthal (Eds.), *Talking sexuality: Parent–adolescent communication.* San Francisco: Jossey-Bass, pp. 93–110.

Kirby, D., Obasi, A. & Laris, B. (2006). *The effectiveness of sex education and HIV interventions in schools in developing countries, preventing HIV/AIDS in young people: A systemic review of the evidence from developing countries.* Geneva: World Health Organization.

Kirby, D., Rolleri, L. & Wilson, M.M. (2007). *Tool to assess the characteristics of effective sex and STD/HIV education programmes.* Washington, DC: Healthy Teen Network.

Kirby D.B. (2008). The impact of abstinence and comprehensive sex and STD/HIV education programs on adolescent sexual behaviour. *Sexuality Research & Social Policy, 5,* 18–27.

Kirby, D.B. (2011). *Sex education: Access and impact on sexual behaviour of young people.* New York: UN Expert Group Meetings on Adolescents, Department of Economic and Social Affairs.

Kirkman, M., Rosenthal, D.A. & Feldman, S.S. (2002). Talking to a tiger: Fathers reveal their difficulties in communicating about sexuality with adolescents. In D.A. Rosenthal & S.S. Feldman (Eds.), *Talking sexuality: Parent–adolescent communication.* San Francisco, CA: Jossey-Bass, pp. 57–74.

Kirkman, M., Rosenthal, D.A. & Feldman, S.S. (2005). Being open with your mouth shut: The meaning of 'openness' in family communication about sexuality. *Sex Education, 5,* 49–66.

Kirkman, M., Rosenthal, D., Mallett, S., Rowe, H. & Hardiman, A. (2010). Reasons women give for contemplating or undergoing abortion: A qualitative investigation in Victoria, Australia. *Sexual & Reproductive Healthcare, 1,* 149–155.

Kirkman, M., Rowe, H., Hardiman, A., Mallett, S. & Rosenthal, D. (2009). Reasons women give for abortion: A review of the literature. *Archives of Women's Mental Health, 12*(6), 365–378.

Kirkman, M., Rowe, H., Hardiman, A. & Rosenthal, D. (2011). Abortion is a difficult solution to a problem: A discursive analysis of interviews with women considering or undergoing abortion in Australia. *Women's Studies International Forum, 34,* 121–129.

Klein, F., Sepekoff, B. & Wolf, T.J. (1985). Sexual orientation: A multi-variable dynamic process. *Journal of Homosexuality, 11,* 35–49.

Klein, J.D. (2005). Adolescent pregnancy: Current trends and issues. *Pediatrics, 116*(1), 281–286.

Knauper, B., Kornik, R., Atkinson, K., Guberman, C. & Aydin, C. (2005). Motivation influences the underestimation of cumulative risk. *Personality and Social Psychology Bulletin, 31,* 1511–1522.

Koh, M. (2014a, 18 March). Sexting is safe. *The New Paper on Sunday.* Retrieved from: http://news.asiaone.com/news/singapore/sexting-safe [Accessed 17 November 2014].

Koh, H. (2014b). The Teen Pregnancy Prevention Program: An evidence-based public health program model. *Journal of Adolescent Health, 54,* S1–S2.

Kolbeins, G. (2006). Pornography and sex among adolescents in Iceland, i Unge, køn og pornografi i Norden – kvantitative studier. Copenhagen: Nordisk Ministerråd, pp. 108–150.

Kontula, O. (2010). The evolution of sex education and students' sexual knowledge in Finland in the 2000s. *Sex Education: Sex, Society and Learning, 10,* 373–386.

Kosciw, J.G., Greytak, E.A., Bartkiewicz, M.J., Boesen, M.J. & Palmer, N.A. (2012). *The 2011 National School Climate Survey: The experiences of lesbian, gay, bisexual and transgender youth in our nation's schools.* New York: GLSEN.

Kranz, F. & Ishai, A. (2006). Face perception is modulated by sexual preference. *Current Biology, 16,* 63–68.

Krug, E.G., Dahlberg, L.L., Mercy, J.A., Zwi, A. & Lozano, R. (2002). *World report on violence and health.* Geneva, World Health Organization.

Krupnick, J.L., Green, B.L., Stockton, P., Goodman, L., Corcoran, C. & Petty, R. (2004). Mental health effects of adolescent trauma exposure in a female college sample: Exploring differential outcomes based on experiences of unique trauma types and dimensions. *Psychiatry, 67,* 264–279.

Kumar, V. (2013). The rise of the romantic ideal. *The Socjournal: A New Media Journal of Sociology and Society, April 12.* Retrieved from: http://www.sociology.org/classroom-controversy/the-rise-of-the-romantic-ideal [Accessed 23 April 2015].

Kunkel, D., Eyal, K., Finnerty, K., Biely, E. & Donnerstein, E. (2005). *Sex on TV 4: A biennial report to the Kaiser Family Foundation.* Menlo Park, CA: Kaiser Family Foundation.

Kunze, E.I. (2010). Sex trafficking via the internet: How international agreements address the problem and fail to go far enough. *Journal of High Technology Law, 10,* 241–289.

L'Engle, K.L., Brown, J.D. & Kenneavy, K. (2006). The mass media are an important context for adolescents' sexual behavior. *Journal of Adolescent Health, 38,* 186–192.

Lam, T.H., Stewart, S.M., Leung, G., Ho, S.Y., Fan, A.H. & Ma, A.L.T. (2002). Sex differences in body satisfaction, feeling fat and pressure to diet among Chinese adolescents in Hong Kong. *European Eating Disorders Review, 10*(5), 347–358.

Lammers, C., Ireland, M., Resnick, M. & Blum, R. (2000). Influences on adolescents' decision to postpone onset of sexual intercourse: A survival analysis of virginity among youths aged 13 to 18 years. *Journal of Adolescent Health, 26*(1), 42–48.

Landor, A., Simons, L.G., Simons, R.L., Brody, G.H. & Gibbons, F.X. (2011). The role of religiosity in the relationship between parents, peers, and adolescent risky sexual behavior. *Journal of Youth and Adolescence, 40,* 296–309.

Latreille, S., Collyer, A. & Temple-Smith, M. (2014). Finding a segue into sex: Do young men want sexual health information from their GP? *Australian Family Physician, 43*(4), 217–221.

Laumann, E., Gagnon, J., Michael, R. & Michaels, S. (1994). *The social organization of sexuality: Sexual practices in the United States.* Chicago: University of Chicago Press.

Layne, L. (2002). *Motherhood lost: The cultural construction of miscarriage and stillbirth in America.* New York: Routledge.

Leadbeater, B. (2001). *Growing up fast: Transitions to early adulthood of inner-city adolescent mothers.* Mahwah, NJ: Lawrence Erlbaum Associates.

Lee, C. & Gramotnev, H. (2006). Predictors and correlates of coping well with early motherhood in the Australian Longitudinal Study on Women's Health. *Psychology, Health & Medicine, 11*(4), 411–424.

Lee, Y. & Styne, D. (2013). Influences on the onset and tempo of puberty in human beings and implications for adolescent psychological development. *Hormones and Behavior, 64,* 250–261.

Leitenberg, H. & Henning, K. (1995). Sexual fantasy. *Psychological Bulletin, 117*(3), 469–496.

Leitz, M.A. & Theriot, M.T. (2005). Adolescent stalking: A review. *Journal of Evidence-Based Social Work, 2*(3), 97–112.

Lenciauskiene, I. & Zaborskis, A. (2008). The effects of family structure, parent-child relationship and parental monitoring on early sexual behaviour among adolescents in nine European countries. *Scandinavian Journal of Public Health, 36,* 607–618.

Lenhart, A. (2009). Teens and sexting: How and why minor teens are sending sexually suggestive nude or nearly nude images via text messaging. *Pew Internet & American Life Project*. Retrieved from: http://www.pewinternet.org/Reports/2009/Teens-and-Sexting.aspx [Accessed 18 July 2013].

Lenhart, A., Ling, R., Campbell, S. & Purcell, K. (2010). Teens and mobile phones. *Pew Internet & American Life Project*. Retrieved from: http://www.pewinternet.org/2010/04/20/teens-and-mobile-phones [Accessed 13 November 2014].

Lescano, C.M., Vazquez, E.A., Brown, L.K., Litvin, E.B., Pugatch, D. & Project SHIELD Study Group. (2006). Condom use with 'casual' and 'main' partners: What's in a name? *Journal of Adolescent Health, 39*(3), 443e.1–443e.7.

Let Them Know. (n.d.). Retrieved from: http://www.letthemknow.org.au [Accessed 27 December 2014].

Leung, C., Moore, S., Karnilowicz, W. & Lung, C.L. (2011). Romantic relationships, relationship styles, coping strategies, and psychological distress among Chinese and Australian young adults. *Social Development, 20*(4), 783–804.

LeVay, S. (1991). A difference in hypothalamic structure between homosexual and heterosexual men. *Science, 253,* 1034–1037.

Lewis, L., Hickey, M., Doherty, D. & Skinner, S. (2009). How do pregnancy outcomes differ in teenage mothers? A Western Australian study. *Medical Journal of Australia, 190,* 537–541.

Lewis, M.A., Patrick, M.E., Mittmann, A. & Kaysen, D.L. (2014). Sex on the beach: The influence of social norms and trip companion on spring break sexual behavior. *Prevention Science, 15,* 408–418.

Li, Z.H., Connolly, D., Jiang, D., Pepler, W. & Craig, W. (2010). Adolescent romantic relationships in China and Canada: A cross-national comparison. *International Journal of Behavioral Development, 34*(2), 113–120.

Liao, L.M. & Creighton, S.M. (2007). Requests for cosmetic genitoplasty: How should healthcare providers respond? *British Medical Journal (Clinical Research Ed.), 334,* 1090–1092.

Liao, L.M., Michala, L. & Creighton, S.M. (2010). Labial surgery for well women: A review of the literature. *BJOG: An International Journal of Obstetrics and Gynaecology, 117*(1), 20–25.

Liddon, N., Michael, S.L., Dittus, P. & Markowitz, L.E. (2013). Maternal underestimation of child's sexual experience: Suggested implications for HPV vaccine uptake at recommended ages. *Journal of Adolescent Health, 53,* 674–676.

Lim, M., Bowring, A., Gold, J., Aitken, C. & Hellard, M. (2012). Trends in sexual behaviour, testing, and knowledge in young people, 2005–2011. *Sexually Transmitted Diseases, 39*(11), 831–834.

Lim, M., Hocking, J., Aitken, C., Fairley, C., Jordan, L. & Hellard, M. (2012). Impact of text and email messaging on the sexual health of young people: A randomized controlled trial. *Journal of Epidemiology and Community Health, 66*(1), 69–74.

Lim, M., Villa, A.M. & Hellard, M. (2014). *Correlation between pornography viewing and sexual behaviours.* Australian Sexual Health Conference, 9–11 October, Sydney, 2014.

Lindberg, L.D. & Maddow-Zimet, I. (2011). *Consequences of sex education on teen and young adult sexual behaviors and outcomes.* New York: The Guttmacher Institute.

Lindenberger, U. & von Oertzen, T. (2006). Variability in cognitive aging: From taxonomy to theory. In F.I.M. Craik & E. Bialystok (Eds.), *Lifespan cognition: Mechanisms of change* (pp. 297–314). Oxford: Oxford University Press.

Lindsay, J., Smith, A.M.A. & Rosenthal, D.A. (1997). *Secondary students, HIV/AIDS & sexual health 1997.* (Monograph series No. 3). Melbourne: Australian Research Centre in Sex, Health and Society, La Trobe University. Retrieved from: http://webstat.latrobe.edu.au/url/hdl.handle.net/1959.9/279427 [Accessed 31 December 2014].

Litras, A., Latreille S. & Temple-Smith, M. (under review). Dr Google, porn and a friend-of-a-friend: Where are young men really getting their sexual health information?

Little, M., Shah, R., Vermeulen, M.J., Gorman, A., Dzendoletas, D. & Ray, J.G. (2005). Adverse perinatal outcomes associated with homelessness and substance use in pregnancy. *Canadian Medical Association Journal, 173,* 615–618.

Littlejohn, P. (1996). *Young mothers: A longitudinal study of young pregnant women in Victoria.* Melbourne: Youth Research Centre, The University of Melbourne.

Lofgren-Mårtenson, L. & Månsson, S.A. (2010). Lust, love, and life: A qualitative study of Swedish adolescents' perceptions and experiences with pornography. *Journal of Sex Research, 47*(6), 568–579.

Longmore, M.A., Manning, W.D. & Giordano, P.C. (2001). Preadolescent parenting strategies and teens' dating and sexual initiation: A longitudinal analysis. *Journal of Marriage and the Family, 63,* 322–335.

Luder, M.T., Pittet, I., Berchtold, A., Akré, C., Michaud, P.-A. & Surís, J.C. (2011). Associations between online pornography and sexual behaviour among adolescents: myth or reality? *Archives of Sexual Behaviour, 40*(5), 1027–1035.

Lyons, H., Giordano, P.C., Manning, W.D. & Longmore, M.A. (2011). Identity, peer relationships, and adolescent girls' sexual behavior: An exploration of the contemporary double standard. *Journal of Sex Research, 48,* 437–439.

Lyra, J. (2003). *Fatherhood in adolescence: The construction of political agenda.* United Nations Division for the Advancement of Women (DAW) in collaboration with International Labour Organization (ILO) Joint United Nations Programmes on HIV/AIDS (UNAIDS), United Nations Development Programme (UNDP) Expert Group Meeting on 'The role of men and boys in achieving gender equality'. 21–24 October 2003, Brasilia, Brazil. Retrieved from: http://www.un.org/womenwatch/daw/egm/men-boys2003/EP14-Lyra.pdf [Accessed 21 November 2014].

Lyra, J. & Medrado, B. (2014). Pregnancy, marriage, and fatherhood adolescents: A critical review of the literature. In A.L. Cherry & M.E. Dillon (Eds.), *International handbook of adolescent pregnancy.* New York: Springer, pp. 103–128.

Ma, C.M.S. & Shek, D.T.L. (2013). Consumption of pornographic materials in early adolescents in Hong Kong. *Journal of Pediatric and Adolescent Gynecology, 26*(3 Suppl), S18–S25.

Macdowall, W., Gibson, L.J., Tanton, C., Mercer, C.H., Lewis, R., Clifton, S., et al. (2013). Lifetime prevalence, associated factors, and circumstances of non-volitional sex in women and men in Britain: Findings from the third National Survey of Sexual Attitudes and Lifestyles (Natsal-3). *Lancet, 382,* 1845–1855.

Magid, D., Douglas, J.M. & Schwartz, J.S. (1996). Doxycycline compared with azithromycin for treating women with genital chlamydia trachomatis infections:

An incremental cost-effectiveness analysis. *Annals of Internal Medicine, 124,* 389–399.

Mahavarkar, S.H., Madhu, C.K. & Mule, V.D. (2008). A comparative study of teenage pregnancy. *Journal of Obstetrics and Gynaecology, 28,* 604–607.

Makinen, M., Puukko-Viertomies, L.R., Lindberg, N., Siimes, M.A. & Aalberg, V. (2012). Body dissatisfaction and body mass in girls and boys transitioning from early to mid-adolescence: Additional role of self-esteem and eating habits. *BMC Psychiatry, Jun 8,* 12–35.

Mangino, J.G. (2008). *Voices of teenage mothers: Their challenges, support systems and successes.* Thesis undertaken for the Doctor of Education, University of Pittsburgh, Pennsylvania, USA.

Manlove, J. (1997). Early motherhood in an intergenerational perspective: The experiences of a British cohort. *Journal of Marriage and the Family, 59,* 263–279.

Manlove, J., Logan, C., Moore, K.A. & Ikramullah, E. (2008). Pathways from family religiosity to adolescent sexual activity and contraceptive use. *Perspectives on Sexual and Reproductive Health, 40,* 105–117.

Manlove, J., Ryan, S. & Franzetta, K. (2004). Contraceptive use and consistency in U.S. teenagers' most recent sexual relationships. *Perspectives on Sexual and Reproductive Health, 36*(6), 265–275.

Manrodt, A. (2014, 1 June). Teens on Tinder: Why high schoolers have invaded the social dating app. *Teen Vogue.* Retrieved from: http://www.teenvogue.com/my-life/2014-05/teens-on-tinder [Accessed 14 November 2014].

Marazziti, D. & Canale, D. (2004). Hormonal changes when falling in love. *Psychoneuroendocrinology, 29*(7), 931–936.

Marin, B.V., Coyle, K.K., Gomez, C.A., Carvajal, S.C. & Kirby, D.B. (2000). Older boyfriends and girlfriends increase sexual initiation in young adolescents. *Journal of Adolescent Health, 27,* 409–418.

Markham, C.M., Lormand, D., Gloppen, K.M., Peskin, M.F., Flores, B., Low, B. & House, L.D. (2010). Connectedness as a predictor of sexual and reproductive health outcomes for youth. *Journal of Adolescent Health, 46*(Suppl) S23–41.

Marks, M. & Fraley, R.C. (2005). The sexual double standard: Fact or fiction? *Sex Roles, 52*(3), 175–186.

Marks, M. & Fraley, R.C. (2006). Confirmation bias and the sexual double standard. *Sex Roles, 54*(1), 19–26.

Marks, M. & Fraley, R.C. (2007). The impact of social interaction on the sexual double standard. *Social Influence, 2*(1), 29–54.

Marshall, W.A. & Tanner, J.M. (1969). Variations in the pattern of pubertal changes in girls. *Archives of Diseases in Childhood, 44,* 291–303.

Marshall, W.A. & Tanner, J.M. (1970). Variations in the pattern of pubertal changes in boys. *Archives of Disease in Childhood, 45,* 13–23.

Marston, C. & Lewis, R. (2014). Anal heterosex among young people and implications for health promotion: A qualitative study in the UK. *BMJ Open, 4*(8).

Martel, L.D., Hawk, S. & Hatfield, E. (2004). Sexual behavior and culture. In C.D. Spielberger (Ed.), *Encyclopedia of applied psychology.* London: Elsevier Academic Press, pp. 385–392.

Martin, D. & Lyon, P. (1972). *Lesbian woman.* San Francisco, CA: Glide.

Martinez, G., Copen, C.E. & Abma, J.C. (2011). *Teenagers in the United States: Sexual activity, contraceptive use, and child-bearing, 2006–2010. National Survey of Family Growth.* (Vital and Health Statistics Series 23, No. 31). Washington, DC: Centers for Disease Control and Prevention, National Centre for Health Statistics.

Martinez, J., Caracedo, R., Furtes, A., Vicario-Molina, I., Fernandez-Fuertes, A. & Orgaz, B. (2014). Sex education in Spain: Teachers' views of obstacles. *Sex Education, 12,* 425–436.

Mason, S. (2010). Braving it out! An illuminative evaluation of the provision of sex and relationship education in two primary schools in England. *Sex Education, 10,* 157–169.

Mathematica Policy Research. (2012). *Identifying programs that impact teen pregnancy, sexually transmitted infections, and associated sexual risk behaviors, review protocol.* Retrieved from: http://www.hhs.gov/ash/oah/oah-initiatives/teen_pregnancy/db/eb-programs-review-v2.pdf [Accessed 23 May 2014].

Mattebo, M., Larsson, M., Tyden, T., Olssen, T. & Häggström-Nordin, E. (2012). Hercules and Barbie? Reflections on the influence of pornography and its spread in the media and society in groups of adolescents in Sweden. *European Journal of Contraception and Reproductive Health Care, 17,* 40–49.

Mayock, P., Bryan, A., Carr, N. & Kitching, K. (2008). *Supporting LGBT lives: A study of mental health and well-being. Gay and Lesbian Equality Network (GLEN) and BeLonGTo.* Retrieved from: http://www.nosp.ie/lgbt_lives_dec_2008.pdf [Accessed 31 December 2014].

Mazza, D., Harrison, C., Taft, A., Brijnath, B., Britt, H., Hobbs, M., *et al.* (2012). Current contraceptive management in Australian general practice: An analysis of BEACH data. *Medical Journal of Australia, 197,* 110–114.

McAdam, N. (1 October, 2013). Alarm over children being sexually exploited in Northern Ireland care homes was raised seven years ago. *Belfast Telegraph.* Retrieved from: http://www.belfasttelegraph.co.uk/news/local-national/northern-ireland/alarm-over-children-being-sexually-exploited-in-northern-ireland-care-homes-was-raised-seven-years-ago-29622491.html [Accessed 20 January 2015].

McBride, K.R. & Fortenberry, J.D. (2010). Heterosexual anal sexuality and anal sex behaviors: A review. *Journal of Sex Research, 47*(2), 123–136.

McCabe, M.P. (2005). Boys want sex, girls want commitment: Does this trade-off still exist? *Sexual and Relationship Therapy, 20*(2), 139–141.

McCabe, M.P. & Ricciardelli, L.A. (2004). A longitudinal study of pubertal timing and extreme body change behaviors among adolescent boys and girls. *Adolescence, 39,* 145–166.

McCarthy, O., Carswell, K., Murray, E., Free, C., Stevenson, F. & Bailey, J.V. (2012). What young people want from a sexual health website: Design and development of sexunzipped. *Journal of Medical Internet Research, 14*(5), e127.

McCauley, H.L., Silverman, J., Broyles, L.M., Decker, M.R., Tancredi, D.J., Zelazny, S. & Miller, E. (2014). Substance use, intimate partner violence and sexual assault among adolescent and young adult female family planning clients. *Journal of Adolescent Health, 54,* S7.

McClain, N.M. & Garrity, S.E. (2011). Sex trafficking and the exploitation of adolescents. *Journal of Obstetric, Gynaecology and Neonatal Nursing, 40*(2), 243–252.

McGivern, R.F., Andersen, J., Byrd, D., Mutter, K.L. & Reilly, J. (2002). Cognitive efficiency on a match to sample task decreases at the onset of puberty in children. *Brain and Cognition, 50*(1), 73–89.

McKay, A. & Bissell, M. (2010). *Sexual health education in the schools: Questions and answers* (3rd edn). Toronto: Sex Information and Education Council of Canada.

McKee, A. (2007). Saying you've been at dad's porn book is part of growing up: Youth, pornography and education. *Metro Magazine, 155,* 118–122.

McKee, M. (2011, 2 October). Teen mags, not parents, teaching sex education. Retrieved from: http://www.smh.com.au/national/health/teen-mags-not-parents-teaching-sex-education-20111001-1l2lq.html [Accessed 17 November 2014].

McNair, R., Prestage, G., Russell, D. & Richters, J. (2014). Lesbian, gay, bisexual and transgender people. In M. Temple-Smith (Ed.), *Sexual health: A multidisciplinary approach.* Melbourne: IP Communications.

McNeely, C., Shew, M., Beuhring, T., Sieving, R., Miller, B.C. & Blum, R.W. (2002). Mothers' influence on the timing of first sex among 14- and 15-year-olds. *Journal of Adolescent Health, 31,* 256–265.

Médecins Sans Frontières. (2013). Generic competition pushing down HIV drug prices, but patents keep newer drugs unaffordable. Retrieved from: http://www.msfaccess.org/about-us/media-room/press-releases/generic-competition-pushing-down-hiv-drug-prices-patents-keep [Accessed 4 July 2014].

MedXSafe (n.d.). Retrieved from: http://medxpatient.com/products/medxsafe [Accessed 27 December 2014].

Meertens, R., Brankovic, I., Ruiter, R.A.C., Lohstroh, E. & Schaalma, H.P. (2013). Dirty love: The effect of cleanliness of the environment on perceived susceptibility for sexually transmitted infections. *Journal of Applied Social Psychology, 43,* E56–E63.

Meier, E.P. & Gray, J. (2014). Facebook photo activity associated with body image disturbance in adolescent girls. *Cyberpsychology, Behavior, and Social Networking, 17*(4), 199–206.

Mendle, J. & Ferrero, J. (2012). Detrimental psychological outcomes associated with pubertal timing in adolescent boys. *Developmental Review, 32*(1), 49–66.

Mercer, C.H., Tanton, C., Prah, P., Erens, B., Sonnenberg, P., Clifton, S., *et al.* (2013). Changes in sexual attitudes and lifestyles in Britain through the life course and over time: Findings from the National Surveys of Sexual Attitudes and Lifestyles (NATSAL). *Lancet, 382,* 1781–1794.

Merghati-Khoei, E., Abolghasemi, N. & Smith, T. (2014). 'Children are sexually innocent': Iranian parents' understanding of children's sexuality. *Archives of Sexual Behavior, 43,* 587–595.

Merki-Feld, G.S. & Gruber, I.M.L. (2014). Broad counseling for adolescents about combined hormonal contraceptive methods: The CHOICE study. *Journal of Adolescent Health, 54,* 404–409.

Meschke, L.L. & Dettmer, K. (2012). 'Don't cross a man's feet': Hmong parent–daughter communication about sexual health. *Sex Education, 12,* 109–123.

Meyer, I.H. (2003). Prejudice, social stress, and mental health in lesbian, gay, and bisexual populations: Conceptual issues and research evidence. *Psychological Bulletin, 129*(5), 674–697.

Mikulincer, M. & Shaver, P.R. (2010). *Attachment in adulthood structure, dynamics, and change*. New York: Guilford Publications.

Miller, S.L. & Maner, J.K. (2010). Scent of a woman: Men's testosterone responses to olfactory ovulation cues. *Psychological Science, 21*(2), 276–283.

Milligan, K. (2002). Quebec's Baby Bonus: Can public policy raise fertility? *Backgrounder*. Toronto, Ontario: CD Howe Institute. Retrieved from: http://www.cdhowe.org/quebecs-baby-bonus-can-public-policy-raise-fertility/9771 [Accessed 13 June 2014].

Milne-Holme, Power, A. & Dennis, B. (1996). *Pregnant futures: Barriers to employment, education and training amongst pregnant and parenting adolescents*. Women's Employment, Education and Training Advisory Group Project. Canberra: Australian Government Publishing Service.

Minichiello, V., Rahman, S., Dune, T., Scott, J. & Dowsett, G. (2013). E-health: Potential benefits and challenges in providing and accessing health services. *BioMed Central Public Health, 13*, 790–797.

Ministry of Social Development. (2010). *The social report 2010*. Retrieved from: http://www.socialreport.msd.govt.nz/people/fertility.html [Accessed 23 May 2014].

Miranda-Diaz, M. & Corcoran, K. (2012). 'All my friends are doing it': The impact of the perception of peer sexuality on adolescents' intent to have sex. *Journal of Evidence-Based Social Work, 9*, 260–264.

Mitchell, A., Patrick, K., Heywood, W., Blackman, P. & Pitts, M. (2014). *Fifth National Survey of Australian Secondary Students and Sexual Health 2013* (ARCSHS Monograph Series No. 97). Melbourne: Australian Research Centre in Sex, Health and Society, La Trobe University.

Mitchell, J., Finkelhor, D. & Wolak, J. (2010). Juvenile prostitution as child maltreatment: Findings from the National Juvenile Prostitution Study. *Child Maltreatment, 15*(1), 18–36.

Mitchell, K. & Wellings, K. (2002). The role of ambiguity in sexual encounters between young people in Britain. *Culture, Health & Sexuality, 4*, 393–408.

Moffitt, T.E. & The E-Risk Study Team (2002). Teen-aged mothers in contemporary Britain. *Journal of Child Psychology and Psychiatry, 42*, 727–742.

Mohammadi, M.R., Mohammad, K., Farahani, F.K., Alikhani, S., Zare, M., Tehrani, F.R., *et al*. (2006). Reproductive knowledge, attitudes and behaviour among adolescent males in Tehran, Iran. *International Family Planning Perspectives, 32*(1), 35–44.

Mohktar, M.M. (2015). *Sexual health and education: Knowledge and behaviour among Malaysian university students*. Unpublished PhD thesis. Melbourne: The University of Melbourne.

Mollborn, S. & Lovegrove, P.J. (2011). How teenage fathers matter for children: Evidence from the ECLS-B. *Journal of Family Issues, 32*(1), 3–30.

Mond, J., van den Berg, P., Boutelle, K., Hannan, P. & Neumark-Sztainer, D. (2011). Obesity, body dissatisfaction, and emotional well-being in early and late adolescence: Findings from the Project EAT study. *Journal of Adolescent Health, 48*(4), 373–378.

Monder, B.R. (2007). After 'our bodies, ourselves'. *Psychoanalytic Psychology, 24*(2), 384–394.

Money, J. & Ehrhardt, A.A. (1972). *Man and woman: Boy and girl.* Baltimore, MD: Johns Hopkins University Press.

Montgomery, M.J. (2005). Psychosocial intimacy and identity: From early adolescence to emerging adulthood. *Journal of Adolescent Research, 20*(3), 346–374.

Moore, S.M. (1995). Girls' understanding and social constructions of menarche. *Journal of Adolescence, 18,* 87–104.

Moore, S.M., Leung, C., Karnilowicz, W. & Lung, C.L. (2012). Characteristics and predictors of romantic relationships in late adolescence and young adulthood in Hong Kong and Australia. *Australian Psychologist, 47*(2), 108–117.

Moore, S.M. & Rosenthal, D.A. (1991). Adolescents' perceptions of friends' and parents' attitudes to sex and sexual risk-taking. *Journal of Community and Applied Social Psychology, 1,* 189–200.

Moore, S.M. & Rosenthal, D.A. (2006). *Sexuality in adolescence: Current trends.* London: Routledge.

Morre, S.A., Valkengoed, I., Jong, A., Boeke, A., Eijk, J., Meijer, C.J. & Vane Den Brule, A.J.C. (1999). Mailed home-obtained urine specimens: A reliable screening approach for detecting asymptomatic chlamydia trachomatis infections. *Journal of Clinical Microbiology, 37,* 976–980.

Morris, D.H., Jones, M.E., Schoemaker, M.J., Ashworth, A. & Swerdlow, A.J. (2011). Familial concordance for age at menarche: Analyses from the Breakthrough Generations study. *Paediatric and Perinatal Epidemiology, 25,* 306–311.

Mozes, A. (2011). Study tracks masturbation trends among U.S. teens. *HealthDay.* Retrieved from: http://consumer.healthday.com/women-s-health-information-34/abortion-news-2/study-tracks-masturbation-trends-among-u-s-teens-655445.html [Accessed 2 September 2014].

Mulford, C. & Giordano, P.C. (2008). Teen dating violence: A closer look at adolescent romantic relationships. *National Institute of Justice Journal (NIJ Journal), 261.* Retrieved from: http://www.nij.gov/journals/261/pages/teen-dating-violence.aspx [Accessed 31 December 2014].

Murnen, S.K. & Kohlman, M.H. (2007). Athletic participation, fraternity membership, and sexual aggression among college men: A meta-analytic review. *Sex Roles, 57,* 145–157.

Murphy, D.A., Blezer, M., Duarko, S.J., Sarr, M., Wilson, C.M., Muenz, L.R. & Adolescent Medicine HIV/AIDS Research Network. (2005). Longitudinal antiretroviral adherence among adolescents infected with human immunodeficiency virus. *Archives of Pediatric & Adolescent Medicine, 159,* 764–770.

Mussen, P.H. & Jones, M.C. (1957). Self-concepts, motivations, and interpersonal attitudes of late and early maturing boys. *Child Development, 28,* 243–256.

Mustanski, B., Lyons, T. & Garcia, S.C. (2011). Internet use and sexual health of young men who have sex with men: A mixed-methods study. *Archives of Sexual Behavior, 40,* 289–300.

Naar-King, S., Silvern, L., Ryan, V. & Sebring, D. (2002). Type and severity of abuse as predictors of psychiatric symptoms in adolescence. *Journal of Family Violence, 17,* 133–150.

Nagy, Z., Westerberg, H. & Klingberg, T. (2004). Maturation of white matter is associated with the development of cognitive functions during childhood. *Journal of Cognitive Neuroscience, 16*(7), 1227–1233.

Naik, A. (2008). *Everyday conversations, every day.* London: Parents Centre/Department for Children, Schools and Families, p. 66.

Nandaweera, N. (2013). *Young women's understanding of the factors affecting their fertility.* Bachelor of Science (Hons) thesis. Melbourne: University of Melbourne.

National AIDS Trust. (n.d.). *People living with HIV in the UK.* Retrieved from: http://www.hivaware.org.uk/facts-myths/hiv-statistics [Accessed 25 April 2015].

National Campaign to Prevent Teen and Unplanned Pregnancy. (2013). Retrieved from: http://thenationalcampaign.org/sites/default/files/resource-primary-download/childbearing-childwelfare.pdf [Accessed 22 November 2014].

National Collaborating Centre for Mental Health. (2011). *Induced abortion and mental health: A systematic review of outcomes of induced abortion, including their prevalence and associated factors.* London: Academy of Medical Royal Colleges.

National Collaborating Centre for Women's and Children's Health. (2005). Press release: *New guidelines on long acting contraception promote greater choice for women.* London: RCOG Press.

National Crime Prevention. (2001). Young people and domestic violence: National research on young people's attitudes and experiences of domestic violence. Canberra: Crime Prevention Branch, CW Attorney-General's Dept.

National Institute of Mental Health. (2011). *The teen brain: Still under construction.* Retrieved from: http://www.nimh.nih.gov/health/publications/the-teen-brain-still-under-construction/index.shtml [Accessed 15 January 2014].

Nayak, M., Byrne, C., Martin, M.S. & Abraham, A.G. (2003). Attitudes towards violence against women: A cross-nation study. *Sex Roles, 49*(7–8), 333–342.

Negriff, S. & Susman, E.J. (2011). Pubertal timing, depression, and externalizing problems: A framework, review, and examination of gender differences. *Journal of Research on Adolescence, 21*(3), 717–746.

Nelson, L.J., Padilla-Walker, L.M. & Carroll, J. (2010). 'I believe it is wrong but I still do it': A comparison of religious young men who do versus do not use pornography. *Psychology of Religion and Spirituality, 2,* 136–147.

Neumark-Sztainer, D., Bauer, K.W., Friend, S., Hannan, P.J., Story, M. & Berge, J.M. (2010). Family weight talk and dieting: How much do they matter for body dissatisfaction and disordered eating behaviors in adolescent girls? *Journal of Adolescent Health, 47*(3), 270–276.

Neumark-Sztainer, D., Paxton, S.J., Hannan, P.J., Haines, J. & Story, M. (2006). Does body satisfaction matter? Five-year longitudinal associations between body satisfaction and health behaviors in adolescent females and males. *Journal of Adolescent Health, 39*(2), 244–251.

Neumark-Sztainer, D., Wall, M., Guo, J., Story, M., Haines, J. & Eisenberg, M. (2006). Obesity, disordered eating, and eating disorders in a longitudinal study of adolescents: How do dieters fare 5 years later? *Journal of the American Dietetic Association, 106*(4), 559–568.

New South Wales Government. (2013). Help for victims of sexual assault. Retrieved from: http://www.victimsservices.justice.nsw.gov.au/sexualassault [Accessed 23 April 2015].

Newman, L. (2002). Sex, gender and culture: Issues in the definition, assessment and treatment of gender identity disorder. *Clinical Child Psychology and Psychiatry, 7*(3), 352–359.

Newton, D., Keogh, M., Temple-Smith, M., Fairley, C., Chen, M., Bayly, C., *et al.* (2012). Australian key informant perceptions of youth-focused sexual health promotion programs. *Sexual Health, 10,* 47–56.

Ng, A.S. & Kaye, K. (2012). *Why it matters: Teen childbearing, single parenthood, and father involvement.* Washington, DC: The National Campaign to Prevent Teen and Unplanned Pregnancy.

NHS Bristol. (2009). Parent attitudes to teenage sexual health, pregnancy and sex, and relationships education: Telephone interviews. MSS Research (Project number MR4689). Retrieved from: https://www.4ypbristol.co.uk/for-parents [Accessed 29 January 2015].

Nisbet, I.A., Wilson, P.H. & Smallbone, S.W. (2004). A prospective longitudinal study of sexual recidivism among adolescent sex offenders. *Sexual Abuse: Journal of Research & Treatment, 16,* 223–234.

Nkosana, J. & Rosenthal, D.A. (2007a). The dynamics of intergenerational sexual relationships: The experience of schoolgirls in Botswana. *Sex Health, 4*(3), 181–187.

Nkosana, J. & Rosenthal, D.A. (2007b). Saying no to intergenerational sex: The experience of schoolgirls in Botswana. *Vulnerable Children and Youth Studies, 2*(1), 1–11.

Noll, J.G. (2005). Does childhood sexual abuse set in motion a cycle of violence against women? What we know and what we need to learn. *Journal of Interpersonal Violence, 20,* 455–462.

Noll, J.G. & Shenk, C.E. (2013). Teen birth rates in sexually abused and neglected females. *Pediatrics, 131*(4), e1181–e1187.

Nonnemaker, J.M., McNeely, C.A. & Blum, R.W. (2003). Public and private domains of religiosity and adolescent health risk behaviors: Evidence from the National Longitudinal Study of Adolescent Health. *Social Science and Medicine, 57,* 2049–2054.

Noonan, L. (2012). Towards a comprehensive curriculum for pregnancy prevention: Combining child support education and sexual education programs. *Journal of Public and International Affairs, 23,* 28–51.

Novembre, J., Galvani, A.P. & Slatkin, M. (2005). The geographic spread of the CCR5 Δ32 HIV-resistance allele. *PLoS Biology, 3,* e339.

Oakeshott, P., Kerry, S., Aghaizu, A., Atherton, H., Taylor-Robinson, D., Simms, I. & Hay, P. (2010). Randomised controlled trial of screening for chlamydia trachomatis to prevent pelvic inflammatory disease: The POPI (prevention of pelvic infection) trial. *British Medical Journal (Clinical Research Edition), 340,* 1642.

Ochiogu, I.N., Miettola, J., Iluka, A.L. & Vaskilampi, T. (2011). Impact of timing of sex education on teenage pregnancy in Nigeria: Cross-sectional survey of secondary school students. *Journal of Community Health, 36,* 375–380.

O'Donnell, L., Myint-U, A., O'Donnell, C.R. & Stueve, A. (2003). Long-term influence of sexual norms and attitudes on timing of sexual initiation among urban minority youth. *Journal of School Health, 73,* 68–75.

O'Donnell, L., O'Donnell, C.R. & Stueve, A. (2001). Early sexual initiation and subsequent sex-related risks among urban minority youth: The reach for health study. *Family Planning Perspectives, 33,* 268–275.

Office for National Statistics. (2013a). Teenage pregnancies at lowest level since records began: Part of conception statistics, England and Wales, 2011 release. Retrieved from: http://www.ons.gov.uk/ons/rel/vsob1/conception-statistics--england-and-wales/2011/sty-conception-estimates-2011.html [Accessed 13 June 2014].

Office for National Statistics. (2013b). Statistical bulletin: Adoptions in England and Wales 2012. Retrieved from: http://www.ons.gov.uk/ons/rel/vsob1/adoptions-in-england-and-wales/2012/stb-adoptions-in-england-and-wales--2012-.html#tab-Key-findings [Accessed 3 April, 2014].

O'Hara, R.E., Gibbons, F.X., Gerrard, M., Li, Z. & Sargent, J.D. (2012). Greater exposure to sexual content in popular movies predicts earlier sexual debut and increased sexual risk taking. *Psychological Science, 23*(9), 984–993.

O'Keefe, G.S. & Clarke-Pearson, K. (2011). Clinical report: The impact of social media on children, adolescents, and families. *Paediatrics, 127,* 800–804.

Ollis, D. (2014). The role of teachers in delivering education about respectful Relationships: Exploring teacher and student perspectives. *Health Education Research, 29,* 702–713.

Ollis, D. & Harrison, L. (in press). Lessons in building capacity in sexuality education using the Health Promoting School Framework: From planning to implementation. *Health Education (special issue).*

Ollis, D., Harrison, L. & Maharaj, C. (2013). *Sexuality education matters: Preparing preservice teachers to teach sexuality education.* Burwood, Victoria, Australia: Deakin University.

Ollis, D., Harrison, L. & Richardson, A. (2012). *Building capacity in sexuality education: The Northern Bay College experience. Report of the first phase of the Sexuality Education and Community Support (SECS) project.* Geelong, Australia: School of Education, Deakin University.

Ong, J., Temple-Smith, M., Wong, W., McNamee, K. & Fairley, K. (2012). Contraception matters: Indicators of poor usage of contraception in sexually active women attending family planning clinics in Victoria, Australia. *BioMed Central Public Health, 12*(1), 1108.

OnlineDatingSafetyTips.com (n.d.). *Safe and successful online dating.* Retrieved from: http://www.onlinedatingsafetytips.com [Accessed 27 December 2014].

Onyeonoro, U.U., Oshi, D.C., Ndimele, E.C., Chuku, N.C., Onyemuchara, I.L., Ezekwere, S.C. & Emelumadu, O.F. (2011). Sources of sex information and its effects on sexual practices among in-school female adolescents in Osisioma Ngwa LGA, South-East Nigeria. *Journal of Pediatric and Adolescent Gynecology, 24,* 294–299.

Orban, L.A., Stein, R., Koenig, L.J., Conner, L.C., Rexhouse, E.L., Lewis, J.V. & LaGrange, R. (2010). Coping strategies of adolescents living with HIV: Disease-specific stressors and responses. *AIDS Care, 22,* 420–430.

Osorio, A., López-del Burgo, C., Carlos, S., Ruiz-Canela, M., Delgado, M. & de Irala, J. (2012). First sexual intercourse and subsequent regret in three developing countries. *Journal of Adolescent Health, 50*(3), 271–278.

O'Sullivan, L. (2005). Sexual coercion in dating relationships: Conceptual and methodological issues. *Sexual and Relationship Therapy, 20,* 3–11.

O'Sullivan, L.F., Udell, W., Montrose, V.A., Antoniello, P. & Hoffman, S. (2010). A cognitive analysis of college students' explanations for engaging in unprotected sexual intercourse. *Archives of Sexual Behavior, 39,* 1121–1131.

Out & Online (n.d.). Retrieved from: https://www.outandonline.org.au [Accessed 24 January 2015].

Owusu-Edusei, K., Chesson, H.W., Gift, T.L., Tao, G., Mahajan, R., Ocfemia, M.C. & Kent, C.K. (2013). The estimated direct medical cost of selected sexually transmitted infections in the United States, 2008. *Sexually Transmissible Diseases, 40,* 197–201.

Pallotta-Chiarolli, M. & Lubowitz, S. (2003). Where are we? How do we? *Journal of Bisexuality, 3*(1), 55–85.

Papadopoulos, L. (2010). *Sexualisation of young people: Review.* Retrieved from: http://dera.ioe.ac.uk/10738/1/sexualisation-young-people.pdf [Accessed 16 December 2014].

Parker, R., Wellings, K. & Lazarus, J.V. (2009). Sexuality education in Europe: An overview of current policies. *Sex Education, 9*(3), 227–242.

Parliament of Victoria, Law Reform Committee. (2013). *Inquiry into sexting.* May 2013.

Parr, C. (2013, September 12). Africa's mobile phone e-learning transformation. *Times Higher Education.* Retrieved from: http://www.timeshighereducation. co.uk/features/africas-mobile-phone-e-learning-transformation/2007120.article [Accessed 4 October 2014].

Parry, T. (2014, 26 March). Beaten, raped and locked in cage by paedophiles at the age of 9: India's modern day slaves. *The Mirror.* Retrieved from: http://www. mirror.co.uk/news/real-life-stories/beaten-raped-locked-cage-paedophiles-3288946 [Accessed 20 January 2015].

Pascoe, C.J. (2007). *Dude, you're a fag: Masculinity and sexuality in high school.* Berkeley, CA: University of California Press.

Pascuzzo, K., Cyr, C. & Moss, E. (2013). Longitudinal association between adolescent attachment, adult romantic attachment, and emotion regulation strategies. *Attachment & Human Development, 15*(1), 83–103.

Patel, A.L., Sachdev, D., Nagpal, P., Chaudhry, U., Sonkar, S.C., Mendiratta, S.L. & Saluja, D. (2010). Prevalence of chlamydia infection among women visiting a gynaecology outpatient department: Evaluation of an in-house PCR assay for detection of chlamydia trachomatis. *Annals of Clinical Microbiology & Antimicrobials, 9,* 24.

Patrick, M., Morgan, N., Maggs, J. & Lefkowitz, E. (2011). 'I got your back': Friends' understandings regarding college student Spring break behavior. *Journal of Youth and Adolescence, 40,* 108–120.

Paul, T., Schiffer, B., Zwarg, T., Kruger, T.H.C., Karama, S., Schedlowski, M. & Forsting, M. (2008). Brain response to visual sexual stimuli in heterosexual and homosexual males. *Human Brain Mapping, 29*(6), 726–735.

Pavlin, N., Parker, R., Fairley, C.K., Gunn, J.M. & Hocking, J. (2008). Take the sex out of STI screening! Views of young women on implementing chlamydia screening in General Practice. *BMC Infectious Diseases, 8,* 62.

Paxton, S.J., Neumark-Sztainer, D., Hannan, P.J. & Eisenberg, M.E. (2006). Body dissatisfaction prospectively predicts depressive mood and low self-esteem in adolescent girls and boys. *Journal of Clinical Child and Adolescent, 35*(4), 539–549.

Payne, K. (Ed.). (1983). *Between ourselves: Letters between mothers and daughters 1750–1982.* Boston, MA: Houghton Mifflin.

Pearce, J., Hynes, P. & Bovarnick, S. (2013). *Trafficked young people: Breaking the wall of silence.* New York: Routledge/Taylor & Francis Group.

Peipert, J.F. (2003). Genital chlamydial infections. *New England Journal of Medicine, 349,* 2424–2430.

Penfold, J. (2012). Tackling unplanned teenage pregnancy and sexual health. *Primary Health Care, 22*(4), 6–7.

Peper, J.S. & Dahl, R.E. (2013). The teenage brain: Surging hormones – brain-behavior interactions during puberty. *Current Directions in Psychological Science, 22*(2), 134–139.

Peppard, J. (2008). Culture wars in South Australia: The sex education debates. *Australian Journal of Social Issues, 43,* 499–516.

Perkins, M. (2014, 16 September). One in five say drunk women partly to blame for rape, survey finds. *Sydney Morning Herald.* Retrieved from: http://www.smh.com.au/national/one-in-five-say-drunk-women-partly-to-blame-for-rape-survey-finds-20140916-10hu5q.html [Accessed 23 April 2015].

Perrin, J.S., Hervé, P.-Y., Leonard, G., Perron, M., Pike, G.B., Pitiot, A., *et al.* (2008). Growth of white matter in the adolescent brain: Role of testosterone and androgen receptor. *Journal of Neuroscience, 28*(38), 9519–9524.

Perrin, J.S., Leonard, G., Perron, M., Pike, G.B., Pitiot, A., Richer, L., *et al.* (2009). Sex differences in the growth of white matter during adolescence. *NeuroImage, 45*(4), 1055–1066.

Persson, A. & Newman, C. (2012). When HIV-positive children grow up: A critical analysis of the transition literature in developed countries. *Qualitative Health Research, 22,* 656–667.

Peskin, H. (1967). Pubertal onset and ego functioning. *Journal of Abnormal Psychology, 72*(1), 1–15.

Petanjek, Z., Judaš, M., Šimić, G., Rašin, M.R., Uylings, H.B.M., *et al.* (2011). Extraordinary neoteny of synaptic spines in the human prefrontal cortex. *Proceedings of the National Academy of Sciences of the USA, 108*(32), 13281–13286.

Peter, J. & Valkenburg, P.M. (2006). Adolescents? Exposure to sexually explicit online material and recreational attitudes towards sex. *Journal of Communication, 56*(4), 639–660.

Petersen, J.L. & Hyde, J.S. (2011). Gender differences in sexual attitudes and behaviors: A review of meta-analytic results and large datasets. *Journal of Sex Research, 48,* 149–165.

Pettifor, A.E., Rees, H.V., Kleinschmidt, I., Steffenson, A.E., MacPhail, C., Hlongwa-Madikizela, L., *et al.* (2005). Young people's sexual health in South Africa: HIV prevalence and sexual behaviors from a nationally representative household survey. *AIDS (London, England), 19*(14), 1525–1534.

Pettijohn, T.F. & Jungeberg, B.J. (2004). Playboy Playmate curves: Changes in facial and body feature preferences across social and economic conditions. *Personality and Social Psychology Bulletin, 30,* 1186–1197.

Pew Consulting (2013). *Teens and technology 2013.* Retrieved from: http://www.pewinternet.org/2013/03/13/teens-and-technology-2013 [Accessed 25 September 2014].

Pew Research (2013, 4 June; updated 2014, 27 May). The global divide on homosexuality. Retrieved from: http://www.pewglobal.org/2013/06/04/the-global-divide-on-homosexuality [Accessed 29 December 2014].

Pew Research Internet Project. (2010). Teens and mobile phones. Retrieved from: http://www.pewinternet.org/2010/04/20/teens-and-mobile-phones [Accessed 25 September 2014].

Phoenix, A. (1991). *Young mothers?* Cambridge: Polity Press.

Pickhardt, C. (2012, 10 September) Adolescence and the teenage crush. Retrieved from: https://www.psychologytoday.com/blog/surviving-your-childs-adolescence/201209/adolescence-and-the-teenage-crush [Accessed 28 April 2015].

Pickhardt, C. (2013, 11 May). Crushes are delicate [Web log comment]. Retrieved from: http://www.psychologytoday.com/blog/surviving-your-childs-adolescence/201209/adolescence-and-the-teenage-crush [Accessed 23 April 2015].

Pilgrim, N.A., Ahmed, S., Gray, R.H., Sekasanvu, J., Lutalo, T., Nalugoda, F. & Wawer, M.J. (2014). Family structure effects on early sexual debut among adolescent girls in Rakai, Uganda. *Vulnerable Children and Youth Studies, 9,* 193–205.

Pilon, S. (2011). Sexual fantasies during adolescence. *The Sex Educator, 17,* 6. Retrieved from: http://publications.msss.gouv.qc.ca/acrobat/f/documentation/2011/11-314-01A.pdf [Accessed 30 December 2014].

Pinquart, M. (2010). Ambivalence in adolescents' decisions about having their first sexual intercourse. *Journal of Sex Research, 47*(5), 440–450.

Pittar, K. (2014, 24 June). Sexting among teenagers more widespread than many parents think. *South China Morning Post.* Retrieved from: http://www.scmp.com/lifestyle/family-education/article/1538979/sexting-among-teenagers-more-widespread-many-parents [Accessed 17 November 2014].

Pitts, M. (2003). Explaining human papilloma virus (HPV). *The Australian Health Consumer, 1,* 30–31. Retrieved from: https://www.chf.org.au/pdfs/ahc/ahc-2003-1-explaining-hpv.pdf [Accessed 4 July 2014].

Pitts, S. & Emans, S.J. (2014). Contraceptive counseling: Does it make a difference? *Journal of Adolescent Health, 54,* 367–368.

Planned Parenthood. (2012, 2 October). *National News.* Half of all teens feel uncomfortable talking to their parents about sex while only 19 percent of parents feel the same, new survey shows. Retrieved from: http://www.plannedparenthood.org/about-us/newsroom/press-releases/half-all-teens-feel-uncomfortable-talking-their-parents-about-sex-while-only-19-percent-parents#sthash.xE1gfLbg.dpuf [Accessed 30 December 2014].

Plummer, D.C. (2001). The quest for modern manhood: Masculine stereotypes, peer culture and the social significance of homophobia. *Journal of Adolescence, 24*(1), 15–24.

Pokharel, S., Kulczycki, A. & Shakyac, S. (2006) School-based sex education in Western Nepal: Uncomfortable for both teachers and students. *Reproductive Health Matters, 14,* 156–161.

Porterfield, S.P. (2005). *Women's lived experience with human papillomavirus.* Unpublished doctoral dissertation. Gainesville, FL: University of Florida.

Potard, C., Courtois, R. & Rusch, E. (2008). The influence of peers on risky sexual behaviour during adolescence. *European Journal of Contraception & Reproductive Health Care, 13,* 264–270.

Poteat, P.V., Espelage, D.L. & Koenig, P.K. (2009). Willingness to remain friends and attend school with lesbian and gay peers: Relational expressions of prejudice among heterosexual youth. *Journal of Youth and Adolescence, 38,* 952–962.

Potoczniak, D., Crosbie-Burnett, M. & Saltzburg, N. (2009). Experiences regarding coming out to parents among African American, Hispanic, and White gay, lesbian, bisexual, transgender, and questioning adolescents. *Journal of Gay & Lesbian Social Services, 21,* 189–205.

Powell, E. (2008). Young people's use of friends and family for sex and relationships information and advice. *Sex Education, 8,* 289–302.

Premier of Victoria (2014, 3 November). New 'sexting' laws commence today. Retrieved from: http://archive.premier.vic.gov.au/2014/media-centre/media-releases/11646-new-sexting-laws-commence-today.html [Accessed 27 December 2014].

Prince, P. & Jordan, R. (2004). Act (67A) in Crimes Legislation Amendment (Telecommunications Offences and Other Measures) Bill 2004. Australian Government Department of Parliamentary Services, Canberra.

Prynne, M. (2014, 5 May). 'Sexting' is new courtship', parents are told. *The Telegraph.* Retrieved from: http://www.telegraph.co.uk/technology/10808862/Sexting-is-new-courtship-parents-are-told.html [Accessed 5 January 2014].

Public Health Agency of Canada (2008). *Canadian guidelines for sexual health education.* Retrieved from: http://www.phac-aspc.gc.ca/std-mts/sti-its/index-eng.php [Accessed 6 April 2015].

Public Health England. (2013, 12 December). Press release: National HPV vaccination coverage remains high and evidence shows programme effective in protecting women's health. Retrieved from: https://www.gov.uk/government/news/national-hpv-vaccination-coverage-remains-high-and-evidence-shows-programme-effective-in-protecting-womens-health [Accessed 4 July 2014].

Public Health England. (2014a). Genital Chlamydia trachomatis. Retrieved from: http://www.hpa.org.uk/Topics/InfectiousDiseases/InfectionsAZ/Chlamydia [Accessed 4 July 2014].

Public Health England. (2014b). Nearly half a million new sexual infections in 2012. Retrieved from: https://www.gov.uk/government/news/nearly-half-a-million-new-sexual-infections-in-2012 [Accessed 9 January 2014].

Pulerwitz, J. & Barker, G. (2008). Measuring attitudes towards gender norms among young men in Brazil: Development and psychometric evaluation of the GEM scale. *Men and Masculinities, 10*(3), 322–338.

Purdie-Vaughns, V. & Eibach, R. (2008). Intersectional invisibility: The ideological sources and social consequences of non-prototypicality. *Sex Roles, 59*(5), 377–391.

Queensland Health. (2010). *Unwanted sex and sexual assault.* Retrieved from: http://www.health.qld.gov.au/istaysafe/lets-talk-about-sex/unwanted-sex.aspx [Accessed 17 May 2014].

Raco, E. (2014, July 1). Aussie teens online. Research Snapshots. Australian Communications and Media Authority (ACMA). Retrieved from: http://www.acma.gov.au/theACMA/engage-blogs/engage-blogs/Research-snapshots/Aussie-teens-online [Accessed 25 September 2014].

Ralph, L., Gould, H., Baker, A. & Greene, F.D. (2014). The role of parents and partners in minors' decisions to have an abortion and anticipated coping after abortion. *Journal of Adolescent Health, 54,* 428–434.

Ramirez, X. (2011). National study reveals striking findings on school sexual harassment. *Care2,* November 7. Retrieved from: http://www.care2.com/causes/national-study-reveals-striking-findings-on-school-sexual-harassment.html#ixzz34qqfbH00 [Accessed 17 June 2014].

Rape, Abuse and Incest National Network. (n.d.). *Ways to reduce your risk of sexual assault.* Retrieved from: http://www.rainn.org/get-information/sexual-assault-prevention [Accessed 5 January 2014].

Raznahan, A., Lee, Y., Stidd, R., Long, R., Greenstein, D., Clasen, L., *et al.* (2010). Longitudinally mapping the influence of sex and androgen signaling on the dynamics of human cortical maturation in adolescence. *Proceedings of the National Academy of Sciences, USA, 107*(39), 16988–16993.

Reilly, C. (2014, 5 November). Unsolicited sexting now illegal under new Victorian laws. *CNET*. Retrieved from: http://www.cnet.com/au/news/unsolicited-sexting-now-illegal-under-new-victorian-laws [Accessed 11 November 2014].

Reist, T. (2013, 15 December). Love me Tinder. *The Sunday Age*, 1–6.

Revzina, N.V. & DiClemente, R.J. (2005). Prevalence and incidence of human papillomavirus infection in women in the USA: A systematic review. *International Journal of STDs and AIDS, 16,* 528–537.

Rhucharoenpornpanich, O., Chamratrithirong, A., Fongkaew, W., Miller, B.A., Cupp, P.K., Rosati, M.J. & Chookhare, W. (2012). Parent-teen communication about sex in urban Thai families. *Journal of Health Communication, 17,* 380–396.

Richters, J., Altman, D., Badcock, P.D., Smith, A.M.A., de Visser, R.O., Grulich, A.E., *et al.* (2014). Sexual identity, sexual attraction and sexual experience: The second Australian study of health and relationships. *Australian and New Zealand Journal of Public Health, 11,* 451–460.

Richters, J., Grulich, A.E., Visser, R.O., Smith, A.M.A. & Rissel, C.E. (2003) Sex in Australia: Contraceptive practices among a representative sample of women. *Australian and New Zealand Journal of Public Health, 27*(2), 210–216.

Rideout, V.J., Foehr, U.G. & Roberts, D.F. (2010). *Generation M2: Media in the lives of 8- to 18-year-olds.* Menlo Park, CA: Henry J. Kaiser Family Foundation.

Riley, E.A., Sitharthan, G., Clemson, L. & Diamond, M. (2011). The needs of gender-variant children and their parents: A parent survey. *International Journal of Sexual Health, 23*(3), 181–195.

Ringli, M., Kurth, S., Huber, R. & Jenni, O.G. (2013). The sleep EEG topography in children and adolescents shows sex differences in language areas. *International Journal of Physiology, 89*(2), 241–245.

Rissel, C.E., Richters, J., Grulich, A.E., deVisser, R.O. & Smith, A.M.A. (2003). Sex in Australia: First experiences of vaginal intercourse and oral sex among a representative sample of adults. *Australian and New Zealand Journal of Public Health, 27,* 131–137.

Ritter, A., Matthew-Simmons, F. & Carragher, N. (2012). *Monograph No 23: Prevalence of and interventions for mental health and alcohol and other drug problems amongst the gay, lesbian, bisexual and transgender community: A review of the literature.* DPMP Monograph Series. Sydney: National Drug and Alcohol Research Centre.

Roberts, B. & Reddy, V. (2008). Pride and prejudice: Public attitudes towards homosexuality. *HSRC Review, 6,* 9–11.

Roberts, C. (2013). Evolutionary psychology, feminism and early sexual development. *Feminist Theory, 14*(3), 295–304.

Roberts, T.A., Auinger, P. & Klein, J.D. (2005). Intimate partner abuse and the reproductive health of sexually active female adolescents. *Journal of Adolescent Health, 36,* 380–385.

Robinson, K.H., Bansel, P., Denson, N., Ovenden, G. & Davies, C. (2014). *Growing up queer: Issues facing young Australians who are gender variant and sexually diverse.* Melbourne: Young and Well Cooperative Research Centre.

Robson, S., Cameron, C.A. & Roberts, C.L. (2006). Birth outcomes for teenage women in New South Wales, 1998–2003. *Australian and New Zealand Journal of Obstetrics and Gynaecology, 46,* 305–310.

Rogala, C. & Tyden, T. (2003). Does pornography influence young women's sexual behavior? *Women's Health Issues, 13,* 39–43.

Rogers, D. (1981). *Adolescents and youth.* Englewood Cliffs, NJ: Prentice-Hall.

Romoren, M., Sundby, J., Velauthapillai, M., Rahman, M., Klouman, E. & Hjortdahl, P. (2007). Chlamydia and gonorrhoea in pregnant Batswana women: Time to discard the syndromic approach? *BMC Infectious Diseases, 7,* 27, doi:10.1186/1471-2334-7-27.

Roney, J.R., Mahler, S.V. & Maestripieri, D. (2003). Behavioral and hormonal responses of men to brief interactions with women. *Evolution and Human Behavior, 24*(6), 365–375.

Ronken, C. & Johnston, H. (2012). *Child sexual assault: Facts and statistics.* Arundel, Queensland: Bravehearts Inc. Retrieved from: http://www.bravehearts.org.au/pages/research_lobbying.php [Accessed 19 January 2015].

Rose, A.J. & Rudolph, K.D. (2006). A review of sex differences in peer relationship processes: Potential trade-offs for the emotional and behavioral development of girls and boys. *Psychological Bulletin, 132*(1), 98–131.

Rosenberg, M. (2004, 10 February). Universities to blame for sex scandals. *Knight Ridder Newspapers.* Retrieved from: HighBeam Research website: http://www.highbeam.com/doc/1G1-113077870.html [Accessed 24 April 2015].

Rosengard, C. (2009).Confronting the intendedness of adolescent rapid repeat pregnancy. *Journal of Adolescent Health, 44*(1), 5–6.

Rosengard, C., Adler, N.E., Gurvey, J.E. & Ellen, J. (2005). Adolescent partner-type experience: Psychosocial and behavioral differences. *Perspectives on Sexual and Reproductive Health, 37*(3), 141–147.

Rosengard, C., Pollock, L., Weitzen, S., Meers, A. & Phipps, M.G. (2006). Concepts of the advantages and disadvantages of teenage childbearing among pregnant adolescents: A qualitative study. *Pediatrics, 118,* 503–510.

Rosenthal, D. & Collis, F. (1997). Australian parents' beliefs about adolescent sexuality and HIV/AIDS. *Journal of HIV/AIDS Prevention & Education in Adolescents & Children, 1,* 57–72.

Rosenthal, D., Moore, S. & Flynn, I. (1991). Adolescent self-efficacy, self-esteem and sexual risk-taking. *Journal of Community and Applied Social Psychology, 1*(2), 77–88.

Rosenthal, D., Rowe, H., Mallett, S., Hardiman, A. & Kirkman, M. (2009). *Understanding women's experiences of unplanned pregnancy and abortion, final report.* Melbourne: Key Centre for Women's Health in Society, Melbourne School of Population Health, The University of Melbourne.

Rosenthal, D. & Smith, A.M.A. (1995). Adolescents and sexually transmissible diseases: Information sources, preferences and trust. *Australian Health Promotion Journal, 5,* 38–44.

Rosetta Foundation. (2014a). Stories from girls who aborted. *TeenBreaks.* Retrieved from: http://www.teenbreaks.com/abortion/girlswhoaborted.cfm [Accessed 22 May 2014].

Rosetta Foundation. (2014b). Birth mother stories. Retrieved from: http://www.teenbreaks.com/adoption/birthmotherstories.cfm [Accessed 22 May 2014].

Rostosky, S.S., Dekhtyar, O., Cupp, P. & Anderman, E. (2008). Sexual self-concept and sexual self-efficacy in adolescents: A possible clue to promoting sexual health? *Journal of Sex Research, 45*(3), 277–286.

Rostosky, S.S., Regnerus, M.D. & Wright, M.L. (2003). Coital debut: The role of religiosity and sex attitudes in the Add Health Survey. *Journal of Sex Research, 40,* 358–367.

Rostosky, S.S., Wilcox, B.L., Wright, M.L.C. & Randall, B.A. (2004). The impact of religiosity on adolescent sexual behaviour: A review of the evidence. *Journal of Adolescent Research, 19,* 677–697.

Rothman, E.F., Miller, E., Terpeluk, A., Glauber, A. & Randel, J. (2011). The proportion of U.S. parents who talk with their adolescent children about dating abuse. *Journal of Adolescent Health, 49,* 216–218.

Roudsari, R.L., Javadnoori, M., Hasanpour, M., Hazavehei, S.M. & Taghipour, A. (2013). Socio-cultural challenges to sexual health education for female students in Iran. *Iran Journal of Reproductive Medicine, 11,* 101–110.

Rowe, H., Kirkman, M., Hardiman, A., Mallett, S. & Rosenthal, D. (2009). Considering abortion: 12-month audit of records of women contacting a Pregnancy Advisory Service. *Medical Journal of Australia, 190,* 69–72.

Rowe, R., Maughan, B., Worthman, C.M., Costello, E.J. & Angold, A. (2004). Testosterone, antisocial behavior, and social dominance in boys: Pubertal development and biosocial interaction. *Biological Psychiatry, 55*(5), 546–552.

Rowlands, I. & Lee, C. (2006). Choosing to have children or choosing to be child-free: Australian students' attitudes towards the decisions of heterosexual and lesbian women. *Australian Psychologist, 41,* 55–59.

Rozbroj, T., Lyons, A., Pitts, M., Mitchell, A. & Christensen, H. (2014). Assessing the applicability of e-therapies for depression, anxiety, and other mood disorders among lesbians and gay men: Analysis of 24 web- and mobile phone-based self-help interventions. *Journal of Medicine and Internet Research, 16*(7), e166.

Rubin, C., Maisonet, M., Kieszak, S., Monteilh, C., Holmes, A., Flanders, D., et al. (2009). Timing of maturation and predictors of menarche in girls enrolled in a contemporary British cohort. *Paediatric and Perinatal Epidemiology, 23*(5), 492–504.

Rudman, L.A., Fetterolf, J.C. & Sanchez, D.T. (2013). What motivates the sexual double standard? More support for male versus female control theory. *Personality and Social Psychology Bulletin, 39*(2), 250–263.

Rudman, L.A. & Mescher, K. (2012). Of animals and objects: Men's implicit dehumanization of women and likelihood of sexual aggression. *Personality and Social Psychology Bulletin, 38*(6), 734–746.

Rudy, B.J., Murphy, D.A., Harris, D.R., Muenz, L. & Ellen, J. (2009). Adolescent trials network for HIVAI. Patient-related risks for nonadherence to antiretroviral therapy among HIV-infected youth in the United States: A study of prevalence and interactions. *AIDS Patient Care and STDS, 23,* 185–194.

Ryan, C., Huebner, D., Diaz, R.M. & Sanchez, J. (2009). Family rejection as a predictor of negative health outcomes in white and Latino lesbian, gay and bisexual young adults. *Pediatrics, 123*(1), 346–352.

Ryan, E. (2010). Sexting: How the state can prevent a moment of indiscretion from leading to a lifetime of unintended consequences for minors and young adults. *Iowa Law Review, 96,* 357–383.

Saewyc, E.M., Homma, Y., Skay, C.L., Bearinger, L.H., Resnick, M.D. & Reis, E. (2009). Protective factors in the lives of bisexual adolescents in North America. *American Journal of Public Health, 99,* 110–117.

Samandari, G. & Speizer, I.S. (2010). Adolescent sexual behavior and reproductive outcomes in Central America: Trends over the past two decades. *International Perspectives on Sexual and Reproductive Health, 36*(1), 26–35.

Sánchez-Martínez, M. & Otero, A. (2009). Factors associated with cell phone use in adolescents in the community of Madrid (Spain). *CyberPsychology & Behavior, 12*(2), 131–137.

Sanders, S.A., Hill, B.J., Yarber, W.L., Graham, C.A., Crosby, R.A. & Milhausen, R.R. (2010). Misclassification bias: Diversity in conceptualisations about having 'had sex'. *Sexual Health, 7*(1), 31–34.

Santelli, J.S., Abraido-Lanza, A.F. & Melnikas, A.J. (2009). Migration, acculturation, and sexual and reproductive health of Latino adolescents. *Journal of Adolescent Health, 44*(1), 3–4.

Santelli, J.S., Speizer, I.S., Avery, A. & Kendall, C. (2006). An exploration of the dimensions of pregnancy intentions among women choosing to terminate pregnancy or to initiate prenatal care in New Orleans, Louisiana. *American Journal of Public Health, 96*(11), 2009–2015.

Satterwhite, C.L., Torrone, E., Meites, E., Dunne, E.F., Mahajan, R., Ocfemia, M., *et al.* (2013). Sexually transmitted infections among U.S. women and men: Prevalence and incidence estimates, 2008. *Sexually Transmissible Diseases, 40,* 187–193.

Sauers, J. (2007). *Sex lives of Australian teenagers.* Sydney: Random House Australia.

Saul, H. (22 November, 2013) Sex app notifies you when you have an STD. *The Independent.* Retrieved from: http://www.independent.co.uk/life-style/gadgets-and-tech/sex-app-notifies-you-when-you-have-an-sti-8956813.html [Accessed 24 July 2014].

Savic, I., Berglund, H. & Lindstrom, P. (2005). Brain response to putative pheromones in homosexual men. *Proceedings of the National Academy of Sciences, USA, 102*(20), 7356–7361.

Savic, I. & Lindstrom, P. (2008). PET and MRI show differences in cerebral asymmetry and functional connectivity between homo-and heterosexual subjects. *Proceedings of the National Academy of Sciences, USA, 105,* 9403–9408.

Savin-Williams, R.C. (2003). Lesbian, gay and bisexual youths' relationships with their parents. In L.D. Garnets & D.C. Kimmel (Eds.), *Psychological perspectives on lesbian, gay and bisexual experiences* (2nd edn). New York: Columbia University Press, pp. 299–326.

Savin-Williams, R.C. (2006). Who's gay? And does it matter? *Current Directions in Psychological Science, 15,* 140–144.

Savin-Williams, R.C. & Joyner, K. (2014). The dubious assessment of gay, lesbian, and bisexual adolescents of Add Health. *Archives of Sexual Behaviour, 43*(3), 413–422.

Sawyer, S.M., Afifi, R.A., Bearinger, L.H., Blakemore, S.-J., Dick, B., Ezeh, A.C. & Patton, G.C. (2012). Adolescence: A foundation for future health. *Lancet, 379,* 1630–1640.

Schaalma, H.P., Abraham C., Gillmore, M.R. & Kok, G. (2004). Sex education as health promotion: What does it take? *Archives of Sexual Behavior, 33,* 259–269.

Schalet, A. (2010). Sexual subjectivity revisited: The significance of relationships in Dutch and American girls' experiences of sexuality. *Gender and Society, 24*(3), 304–329.

Schalet, A.T. (2011). *Not under my roof: Parents, teens, and the culture of sex.* Chicago, IL: University of Chicago Press.

Scheil, W., Scott, J., Catcheside, B., Sage, L. & Kennare, R. (2013). *Pregnancy outcomes in South Australia 2011.* Adelaide: Pregnancy Outcome Unit, SA Health, Government of South Australia.

Schofield, M. (1968). *The sexual behaviour of young people.* Harmondsworth: Penguin.

Schultz, K.M., Molenda-Figueira, H.A. & Sisk, C.L. (2009). Back to the future: The organizational activational hypothesis adapted to puberty and adolescence. *Hormones and Behavior, 5*(55), 597–604.

Schwartz, D.H., Romans, S.E., Meiyappan, S., De Souza, M.J. & Einstein, G. (2012). The role of ovarian steroid hormones in mood. *Hormones and Behavior, 62*(4), 448–454.

Secor-Turner, M., Sieving, R.E., Eisenberg, M.E. & Skay, C. (2011). Associations between sexually experienced adolescents' sources of information about sex and sexual risk outcomes. *Sex Education: Sexuality, Society and Learning, 11,* 489–500.

Segalowitz, S.J. & Davies, P.L. (2004). Charting the maturation of the frontal lobe: an electrophysiological strategy. *Brain and Cognition, 55*(1), 116–133.

Seiffge-Krenke, I., Bosma, H., Chau, C., Cok, F., Gillespie, C., Loncaric, D., *et al.* (2010). All they need is love? Placing romantic stress in the context of other stressors: A 17-nation study. *International Journal of Behavioral Development, 34*(2), 106–112.

Selemon, L.D. (2013). A role for synaptic plasticity in the adolescent development of executive function. *Translational Psychiatry, 3*(3), e238.

Seminara, S.B., Messager, S., Chatzidaki, E.E., Thresher, R.R., Acierno Jr., J.S., Shagoury, J.K., *et al.* (2003). The GPR54 gene as a regulator of puberty. *New England Journal of Medicine, 349,* 1614–1627.

Semiz, S., Kurt, F., Kurt, D.T., Zencir, M. & Sevinç, Ö. (2009). Factors affecting onset of puberty in Denizli province in Turkey. *Turkish Journal of Pediatrics, 51,* 49–55.

Sex Education Forum Survey. (2008). Evidence. Retrieved from: http://www.sexeducationforum.org.uk/evidence.aspx [Accessed 24 January 2014].

Shacklock, G. (2007). Parenting students in secondary school settings: The challenge of the 'dilemma of difference'. TASA & SAANZ Joint Conference, 4–7 December 2007, Auckland.

Shaw, P., Greenstein, D., Lerch, J., Clasen, L., Lenroot, R., Gogtay, N., *et al.* (2006). Intellectual ability and cortical development in children and adolescents. *Nature, 440*(7084), 676–679.

Shaw, P., Sharp, W.S., Morrison, M., Eckstrand, K., Greenstein, D.K., Clasen, L.S., *et al.* (2009). Psychostimulant treatment and the developing cortex in attention deficit hyperactivity disorder. *American Journal of Psychiatry, 166*(1), 58–63.

Shearer, D.L. (2000). Cognitive ability and its association with early childbearing and second teen births. *Dissertation Abstracts International Section B: The Sciences & Engineering, 60,* 5466.

Shelton, J.D. (2010). Masturbation: Breaking the silence. *International Perspectives in Sexual and Reproductive Health, 36,* 157–158.

Sherbet Research. (2009). *Customer voice research: sex and relationships education.* Research Report DCSF-RR175. London: Department for Children, Schools and Families.

Shtarkshall, R.A., Carmel, S., Jaffe-Hirschfield, D. & Woloski-Wruble, A. (2009). Sexual milestones and factors associated with coitus initiation among Israeli high school students. *Archives of Sexual Behavior, 38*(4), 591–604.

Sieving, R.E., Eisenberg, M.E., Pettingell, S. & Skay, C. (2006). Friends' influence on adolescents' first sexual intercourse. *Perspectives on Sexual Health, 38,* 175–180.

Silventoinen, K., Haukka, J., Dunkel, L., Tynelius, P. & Rasmussen, F. (2008). Genetics of pubertal timing and its associations with relative weight in childhood and adult height: The Swedish young male twins study. *Pediatrics, 121,* 885–889.

Simon, L. & Daneback, K. (2013). Adolescents' use of the internet for sex education: A thematic and critical review of the literature. *International Journal of Sexual Health, 25*(4), 305–319.

Sinkinson, M. (2009). 'Sexuality isn't just about sex': Pre-service teachers' shifting constructs of sexuality education. *Sex Education, 9,* 421–436.

Sipsma, H., Divney, A.A., Niccolai, L.M., Gordon, D., Magriples, U. & Kershaw, T.S. (2012). Pregnancy desire among a sample of young couples who are expecting a baby. *Perspectives on Sexual and Reproductive Health, 44*(4), 244–251.

Sipsma, H.L., Ickovics, J.R. & Kershaw, T.S. (2011). Adolescent pregnancy desire and pregnancy incidence. *Women's Health Issues, 21*(2), 110–116.

Sisk, C. & Foster, D. (2004). The neural basis of puberty and adolescence. *Nature Neuroscience, 7,* 1040–1047.

Skinner, S.R., Smith, J., Fenwick, J., Fyfe, S. & Hendriks, J. (2008). Perceptions and experiences of first sexual intercourse in Australian adolescent females. *Journal of Adolescent Health, 43*(6), 593–599.

Skoog, T., Stattin, H. & Kerr, M. (2009). The role of pubertal timing in what adolescent boys do online. *Journal of Research on Adolescence, 19*(1), 1–7.

Slane, A. (2009). Sexting, teens and a proposed offence of invasion of privacy. Retrieved from: www.iposgoode.ca/2009/03/sexting-teens-and-a-proposed-offence-of-invasion-of-privacy [Accessed 20 November 2014].

Slowinski, K. & Hume, A. (2001). *Unplanned teenage pregnancy and the support of young mothers. Part C: Statistics.* Adelaide: Department of Human Services. Retrieved from: www.sapo.org.au/binary/binary1101/Teen.pdf [Accessed 13 June 2014].

Smith, A., Schlichthorst, M., Mitchell, A., Walsh, J., Lyons, A., Blackman, P. & Pitts, M. (2011). *Sexuality education in Australian secondary schools: Results of the 1st national survey of Australian secondary teachers of sexuality education 2010.* Melbourne: Australian Research Centre in Sex Health and Society, La Trobe University.

Smith, A.M.A., Rissel, C.E., Richters, J., Grulich, A.E. & de Visser, R.O. (2003). Sex in Australia: Reproductive experiences and reproductive health among a representative sample of women. *Australian & New Zealand Journal of Public Health, 27*(2), 204–209.

Smith, A.M.A. & Rosenthal, D. (1997). Sex, alcohol and drugs? Young people's experience of Schoolies Week. *Australian and New Zealand Journal of Public Health, 21,* 175–180.

Smith, D.M. & Elander, J. (2006). Effects of area and family deprivation on risk factors for teenage pregnancy among 13–15-year-old girls. *Psychology, Health and Medicine, 11*(4), 399–410.

Smith, J.L., Fenwick, J., Skinner, R., Hallet, J., Merriman, G. & Marshall, L. (2012). Sex, condoms and sexually transmissible infections: A qualitative study of sexual health in young Australian men. *Archives of Sexual Behavior, 41,* 487–495.

Smith, J.L., Skinner, S.R. & Fenwick, J. (2011). How Australian female adolescents prioritize pregnancy protection: A grounded theory study of contraceptive histories. *Journal of Adolescent Research, 26*(5), 617–644.

Smith, P.B., Realini, J.P., Buzi, R.S. & Martinez, M. (2011). Students' experiences and perceived benefits of a sex education curriculum: A qualitative analysis. *Journal of Sex & Marital Therapy, 37,* 270–285.

Snapp, S., Cheney, B., Galiani, M. & Lento, R. (2012, March). The role of gender in determining sexual motives in a hookup. Paper presented at the 14th Society for Adolescent Research Biennial Meeting, Vancouver, Canada.

Soller, B. (2014). Caught in a bad romance: Adolescent romantic relationships and mental health. *Journal of Health and Social Behavior, 55*(1), 56–72.

Sowell, E.R., Delis, D., Stiles, J. & Jernigan, T.L. (2001). Improved memory functioning and frontal lobe maturation between childhood and adolescence: A structural MRI study. *Journal of the International Neuropsychological Society (JINS), 7*(3), 312–322.

Spitzer, R.L. (1981). The diagnostic status of homosexuality in DSM III: A reformulation of the issues. *American Journal of Psychiatry, 138,* 210–215.

Sprecher, S. (2014). Evidence of change in men's versus women's emotional reactions to first sexual intercourse: A 23-year study in a human sexuality course at a midwestern university. *Journal of Sex Research, 51*(4), 466–472.

Sprecher, S., Treger, S. & Sakaluk, J.K. (2013). Premarital sexual standards and sociosexuality: Gender, ethnicity, and cohort differences. *Archives of Sexual Behavior, 42*(8), 1395–1405.

Stanwood, G.D. & Levitt, P. (2004). Drug exposure early in life: Functional repercussions of changing neuropharmacology during sensitive periods of brain development. *Current Opinion in Pharmacology, 4,* 65–71.

Stark, J. (13 November 2011). Schoolies get what they want: Booze and risky sex. *Brisbane Times,* Fairfax Media.

Stark, J. (2014, 4 July). Calls to help sex-change kids as demand for gender reassignment soars. *The Sydney Morning Herald.* Retrieved from: http://www.smh.com.au/national/calls-to-help-sexchange-kids-as-demand-for-gender-reassignment-soars-20140704-zsvz7.html [Accessed 24 January 2015].

Statistics New Zealand (2003). Teenage fertility in New Zealand. *Key Statistics, September.* Retrieved from: http://www.stats.govt.nz/browse_for_stats/population/births/teenage-fertility-in-nz.aspx [Accessed 23 May 2014].

Stein, J.H. & Reiser, L.W. (1994). A study of white middle-class adolescent boys' responses to 'semenarche' (the first ejaculation). *Journal of Youth & Adolescence, 23*(3), 373–384.

Steinmetz, K. (2013, 12 November). (No) condom culture: Why teens aren't practicing safe sex. *Time Magazine.* Retrieved from: http://healthland.time.com/2013/11/12/no-condom-culture-why-teens-arent-practicing-safe-sex [Accessed 29 November 2014].

Stelio, N. (2014, 13 April). The full bush Brazilian. *The Sydney Morning Herald Life and Style Magazine.* Retrieved from: http://www.smh.com.au/lifestyle/beauty/the-full-bush-brazilian-20140413-36lbf.html [Accessed 19 January 2015].

Stice, E., Presnell, K. & Bearman, S.K. (2001). Relation of early menarche to depression, eating disorders, substance abuse, and comorbid psychopathology among adolescent girls. *Developmental Psychology, 37,* 608–619.

Strasburger, V.C., Wilson, B.J. & Jordan, A.B. (2009). *Children, adolescents, and the media* (2nd edn). Thousand Oaks, CA: Sage.

Štulhofer, A., Busko V. & Schmidt, G. (2012). Adolescent exposure to pornography and relationship intimacy in young adulthood. *Psychology & Sexuality, 3*(2), 95–107.

Stutterheim, S.E., Bos, A.E.R. & Schaalma, H.P. (2008). *Positive living under stigma.* Enschede: AIDS Fonds.

Styne, D. & Grumbach, M.M. (2011). Puberty: Ontogeny, neuroendocrinology, physiology, and disorders. In S. Melmed, K.S. Polonsky, P.R. Larsen & H.M. Kronenberg (Eds.), *Williams textbook of endocrinology* (12th edn). Philadelphia, PA: Saunders Elsevier, pp. 969–1166.

Su, J.-Y., Holt, J., Payne, R., Gates, K., Ewing, A. & Ryder, N. (2014, October). Effectiveness of using GrindR broadcast to increase syphilis testing among men who have sex with men in Darwin, Australia. Paper presented at the Australasian Sexual Health Conference, Sydney, Australia.

Sutton, H. (1944). *Lectures on preventive medicine.* Sydney: Consolidated Press.

Swann, C., Bowe, K., McCormick, G. & Kosmin, M. (2003). *Teenage pregnancy and parenthood: A review of reviews, evidence briefing.* London: Health Development Agency, Department of Health.

Sychareun, V., Phengsavanh, A., Hansana, V., Chaleunvong, K., Kounnavong, S., Sawhney, M. & Durham, J. (2013). Predictors of premarital sexual activity among unmarried youth in Vientiane, Lao PDR: The role of parent–youth interactions and peer influence. *Global Public Health, 8,* 958–975.

Symons, E.K. (2004a, 15 September). AFL (Australian Football League) standing still on spate of sex assaults. *The Australian,* p. 3.

Symons, E.K. (2004b, 3 March). Degrading culture knows no boundaries. *The Australian,* p. 12.

Szymanski, D.M. & Stewart-Richardson, D.N. (2014). Psychological, relational, and sexual correlates of pornography use on young adult heterosexual men in romantic relationships. *Journal of Men's Studies, 22*(1), 64–82.

Tang, N., Bensman, L. & Hatfield, E. (2012). The impact of culture and gender on sexual motives: Differences between Chinese and North Americans. *International Journal of Intercultural Relations, 36*(2), 286–294.

Tannen, D. (2007). *You just don't understand: Women and men in conversation.* New York: Harper Collins.

Tappé, M., Bensman, L., Hayashi, K. & Hatfield, E. (2013). Gender differences in receptivity to sexual offers: A new research prototype. *Interpersona: International Journal on Personal Relationships, 7*(2), 323–344.

Tarkowski,T.A., Koumans, E.H., Sawyer, M., Pierce, A., Black, C.M., Papp, J.R., et al. (2004). Epidemiology of human papillomavirus infection and abnormal cytologic test results in an urban adolescent population. *Journal of infectious Diseases, 189,* 46–50.

Temple, J.R., Paul, J.A., van den Berg, P., Le, V.D., McElhany, A. & Temple, B.W. (2012). Teen sexting and its association with sexual behaviors. *Archives of Pediatric and Adolescent Medicine, 166,* 828–833.

Temple, J., Vi, D.L., Van den Berg, P., Ling, Y., Paul, J. & Temple, B. (2014).Teen sexting and psychosocial health. *Journal of Adolescence, 37,* 33–36.

Temple-Smith, M., Hopkins, C., Fairley, C., Tomnay, J., Pavlin, N., Parker, R., *et al.* (2010). The right thing to do: Patients' views and experiences of telling partners about chlamydia. *Family Practice, 27,* 418–423.

Tharp, A.T., DeGue, S., Valle, L.A., Brookmeyer, K.A., Massetti, G.M. & Matjasko, J.L. (2013). A systematic qualitative review of risk and protective factors for sexual violence perpetration. *Trauma Violence Abuse, 4,* 133–167.

The Hormone Factory. (n.d.). Retrieved from: www.thehormonefactory.com [Accessed 27 December 2014].

The International Association for the Study of Sexuality, Culture and Society. (2014). About IASSCS. Retrieved from: http://iasscs.org/our-aims-and-objectives [Accessed 20 June 2014].

The Kirby Institute. (2011). *HIV, viral hepatitis and sexually transmissible infections in Australia Annual Surveillance Report 2011.* Sydney, NSW: The Kirby Institute, The University of New South Wales.

The Kirby Institute. (2013). *HIV, viral hepatitis and sexually transmissible infections in Australia Annual Surveillance Report 2013.* Sydney, NSW: The Kirby Institute, The University of New South Wales.

The Smith Family. (2014). Back to school for young Gippsland mums. Retrieved from: http://www.thesmithfamily.com.au/media-centre/2014/02/10/11/20/05-Feb-2014-Back-to-School-for-young-Gippsland-mums [Accessed 22 February 2014].

TheSomebodytoknow. (2012, September 7). My story: Struggling, bullying, suicide, self harm [video file]. Retrieved from: https://www.youtube.com/watch?v=vOHXGNx-E7E [Accessed 17 May 2014].

Think U Know. (n.d.). Retrieved from: http://www.thinkuknow.co.uk [Accessed 16 January 2014].

Thornburg, H.D. (1981). The amount of sex information learning obtained during early adolescence. *Journal of Early Adolescence, 1,* 71–183.

Thorsen, C., Aneblom, G. & Gemzell-Danielsson, K. (2006). Perceptions of contraception, non-protection and induced abortion among a sample of urban Swedish teenage girls: Focus group discussions. *European Journal of Contraception and Reproductive Health Care, 11*(4), 302–309.

Thurlow, C. (2001). Naming the 'outsider within': Homophobic pejoratives and the verbal abuse of lesbian, gay and bisexual high-school pupils. *Journal of Adolescence, 24*(1), 25–38.

Tiggemann, M. & Hodgson, S. (2008). The hairlessness norm extended: Reasons for and predictors of women's body hair removal at different body sites. *Sex Roles, 59*(11/12), 889–897.

Tiggemann, M. & Lynch, J.E. (2001). Body image across the life span in adult women: The role of self-objectification. *Developmental Psychology, 37*(2), 243–253.

Timmons, A. (2014). Sexy but not sexual: An examination of the sexual narratives of African American adolescent females (Doctoral dissertation). Retrieved from http://via.library.depaul.edu/csh_etd/85 [Accessed 19 January 2015].

Tinder. (n.d.). Retrieved from: http://www.gotinder.com/blog [Accessed 14 October 2014].

Tolman, D.L. (2005). *Dilemmas of desire: Teenage girls talk about sexuality.* Cambridge, MA: Harvard University Press.

Tolman, D.L. (2012). Female adolescents, sexual empowerment and desire: A missing discourse of gender enquiry. *Sex Roles, 66,* 746–757.

Tornello, S.L., Riskind, R.G. & Patterson, C.J. (2014). Sexual and reproductive health among sexual minority female youth in the United States. Oral Research Presentation, GLMA: Health Professionals Advancing LGBT Equality, Baltimore, MD.

Townsend, C.L., Cortina-Borja, M., Peckham, C.S., de Ruiter, A., Lyall, H. & Tookey, P.A. (2008). Low rates of mother-to-child transmission of HIV following effective pregnancy interventions in the United Kingdom and Ireland, 2000–2006. *AIDS, 22,* 973–981.

Townsend, S. (1982). *The secret diary of Adrian Mole aged 13 3/4.* London: Methuen.

Tracy, J.L., Shaver, P.R., Albino, A.W. & Cooper, M.L. (2003). Attachment styles and adolescent sexuality. In P. Florsheim (Ed.), *Adolescent romance and sexual behavior: Theory, research, and practical implications.* Mahwah, NJ: Lawrence Erlbaum Associates, pp. 137–159.

Trickett, P., Noll, J. & Putnam, F. (2011). The impact of sexual abuse on female development: Lessons from a multigenerational, longitudinal research study. *Developmental Psychology, 23*(2), 453–476.

Trussell, J. (1988). Teenage pregnancy in the United States. *Family Planning Perspectives, 20,* 262–272.

Trussell, J. & Wynn, L.L. (2008). Reducing unintended pregnancy in the United States. *Contraception, 77,* 1–5.

Tsui-Sui, A.K. & Manczak, M. (2013). Family influences on adolescents' birth control and condom use, likelihood of sexually transmitted infections. *Journal of School Nursing, 29,* 61–70.

Turner, K.M. (2004). Young women's views on teenage motherhood: A possible explanation for the relationship between socio-economic background and teenage pregnancy outcome? *Journal of Youth Studies, 7,* 221–238.

Tyden, T., Olsson, S-E. & Häggström-Nordin, E. (2001). Improved use of contraceptives, attitudes towards pornography, and sexual harassment among female university students. *Women's Health Issues, 11,* 87–94.

Tyden, T. & Rogala, C. (2004). Sexual behaviour among young men in Sweden and the impact of pornography. *International Journal of STD & AIDS, 15,* 590–593.

Tyler, C.P., Whiteman, M.K., Kraft, J.M., Zapata, L.B., Hillis, S.D., Curtis, K.M., et al. (2014). Dual use of condoms with other contraceptive methods among adolescents and young women in the United States. *Journal of Adolescent Health, 54,* 169–175.

Udry, J.R. (1988). Biological predispositions and social control in adolescent sexual behavior. *American Sociological Review, 53,* 709–722.

Udry, J.R. (2000). Biological limits of gender construction. *American Sociological Review, 65,* 443–457.

Udry, J.R., Talbert, L.M. & Morris, N.M. (1986). Biosocial foundations for adolescent female sexuality. *Demography 23*(2), 217–230.

UK Government. (2014). *The National Curriculum.* Retrieved from: https://www.gov.uk/national-curriculum/other-compulsory-subjects [Accessed 3 November 2014].

UNAIDS. (2008). *2008 Report on the global AIDS epidemic.* Geneva: UNAIDS.

UNAIDS. (2012). *Global report: UNAIDS report on the global AIDS epidemic 2012.* Retrieved from: http://www.unaids.org/en/resources/campaigns/20121120_globalreport2012/globalreport [Accessed 10 February 2014].

Underhill, K., Montgomery, P. & Operario, D. (2007). Sexual abstinence only programmes to prevent HIV infection in high income countries: Systematic review. *British Medical Journal, 335,* 248–252.

UNESCO (United Nations Educational, Scientific and Cultural Organization). (2009). *International technical guidance on sexuality education: An evidence-informed approach for schools, teachers and health educators.* Retrieved from: http://unesdoc.unesco.org/images/0018/001832/183281e.pdf [Accessed 3 November 2014].

UNICEF. (2001). *Early marriage: Child spouses.* Florence: United Nations Children's Fund, Innocenti Research Centre.

UNICEF. (2006). *The state of the world's children: Excluded and invisible.* Retrieved from: http://www.unicef.org/sowc06/pdfs/sowc06_fullreport.pdf [Accessed 20 January 2015].

UNICEF. (2012). *Progress for children: A report card on adolescents.* Retrieved from: http://www.unicef.org/publications/index_62280.html [Accessed 22 May 2014].

United Nations (2000). *Optimal protocol on the sale of children, child prostitution and child pornography.* Retrieved from: http://www.ohchr.org/EN/ProfessionalInterest/Pages/OPSCCRC.aspx [Accessed 20 January 2015].

United Nations Youth. (2014). *Young people and HIV.* Retrieved from: http://www.un.org/esa/socdev/documents/youth/fact-sheets/youth-hiv.pdf [Accessed 4 July 2014].

Upadhyay, U.D. & Hindin, M.J. (2006). Do perceptions of friends' behaviors affect age at first sex? Evidence from Cebu, Philippines. *Journal of Adolescent Health, 39,* 570–577.

US Department of State. (2009). *Trafficking in persons report 2010.* Retrieved from: http://www.state.gov/g/tip/rls/tiprpt/2010 [Accessed 16 January 2014].

Van den Broek, I.V.F., van Bergen, J.E.A.M., Brouwers, E.E.H.G., Fennema, J.S.A., Gotz, H.M., Hoebe, C.J.P.A, et al. (2012). Effectiveness of yearly, register based screening for chlamydia in the Netherlands: Controlled trial with randomised stepped wedge implementation. *BMJ (Clinical Research Edition), 345,* e4316.

Veneziano, C. & Veneziano, L. (2002). Adolescent sex offenders: A review of the literature. *Trauma Violence Abuse, 3,* 247–260.

Ventura, S.J., Curtin, S.C., Abma, J.C. & Henshaw, S.K. (2012). Estimated pregnancy rates and rates of pregnancy outcomes for the United States, 1990–2008. *National Vital Statistics Reports, 60*(7). Hyattsville, MD: National Center for Health Statistics.

Victorian Department of Education and Early Childhood Development. (2008). *Catching on Everywhere: Sexuality education program for Victorian schools.* Melbourne: Student Learning Programs Division, Office for Government School Education.

Vrangalova, Z. (2014, 3 March). Is our sexual double standard going away? *Psychology Today* [Web blog post]. Retrieved from: http://www.psychologytoday.com/blog/strictly-casual/201403/is-our-sexual-double-standard-going-away [Accessed 24 April 2015].

Vuttanont, U., Greenhalgh, T., Griffin, M. & Boynton, P. (2006). 'Smart boys' and 'sweet girls' – sex education needs in Thai teenagers: A mixed-method study. *The Lancet, 368,* 2068–2080.

Wade, L. & Heldman, C. (2012). Hooking up and opting out: Negotiating sex in the first year of college. In L.M. Carpenter & J. DeLamater (Eds.), *Sex for life: From virginity to Viagra, how sexuality changes throughout our lives.* New York: New York University Press.

Walker, J. & Milton, J. (2006). Teachers' and parents' roles in the sexuality education of primary school children: A comparison of experiences in Leeds, UK and in Sydney, Australia. *Sex Education, 6,* 415–428.

Walker, S.J. (2012). *Sexting and young people: A qualitative study.* Masters Research thesis. Melbourne: Medicine, Dentistry & Health Sciences – General Practice, The University of Melbourne.

Walker, S., Sanci, L. & Temple-Smith, M. (2013). Sexting: Young women and men's view on its nature and origins. *Journal of Adolescent Health, 52,* 697–701.

Walker, S., Temple-Smith, M., Higgs, P. & Sanci, L. (2015). 'It's always just there in your face': Australian young people's views on porn. *Sexual Health.* Retrieved from: http://www.publish.csiro.au/nid/164.htm [Accessed 4 May 2015].

Walsh, J. (2011). *Talk soon. Talk often: A guide for parents talking to their kids about sex.* Government of Western Australia, Department of Health, Australia.

Walsh, K., Latzman, N.E. & Latzman, R.D. (2014). Pathway from child sexual and physical abuse to risky sex among emerging adults: The role of trauma-related intrusions and alcohol problems. *Journal of Adolescent Health, 54,* 442–448.

Wang, B., Stanton, B., Li, X., Cottrell, L., Deveaux, L. & Kaljee, L. (2013). The influence of parental monitoring and parent-adolescent communication on Bahamian adolescent risk involvement: A three-year longitudinal examination. *Social Science and Medicine, 18*(Suppl 1), S69–74.

Ward, E.G. (2005). Homophobia, hypermasculinity and the U.S. black church. *Culture, Health and Sexuality, 5,* 493–504.

Warwick, I., Aggleton, P. & Douglas, N. (2001). Playing it safe: Addressing the emotional and physical health of lesbian and gay pupils in the U.K. *Journal of Adolescence, 24*(1), 129–140.

Weaver, E., Horyniak, D., Jenkinson, R., Dietze, P. & Lim, M. (2013). 'Let's get wasted' and other apps: Characteristics, acceptability and use of alcohol-related smartphone applications. *Journal of Medical Internet Research Mobile Health and Ubiquitous Health, 1*(1), e9.

Weaver, H., Smith, G. & Kippax, S. (2005). School-based sex education policies and indicators of sexual health among young people: A comparison of the Netherlands, France, Australia and the United States. *Sex Education, 5,* 171–188.

Webster, G.D. (2008). Playboy Playmates, the Dow Jones, consumer sentiment, 9/11, and the Doomsday Clock: A critical examination of the Environmental Security Hypothesis. *Journal of Social, Evolutionary, and Cultural Psychology, 2*(2), 23–41.

Weeks, J. (1977). *Coming out: Homosexual politics in Britain from the nineteenth century to the present.* London: Quartet.

Weinberg, M.S., Williams, C.J., Kleiner, S. & Irizarry, Y. (2010). Pornography, normalization, and empowerment. *Archives of Sexual Behavior, 39,* 1389–1401.

Weinshenker, N. (2010). Teenagers and body image: What's typical and what's not. Retrieved from: http://www.education.com/print/Ref_Adolescents_Body [Accessed 31 December 2014].

Weiss, R. & Samenow, C.P. (2010). Smart phones, social networking, sexting and problematic sexual behaviours: A call for research. *Sexual Addiction & Compulsivity, 17,* 241–246.

Wekerle, C. & Avgoustis, E. (2003). *Child maltreatment, adolescent dating and adolescent dating violence.* Mahwah, NJ: Lawrence Erlbaum Associates.

Wellings, K. (2008). Sexual health. In P. Van Look (Ed.), *Sexual and reproductive health: A public health perspective.* Amsterdam: Elsevier.

Wellings, K., Collumbien, M., Slaymaker, E., Singh, S., Hodges, Z., Patel, D. & Bajos, N. (2006). Sexual behaviour in context: A global perspective. *The Lancet, 368*(9548), 1706–1728.

Welsh, D.P., Grello, C.P. & Harper, M.S. (2003). When love hurts: Depression and adolescent romantic relationships. In P. Florsheim (Ed.), *Adolescent romantic relations and sexual behavior: Theory, research and practical implications.* Mahwah, NJ: Lawrence Erlbaum Associates, pp. 185–212.

West, J., Lister, E., Hall, P.C, Crookston, B.T., Rivera Snow P., Zvietcovich M.E. & West, R.P. (2014). Sexting among Peruvian adolescents. *BMC Public Health, 14,* 811. Retrieved from: http://www.biomedcentral.com/1471–2458/14/811 [Accessed 31 December 2014].

Wheeler, S.B. (2010). Effects of self-esteem and academic performance on adolescent decision-making: An examination of early sexual intercourse and illegal substance use. *Journal of Adolescent Health, 47*(6), 582–590.

Whitbeck, L.B. (2009). *Mental health and emerging adulthood among homeless young people.* New York: Psychology Press.

Whitbeck, L., Chen, X. & Johnson, K. (2006). Food insecurity among homeless and runaway adolescents. *Public Health Nutrition, 9*(1), 47–52.

Whitbeck, L.B., Johnson, K.D., Hoyt, D.R. & Cauce, A.M. (2004). Mental disorder and comorbidity among runaway and homeless adolescents. *Journal of Adolescent Health, 35,* 132–140.

White, L. (2013). The function of ethnicity, income level, and menstrual taboos in postmenarcheal adolescents' understanding of menarche and menstruation. *Sex Roles, 68*(1), 65–76.

WHO. (2001). *The second decade: Improving adolescent health and development.* Geneva: World Health Organization. Retrieved from: http://www.who.int/maternal_child_adolescent/documents/frh_adh_98_18/en [Accessed 29 January 2015].

WHO. (2005). *Sexual and reproductive health of adolescents and youths in Malaysia: A review of literature and projects 2005.* Geneva: World Health Organization.

WHO. (2007a). *Helping parents in developing countries improve adolescent health.* Geneva: Department of Child and Adolescent Health and Development.

WHO. (2007b). Misperceptions amongst boys in the Islamic Republic of Iran about sexual and reproductive health. *Social Science Research Policy Briefs.* Retrieved from: http://whqlibdoc.who.int/hq/2007/WHO_RHR_HRP_07.20_eng.pdf [Accessed 24 January 2014].

WHO. (2008). Adolescent pregnancy. *MPS Notes, 1*(1): 1–4.

WHO. (2011). *UNAIDS World AIDS Day Report 2012*. Retrieved from: http://www.unaids.org/sites/default/files/media_asset/JC2434_WorldAIDSday_results_en_1.pdf [Accessed 29 January 2015].

WHO. (2012). *Global incidence and prevalence of selected curable sexually transmitted infections: 2008*. Geneva: World Health Organization.

WHO. (2013a). Female genital mutilation: What it is and why it continues. In *Elimination of female genital mutilation: An interagency statement*. Geneva: World Health Organization, pp. 4–7. Retrieved from: http://whqlibdoc.who.int/publications/2008/9789241596442_eng.pdf?ua=1 [Accessed 31 December 2014].

WHO. (2013b). *Global update on HIV treatment 2013: Results, impact and opportunities. WHO report in partnership with UNICEF and UNAIDS*. Geneva: World Health Organization.

WHO. (2013c). *Sexual and reproductive health: Global and regional estimates of violence against women – prevalence and health effects of intimate partner violence and non-partner sexual violence*. Retrieved from: http://www.who.int/reproductivehealth/publications/violence/9789241564625/en [Accessed 29 January 2015].

WHO. (2014a). *Sexual and reproductive health: Gender and human rights*. Retrieved from: http://www.who.int/reproductivehealth/topics/gender_rights/sexual_health/en [Accessed 20 December 2014].

WHO. (2014b). Human papillomavirus vaccines: WHO position paper. *WHO Weekly Epidemiological Record, 43*(89), 465–492.

WHO. (2014c). *Maternal, newborn, child and adolescent health: Adolescent pregnancy*. Retrieved from: http://www.who.int/maternal_child_adolescent/topics/maternal/adolescent_pregnancy/en/ [Accessed 27 February 2014].

Widman, L., Neal, J., Choukas-Bradley, S. & Prinstein, M.J. (2013). Safe sext: Use of technology to communicate about sexual health with dating partners. *Journal of Adolescent Health, 54*(5), 612–614.

Widman, L., Nesi, J., Choukas-Bradley, S. & Prinstein, M.J. (2014). Safe sext: Adolescents' use of technology to communicate about sexual health with dating partners. *Journal of Adolescent Health, 54*, 612–614.

Widman, L., Welsh, D.P., McNulty, J.K. & Little, K.C. (2006). Sexual communication and contraceptive use in adolescent dating couples. *Journal of Adolescent Health, 39*(6), 893–899.

Widmer, E.D. (1997). Influence of older siblings on initiation of sexual intercourse. *Journal of Marriage and the Family, 59*, 928–938.

Wight, D. (2011). The effectiveness of school-based sex education: What do rigorous evaluations in Britain tell us? *Education and Health, 29*(4), 67–73.

Wight, D. & Fullerton, D. (2013). A review of interventions with parents to promote the sexual health of their children. *Journal of Adolescent Health, 52*, 4–47.

Wight, D., Williamson, L. & Henderson, M. (2006). Parental influences on young people's sexual behaviour: A longitudinal analysis. *Journal of Adolescence, 29*, 473–494.

WikiHow. (n.d.). *How to prevent a potential rape: 26 steps*. Retrieved from: http://www.wikihow.com/Prevent-a-Potential-Rape [Accessed 15 January 2015].

Wikipedia (2014). *Hypomania*. Retrieved from: http://en.wikipedia.org/wiki/Hypomania [Accessed 14 January 2014].

Wilkinson, T.A., Vargas, G., Fahey, N., Suther, E. & Silverstein, M. (2014). 'I'll see what I can do': What adolescents experience when requesting emergency contraception. *Journal of Adolescent Health, 54,* 14–19.

Williams, C. (2005). Framing the fetus in medical work: Representations and practices. *Social Science & Medicine, 60,* 2085–2095.

Williams, P.L., Sergeyev, O., Lee, M.M., Korrick, S.A., Burns, J.S., Humblet, O., *et al.* (2010). Blood lead levels and delayed onset of puberty in a longitudinal study of Russian boys. *Pediatrics, 125,* 1088–1096.

Williamson, C. & Prior, M. (2009). Domestic minor sex trafficking: A network of underground players in the Midwest. *Journal of Child and Adolescent Trauma, 2,* 45–61.

Wilton, T. (2000). *Sexualities in health and social care: A textbook.* Buckingham: Open University Press.

Withington, T., Ogilvie, J. & Watt, B. (2013). A brief report of the characteristics of adolescents with identified sexually abusive behaviours referred to a forensic child and youth mental health service. *Sexual Abuse in Australia and New Zealand, 5,* 40–44.

Witt, E.D. (2007). Puberty, hormones, and sex differences in alcohol abuse and dependence. *Neurotoxicology and Teratology, 29*(1), 81–95.

Witthaus, D. (2010). *Beyond 'that's so gay': Challenging homophobia in Australian schools.* Cheltenham, Victoria: Hawker Brownlow Education.

Wolf, N. (2012). Amanda Todd's suicide and social media's sexualisation of youth culture. *The Guardian.* Retrieved from: http://www.theguardian.com/commentisfree/2012/oct/26/amanda-todd-suicide-social-media-sexualisation [Accessed 17 May 2014].

Wong, C. & Tang, C. (2004). Coming out experiences and psychological distress of Chinese homosexual men in Hong Kong. *Archives of Sexual Behavior, 33*(2), 149–157.

Wood, E.B., Hutchinson, M.K., Kahwa, E., Hewitt, H. & Waldron, N. (2011). Jamaican adolescent girls with older male sexual partners. *Journal of Nursing Scholarship, 43,* 396–404.

Woodward, L.J., Fergusson, D.M. & Horwood, L.J. (2001). Risk factor and life processes associated with teenage pregnancy: Results of a prospective study from birth to 20 years. *Journal of Marriage and Family, 63,* 1170–1184.

Woody, J.D., D'Souza, H.J. & Russel, R. (2003). Emotions and motivations in first adolescent intercourse: An exploratory study based on object relations theory. *Canadian Journal of Human Sexuality, 12,* 35–51.

World Bank. (2013a). *Adolescent fertility rate (births per 1,000 women ages 15–19).* Retrieved from: http://data.worldbank.org/indicator/SP.ADO.TFRT [Accessed 23 May 2014].

World Bank. (2013b). *Fertility rate, total (births per woman).* Retrieved from: http://data.worldbank.org/indicator/SP.DYN.TFRT.IN [Accessed 24 January 2015].

Wu, D. (2003, 19 December). Survey reveals sexual behavior and attitudes. *Taipei Times,* p. 4.

Wu, T., Mendola, P. & Buck, G.M. (2002). Ethnic differences in the presence of secondary sex characteristics and menarche among US girls: The Third National Health and Nutrition Examination Survey, 1988–1994. *Pediatrics, 110,* 752–757.

Xie, Y., Chen, Y.A. & DeBellis, M.D. (2012). The relationship of age, gender, and IQ with the brainstem and thalamus in healthy children and adolescents: A magnetic resonance imaging volumetric study. *Journal of Child Neurology, 27*(3), 325–331.

Yahoo Answers. (2010). What's your opinion on premarital sex? Retrieved from: https://answers.yahoo.com/search/search_result?fr=uh3_answers_vert_gs& type=2button&p=what%27s%20your%20°pinion%20°n%20premarital%20 sex%3F [Accessed 12 January 2015].

Yeung, D.Y., Tang, C.S. & Lee, A.M. (2005). Psychosocial and cultural factors influencing anticipations of menarche: A study on Chinese pre-menarcheal teenage girls. *Journal of Adolescent Research, 20,* 118–135.

Yeung, T.H, Horyniak, D., Vella, A., Hellard, M. & Lim, M. (2014). Prevalence, correlates and attitudes towards sexting among young people in Melbourne, Australia. *Sexual Health, 11*(4), 332–339.

Your Sex Health. (n.d.). Retrieved from: www.yoursexhealth.org.au [Accessed 27 December 2014].

Youth Risk Behavior Surveillances. (2004). Youth risk behavior surveillance: United States, 2003. *Morbidity and Mortality Weekly Report, 53,* No. SS-2.

Yu, C.K-C. & Fu, W. (2011). Sex dreams, wet dreams and nocturnal emissions. *Dreaming, 21*(3), 197–212.

Yu, J. (2012). Teenage sexual attitudes and behaviour in China: A literature review. *Health and Social Care in the Community, 20*(6), 561–582.

Yu, X., Guo, S. & Sun, Y. (2013). Sexual behaviours and associated risks in Chinese young people: A meta-analysis. *Sexual Health, 10*(5), 424–433.

Yusuf, F. & Siedlecky, S. (2007). Patterns of contraceptive use in Australia: Analysis of the 2001 National Health Survey. *Journal of Biosocial Science, 39,* 735–744.

Zabin, L.S., Emerson, M.R. & Rowland, D.L. (2005). Childhood sexual abuse and early menarche: The direction of their relationship and its implications. *Journal of Adolescent Health, 36*(5), 393–400.

Zawacki, T., Abbey, A., Buck, P.O., McAuslan, P. & Clinton-Sherrod, A.M. (2003). Perpetrators of alcohol-involved sexual assaults: How do they differ from other sexual assault perpetrators and nonperpetrators? *Aggressive Behavior, 29,* 366–380.

Zhang, L.Y., Li, X.M., Shah, I.H., Baldwin, W. & Stanton, B. (2007). Parent-adolescent sex communication in China. *European Journal of Contraception and Reproductive Health Care, 12,* 138–147.

Zhao, Y., Montoro, R., Igartua, K. & Thombs, B.D. (2010). Suicidal ideation and attempt among adolescents reporting 'unsure' sexual identity or heterosexual identity plus same-sex attraction or behavior: Forgotten groups? *Journal of the American Academy of Child and Adolescent Psychiatry, 49*(2), 104–113.

Ziegler, T.E. (2007). Female sexual motivation during non-fertile periods: A primate phenomenon. *Hormones and Behavior, 51*(1), 1–2.

Zimmer-Gembeck, M.J. & Helfand, M. (2008). Ten years of longitudinal research on U.S. adolescent sexual behavior: Developmental correlates of sexual intercourse, and the importance of age, gender and ethnic background. *Developmental Review, 28,* 153–224.

Zimmer-Gembeck, M.J., Siebenbruner, J. & Collins, W.A. (2001). Diverse aspects of dating: Associations with psychosocial functioning from early to middle adolescence. *Journal of Adolescence, 24*(3), 313–336.

Zimmer-Gembeck, M., Siebenbruner, J. & Collins, W. (2004). A prospective study of intraindividual and peer influences on adolescents' heterosexual romantic and sexual behavior. *Archives of Sexual Behavior, 33*(4), 381–394.

Zou, H., Tabrizi, S., Grulich, A.E., Garland, S.M., Hocking, J.M., Bradshaw, C.S., *et al.* (2014). Early acquisition of anogenital human papillomavirus among teenage men who have sex with men. *Journal of Infectious Diseases Advance Access, 209*(5), 642–651.

INDEX

promotion 137; sexual identity 101; sexual initiation 10; sexual self-esteem 160; social media 122, 123; text messaging 136; unwanted sex 250–251, 252, 261; views on mothers 226–227; virginity 23; websites as source of information about sex 118; withdrawal method 15

Australian Football League (AFL) 262

Austria 96

Ayers, S. 58

bacteria 193, 212

Baker, J. 123

Bale, C. 146

Balfe, M. 209, 211

Baltic States 95

Bansel, P. 164

Bauman, L.J. 204–205, 207

Baumeister, R.F. 143–144, 147, 189

beauty 56, 118–119, 206–207

Becker, J.B. 52–53

Beckett, R. 267

Beech, A. 260, 266

Being Brendo 137

Bennett, T. 267

Bensman, L. 141

Bercaw-Pratt, J.L. 61

Berge, J. 57–58

Berkeley Growth Study 49

Berman, R. 204–205, 207

Bettelheim, B. 21–22

Biddlecom, A. 76–77

biology 4, 34–67; genital development 59–60; homosexuality 170–171; sex differences 35–38; timing of puberty 47–51; *see also* brain; hormones; puberty

birth rates 214, 215, 217, 221

bisexuality 101, 165, 167–169, 171; health and wellbeing 181–182, 183; HIV/AIDS 196; prevalence 173; sexually transmissible infections 192

Bissell, M. 109

Blakemore, S.J. 44

blogs 119, 123

body dissatisfaction 53–55, 57, 58–59

body image 47, 50, 53–62, 118

Bogaert, A.F. 156

Bogt, T.T. 75

Boonstra, H.D. 108

Botswana 91

Bovarnick, S. 246

Bowring, A. 10

Boyar, R. 100, 104, 134–135, 204

Boynton, P. 103

boys/young men: adolescent sex offenders 265–267; attitudinal stereotypes 139–140; biological differences 35–37; body dissatisfaction 54–55, 57; brain 41; casual sex 9; changes in goals 7; communication with parents 71, 82–84; contraception 32; conversational motives 162–163; cultural issues 25; double standard 24, 149–152; first ejaculation 46, 65–66; gender inequalities 272; hormones 52; masturbation 17–18; media influences 118; motives for sex 140–143; numbers of sexually active 10–11; oral sex 13; parental influence 77; partners 19–20; peer influence 89–90; perpetrators of sexual violence 261–262; pornography 129–130; puberty 38–41, 45, 46–51; resocialization of 269; romantic relationships 153–154, 159; sex drive 143–149; sex education 105; sexting 127, 128; sexual abuse 242; sexual exploitation 246; sexual fantasies 16; sexual harassment 257; sexual initiation 9–10; sexual self-concept 160; sexually transmissible infections 193, 199, 210–211; social media 124; staying safe 263–264; unwanted sex 23, 248, 251, 255, 264–265; views on sexual violence 249

Bradley, H. 200

brain 2, 35, 41–45, 67, 273; early maturation 51; homosexuality 170–171; hormones 36–37, 52